Praise for Lisa Kelly's

Triumphs From Notre Dame:
Echoes of Her Loyal Sons and Daughters

"Lisa writes the untold stories of the young men and women whose lives were shaped and molded by Notre Dame. So often we only hear of their brief accomplishments on the field, but there is so much more to these outstanding individuals. Lisa brings us the humanistic, passionate and trying stories of these men and women – the stories that mirror the morals, ethics and character that Notre Dame expounds. Thank you, Lisa."

~Darrell "Flash" Gordon

"The men and women featured in this book are special individuals and represent all that is great about Notre Dame. These men and women are significant and they have strived each day to make an impact and difference in all things that they touch. They were and as far as I'm concerned remain Notre Dame student-athletes and I'm proud to have touched many of their lives. Lisa, thank you for your work and sharing with the Notre Dame Family what you so appropriately have named, "*Triumphs From Notre Dame: Echoes of Her Loyal Sons and Daughters.*"

~Lou Holtz, former Notre Dame Football Head Coach

"Karen Robinson Keyes represents all the values and ideals that Notre Dame stands for. She made an impact on our team and her legacy lives on through her and her husband Kevin's generosity. Lisa Kelly did a masterful job of telling the story of how the Notre Dame values affect our lives forever. Karen's story speaks to the heart of what being a student-athlete at Notre Dame is like."

~Muffet McGraw, Notre Dame Women's Basketball Head Coach

"The University of Notre Dame affords those who are blessed to attend a phenomenal opportunity. Not just in terms of personal accolades or successes, but rather in the fundamental growth and development of individuals as they journey along a path that will undoubtedly change their lives forever. Lisa perfectly captures the spirit of this journey through the eyes of my Notre Dame brothers and sisters in the eloquently written *Triumphs from Notre Dame – Echoes of Her Loyal Sons and Daughters*. Outstanding!"

~Oscar McBride

Triumphs From Notre Dame:

Echoes of Her Loyal Sons and Daughters

Lisa Kelly

Notre Dame alumna and author, Lisa Kelly.
(Photographer: Lynne Gilbert)

Triumphs From Notre Dame:

Echoes of Her Loyal Sons and Daughters

Lisa Kelly

Triumphs From Notre Dame
Echoes of Her Loyal Sons and Daughters
Lisa Kelly
Kelly Creations, LLC

Published by Kelly Creations, LLC
Copyright ©2016 Lisa Kelly
All rights reserved.

No part of this publication may be reproduced, stored in a retrieval system, or transmitted in any form or by any means, electronic, mechanical, photocopying, recording, scanning, or otherwise, except as permitted under Section 107 or 108 of the 1976 United States Copyright Act, without the prior written permission of the Publisher. Requests to the Publisher for permission should be addressed to Permissions Department, Kelly Creations, LLC, LKND93@sbcglobal.net. Portions of some of these chapters appeared online as "Where Are They Now" player interviews on NoCoastBias.com, HerLoyalSons.com, UHND.com and IrishEyes.com under the byline of The Men We Became author Lisa Kelly.

Content Editor: Catherine Russell
Copy Editor: Mary Ann Falkenberg
Front cover design: Bridget J. Reynolds
Front Cover Photos: Lynne Gilbert, Lisa Kelly, Mike Miller and Tracey Saraceni
Back cover photo: Tracey Saraceni

Library of Congress Cataloging-in-Publication Data
Library of Congress Control Number: 2020912424
Lisa Kelly
Triumphs From Notre Dame: Echoes of Her Loyal Sons and Daughters
ISBN: 978-1-7353488-2-7
Library of Congress subject headings:
1. SPO019000   SPORTS & RECREATION / History   2. SPO015000 SPORTS & RECREATION / Football   3. SPO000000   SPORTS & RECREATION / General

2016

ATTENTION CORPORATIONS, UNIVERSITIES, COLLEGES AND PROFESSIONAL ORGANIZATIONS: Quantity discounts are available on bulk purchases of this book for educational, gift purposes, or as premiums for increasing magazine subscriptions or renewals. Special books or book excerpts can also be created to fit specific needs. For information, please contact Kelly Creations, LLC, LKND93@sbcglobal.net.

For more information visit:
TheMenWeBecame.com, Facebook.com/EchoesFromNotreDame
and Twitter.com/echoesfromnd

Dedication

*To my husband, Jim, and my children, Michael and Caitlyn.
Thank you for continuing to listen to me tell countless Notre Dame stories,
and for always supporting me as I chase my crazy dreams!*

"For those who know Notre Dame, no explanation's necessary. For those who don't, no explanation will suffice."

~Coach Lou Holtz

Table of Contents

Dedication vii
Foreword by Reggie Brooks.. xi

Introduction 1
The Evolution of the Student-Athlete at Notre Dame 3

1. The Composer: John Scully.. 7
2. The Game Changer: Clint Johnson 17
3. The Stunt Coordinator: Stephen Pope....................................... 30
4. The Business Developer: Eddie Hartwell 51
5. The Concerned Citizen: Dr. Charles Thomas Jr. 65
6. The World Champion: Shannon Boxx 83
7. The Lifelong Learner: Brett Bruininks 96
8. The Family Man: Bill Hackett... 117
9. The Medical Salesman: Rich Thomann 129
10. The Great Adventurer: Elizabeth Wagner 142
11. The Shaper of Men: Torrian Jones 156
12. The Chief Marketing Officer: Denise (Chabot) Karkos 172
13. The US Marshal: Eric Gregoire 184
14. The Harlem Stuntman: Jeremy Sample 199
15. The Skill Developer: Raki Nelson.. 211
16. The Sporting Event Curator: Mike O'Connell........................ 221
17. The Golf Pro: Chris O'Connell 233
18. The Sideline Reporter & Coach: Karen (Robinson) Keyes..... 244
19. The Mental Motivator: Charles Stafford 258
20. The Guidance Counselor: Martin 'Marty' Olosky 271
21. The Radio Guy: Joe Fredrick 279

22. The Ace Runner: Molly Huddle	292
23. The Sports Marketer: Mary O'Connor	301
24. The Baseball Mentor: Chris Michalak	308
Epilogue	325
About the Author	326

Foreword

"For those who know Notre Dame, no explanation's necessary. For those who don't, no explanation will suffice."

– Coach Lou Holtz

I had the pleasure and pain of playing intercollegiate football at the University of Notre Dame under Louis Leo Holtz. I have always been intrigued by the above quote. It took me 15 years to truly get it. Notre Dame is more than a college campus in northern Indiana, it is a collective of individuals bound by experiences few can comprehend. Having been a student-athlete and now an employee for the last 15 years, I have a much broader perspective of Our Lady's University. My experience as a student-athlete at Notre Dame was mixed. I had difficulties early in my stay at Notre Dame. . . athletically, academically, socially and culturally. I struggled to find my way. I did not see a lot of playing time as a freshman and was moved to defensive back as a sophomore. As many who attended Notre Dame will tell you, the academic rigor was high and expectation to compete in the classroom was a constant. While I was a strong student in high school, I was not prepared for the academic pace of college. Coming from Tulsa, OK, I was not used to the varying cultural and social dynamic of Notre Dame. I was a young black Pentecostal in a predominately black community, thrust into a predominately white Catholic institution. I was not an outgoing person, and seldom left the confines of north Tulsa. As many know, Notre Dame is truly a national if not international institution. I found myself in a male-only dormitory with people from every part of the country. Talk about a fish out of water. I did not adapt well early on. I had to learn the hard way, that **you do not come to Notre Dame to change it, you come to Notre Dame to be shaped by it**.

My father always told me that you honor your commitments and you finish what you start. Once I opened my mind and changed my perspective a whole new world opened up to me. I engaged a little more not only with the campus community but also with my teammates and coaches. I developed a greater awareness of the importance of being a member of something bigger than yourself. I went on to enjoy success on the field, my grades improved and I would find my wife (Proverbs 18:22) of the past 25 years. I still encountered difficult situations and learned tough lessons but I now had my Notre Dame family as a support structure. Notre Dame is not for everyone and there is no easy way to navigate the challenging road through its hollowed grounds, but the *spirit of Notre Dame* is in the people. Now that I am back at Notre Dame working in the athletics department I have a greater appreciation for those difficult times. I also cherish those moments that have come to define me as a man as well as shape my current perspective. I have come to realize that my role at the University is to further that spirit of family, assist our current student-athletes in navigating the challenging experience of being at Notre Dame and encourage our former student-athletes to be emboldened in sharing their own experience, good and bad, with the world.

Through our shared experiences this is how ***WE ARE ND!***

Reggie Brooks
Running Back
University of Notre Dame du Lac '93

Introduction

College athletics have made great strides in the last century, but at many schools we are witnessing a shift in what it is to be a student-athlete; schools that diminish the importance of being a student first and an athlete second. In my first two books of the *Echoes From Notre Dame* book series (*Echoes from the End Zone: The Men We Became*, and *The Men We Became: More Echoes from the End Zone*), I told the stories of 55 student-athletes and how the *Notre Dame Value Stream* guided them on their journeys to and through Notre Dame and onto the rest of their lives. The *Notre Dame Value Stream*, as I developed in my first book, is the value system that Notre Dame students learn through their academics, athletics and spiritual life which prepares them for what life will put in front of them. The *Notre Dame Value Stream* is all about hard work, core values and treating others as you wish to be treated. It's about learning how to live in a fashion that takes care of yourself and others. In this book, I examine a new group of student-athletes.

The gap between success and failure for a student-athlete is narrow. That narrow gap can be an injury, an attitude, or a behavior; one slight variable can either push a student-athlete to success, or plummet him to the depths of failure. What I've observed through my research and interviews with these student-athletes is that Notre Dame does everything in Her power to prepare Her student-athletes for success.

Our Lady's University may not be able to control a student-athlete's attitude, behavior, or injuries; but She can provide Her student-athletes with a toolbox full of the right people and resources to give them their best chance at achieving success both on and off the field. Notre Dame is by no means perfect, and not every student-athlete who passes through Her doors will be successful. Our Lady's University recognizes the pitfalls that await student-athletes once they step on campus to begin their collegiate career, and She does everything within Her power to guide them toward success, often via a path less traveled by the masses.

In 1972 Notre Dame student life changed forever when the first women undergraduate students were admitted to the University. And, Notre Dame athletics changed forever when the first female student-athletes wanted to play a team sport and joined the Athletic Department. In this volume of the *Echoes From Notre Dame* book series, I have diversified the selection of student-athletes to include more than just football players. I love football as much as the next guy (or girl), but I felt it was time to spread my wings a bit, and expand my coverage into other sports. In the pages that follow you will see the journeys of male and female student-athletes from football, basketball, hockey, baseball, golf, women's soccer, women's basketball, women's track and field, and a woman who was a student manager for the football team. I hope you enjoy the stories from this next group of Notre Dame student-athletes and how the *Notre Dame Value Stream* guided them to become the best possible version of themselves, and to bring out the best possible version of those around them. Student-athlete life is not easy, but with Our Lady and the *Notre Dame Value Stream* to support them, anything is possible.

Lisa Kelly
University of Notre Dame du Lac '93
Author, *Echoes From Notre Dame* book series

The Evolution of the Student-Athlete at Notre Dame

"I didn't know what in the hell I was doing when I first took the job," said Mike DeCicco, a mechanical engineering professor at Notre Dame back in 1964 when he accepted Father Joyce's offer to become the Chief Academic Advisor of Student-Athletes, a newly created position. Notre Dame executive vice president Rev. Edmund P. Joyce C.S.C. and then President Father Theodore Hesburgh had a vision and felt a moral commitment that the University's excellence in athletics wasn't good enough. This was Notre Dame and Our Lady of Victory was ready to create a new era in collegiate sports. No - these young men would become much more than mere "jocks" – instead now and forever known as "Notre Dame Student-Athletes".

In a 1988 interview with *Blue & Gold Illustrated*, Mike recalled he had no idea what to do, but it was clear that Hesburgh and Joyce would know success when they saw it. "There was no template or benchmark for success. I'd sit down with a kid and ask how his schoolwork was going. He'd say, 'Okay.' I'd say, 'Fine.' And that was that. Then when grades would be posted, I'd discover a lot were not doing as well as they said they were." Mike quickly learned he had to stay on top of each student-athlete's progress on a weekly basis, not once they were in academic trouble.

Mike created a methodology that would become the model for the best universities, and a standard to be adopted by the NCAA. During Mike's time as the ND Athletic Department's Chief Academic Advisor, 99% of student-athletes who were enrolled and stayed in school for four years graduated. When women came to Notre Dame in 1972, female student-athletes were offered the same academic support that was available to the male student-athletes. And in 1988, Notre Dame became the first school ever to win a football national title while at the same time graduating 100% of its players. For the 59 other College Football Association member institutions who returned results that year, the graduation rate was 50.7 percent.

Mike always credited Father Joyce and Father Hesburgh for having the vision to create a position that many felt was unnecessary. "They recognized the constraints and time-factor difficulties student-athletes would eventually have with the increased emphasis on intercollegiate sports," Mike said. The three of them felt that if they were asking athletes to give their service and energy to the University, the University at the very least could assure them an equal chance to earn a degree along with the rest of their fellow classmates.

Mike's team set up tutorial services and a ten day orientation program which taught time management and proper study habits, and a summer school program; all of which have been a mandatory part of the academic year of a student-athlete for years. Luther Bradley and Marv Russell, two of the former student-athletes featured in my first book, *Echoes From the End Zone: The Men We Became*, recalled Mike's role in their lives. "Two-months before we arrived on campus to start summer camp, we received a letter from this guy named Mike outlining academic expectations and what he and his team would do to insure our success in school."

Marv recalled, "I was a good student, studying theology which is a very tough major at a religious school like ND. Coach DeCicco (also the Notre Dame Fencing Coach) called me into his office and told me what it was going to take to be successful. He said 'Marv, this is how it's going to be. The minute I suspect you are not cutting it or you're having problems, we are going to reassess your major.' He said, 'I want you to meet with a graduate assistant every two weeks to assess your progress. Remember: you will get no breaks or special consideration.' I did what I was told and I was successful. Forty years later I saw Coach at a Notre Dame function and he still recalled that story. What made me feel great was when he said, 'I'm proud of you Marv and what you have accomplished.'"

Luther was focused on business as his major. He and Marv laughed at Luther's story of being called into Coach DeCicco's office for a chat, "You remember that fencing sword he had mounted over his desk? I walked into his office and sat down and all he said was, 'You see the sword behind me? If you don't get busy and study harder, you are going to find that sword up your ass.' Coach never minced words." Luther said, "I wasn't doing that bad in class, but he felt I wasn't working to my potential. He wanted our best just like Ara did on the field." Both Luther and Marv said what was even more important was if you weren't performing in the classroom you could bet Ara knew and it was likely Moose Krause the AD knew and you were going to hear from all of them.

The students interviewed in this book all realize how they benefited from the evolution of the Notre Dame "student-athlete" concept. Notre Dame is not an easy place for any student, let alone for those who have the additional demands of athletics. Without this visionary program, many athletes would be left by the wayside, as they are at so many other schools. Today, thanks to the leadership of Mike DeCicco, Father Hesburgh and Father Joyce, Notre Dame consistently leads NCAA schools in graduation rates and overall academic performance.

Coach DeCicco passed away in the spring of 2013. His impact on Notre Dame and the NCAA schools will be a legacy for decades to come. Notre Dame student-athletes owe a debt of thanks to this Loyal Son.

Mike DeCicco was Notre Dame at its finest – he was the *Notre Dame Value Stream* at work.[1]

Mike DeCicco quotes taken from: http://notredame.247sports.com/Article/Notre-Dame-Mourns-Death-Of-Mike-DeCicco-123852.

John Scully (Photo courtesy of Matt Cashore.)

CHAPTER ONE

The Composer
John Scully
(Notre Dame Football – Class of 1981)

There is something special about the University of Notre Dame. It embodies a spirit that is difficult to put one's finger on, let alone describe; something that brilliantly shines and sparkles in the light. It is a place that so many of us love, so incredibly deeply, and yet very few of us can ever seem to do it justice, when trying to put into words what Notre Dame means to us. Not so for John Scully. In two short days, John penned a song that for so many eloquently describes what Notre Dame truly is, finishing the chorus somewhere between I-294 and I-55, on the drive to his producer's studio. A song that countless Notre Dame fans will immediately recognize in the first few notes. A song that so fully embodies the spirit of Notre Dame that it will make the hairs on your arms stand up. How did a second generation immigrant from Ireland make his way from Huntington, NY, to play football for the University of Notre Dame, and eventually go on to pen one of the most iconic songs ever written about the spirit of Notre Dame? This is John Scully's story.

The Notre Dame Years

> *"The biggest reason why I ended up at Notre Dame was because they had actively recruited me. I do think, however, that part of why I ended up at Notre Dame was because I am second generation Irish. All of my grandparents emigrated from Ireland in the 1920s, and when you move to a strange land, you latch on to things that are familiar. My paternal grandparents and my father latched on to Notre Dame. My dad helped steer me towards Notre Dame, not in a persuasive manner, but rather in an influential one. I very nearly went to Penn State University due to the fact that they have an excellent music school. At the time, an NFL player named Mike Reid (who was a Penn State graduate and had been drafted by the Cincinnati Bengals) had just graduated from Penn State, and he was also a music major (Reid went on to be a big song writer in Nashville years later). In the 70s, when I was being recruited to play football in college, Penn State was THE school on the East Coast. It was the place where everyone wanted to be. Notre Dame had more of a national appeal, though, and I thought it would likely give me more options than Penn State."*

> *"I took four official visits: Penn State, Pittsburgh, Ohio State, and Notre Dame. My visit to Ohio State was interesting as it was the first recruiting weekend of the season, and I was the only recruit on campus that weekend. As a result, I got to spend a lot of one-on-one time with their head coach, Woody Hayes, which was truly a unique experience as far as recruiting weekends go. When I took my visit to Notre Dame, I stayed with Leo Driscoll, who I had gone to high school with (he was a couple of years older than me). He was a walk-on at Notre Dame, and pretty much his entire family had gone to Notre Dame."*

When you play a Division I sport at a school like Notre Dame, you were probably one of the best in your sport at your respective high school. Which probably lead you to believe that you would arrive on campus and make an instant contribution to the team. However, transitioning from playing sports in high school to playing sports at the collegiate level is not always easy. Having that confidence, that you will make a difference upon arrival, will help you make the transition. But, having the resolve to pick yourself up after you've been knocked down is also very helpful.

> *"My first year at Notre Dame was quite challenging, to say the least. I was hurt for most of my freshman year (I had an ankle injury, a detached ligament, which ironically wasn't repaired until 15 years later when I retired from the NFL), and I spent most of the year limping around campus, which made me feel very ostracized from the team. For most New Yorkers (John is from Huntington, NY), the Hudson River is the most western part of civilization; so moving as far west as South Bend, IN, was quite a culture shock for me as well."* As a result of being injured that first year, John was able to dig right into his studies, and get a jump start on his Notre Dame education. *"I studied Sociology at Notre Dame, and received an excellent liberal arts education. I also was able to take a healthy smattering of music courses, including several music theory courses."*

Legendary and college football coaches go hand-in-hand at the University of Notre Dame. As you stand in the sports section of the bookstore, there are plenty of books on the storied Notre Dame coaches on the shelves: Knute Rockne, Frank Leahy, Ara Parseghian, Dan Devine, and Lou Holtz, to name a few. If you played football at Notre Dame as you sailed down the *Notre Dame Value Stream*, you are considered in most people's eyes one of the lucky ones. But if you played football at Notre Dame under one of the legends, lucky is an understatement. John was fortunate to play under one of those fabled Notre Dame coaches, Dan Devine, but it took a while for John to get in Devine's line of sight.

> *"I was sort of the invisible man to Devine and the rest of the coaches my first couple of years on the team. I was hurt my freshman year with an ankle injury, and then my sophomore year I wasn't on the varsity team yet. Coach Devine was, however, instrumental in helping me with my football career, and getting me recognized in a way that spring-boarded me out of college and into the NFL. I have nothing but good things to say about Coach Devine and all he did to help me develop into an NFL caliber player. Coach Devine taught us endless lessons, not only on, but off the field as well. The one that I still use today is to always show up early. He taught us that if you show up on time, you're actually late; in order to be on time, always show up early. This simple rule is one that I've used in all aspects of my life. It may sound like a very simple rule, but for so many people it is a very hard rule to follow."*

The greatest lesson I took away from that season was the importance of raising expectations; set expectations at a level where everyone believes they have something important to live up to.

Not only was John fortuitous enough to have played under head coach Dan Devine, he also was a member of the 1977 National Championship team. John shared with me what it was like to be a part of such an incredible team, and the lasting impact that year had on him.

> *"I was not a starter during the '77 championship season, but I did get in for five minutes of the Georgia Tech game, as we were winning by an obscene amount of points. I also had the opportunity to practice against the first team defense that season, and probably learned more about football (and self-preservation) in that single year than I did in any year before or after. It was an incredible experience. The greatest lesson I took away from that season was the importance of raising expectations; set expectations at a level where everyone believes they have something important to live up to. We weren't just expected to win by our coaches, but each and every one of us expected ourselves to win, and our teammates as well. It's one thing to aspire to it, but to be as close to excellence as I was that year, I learned what we should be shooting for every year, and what the level of achievement needed to be, both on and off the field. I have used that in my life both in my football career, and after."*

> *"Two of my favorite Notre Dame Football moments occurred while playing against the University of Michigan Wolverines, during the 1979 and 1980 seasons. I got to start against Michigan during both of those seasons. In 1979 we played Michigan away in Ann Arbor, and we won with time running out on the clock by blocking a Michigan field goal. In 1980 we played Michigan at home in South Bend, and we beat them with time running out on the clock, on a field goal that we made. As hard as those losses were for Michigan, they were equally as thrilling for us."*

Being a student-athlete at a school like Notre Dame is rigorous both on and off the field. You are physically exhausted from giving 110% during practice and in games, and then you immediately have to turn around and hit the books in order to remain successful in your academic studies. One thing that can help keep you focused on your academics, though, is pursuing an academic track that you are passionate about. This is not always an easy path to discern, at 18 years of age, but John figured it out pretty quickly and took advantage of it.

> *"It was very challenging to be a student-athlete at Notre Dame. People think I'm naturally good at everything I do, but really I only do well at things that I'm 'good' at and that I 'like' to do. While I did very much enjoy some of my classes, I definitely didn't like all of them. Class at times was just a necessary obligation, and I sure am glad it is in the rear view mirror. Being a scholarship athlete just layers complications on top of the complexities of football.*

> *You're always short on time, and you still have to get your school work done after you complete your football obligations."*

> *"It absolutely prepared me for life after college. Along the same lines of Coach Devine's lessons on arriving early, I still have nightmares about turning in an assignment or paper late. I think for me, part of being a student-athlete at Notre Dame was growing up, and the realization that there are two sets of tasks you must complete every day: football and academics. And some of those tasks are ones you want to do, and some of those tasks are ones you have to do. I learned the importance of getting your obligations done first, so that you can move on to the things you want to do."*

The college years tend to go by quickly, often much more swiftly than any student ever anticipates, and then it's time once again to figure out what path to venture down. As a student-athlete, you learn on your journey down the *Notre Dame Value Stream* that academics are your top priority; it's the reason you go to college. But in the back of your mind, the ultimate goal is to play your sport at the next level, and for John, his mindset was no different. John talks about what his NFL draft was like, and what it was like to play football in the National Football League (NFL).

The Professional Years

> *"My NFL draft was actually pretty horrible. You're only as informed as the information you receive from other people. The consensus was that I was going to be drafted in the first or second round, and I didn't end up being drafted until the end of the fourth round. To call it anti-climatic would have been the understatement of the year. In retrospect, though, I was drafted exactly where I should have been given the talent and competition in that year's draft. I just wish I would have had that information prior to going into the draft. It would have saved me from getting knocked down and having to get back up again."*

> *"I am very grateful to have had the opportunity to play in the NFL, and I'm so glad that I did it. I played with some tremendous guys down in Atlanta, and my time there was filled with so many wonderful memories. It was, though, more of a nine-to-five job than most people give it credit for. We basically kept nine-to-five hours. You picked up your buddy, drove out to camp, had meetings, lifted weights, and practiced. We kept a very strict daily schedule. There was a lot of drudgery to that strict schedule as well. I'm not crying the blues by any stretch of the imagination, but it wasn't as magical as many people ascribe it to be."*

> *"Once you make it to the NFL, your motivations are quite different from what they were when you played at the college level. You're thrust into a new mix*

of people, philosophies and cultures; what you get could be really fantastic, or quite miserable. I was fortunate that the culture in Atlanta was really fantastic, and some of my best friends are the guys whom I played with in Atlanta. But, it is very different from the atmosphere of playing college football."

For so many people, the old adage that the NFL stands for "Not For Long," rings painfully true; not so for John. John played for ten years in the NFL for the Atlanta Falcons, playing in 112 games, and starting in 82 of them. However, a body can only take the beating the NFL serves up for so long, especially for John who suffered broken fingers, cracked ribs, and broken legs and ankles during his ten years in the NFL. At that point, it was time for him to choose a life direction that was a bit less harmful to his body.

Today

"Following my NFL career, I moved my family back to Joliet, IL so that my wife and children could be near my wife's family; I got into the music production business with Jim Tullio, who was a prolific producer in the music business. Our primary focus was on recording projects, and we did tons and tons of jingles for TV and radio. You might recognize a few of our clients: McDonalds, State Farm, and Ace Hardware."

"It was very fortunate that I met him in Chicago, and we had a lot in common outside of music as we were both from the east coast: Jim from New Jersey and I from New York. We produced a gigantic amount of music together from the early 1990s until 2000. It was great because the work mostly consisted of advertising jingles or corporate videos, as that was where the money was, and it allowed me to keep a flexible schedule. This schedule made it possible to be present in my girls' lives in a way many fathers were not able. I got to take my girls to and from school, coach them, and really contribute to the raising of them alongside my wife. The 90s were a great time for me."

"Beyond the music part of creating jingles was the business aspect of the music industry, which eventually got squirrelly, and I became fed up with that. Once the girls got older, I also needed a career that would take up more of my time, so in the year 2000 I left the music industry and got into the insurance business. I started on the ground floor and was able to work my way up pretty quickly. In the first five years I became a national account executive for corporate AIG. In the next seven or eight years I did a lot of corporate work, and then I went off on my own four years ago and started my own consulting business. I consult very broadly in the insurance space: business-to-business relationships consisting of distribution, product marketing and technology."

If you've ever been to a Notre Dame Football game in the last ten years, you've probably heard the song "Here Come the Irish." But did you know that it was written by a former Notre Dame Football player? John told me the story of how the song was written, and how it magically became a song that is near and dear to every Notre Dame alumni and fan.

> "When Jim Tullio and I were knee-deep in producing music, I knew there was something special I wanted to work on. We had done a project for the Chicago Bulls at the end of Michael Jordan's career, and Jim asked me what I wanted to do next, and I told Jim I wanted to do something for Notre Dame. We weren't solicited by the University, it was a passion project of sorts, and what resulted was nothing short of magical."

> Well I remember the leaves a fallin'
> And far off music like pipes a callin'
> And I remember the golden morning
> I saw the long ranks as they were forming
> And there's a magic in the sound of their name
> Here come the Irish of Notre Dame
> The pilgrims follow by the sacred waters
> And arm in arm go the sons and daughters
> The drums are rolling and forward bound
> They're calling spirits up from the ground
> And there's a magic in the sound of their name
> Here come the Irish of Notre Dame

> "I tossed it over to the athletic department to get their reaction, and the next thing I knew Bob Davie was calling and thanking me, and asking me about the song. It just sort of sprang up from the ground, and the rest is, as they say, history."

> "The song continues to keep me very involved with Notre Dame. Recently, I did a short program for the ND Women Connect group over at the Stayer Center. Both of my daughters have also graduated from Notre Dame, Britt in 2010, and Annie in 2011. Britt sang the song (Here Come the Irish) for me on campus, at an event, as Cathy Richardson (who originally recorded the song for us) was traveling with Jefferson Starship."

> "Cathy Richardson? She's the real deal. I wrote a song for another institution, and asked Cathy to come in and sing it. She came in, learned the song, and sang it like she's been singing it her entire life. Cathy has been an absolute pleasure to work with."

I also had the chance to speak to Cathy Richardson, whose incredible voice brought John's song, "Here Come the Irish" to life, and she explained to me how she came to work with John.

> *"John Scully (Notre Dame center, 1977-1980) and Jim Tullio wrote the song together. Jim was a (Grammy Award winning) producer friend of mine that I had worked with in Chicago. John had written this beautiful song about Notre Dame and he and Jim just hired me to sing it. At the time (1997) I was doing a lot of commercial recording sessions. People would write songs and then would hire me to sing them. That's how I got involved on the 'Here Come the Irish of Notre Dame' project; I was hired as a session singer. After we recorded it I never really heard anything about it and then 10 years later I got a call from the school. They said, 'Do you have any idea how popular this song is?' and I had absolutely no idea. They asked me to come and sing it at a basketball pep rally and it was an incredible experience. I felt like I was the Notre Dame 'Beatles.' The response that I got from the audience literally blew me away. I started going to the school and doing performances at special events. You don't even have to be affiliated with the school to be affected that way. I know for people who go to Notre Dame, the way that they feel about the school is different than how most people feel about their college or university. It's just different. I can't put it into words. It's more than just pride. It's a spiritual thing. Music transcends those sorts of titles and boxes that we put ourselves into because I'm not a Notre Dame graduate or Catholic and I still can feel the impact of the Notre Dame spirit."*

When I interview fellow authors, I always ask them what they are reading, or for them to share their favorite books with me. And so when I interviewed John, a musician, I couldn't resist asking him what kind of music he listens to. Here's what he had to say.

> *"Back when I used to play football, I got used to dividing my year in half. Half of the year I would focus on football, and then the other half of the year I would focus on music. So as a result of that, I have a tendency to get away from music for a period of time, and then I get back into it. Right now I'm in one of my 'off music' periods, but there really isn't a genre of music that I can't find something to listen to. I listen to anything from genuine country music all the way to rap. Every genre of music has its top 10% where all of the good stuff lives; I enjoy listening to good music of any kind!"*

So many young people aspire to chase their dreams of playing sports at the Division I level. It's not an easy journey to embark upon, but who better to ask for some words of wisdom than someone who has been there before and succeeded.

John shared with me his words of wisdom on how to be successful as a student-athlete at a Division I school.

> "The message I would give to student-athletes aspiring to have a career in sports is that playing sports at the professional level can be a fleeting goal for any number of reasons. And although it wasn't particularly thrilling for me to pay attention to my academic studies, in retrospect, I probably should have done much better. The idea of actually getting a degree should be of supreme importance as you will use it for the rest of your life, and there will be a rest of your life."

> "As far as advice for boys and young men wanting to play football, I've heard so many stories about former players suffering from concussion syndrome and other maladies. I know, first hand, how dangerous the sport is. For example, I just had both of my shoulders replaced, I've had knee surgery and a broken leg. But, I think that in sports, as in life, you have to keep everything in balance. And if you run away from things, there is a peril in that as well. There isn't a better exercise than football for teaching you how to work with other people, and you will need to work with people for the rest of your life, at one time or another.

John currently lives in Joliet, IL, with his wife Annette, and they have two daughters, Britt Florin and Annie Scully, both of whom are Notre Dame graduates.

John Scully's Lessons from the Notre Dame Value Stream:

- Always show up early. As I was taught by Coach Dan Devine, if you show up on time, you're actually late; in order to be on time, always show up early. This simple rule is one I've used in all aspects of my life. It may sound like a very simple rule, but for so many people it's a very hard rule to follow.

- Get your college degree. Although it wasn't particularly thrilling for me to pay attention to my academic studies, in retrospect, I probably should have done much better. The idea of actually getting a degree should be of supreme importance as you will use it for the rest of your life, and there will be a rest of your life.

- Sports is such a great teacher for life. There isn't a better exercise that playing on a team for teaching you how to work with other people, and you will need to work with people for the rest of your life, at one time or another.

John Scully. (Photo courtesy of Matt Cashore.)

Senior split end, Clint Johnson, returns the only Purdue kickoff for the day.
He returned the ball 53 yards on the kick.
(Photo by Brian McDonough, courtesy of Notre Dame Archives.)

CHAPTER TWO

The Game Changer

Clint Johnson

(Notre Dame Football – Class of 1994)

*L*ife is a wonderful and often unexpected journey. We set out on one path, convinced that we are absolutely positive as to where we are headed, and almost without fail get diverted onto a new path that while unplanned, is more incredible than we ever could have dreamed. On Thanksgiving evening of 2016, Clint Johnson, former University of Notre Dame wide receiver, was offered the head coaching position at Oak Ridge High School in Orlando, FL. Clint took over as head coach for Kenard Lang, who stepped down from his post on November 7th due to chronic back problems following a 3-7 season. He may not have planned to be on this particular path, and yet at the same time can't imagine being anywhere else. How does a young man who started out playing pickup football games in Paducah, KY, become the head football coach at Oak Ridge High School? This is Clint Johnson's story.

"As a boy growing up in Paducah, KY, I was exposed to football at a very early age. It was a way of life for me, from pickup games at the abandoned fire station lot to youth football. I absolutely lived for the game. The local high school, Paducah Tilghman, was a breeding ground for athletes and became a perennial contender for state championships. It is this environment and culture that was engrained in me, and it was all that I wanted to be. I was raised by my grandparents and my (single) mom. When I was 12-years-old, my mom accepted a job in Altamonte Springs, FL (a suburb of Orlando), and I embarked on a new and unexpected journey. Through new friendships and church relationships, my mom was told about the local Pop Warner Youth Football program. She signed me up to play and my Florida football journey began. Immediately I experienced some success, as I was faster than any of the other 13-year-olds in my division. Pop Warner playing restrictions were governed by the player's weight. I grew rapidly between my 7th and 8th grade year, and so in order to meet my weigh-in for Saturday football games, I remember taking tuna fish and crackers for lunch during the school week. It was right about then that the high school coaches started to show up at my Saturday morning games."

"Upon completing middle school, I entered Lake Brantley High School. I was Lake Brantley's first black quarterback. I had an outstanding freshman year, which included beating our rival school's freshmen team, which hadn't happened for five years. I was moved to the varsity squad in the spring of my freshman year, and became the varsity quarterback as a sophomore. I enjoyed a successful sophomore season until I broke the thumb on my throwing hand. Expectations were high for me as I entered my junior season. Lake Brantley High School had never won a district championship or been to the state playoffs. That year, we won both the district and conference championships, and went to the playoffs. My name began to spread and the recruiting letters and coaches started to show up. In the spring of my junior year, heading into my senior year, the scouts would line the field to watch me practice. In those days, most families had micro-cassette answering machines. Every day I would come home from school to a completely full micro-cassette that could no longer record any more messages. In addition to that, I was receiving recruiting mail daily. Going into my senior season I was ranked, depending on the publication, either the number one or number two option quarterback. Ironically,

I never played cornerback in my high school career, but I was also ranked as one of the top ten cornerbacks in the nation."

"Recruiting in the late 1980s wasn't at all like it is today. Back then, Tom Lemming's Top 100 list was the end all, be all. All of the high school football players being recruited would anxiously wait for the Tom Lemming report to come out, to see where you were ranked. When I was coming out in 1990, the top three option running quarterbacks were Mill 'The Thrill' Coleman (Michigan State), Corey Sawyer (FSU) and myself. Since I was so highly ranked, I was aggressively recruited by several schools. The first school that actively pursued me was Florida State (Coach Billy Sexton). The most intense pursuit to get me was the University of Colorado. Coach Gary Barnett was at my house just about every other week, selling me on all of the things that the University of Colorado had to offer. When I made my trip to Boulder, I flew into Denver. I landed at the airport and the pilot announced that it was 12 degrees. I didn't even know it could actually get that cold, and the only jacket I had was my high school letterman jacket. Darian Hagan, who finished 5th in the 1989 Heisman Trophy voting was my host when I made my trip to CU, and Colorado was the only school that had their University President directly call me to recruit me to come to his school."

"The next school that was pursuing me was the University of Arizona. The very first official recruiting trip that I took was to Arizona, and their head coach, Dick Tomey, actually drove me around everywhere during my visit. Colorado was my second visit, Georgia was my third, Notre Dame was my fourth and Michigan was my fifth visit. Andre Hastings, the offensive player of the year that year, was also visiting Michigan when I did. As a Florida kid, the local Florida schools were also pursing me. The University of Miami didn't recruit me very hard, but Florida State started calling towards the end of my sophomore year, beginning of my junior year, and Billy Sexton was their running backs coach. The University of Florida was also recruiting me pretty heavily, but they were on probation at the time for recruiting violations, and I wasn't interested in going to a school that was on probation and couldn't play in any bowl games. Steve Spurrier was coming in as their new head coach from Duke, but it wasn't enough to get me there. The violations were just too much of a barrier for me."

"The players whom I idolized in high school were Jamelle Holloway and Charles Johnson, who both went to the University of Oklahoma (OU). I recorded all of the OU games because I wanted to be just like Jamelle Holloway. I had his pictures all over my wall. I wanted to be the best option quarterback in the nation. I only played defense one time during my high school career. It was in a game against our rival, Lake Mary High School, during my senior season. We had scored the go-ahead score at the end of the game and my coach put me in as a free safety and told me to stay back just in case they threw a long ball. Sure enough, they threw a long ball, and I caught it for an interception and ran it for 60 yards. That one play earned me defensive player of the week and got my coach and I invited to this big dinner in Orlando for all of the players of the week. My coach thought it was hysterical that one play got us invited to this fancy steak dinner. In fact, in one high school football publication I was ranked as the number nine cornerback, even though I never played cornerback in high school. I was getting a lot of attention for being a big time athlete."

> **"Winners embrace hard work. They love the discipline of it, the trade-off they're making to win. Losers, on the other hand, see it as punishment. And that's the difference." - Coach Lou Holtz**

"Recruiting was very hectic for me, however, a few recruiters stood out: Vinny Cerrato of Notre Dame and Gary Barnett of Colorado. Vinny Cerrato very quickly rose to the top. Vinny was silky smooth, and he won my mom over almost instantly. He was the only recruiter my mom would allow in the house to take his shoes off. Vinny would flash the 1988 National Championship ring around as much as he possibly could. Once he convinced my mom that Notre Dame was the best place for her son, the rest was history. When I made the trip to Notre Dame for my official visit, I didn't even own a coat and it was January in South Bend. The late great Rodney Culver, along with Derek Brown, were my recruiting hosts. Rodney was an amazing person, unbelievable host and outstanding leader. He sold me on Notre Dame the very first night I was there. The next morning was my meeting with Coach Holtz. I sat there, completely in awe and focused on every word Coach Holtz said. It was almost inconceivable to me that I was sitting in the office of one the best college coaches at one of the most historic college football programs in the nation. I was a kid who was born in Paducah, Kentucky (the middle of nowhere) and now I'm sitting with Lou Holtz. It was surreal. I remember Coach Holtz handing me a very small container with a mustard seed in it and telling me, if I believed and had faith in him and NOTRE DAME, together we would accomplish GREAT THINGS! I was sold! I committed on the spot, despite having an official visit scheduled to the University of Michigan the following week."

The Notre Dame Years

> *"It's funny, as I think back on my time at Notre Dame, I can vividly remember the first real big snow that we had. It was during the offseason of my freshman year and I had pulled my groin running track. We had early morning football workouts in the offseason, and the walk from Pangborn Hall to Loftus was very long. I was sound asleep and my phone was ringing off the hook at 5:55 am. I answered the phone and heard:*
>
> > *'Clint?'*
> > *'Yes.'*
> > *'This is Coach Hayes.'*
> > *'Yes.'*
> > *'Where are you?'*
> > *'In my room.' (You called me!!)*
> > *'Get your ass to Loftus RIGHT NOW!'*
> > *'But I'm hurt!!'*
> > *'Get over here RIGHT NOW!'*
>
> *"I limped all the way over there, and they put me on an exercise bike for about five minutes before they called practice."*

One of the best parts of looking back on your collegiate years is how wonderful things look in hindsight. Yes, the work you put in was grueling and the hours were tremendously long, but the camaraderie and the time spent with teammates and classmates filled you up each day, and gave you the strength to put in the work once again the next day. This incredible work ethic, imparted upon Her students and student-athletes along the *Notre Dame Value Stream*, not only afforded them to be successful during their years at Notre Dame, but in their time afterwards as well. Clint shared with me some of his favorite memories from his days at Notre Dame.

> *"On the field, my favorite memory was when we played Stanford my senior year. Playing on the road at Stanford against head coach Bill Walsh was a really big deal for me. And then, having a 106 yard kickoff return that day, that was huge. I was named the ABC player of the game, and then the next week I made it into Sports Illustrated. That is my biggest highlight of my playing days at Notre Dame, hands down. Student-wise, graduation day was my favorite off the field Notre Dame memory. Realizing that I was receiving my degree from the University of Notre Dame was an amazing feeling. You didn't really get acknowledged at graduation, they didn't call out your names individually, but rather by each school. But the fact that you met all of your*

> *requirements, graduated, and were heading out into the world; that was an incredible day. One other favorite memory of mine would have to be coming out of the tunnel for my first home game my freshman year. My first home game was against Michigan in 1990, under the lights, and coming out of the tunnel to that packed stadium was truly unforgettable."*

As a high school student-athlete who is focused on playing at the Division I level, you must excel at both your academics and athletics in order to even get an opportunity to play at the next level. But once you get to that Division I program, no matter how prepared you think you are, it is still quite a culture shock, and quite an adjustment to acclimate to the pressures of playing at the next level. Thankfully when you attend the University of Notre Dame, you have the *Notre Dame Value Stream* to carry you through the rough waters that you are sure to encounter during your time under the Dome. Nothing worth having is ever easy, but it helps when you have an incredible support system to carry you through the tough times, and to show you how to reach the summit of your dreams.

> *"Being a student-athlete at Notre Dame was tough, especially your freshman year. I came into Notre Dame thinking I was a pretty good student. I can remember those first exams and mid-terms that I took freshman year, and how I totally bombed them. I had a meeting with my academic advisor and with my coach Skip Holtz, and they both told me, 'Clint, we don't know if you're going to make it.' I had a 0.8 GPA after my midterm exams. 'We don't know what's going to happen, Clint, but it doesn't look good.' Here I was, the first time away from home, trying to get adjusted to the football schedule, practice, going to class, and study hall. Everything was just so taxing. In high school you didn't have all of the requirements that you have as a student-athlete at the collegiate level, and then you add all of the freedoms that come with going away to college. It was a difficult adjustment, but by the end of the first semester, I had brought my grades up to a 2.8. When I met with my advisor at the end of the semester he said, 'Clint, I have to tell you, I've never seen anyone turn it around the way you turned it around this semester.' By making this remarkable turnaround, I proved to myself that I could do the work. My high school was pretty strong, but college academics were another level entirely."*

> *"I started my time at Notre Dame studying business, along with Lake Dawson. It was tough to try and stay focused. To go to practice, learn your plays, satisfy everything that you needed to accomplish on the field and for your coaches, and then turn around and compete with your academic peers in the classroom; it was quite a challenge. I really liked my business classes. Marketing was good, accounting was doable, and then I got to finance and I just*

couldn't wrap my brain around finance. Oh, and statistics was the class from hell. <laughs> So I, along with Lake, changed majors and became communications majors. We decided that being on TV, and broadcasting sports on a network such as ESPN, seemed more fun and more aligned with what we enjoyed and what we wanted to do long term."

When you play for a head coach as colorful as Lou Holtz, you are sure to have at least one, but more likely countless, memorable moments with coach. To pick a favorite "Coach Holtz moment" is all but impossible, but I've discovered that his lads all jump at the chance to share some fun memories of their favorite coach. He may have been incredibly tough on them back in the day, but in hindsight, he gave them exactly what they needed to be successful, and even today they would run through a wall for him if he asked them. Here are Clint's favorite memories of his beloved coach.

> ***"Clint, you are not helping Notre Dame, you're helping the other team; you might as well go stand on the other sideline."***
> ***- Coach Lou Holtz***

"My favorite memory of Coach Holtz happened my freshman year. I was shuffling between the quarterback and receiver positions. We were doing our final scrimmage before the season began and I remember fumbling the snap. I pulled out from under center too quickly and dropped the ball. Coach Holtz just about lost his mind. He yelled at me, 'Clint, you are not helping Notre Dame, you're helping the other team; you might as well go stand on the other sideline.' Such a classic Coach Holtz moment. I also remember when we were preparing to play the University of Florida in the Sugar Bowl my sophomore year (January 1992). All week long the media had been clamoring that we didn't belong in the game, but Coach Holtz wouldn't hear it. He told us, 'If I can get Spurrier to slam his visor down, we've got this.' And sure enough, once we saw Spurrier slam his visor down, and start to jump up and down, we knew we had it. We knew we had won and we started celebrating. That was a great game for us."

"Coach Holtz gave us so many amazing pregame speeches. Obviously, he had a way of conveying his message and getting it across to us quite thoroughly. Ultimately, what sold me on Notre Dame was Coach Holtz and his mustard seed story. I was visiting Notre Dame, and was in his office, when he pulled out this mustard seed. He told me, if you have as much faith in me as the size of this mustard seed, we're going to do great things. I came from a small town in Kentucky, and ended up in Orlando, FL. with my mom, and I never in a million years thought I'd be good enough to play football at a school like Michigan or Notre Dame. Having the opportunity to play football for Coach

> Holtz at Notre Dame, those were some of the best years of my life. Such a tremendous opportunity and blessing for me."

Just when you feel you've mastered balancing the academic work with the rigors of Division I college athletics, graduation day is upon you and it's time to move on. The time you spend in college is so pivotal, as far as setting you up with the tools needed to be successful in the rest of your life. But there comes a time when you have to cut the cord, and head out into the world, and see what you're really made of. Thankfully, for Notre Dame graduates, the *Notre Dame Value Stream* stays with you for all of your days, constantly giving you the guidance you need, in good times as well as in bad.

> "When I was getting ready to graduate from Notre Dame, I was in a catch 22 situation. Everyone around me was preparing for the NFL draft, and I too wanted to get my opportunity to play in the NFL. But, I was also eligible to come back and play for a fifth year. Coach (George) Kelly let me know that I was cleared and could come back and play another year at Notre Dame if I wanted to, but I had also talked to some NFL agents in order to help me decide which route I wanted to take. In the end, I felt I had an opportunity to get drafted. I wasn't sure where in the draft I'd get chosen, but worst case I felt I'd go in one of the late rounds. I did all of the NFL workouts and spoke with all of the people I needed to speak to. Then Coach Holtz called me into his office and he asked me, 'Okay Clint, what are you going to do? And I said, 'Coach, I'm going to take my chance and see what I can do in the league.' He said, 'If it doesn't work out, you can always come back.' Sure enough, I did all the workouts and went through the draft process. Draft day came and I thought, okay, here we go. You sit there and watch pick after pick, and my name never got called. As soon as the draft ended, my phone started ringing off the hook. The Cincinnati Bengals, Atlanta Falcons and Indianapolis Colts were all interested in me."

> "Former Notre Dame Coach Joe Wessel was coaching with the Bengals, which meant there was an instant connection for me there. Another former Notre Dame special teams coach was with the Atlanta Falcons, which meant I had a connection there as well. In addition to that, the general manager from Atlanta had come to meet with me before the draft, and so my relationship with the Falcons was the most established of the three teams who were interested in me. When the official offers came in, the offer from the Falcons was the highest. Not only that, they ran the run and shoot system with their wide receivers, which was perfect for a small, fast receiver like myself. And so that's where I went. June Jones was the head coach of the Falcons at the time, along

> with quarterback coach Darrel 'Mouse' Davis, who was the 'godfather' of the run and shoot offense, which was the system that won the Heisman for Andre Ware. My decision was made, I was headed to Atlanta. With my head in the clouds and my sights set on success, I headed off to training camp. Everything was going great until the last week of training camp, when I aggravated the same groin injury that I suffered my freshman year at Notre Dame. And so there I was, and there wasn't anything I could do about it. It became a numbers situation at that point, and that last week of camp I was released and I returned to Orlando."

> "Following being released by the Falcons, I received a call about an opportunity to play for the World Football League (NFL Europe). The agent I had hired (who was also working with Irv Smith, Lake Dawson and Jeff Burris) ended up separating from his partner, and in the confusion neglected to submit my paperwork on time to the World Football League, which I was unaware of. When draft day came for the WFL, they called me and asked me if I was still interested in playing in the league, because they never received my paperwork. As a result, I wasn't qualified to be a part of the draft, and I missed out on yet another opportunity. Then I was contacted by Jeff Reinebold. Reinebold, who was from South Bend, and I had gotten to know each other when I was a student at Notre Dame. He had moved to a new coaching position with the Edmonton Eskimos in 1995, and asked if I was interested in playing in Canada. I was signed to a CFL contract with the Edmonton Eskimos and left for training camp in the summer of 1996. Once again, I thought things were moving in the right direction. Camp was going great. During one of the morning sessions, we were practicing and the grass was a little high and wet. I was running a route and cut sharply. My cleats slid, I did a split and tore the same groin I previously injured. That, officially, was the end of my football career."

You never know when that fork in the road is going to present itself, but once it does, the choice to change paths can often be as clear as day. And for Clint, his next move was an obvious one, and he set out charting his next path in life.

Today

> "At that point I changed my course and went to Law School at Valparaiso University School of Law. Upon completing my law degree, I returned to Orlando and practiced law for approximately 10 years. I started out as a prosecutor, then transitioned to private practice and focused on criminal defense, civil law, personal injury, and wrongful death. The practice of law is a rewarding experience, and I met a lot of interesting people. When I was

in training camp with the Atlanta Falcons, the OJ Simpson chase happened. I remember sitting and watching the case. It was so interesting to me. I was inspired by Attorney Johnnie Cochran. Becoming a lawyer was a great way for me to still be in a competitive environment, to be in a job where you essentially were trying to 'one up' the opposing lawyer on a daily basis. When you go into the courtroom, it's one-on-one, it's you against the other lawyer. It came down to who was prepared, who knew their opponent's weaknesses and who knew how to strategize."

I have this crazy idea that my purpose is bigger than me.

While Clint not only enjoyed life as a lawyer, but thrived in the role, he once again faced a fork in the road, and decided to adjust his path one more time.

"I had experienced so much, and at the same time had dealt with so much in the legal world. And while I enjoyed it, I decided that it was time for a change. I wanted to get back to my roots, and my roots were firmly planted in football. I reached out to a guy I knew from Orlando, who was working at Oak Ridge High School. He told me that the head coach of their football team was Elijah Williams, and he connected me with Coach Williams. Williams had been a captain at the University of Florida back in the day, and my contact flat out told me, 'there is no way he is going to let you coach the receivers, he likes to control the offense. But I wanted to give it a try anyways. So I got an introduction to Coach Williams, and initially that's exactly how he was, but honestly, that's how most head coaches are. They want you to know it's their show and that they are in charge. I was okay with humbling myself and I wanted to learn the coaching system. It was a challenge for me, but I was up for it. That season was a great experience for me. I learned everything I could and soaked it all up like a sponge. We went 8-2, and ended up losing to Manatee High School in the playoffs."

"During that season at Oak Ridge High School, I was being courted by my old high school (Lake Brantley). It was quite an honor. My jersey is retired there, I was the first black quarterback, the first black homecoming king, we won the first district championship, and the current athletic director there is a Notre Dame alum. She kept telling me that they were interested in talking to me. At the time, the current head coach at Lake Brantley high school had been the defensive coordinator back when I played there, and he had decided to step down. Since I graduated from Lake Brantley in 1990 they continued in their quest for excellence, and their football team was perennially in the playoffs. The culture that had been created there was one in which they were expected to be in the playoffs every year. I was informed that some of the

boosters, as well as players were ready for a change; they wanted something new. The current coach had been running the same offense, and the same option plays for all these years. They were ready for something fresh and new, and they were interested in me interviewing for their new head coach."

"When it came time for me to interview for the job, I made sure I was 100% prepared for everything. The principal and athletic director interviewed me, and afterwards they told me I was the best interviewee they had ever seen. I was in there for an hour and a half. I felt so good walking out of there. I thought I was a shoe in for the job. But instead they gave the job to the guy who was the quarterback right before me. Lake Brantley has never had a black head coach. I was extremely grateful for the opportunity. The principal told me there was no doubt in his mind that I'd be a head coach somewhere, but they had decided to give the job to someone else."

"While all of this was happening, my old high school baseball coach, who was now the Head Baseball Coach at Colonial high school introduced me to the athletic director at Colonial high school, who was a huge Notre Dame fan and discovered I had interviewed for the job at Lake Brantley, which prompted him to call me in for an interview. I sat down with him and he told me straight out, you're my guy. Colonial's football program was struggling and was attempting to 'change the culture' of the program. And so I took the job. I didn't have a lot of athletes at my disposal. I learned a lot on the fly, having to do everything myself. I didn't have a complete coaching staff. My spring football season consisted of me and one other coach. We were literally coaching every position, doing everything that needed to be done to get ready for the football season. It was so chaotic. I found additional coaches prior to the season, and we were fortunate to get some additional players. We finished the season with a better record than their previous two seasons. Additionally, we won 'The Boot Game,' which is a huge rivalry game against University High School. Colonial had lost the game 10 years in a row. Meanwhile, Oak Ridge also hired a different coach for that same season, which resulted in a losing season. The Oak Ridge head coach resigned immediately after the last game. I was contacted to see if I was interested in returning to Oak Ridge as the head coach. I felt Oak Ridge was the place where I already had established relationships with the kids, faculty and administration. I felt I could make an impact there."

"And so here I am, 20 plus years post Notre Dame, and after 10 successful years of practicing law, I find myself gravitated back to the game that gave me so many unbelievable experiences. I've been blessed in so many ways. Many coaches go their entire career and never become a head coach. I was blessed to be named the head football coach of two high schools in the same year. On Thanksgiving night, in 2016, I was blessed to be offered a position as the head football coach for Oak Ridge High School. My football life and journey continues to take me on a fairytale adventure that could only be conceived in the mind of Walt Disney."

Working with young men to help them fulfill their dreams is one of the most rewarding things I've ever experienced. Changing their mind set, their drive, their ambition is my passion.

As a head football coach at the high school level, Clint spends a great deal of his time mentoring young men who aspire to play football at the next level. Clint shared with me his words of wisdom for student-athletes, as they prepare themselves to make the leap to play at the Division I level.

"Most high school student-athletes don't take their freshmen and sophomore years seriously. They end up digging themselves into a hole and spend their junior and senior years trying to dig out. What they need to realize is they are student-athletes, and without the academic side, there isn't an athletic side. Kids get so wrapped up in recruiting and social media. Everything is built around who gets what offers, and then they turn around and use it as a bullying technique. Just because someone else doesn't have a particular offer, they must not be as good. Kids get worried about the wrong things way too early. What they need to realize is that they can only play for one school at one time. They need to stay focused on the daily tasks. It may seem mundane to them, but their high school years will be over quicker than they realize, and then they'll be looking back wishing they had one more game. The most important thing is to work hard while you have the chance. Control what you can control."

"I work on three things with my student-athletes: Believe, Commit, Work. We discuss them every day. If you believe in yourself and your team you will put in the effort. If you're committed to the team, you do it for the guy next to you. If you're willing to put in the work, and can out work the guy across from you, you will be successful. We put our focus on doing it for each other. I had Michael Bennett, from the Seattle Seahawks, come speak to my team, and he asked them what their record was. Quietly they said 3-7. He responded, 'Don't mumble it, say it with pride.' Bennett told them a story about his old high school, he asked them the same question, and their record was 2-7. He told them they needed to step up and own it. 'Look to your left, look to your right, and own it. Enough is enough. Hold the guy next to you accountable.' The next year, his old high school team went 10-0. It can be done. You've got to want it."

Clint currently lives in Orlando, Florida, with his children, Christion (19) a college freshman, Cameron (14) and Sophia (13) and loves being back in his beloved football world, where he can mold and shape the lives of young men. *"Working with young men to help them fulfill their dreams is one of the most rewarding things I've ever experienced. Changing their mind set, their drive, and their ambition is my passion."*

Coach Clint Johnson (Photo courtesy of AmpUp Media.)

Clint Johnson's Lessons from the Notre Dame Value Stream:

- When you get to high school, take your classes seriously. Most high school student-athletes don't take their freshmen and sophomore years seriously. They end up digging themselves into a hole and spend their junior and senior years trying to dig out. What they need to realize is they are student-athletes, and without the academic side, there isn't an athletic side.

- Step back from social media, and stop comparing yourself to your peers. Kids get so wrapped up in recruiting and social media. Everything is built around who gets what offers, and then they turn around and use it as a bullying technique. Just because someone else doesn't have a particular offer, they must not be as good. Kids get worried about the wrong things way too early. What they need to realize is that they can only play for one school at one time. They need to stay focused on the daily tasks.

- In sports as well as in life, follow these three things: Believe, Commit, Work. I discuss them every day with my student-athletes. If you believe in yourself and your team you will put in the effort. If you're committed to the team, you do it for the guy next to you. If you're willing to put in the work, and can out work the guy across from you, you will be successful. We put our focus on doing it for each other. These are important in sports, as well as in the workplace.

Portrait of football player Stephen Pope in uniform, 1992.
(Photo courtesy of Notre Dame Archives.)

CHAPTER THREE

The Stunt Coordinator

Stephen Pope

(Notre Dame Football – Class of 1994)

Stephen Pope, the son of an Army doctor, started out life as many "Army brats" do, moving from city to city as his father served his country. After moving from the state of Washington to Missouri, and back to Washington again, his dad settled the family permanently in Washington and set out to serve the families of his local community as a pediatrician. His father's philosophy of raising kids who were well-rounded "renaissance men" of sorts served Stephen and his brother Dave well as they both headed off to Notre Dame, not to play football, but to study something in the areas of science and math. How did a young man from Chehalis, WA, who was specifically told by his parents that he could not play the game of football end up playing football for the University of Notre Dame? This is Stephen Pope's story.

> "I grew up in Chehalis, WA, for the majority of my childhood. My dad was in the Army and I was born in Seattle, where my dad was finishing medical school and working at Madigan Army Medical Center. We moved to Fort Leonardwood, MO, when I was in Kindergarten and lived there for two years. When I was in second grade we moved back to Washington and lived in a small town called Adna. They had grades K-12 in one building, and the town had a population of 800. And then when I was in 6th grade we moved to the 'big town' of Chehalis, which had a population of around four to five thousand people. I didn't start playing football until my junior year of high school, which is pretty late in the grand scheme of things. I have a twin brother (Dave) and my parents had told both of us that we were not going to play football, but in hindsight they were just saying that, they didn't really mean it. My brother and I were both very good athletes. We played soccer, basketball, baseball, ran track and eventually played football. Our primary sports were soccer, basketball and track. When my brother and I got to high school, we both wanted to play football, but my dad was a pediatrician and he told us no. He didn't want us to get hurt. He kept giving us all of these medical reasons as to why we shouldn't play football. The next year, when we were sophomores, my brother just went ahead and tried out for the football team without even telling me or my parents. We both played select soccer in the fall (select soccer is the next step above recreational soccer), and one day my brother didn't show up to soccer practice. I got home that night and he told me he had joined the football team. 'Dude, really? What's up with the top secret joining the football team and not telling me? I want to play football, too, but now tryouts are over.'"

> **My parents, being highly intellectual people, didn't care whether or not we played sports in college. They wanted us to go to college to get an education.**

> "The following year, when we were juniors, I also joined the football team and played high school football for two years. I was getting recruited by colleges for basketball and track, along with my brother, but neither of us were really getting any looks for football based on the fact that we hadn't been playing for that long. Both my brother and I were competing at the state level in both basketball and track. Dave was being recruited by the University of Florida and the University of Texas for track, and football-wise we were getting a few casual looks from Pac 10 schools, mostly because they had seen our speed

at track meets. The University of Washington was the only school who was seriously looking at us for football, in the outside linebacker spot. They ran this hybrid outside linebacker/safety position, and they knew we both could run. Washington told us, 'We like to take track athletes, put 20 or 30 pounds on them, and then let them run around and hit people. But, in order to play for us, you'll have to redshirt your freshman year and then you'll be on scholarship your sophomore year.' My parents, being highly intellectual people, didn't care whether or not we played sports in college. They wanted us to go to college to get an education."

"During the college recruiting process, Dave and I both got minority recruiting letters[2] from the University of Notre Dame. My brother and I were very strong in both math and science and had goals of one day becoming engineers and working for NASA, so we liked the idea of looking at a school like ND. Notre Dame flew us both out to take a look at the school (for academics) on a minority recruiting trip. While we were there we inquired about the possibility of playing basketball at Notre Dame, but at the time the basketball team only took one walk-on per year (to travel). Notre Dame did have a great cross country team, but basketball wasn't really going to be an option for us. Then we decided to stop by the football office and see what our chances would be of playing football as a walk-on. Neither one of us knew that Notre Dame had such a long tradition of playing walk-ons on the football team. And then there was the fact that prior to our visit to Notre Dame I thought ND was in Northern California near Stanford. I had no idea that Notre Dame was in Indiana until my mom told me."

"My brother and I visited Notre Dame during the spring break of our senior year in high school, and we happened to be there for the last scrimmage before the Blue and Gold game. We talked to several of the coaches and the intake guy and were told, 'We pretty much take everybody. You'll be on the practice squad until we can assess your ability.' We went to this scrimmage, and it was snowing in April! We both looked at each other, and said to our mom; 'Mom, it's April, and it's snowing!'" And so, two twin brothers who had only played football for three years and two years respectively, decided to go to Notre Dame on academic scholarships earmarked for minorities, and both tried out for the football team. "We graduated from high school at the beginning of June, and at the end of June we went to Notre Dame for

---

Dave and I both received small monetary scholarships for being minority students interested in math or science. However, neither one of us received a football scholarship from Notre Dame, we were both walk-ons.

an engineering camp, which also gave us the opportunity to work out with the football team while we were there. Lake Dawson, who was also from Washington, and I had competed against each other in track back in high school. We kind of knew each other as we both ran the hurdles, so when I ran into him it was nice to see a familiar face."

"It was interesting to come into football camp as a guy from a small town who was not heavily recruited. My parents believed that athletics were an important part of the academic process as they helped you to become a well-rounded person; you need to use every part of your body. My dad was definitely a renaissance man. He would tell me, 'If you want to be an engineer, all of your electives should be in art, so that you don't become one sided in your studies.' And so, as a result of my dad's guidance, all of my electives at Notre Dame were in theater. He also told me, 'And if you happen to also be a good athlete on top of it, well that's great.' My dad played basketball at Gonzaga, and my mom played basketball and ran track at Colorado for one year (and stopped because of the social structure of women's sports at the time), so my brother and I came from an athletic household. Coming into football camp, I knew that the majority of the guys there were on scholarship, but I was going to give it my all to try and make the squad. I was a defensive end in high school, because I was tall and fast, and I was in a small town league that mainly ran the ball. I walked into camp weighing 195 pounds, and was really fast, and they moved me to defensive back and taught me how to back pedal."

"Here I am at Notre Dame summer football camp competing with the likes of Tom Carter, Lake Dawson, Jeff Burris, and John Covington; these guys are looking at me and asking, 'Who is this guy? Where is he from? Where have you been?' To which I responded, 'Chehalis, Washington. . . and I know Lake!' I was 6'3", weighed 195 pounds, and could really run. My brother had a bigger frame, and at 6'5", 210 pounds, they put him at outside linebacker and bulked him up to 230 pounds by the end of his freshman year, but he was able to keep his field speed. The two of us came into that summer football camp and everyone wanted to know who the 'f-ck' we were. 'You two are good, why didn't you get recruited by everyone?' We tried to explain that we were from a small town, but no one was listening. My coaches and parents, coming from a small town, didn't know anything about the recruiting process. My parents would rather I be a scientist than play football. Football for us was a means to an end but once we got to Notre Dame, and were in this amazing situation, we gave it our best and we both made the team. Coach Hayes was the outside linebacker coach at Notre Dame at the time, and had players such as Devon McDonald (senior), Andre Jones (senior), and Karmeeleyah McGill (junior) playing for him. Coach Hayes, who had played outside backer in the pros, looked at my brother and told him at the end of that first summer camp, 'You're going to go pro.' And my brother said, 'What do you mean? I want to run track. Is there a track team here?' My brother really did love track, and his love of track finally won out, and he transferred to Azusa Pacific University, out in California, after our freshmen year. He really wanted to run decathlons, and that's where Dave Johnson was training. My brother ended up having a long track career, and went to three Olympic Trials. Coach Hayes tried as hard as he could to get him to stay, but football wasn't his true love."

The Notre Dame Years

"We came to Notre Dame, made the scout squad, and made the travel team our freshman year. I didn't get any playing minutes that first year, but my brother got some minutes on kickoff coverage. My goal with football was to use it to help make myself a well-rounded person. At the time, Notre Dame was one of the top three programs in the country, and every year they were competing for the national title. Playing football at Notre Dame was more of a continual test for me. 'Okay, I made the team. Now I need to work into getting playing time, so that I can get a scholarship.' Unfortunately, I got hurt during spring ball after only one season at Notre Dame, and my glory days came and went just like that. I didn't really get along with my position coach, as he tended to look down on me as a walk-on. He treated me like, 'How dare you think you can come in here as a walk-on and play on this team.' He pretty much used me as a tackling dummy. At the end of my freshman season, he left and Coach Cooper took over. Coach Cooper came in (as we were starting winter workouts) and told us, 'I'm the new coach. I've watched tape on everyone, and you've all got a clean slate. If you can play, you'll play.' Going into spring camp the defensive backfield on the team pretty much consisted entirely of my class, other than Greg Davis, who was coming back as a fifth year senior. On the depth chart, I was the number two strong safety behind Greg Davis. Tom Carter and John Covington were at free safety. Willie Clark was playing cornerback. This was my time to shine."

"Spring ball had been going very well for me. In the scrimmage before, I had an interception. We were in Loftus scrimmaging because there was two feet of snow outside – <Stephen laughed as he told me>, and it was the last scrimmage before the spring game. The call was a safety blitz and I blew up Rick Mirer, but somehow he was still able to twist and get the pass off (which was incomplete, by-the-way). Unfortunately as he twisted, I got my foot stuck in the turf and *tore up my left knee/ACL. This was a pads on, no holding back scrimmage. I had just nearly sacked our starting quarterback Rick Mirer and was most likely going to start on special teams in the fall, and I destroyed my knee. I had finally legitimized myself, and on one play I destroyed myself. I had surgery on August 4th and was out my entire sophomore season rehabbing, which meant no scholarship. I spoke with my coaches after my surgery and they told me to go through the rehab protocol, and we'll see where you are when you're healthy. As my class was so deep at defensive backs, not to mention the underclassmen that came in behind me, I started to think I was never going to get to play again."*

"After rehab was complete and I was fully recovered, I had bulked up to around 215-220 pounds (as the result of spending four hours a day in the weight room, because I had nothing else to do). They told me that if I could put on another 5-10 pounds, that they could use me at outside linebacker, where they were light; but this was a mistake. Unlike my brother, I just couldn't put weight on. I was getting hammered at outside linebacker by the likes of Irv Smith and Oscar McBride. They were handling me every day at practice. As hard as I tried, I just could not stop them. At the end of spring ball, they moved me back to short side corner, and as we were heading into the fall of my junior year they had me on special teams and nickel back. During the third game of the season, we were facing Michigan State University, in East Lansing. On kickoff coverage, this guy blocked me and knocked me out; I blew out my right knee. So at that point, with as much depth as there was in my class, and the two classes now behind me, I decided to hang up my cleats. It was a very difficult decision. I spoke with Coach Holtz and let him know that I was not coming back, and he had some really great words of advice for me. He started by saying, 'I see you're doing well in class,' and I thought, 'Whoa, he actually knew who I was.' He was always invested in me, even though I wasn't a star player. Obviously my position coaches knew who I was, but I was pretty blown away that Coach Holtz not only knew me, but knew what I was doing both on and off the field. Because really, up until that point, the only contact I had with Coach Holtz was him yelling at me."

As a young man who tried to develop himself both academically and athletically, Stephen had an impressive work ethic. He not only tried to improve himself, but those around him as well. Stephen's next story shows as a walk-on, this work ethic can at times be taken the wrong way by coaches and teammates. But at the end of the day, clarity usually surfaces through the current of the *Notre Dame Value Stream*, and the challenge brought forth makes everyone step up their game to the next level.

***And to be honest, the guys on offense were getting kind of lazy,
so I come in and hit the running back.***

> "During spring ball my sophomore year, we were already looking ahead to fall ball and preparing for the first game of the season. As a defensive player on the scout team, we were tasked with running a particular team's offense, and on this particular day we were running Northwestern's defense, as they were the first game of the season. This particular practice was a half speed practice. Basically, you were walking through the plays on the field. After walking through a couple of plays, we moved to running plays at full speed with the caveat that nobody hits the ground. Well f-ck, man. I know exactly what they're going to run. And to be honest, the guys on offense were getting kind of lazy, so I come in and hit the running back. I don't knock him down, just hit him squarely, but apparently that was too much. Then I hear the coaches yell, 'Pope, what are you doing?! That's not your assignment. Run the defense g-d d-mnit.' And I reply, 'But coach, he did such and such, and so that's why I did this.' It was the first time I had ever talked back to a coach. Coach Holtz looks directly at me and says, 'Run the g-d d-mn defense or get out of here.' Yep, that was the gist of it. Then Skip Holtz comes over and starts berating the running back, and after that goes back over to speak with Coach Holtz. At least someone recognized that I wasn't being a jerk, I was merely trying to help the offense get better."

A team is made up of players with not only diverse talent levels, but diverse personalities as well. This can be good, as it helps each player to grow based on their teammates pushing them on; it can be challenging as well. The *Notre Dame Value Stream* knows exactly what to do to take this diversity and turn it into something incredible.

> "Ricky Watters, Tony Brooks, Andre Jones and Todd Lyght were the rock stars of Notre Dame when I came in as a freshman. They were seniors that year, and had just won the national championship the year before. I was lined up across from Ricky my freshman year, and I was pretty uneducated when it came to Notre Dame Football. Yes, they had won the national title the year before, but I didn't follow Notre Dame Football. They weren't my squad, I followed west coast teams. As a result of my not knowing who the 'star players' were, Ricky thought I had disrespected him. And so as a result of him thinking I had disrespected him, in my mind it was his goal every practice to knock me out. I thought he had this personal vendetta against me."

As a walk-on, you had to prove yourself every day.

"This one day at practice, we're having this scout team moment where coach is getting on us. He is screaming at the defense to run the play because he's trying to get his rock stars to actually practice. Meanwhile, Ricky Watters and Todd Lyght and Andre Jones are telling us, 'we're seniors. We won a national championship. We're not getting hurt, we're going pro. We are not going to practice hard.' And they let it be known. And Coach Holtz says to them, 'yeah, you won in '88, but guess what? This isn't '88, and if you actually practice, you have the chance to win it again.' So I am lined up across from Ricky. It's a full speed; nobody goes to the ground practice. I'm playing free safety. When we run the play I wrap Ricky up, and he f-cking throws an elbow to my chin and knocks me down, and runs all the way down the field. I'm thinking to myself, 'what the f-ck was that? I'm being the dude, and coming in, and helping you out.' We're doing repetition drills, and so we line back up to run it again, and what do I do? I don't just wrap him up or knock him down, but I f-cking rock him, and drive him back six yards, and now he's hot. He immediately comes after me, 'who the f-ck are you? How dare you?' and I just say, 'dude, whatever,' and walk away. I knew I was a good athlete, and a smart guy; I also knew I could play at Notre Dame if given the chance. As a walk-on, you had to prove yourself every day."

"Willie Clark lived in my dorm (Morrissey Hall) and then we were roommates for two years. He was a guy who would sleep through class (and still do well), and was incredibly fast on the field, oozing with physical talent. He could walk into practice in flip flops and then turn around and run a killer 40. He was an exceptionally smart guy, however his goals were different than mine: he wanted to go pro after his junior year. We had quite the football crew in Morrissey: myself, Willie Clark, Greg Davis, and Kevin McDougal. I knew that if I could make it through my freshman, sophomore and junior years as a walk on, that I could get a scholarship for my senior year which would take some of the pressure off. I also knew that one out of five seniors from Division I schools made the pros, and at Notre Dame that number was one out of three seniors. I never had really thought about going pro until Coach Holtz threw out the one in three stat; that made me pause. Going into my junior year, I started to look around. I'm better than that guy, and I'm better than that guy; if nothing else, I can go through the free agent process. I already have the mental capacity to stick it out as a walk on at Notre Dame; surely I can go through the rigors of the NFL. And then I got hurt."

Being a student-athlete at Notre Dame is a challenge no matter what you are studying. But being a student-athlete at Notre Dame who is playing on the football team, and trying to complete a degree in engineering, is more than just "challenging" to say the least. Fortunately for student-athletes who choose to embark on such a demanding path, both on and off the field, the *Notre Dame Value Stream* is there to show them how to put in the necessary hard work to succeed at such a high level.

> *"I have a very skewed look at what it was like to be a student-athlete at Notre Dame because I was trying to make it as a ND football walk-on and study engineering at the same time."* What does that mean you ask? *"That meant being in a higher level math class at 8 am, taking advanced science classes, and trying to fit labs into your schedule, which usually met when you were supposed to be at football practice. It definitely was extremely challenging, trying to be a successful student and a successful athlete at a school like Notre Dame. You have to be quite organized, you have to accept the fact that you are going to be tired all of the time, and you have to find a way to motivate yourself to keep moving forward."*

> *"For me, I talked to my dad a lot. We didn't necessarily talk about the dynamic of being a student-athlete, instead we talked about being a good student and oh yeah, playing a sport, too. For me, and my dad as well, the focus was never on athletics; the focus was on academics. When I went out on that field, I had something to prove to myself and my teammates, but I didn't have to perform in order to keep my scholarship as I was a walk-on. The great thing about that was it allowed me to focus on my studies; I didn't have anything to lose. The coaches were happy to have me on the team. I was the guy who ran the scout defense, because the coaches knew I was smart enough to handle it. I happily accepted that role because I understood its importance. I was helping the team win games by preparing the offense for what they were going to see the next week. And the benefit of being a walk-on was that anything good I did was a bonus. The coaches weren't necessarily looking to me to fill spots. Everything I did was a bonus for the team, which allowed me to focus on my academics more than the scholarship guys were able to do. I didn't have to fight through the type of adversity that the scholarship athletes had to go through."*

Yep, that's Notre Dame; they never close.

> *"The main thing that helped me get through the rigors of Notre Dame was the bond that I shared with the guys. We still talk about that today. We played an incredibly difficult sport, for a top tier program, and at an incredibly difficult school where ethics were critical. And oh, by the way, the winters were brutal. The only time I missed a class because of the snow was during my senior year. I lived off campus, and we had a week where the average*

temperature was -30F, and two nights it got down to -50F and they closed everything down. They told the whole town, 'Don't go out on the roads.' No public offices are open, basically everything is closed. I would go outside and turn on my beat-up 1982 Audi twice a day just to make sure it would still start, but that was as far as I got from the house. The professors would come in and put notes on their doors, 'While the university is still open, we will not be having class today.' Yep, that's Notre Dame; they never close."

You realize that you are who you are, and where you are, because of the trials and tribulations that you went through at Notre Dame.

"One of the greatest things that playing on a team does for you is it builds an incredible camaraderie between you and your teammates. You didn't always get along with everyone, and that was okay. But when you're at a school like Notre Dame, where everyone is smart and school is still kicking your butt, you have a shared feeling of accomplishment with your fellow teammates that you made it through and are thrilled just to have survived. The academic and geographic environment at Notre Dame built a bond in itself, and then you added the team camaraderie and tradition on top of that, and what you got was amazing. Plain and simple, being a student-athlete at Notre Dame was incredible. Being a part of what people identify Notre Dame to be (football), is just indescribable. I feel very fortunate to be able to say I played football at Notre Dame. I have an immeasurable amount of love for Notre Dame. When you go through what we went through at Notre Dame, and then you achieve the perspective of being 10 or 20 years out, you realize that you are who you are, and where you are, because of the trials and tribulations that you went through at Notre Dame."

"As a football player and an engineer, I was oftentimes a lone wolf. There weren't too many of my teammates trying to accomplish what I was trying to do. I was majoring in a hybrid degree: Computer Science and Engineering, which was a brand new degree program at a time when the internet was just beginning. I chose this degree program because I wanted to work for NASA post-graduation. I could see that computers were going to be our future, so I decided my best path at Notre Dame was to study computer science and to study how to engineer or design computers. In hindsight, I should have gotten a degree in electrical or mechanical engineering. And if I had, I probably would have stuck with it. What I was learning in my computer science classes was more programming and artificial intelligence, and less of the engineering I had hoped for. I had an internship in Atlanta with a tech company. I liked

> it but I didn't feel as if they had me applying anything that I was learning in school to real world projects or situations. I just couldn't see the bridge from my degree to a future job."

Back when Stephen started his journey at Notre Dame, his father had told him to take electives that were in a completely different discipline from what he was majoring in and that's exactly what he did. Stephen may not have understood how important this was going to be for him long term, but the *Notre Dame Value Stream* most certainly did.

> "All of the electives that I took while I was studying engineering were in theater. I had my internship in Atlanta between my sophomore and junior year, and then at the end of my junior year I walked into my counselor's office and said, 'I no longer want to pursue a degree in Computer Science/Engineering. And, I'm done playing football. I want to get out of South Bend. What can I switch my major to and still graduate on time?' With all of the electives that I had in theater, my counselor told me I could switch to a theater degree and still graduate on time. And I said, 'Done.' In order to pull it off I had to go to summer school, and my counselor knocked down my language requirement to one year, which I was able to complete in the summer school program. I took all theater classes my senior year and graduated on time with a degree in theater."

Today

> "I really never did have any aspirations to go pro, other than Coach Holtz putting the idea in my head with his one in three statistic. After getting injured and switching my major, I graduated with my degree in theater and moved out to California to live with my brother (who graduated from Azusa Pacific University) in Glendora. At that point, I really wasn't sure what to do with myself. I knew I was smart, and I had just graduated from Notre Dame, but I didn't have a job, and I didn't know what I was marketable at. My girlfriend (when I was in undergrad) was a law student at Notre Dame, and I had helped her with about half of her homework, and so I decided to apply to law school in California (USC, UCLA, Loyola-Marymount). She had graduated from law school at the same time that I graduated from Notre Dame, and had gotten a clerkship in the Washington, D.C./Baltimore area. (She was from New York.) I applied to law school, and got accepted at USC and decided to defer for a year to give myself some headspace to figure out what I wanted to do. At least I had a backup plan while I figured my life out. In the meantime, I worked for UPS loading planes on the night shift at the airport in Ontario, CA., and played a lot of basketball at Venice Beach."

"And then I got to thinking, 'Hey, I'm living in a movie town. I don't know anything about the movie business, but I need a job. I need a steady job so that I can pay my rent and figure out what I'm going to do with myself. One of my friends who lived in Morrissey Hall was Ben Finley. His dad lived in California (Ben Finley, Sr.) and so I called him and said, 'Hey, I've moved to California and I need a job. I'll do anything; file papers, bring coffee, anything.' He had connections to a woman who was a locations manager, and she called me the next day and told me to come to one of her locations. I went in the next day and started working on music videos and commercials. I learned very quickly that music videos and commercials were not what I wanted to do. <laughs> Then I got an opportunity on a low budget movie, and that was much better. After working for about a year, I decided that law school was not something that I wanted to do. I really enjoyed the freelance lifestyle. Every day I was in a different place. While I did not like music videos and commercials, I liked working in TV, and I really liked working on movies; that's what I continued to pursue. Those are coveted spots, though."

"At this point my girlfriend and I were no longer together. I was working all the time in Los Angeles, and she was frustrated with my not moving back to the East Coast. I was trying to work my way back to New York, but she could not see any progress and so she was focusing on her law career in Baltimore. I met an assistant director on a job in Los Angeles who was from New York, and I had told her, 'If you ever have any jobs in New York, I'd love to move to New York.' Two weeks later she called me up as she was starting a low budget job in New York and asked me if I wanted to be a part of it. It was only an 8 week job, but I packed up all of my stuff and moved to New York. I couch surfed for about six or seven months, and tried once more to get back together with my ex, but she had already moved on. She was working for a judge, and I was still couch surfing. She wanted to marry a professional man, and she just didn't see that in me at that point, or in my future for that matter."

"So there I was, couch surfing my way through New York, and trying to figure out how to make it. After working a few low budget movies in New York as a production assistant (PA), I learned how expensive it was to live in New York. I was making enough money to pay the rent every month, but didn't have the money needed to get the apartment (first and last month's rent and a security deposit); I was very quickly wearing out my welcome with my friends. I was driving production trucks, and a lot of the time ended up sleeping in the truck and taking a bird bath in the bathroom at work. And then one day my dad called and said,

'Did you know your grandmother's youngest sister lives in Brooklyn?'
'What?! What are you talking about? I've been here for six months and you're just telling me this now?!'
'Well,' he said, 'she's a little crazy so I've never brought her up, but here's her number. She said you can live with her.'

"And so I moved in with my Great Aunt Lugenia. She was old and had a lot of history, which I absolutely loved. She was a black woman from the old south, and a member of the Republican Party (since she had gotten into politics at 16 years old), because that was the party of Abraham Lincoln. Her goal was to bring the Republican Party back to where it was, before everyone jumped to the Democratic Party back in the 1960s. Her involvement in the Abolitionist Movement was fascinating to me and she got me into politics, taking me to Young Republican meetings. She had made the Abolitionist Honor Role, which was the list of names of all the white families that were abolitionists and were helping out the cause back in the day. I basically moved in with her and became her cook and chauffeur, in addition to working 80 hours a week as a PA. She didn't really have a spare room for me to sleep in, it was her sitting room filled with her antique furniture, so I was sleeping on her couch. Many nights I wouldn't get in from work until 4 am, and then she'd wake me up at 6:45 am to make her coffee, which was pretty rough."

Oh, so you're a real athlete.

"At my second job in New York I met George Aguilar who was a stunt coordinator. Up until that point I had only worked on a few low budget indie films, which are basically two talking heads in a room, and maybe two locations because they can't pay location fees. George and I started talking and he said, 'You're an athlete, aren't you? Do you play basketball?' And I said, 'Yeah, I play basketball.' He asked, 'Did you play basketball in college?' And I told him, 'No, I played football at Notre Dame.' And he replied, 'Oh, so you're a real athlete.' As it turned out, he had played basketball at Virginia Tech his freshman year, but saw the writing on the wall that he probably wouldn't come off the bench until his senior year (he was an undersized point guard), and transferred to Regis College in Colorado. Then he went on to play basketball in Argentina for six or seven years, so he was a legitimate athlete as well. (He was originally from the Washington, D.C. area, and was about 10 years older than me.) He told me I should think about doing stunts, instead of working as a PA. I asked him what that meant, and he explained that he was a stunt coordinator, so it was his job to hire all of the stunt men/women to do the stunts for the actors. And here I thought all this time that the actors did all of their own stunts. At the time, I was still a little naïve in regards to the film business. As my dad says, I'm a little slow on the uptake. After George explained to me what he did I told him, 'Sign me up, man!'"

"My first day on set doing stunts it was me and this guy Phil Nielson. It was the first season of Oz, and we were supposed to be arresting Rick Fox. They needed a big guy to play the role because Rick Fox is really tall, and they told me, 'You'd be great as a cop.' My second day on set, we were filming the Oz season finale, which was a riot scene. It was me and 30 other stunt guys, and our job was to beat the crap out of each other for two days. After that I thought to myself, 'Oh yes, I'm going to do stunts. I get to be physical and athletic at work and get paid for it? I'm in.' After working a couple of stunt roles, I started to wonder, what's the end game in all of this? There's definitely a life span of being a stunt man, because physically you cannot do it forever. George explained to me that the next destination in the path of a stunt man was to become a stunt coordinator, which is what he was. I am very fortunate that I met George when I did. We had so much in common, as we were both athletes and both played sports. We instantly understood each other's energy. One day, one of the other stunt men told me, 'You can't just call the stunt coordinator whenever you want to.' And I said 'Why not? He's the one who brought me into the business, and it's in his best interest to make sure that I am doing the right thing. Otherwise, if I do something wrong and look like a jerk, it reflects poorly on him. So I'm going to ask him questions.' And George understood where I was coming from implicitly. We were a team, and we looked out for each other."

There has to be an amount of trust built before I can just blindly do something and end up getting wrecked.

"As a stunt man or stunt woman you don't have an agent like an actor does. You have to put your face in front of stunt coordinators, give them your headshot, chat them up for five or ten minutes and hope they remember you. There is a cliquishness in the stunt world. And as a result of not having an agent, many stunt men and stunt women try to show loyalty to one stunt coordinator, which can help you land more jobs. The stunt coordinators are revered in the stunt industry. They are the end all be all, but that's not how I viewed stunt coordinators. If my coordinator told me something that was not in my best interest, I would push back. I never took anything at face value, I always asked questions. My peers kept telling me, 'Don't question the stunt coordinator!' But I never bought into that mentality. There has to *be an amount of trust built before I can just blindly do something and end up getting wrecked. That just wasn't my philosophy. And now, as a seasoned stunt professional, and stunt coordinator myself, I tell my stunt guys all the time, question anything that doesn't feel right to you. Don't be a jerk about it, but also don't be afraid to ask questions. Everything should be open for discussion. I think that philosophy comes from my playing sports. You have to have a healthy respect for your coach, but at the same time, your coach isn't god. He has to earn your respect from his record and his knowledge. And then, and only then, if you see that he is going to lead you, are you going to buy into his system or philosophy."*

"Today, working in the stunt industry is a career path. Back in 1996, it wasn't like that. There were a couple of 'stunt families,' and a stunt community in Los Angeles, but in New York, there were only about 10 or 15 people doing stunts. Now there are over 300 people in the industry in New York. Back then it was people who had been dreaming of becoming stunt men since they were 15 years old because somehow they had been exposed to the film industry; which was weird for me, because I didn't even know the stunt industry existed. Now it's a career path. A lot of guys who were in the x-games, and guys who were martial artists, NASCAR drivers and gymnasts are now doing stunt work on movies because they have learned that they can make significant money doing it. Fifteen years ago there was this huge influx of people into the stunt industry, with each subset of people having very specific skills. This is great for the stunt coordinators, because now they have a pool of people to hire from, each with very diverse talent offerings."

I liked recruiting athletes who had played at the college level or beyond into the stunt world, because I knew I was going to get better performance from them based on the work ethic that was already instilled in them.

"When I was doing 'Freedomland' with Samuel Jackson and Julianne Moore, Moore was playing a white woman who was a drug addict, whose baby was stolen. She was claiming that the baby was stolen by someone from the projects, when in reality she was just high. Samuel Jackson was playing the investigating officer. In the film we had this riot scene, and at the time in New York we only had three black stunt guys, and I needed 10 for the scene. Not too long before I started working on this project I had reconnected with Jeremy Sample. He had told me he was looking to change his career path and so I decided to give him a call and see if he'd be interested in giving the stunt business a shot. 'Hey, can you take a week or two off? I have a stunt role that I think you'd be great for, and you can go back to the office and brag about *being in a movie.' Jeremy had actually already quit his job and was working as a personal trainer at a body building gym training athletes, and so he jumped at the chance to give the stunt business a try. At that time, a lot of stunt men were the 'weekend warrior' type of athletes, who were decent high school athletes but had never played at a high level. I liked recruiting athletes who had played at the college level or beyond into the stunt world, because I knew I was going to get better performance from them based on the work ethic that was already instilled in them."*

"I have a grading system I use when recruiting athletes to become stunt people. I ask them, 'Were you a high school athlete? Division II? NAIA? Division I? Pro athlete?' That's the criteria I use to categorize them. I basically look at athletes from a coaching standpoint. Some people come from traditional sports, but a lot of them do not. Fortunately we've been able to bring in a lot of high performing athletes into the stunt business, and have brought the level of stunts up. George and I have always tried to bring in the higher level athletes. When George brought me into the stunt coordinating business, the talent pool didn't always have the skill sets that we were looking for, so we started to go out and recruit exactly what we needed."

> **My athletic career definitely lead me to where I am today as a stunt coordinator.**

"For me, the stunt business was the perfect fit because in addition to being very physical, it is very technical as well. You have to set up wire rigs and car crashes, and you have to be able to set them up in a way that they are repeatable. You also have to make sure that your stunt men and women walk away from the set each day. You don't want to send anyone to the hospital. The stunt business was a great for me as it let me be an athlete and a performer. And now as a coordinator, it is very cerebral, which was a great next challenge for me. At this point, I feel like I have most of the knowledge that I need. Yes, there is always new technology to learn, but there will always be new technology. It's all about taking the knowledge you have into each job, and applying it a little differently to each specific situation. Most jobs have some similarities, but they also have their own complexities and differences. Based on the environment, you get to be creative, and come up with weird stuff to make the scene work. My athletic career definitely lead me to where I am today as a stunt coordinator."

While Stephen's football career may have ended years ago, as he reminisces with me about his favorite memories from his time at Notre Dame, they seem as if they happened just yesterday. It's so wonderful to see the guys light up as they share their most memorable moments from their days of playing football at Notre Dame. It makes it even more evident to me how much the *Notre Dame Value Stream* cares for Her students, and student-athletes, and how Coach Holtz's adage of "Give me four years, I'll give you forty" not only applies to the relationship between Coach Holtz and his players, but also to the relationship between the University and Her students.

> "My favorite football memory was the game we played at Soldier Field against Northwestern. I was starting on special teams, and it was the first time I had gotten a start. I also have plenty of incredible memories of hanging with the guys in the dorm, and having pizza, but that was the best football moment hands down. And then of course, there's the Orange Bowl game when we played Colorado. The 'clipping game.' If we would have won that game, we would have won the national championship outright that year. But as it was, the NCAA ended up having co-champions that year. By the way, that clip on Rocket's amazing touchdown play wasn't clipping. The ref who made the call was 15 yards past where the play happened! I felt so bad for Rocket. It would have been a great way for him to go out, had the touchdown counted and we'd won the game. But I digress. Playing in the Orange Bowl was such an electric environment. I got to travel with the team, but because I wasn't playing or dressing I got to hang out and be a student/fan for a change, which was awesome. And then I got to be on the sideline during the game, which was unbelievable in a game like that."

As we talked about Stephen's path into the stunt business, I became curious as to what job has been his favorite so far. Stephen talks about the coveted roles in the stunt business, and his favorite project to work on so far.

> "In the stunt business, the big jobs are all skewed towards superheroes, or movies such as 'The Fast and the Furious,' which I personally find very frustrating. Superheroes are great, but everyone right now wants to work on a superhero movie; well, except for me. If I never coordinate a Marvel movie, that would be okay. I've been fortunate. Every once in a while I get to work on a prestige project. Movies that make you say, 'Oh, I was a part of that!' I got to work on 'Detroit' with Kathryn Bigelow. I had the chance to work on 'Selma,' and 'A Wrinkle in Time' with Ava DuVernay; man, she's a force. She's someone that knows where she's going with her projects. She's a force of human nature. Selma was such a historic piece. My grandmother's family is actually from Selma, so getting to work on the movie was very special for me. I was working on the movie 'Goosebumps' in Atlanta when I got the call for 'Selma.' They were also shooting 'Selma' in Atlanta, so it worked out that I

could do both which was very important for me. I feel very fortunate to have been able to be a part of 'Selma.'"

"The way I see the stunt industry is, every movie needs stunt people. Dramas and romantic comedies need stunts as much as action films. It could be as simple as, I need my actor running across the street and a cab stops short. You'd need to have a stunt person to be the cab driver because they have the safety training and mindset. I did four seasons of 'Boardwalk Empire.' For me, that was my stunt classroom or film school. The directing producer for 'Boardwalk Empire,' Tim Van Patten, was so incredible to work with because I got to see and learn so much more than just stunts. I got to see him work on the tandem units, work on the scripts with the writers, and handle any clean up shots. He is just an amazing human, a really great director. 'Boardwalk Empire' was the show where I really went to town learning film. I already knew stunts, so this really helped me grow in my knowledge of the film business as a whole. It was like being in film school, talking to people every day on set. They helped shape the way I look at film. George is now a stunt coordinator and second unit director for Martin Scorsese. Martin is a living movie icon, a walking film encyclopedia. He was involved in the creation of 'Boardwalk Empire' which was a critically acclaimed show year in and year out."

"When I worked on 'A Wrinkle in Time,' I was in Los Angeles and had to hire all of these LA people. The stunt business in Los Angeles has such a different vibe and dynamic compared to the stunt business in New York City. The majority of people who are stunt performers and coordinators in Los Angeles want to work on the flashy jobs with the big stunts. There is a stunt crew called 8711, and they do movies like 'The Matrix' and they are the hottest thing in LA. They are always looking to work on the biggest, most action packed thing out there, which is very much the LA mentality. In New York City, the stunt performers want to work on the best project out there, not the most action packed. In NYC, they are looking for quality over quantity. Don't get me wrong, I have worked on some action-packed projects, such as '22 Jump Street,' but that was more of an action comedy. I'd rather do projects such as that, as opposed to working on a Marvel film."

As with so many students and student-athletes who come out of Notre Dame, Stephen has some philanthropic endeavors which he holds close to his heart.

"I have four kids, three boys ages 19, 16 and 13 and a daughter who is 8-years-old. I take them with me and we volunteer locally here in New York with an organization called the Sato Project. (**www.thesatoproject.org**) 'The Sato Project is dedicated to rescuing abused and abandoned dogs in Puerto

Rico, locally referred to as 'satos.' Since its inception in 2011, The Sato Project has largely focused its efforts on a place unfortunately known as 'Dead Dog Beach,' in the municipality of Yabucoa, one of the island's poorest. We have rescued over 2,000 dogs to date, rehabilitated them with the highest standards of veterinary care and placed them in loving homes in the mainland U.S.' The woman who runs the program, Chrissy Beckles, is a former Golden Glove Boxer, and in 2011 she started the Sato Project. She brings about 30 dogs to the United States every month and finds them all good homes."

"I also help out with my dad's foundation, which is a respite center that he runs in Washington. I wish I could help him more with it, but with me being in New York and him being in Washington it's kind of difficult. My dad is such an amazing person. He became a doctor in order to serve others; it's what makes him the man that he is. I am fortunate to have parents that I love and highly respect. I don't put him on a pedestal because he is my dad, but he is truly an incredible person. When he sold his medical practice, he opened the respite center: Pope's Kids Place. They serve children from disadvantaged communities. They have a pediatric center for kids who have debilitating conditions, who have to stay to receive treatments for multiple days. They are typically not kids with terminal illnesses, but kids who need treatments that take more than just one afternoon or one day."

"For families from disadvantaged families, without my dad's help their children would not be able to receive the care that they need. In Louis County, South of Olympia, my dad has worked tirelessly for at least the last 10 years to build up this respite center. They have eight beds, a full mental health center, a rehab center, and have recently acquired another piece of property where they are going to be able to expand and offer more services. He's also been working to secure endowments from local corporations to help keep the doors open instead of having to fundraise all of the time. As a family, we want to make sure it doesn't fail, not because it has our name on it, but because it is serving a purpose. My dad is doing everything he can now to make sure the center succeeds long after he's gone, because without it the children of Louis County won't have anywhere to go to receive these necessary services. My dad is such an inspirational human. I hope that one day someone will write a book about him. He's one of those people you just aspire to be like."

When looking for advice, it is important to look to someone who has taken the same journey you are about to embark upon. Stephen shares his thoughts on the challenges of being a student-athlete, and his advice on how to best navigate the sometime choppy water.

As a student, when you get to college, one of the biggest hurdles for students in general is the whole concept of being self-disciplined.

"I don't know what the culture is like today for student-athletes in regards to asking for help, but when you start feeling the academic pressure and think you are falling behind, or you start having trouble on the field, ask for help. So often people wait too long to ask for help, and then when they finally do it's too late. Do your best to stay on top of things and to get ahead of problems before they get out of hand. I remember people telling us just that, and so many of us did not listen, and the next thing you know you're sitting out a semester because you're on academic probation. You're thinking to yourself, 'How did I get here?' Well, all of the signs were there. As a student, when you get to college, one of the biggest hurdles for students in general is the whole concept of being self-disciplined. You can have the best of study habits and still not do well if you aren't self-disciplined, and have a good grasp on time management. You start thinking to yourself, 'This is how I've always done things and suddenly it's not working. What do I do now?' Feeling the pressures of college and not asking for help because you think you are a smart person and should have this all figured out can be a recipe for disaster. Whether it's your freshman year or your junior year, always ask for help."

"And then as a student-athlete, you not only have to stay on top of your academics, but your athletics as well. Always ask for help, even if you don't think you need it. Even if it's just to check in with a professor or advisor, ask for their counsel and advice. There is a reason why your coaches and advisors want you to check in with them. They want to make sure you are staying on top of things. Once you fall behind it is almost impossible to catch up. Always do your best to at least stay on top of things, if not get ahead of things. My last piece of advice is, unless you are going to Medical School or Law School, just graduate. No one will care what your grade point average is. People will care much more about your work experience than if you got a C in Chemistry back in college."

"I did exceptionally well in high school. I had a 3.8 grade point average, and A's in both Honors Calculus and my science classes. I got to college and said 'What?!' The whole idea of being in a Calculus lecture at 8 am with 200 people was pretty overwhelming. And then you realize, 'Oh, so I'm supposed to be taking notes of all this?' I was very lucky that I went to Notre Dame the summer before my freshman year and attended that engineering camp. That was very helpful in preparing me for the rigors of life as a student, and then student-athlete, at Notre Dame."

When he's not off on a movie set, Stephen lives in Brooklyn, NY, with his four children (three boys ages 19, 16 and 13 and a daughter who is 8-years-old).

Stephen Pope

Stephen Pope's Lessons from the Notre Dame Value Stream:

- Don't focus on just your academics, or just your sports. Focus on learning many different things in order to make yourself a well-rounded person, or 'renaissance man' of sorts.

- To be successful as a student and an athlete at a top university is challenging. You have to be quite organized, you have to accept the fact that you are going to be tired all of the time, and you have to find a way to motivate yourself to keep moving forward.

- Don't be afraid to ask for help. If you start feeling the academic pressure and think you are falling behind, or you start having trouble on the field, ask for help. So often people wait too long to ask for help, and then when they finally do it's too late. Do your best to stay on top of things and to get ahead of problems before they get out of hand.

Portrait of baseball player Edwin Hartwell in uniform, September 1989.
(Photo courtesy of Notre Dame Archives.)

CHAPTER FOUR

The Business Developer

Edwin Hartwell

(Notre Dame Baseball – Class of 1993)

"They called him the Deacon, because he cheered like someone in church."
– Craig Counsell on Edwin Hartwell

For Edwin (Eddie) Hartwell, playing sports at the collegiate level was never really on his radar. His father had explained to him, "If you go to college on a sports scholarship, they own you. But if you go to college on an academic scholarship, you are in complete control of the situation; you always want to be the one in control." As a result of these sage words of wisdom, Eddie spent his high school years with a primary focus on academics, and a secondary focus on his athletics. While he knew that he excelled at sports, he wanted his ticket to the next level to be based on the merits of his intelligence, and not his athletic prowess. This is Eddie Hartwell's story.

> "When I was about six years old, my father and I were watching the Little League World Series at our home in Pontiac, MI. My father, who was pretty knowledgeable about baseball, had played for a short stint and tried out with the Pittsburgh Pirates, was explaining to me how great baseball is and that these kids are the best players in the country. Then, in the middle of the game, I blurted out that I didn't think the players were that good, not recognizing that the players were only 12-year-old kids. What did my dad say to me, a kid who at that point hadn't even played baseball yet? He said, 'Put up or shut up,' and I did. I started playing tee ball the next summer for the Bloomfield Beaches and Boats, and I never looked back. My parents got divorced when I was 8-years-old, and I moved to Fort Worth, TX with my dad, who was a middle school English teacher at Wedgwood Middle School. Now as you can imagine, football in Texas is much bigger than baseball. Back in Michigan I had already been playing pee wee football since I was about five years old, so it was an easy transition for me to continue playing football when we moved to Texas for the Ridglea Roughnecks in Fort Worth, but I continued to play baseball as well."

> "When I first starting playing football I was a quarterback, and then I became a running back and a linebacker later on. By the time I got to high school at Fort Worth Country Day I was strictly a running back and linebacker. I never really loved football, it was merely a means to an end. My dad told me, 'You can play football or baseball, but you need to have strong academics. If you play college football on a scholarship, they own you. Never let them own you. Don't knock it if it's your way out, but if you have the brains, and you have the ability to get good grades, you are in control.' And so from that point on, my main quest was to excel at my studies, and sports came second. Both of my parents were teachers, along with two of my grandparents, two cousins, two aunts, and a sister so that really wasn't so much my choice as much as it was a dictate from them. If I didn't get good grades, I'd hear about if from someone."

> "Back then, baseball wasn't really a big deal, especially not in Texas. I played summer ball, but they didn't have travel leagues back then. I played against some pretty good players: Calvin Murray (first round pick with the Giants), Chris Messick and Steve Gilbralter. I didn't play at an elite level until my junior year in high school, at which point I ran into Todd Van Poppel. I actually played pretty well, in both football and baseball, and was

getting some looks from some top universities. As far as football went I was being looked at by Columbia, UCLA, the Naval Academy and Stanford. And baseball wise, I was being recruited by Amherst, and took an official visit there. Notre Dame, however, was not looking at me for football or baseball, but I had thrown them on my list for academic reasons. There were some people at my high school who were way into Notre Dame, and ND reached out to me to come visit for a *minority recruitment weekend (they were looking for minority kids who had decent grades). This was of interest to me and so my principal signed me up and I took the trip. Notre Dame flew me up there to visit in the spring. When I asked where we were going, and they said South Bend, I thought, 'Where?' I had no idea that Notre Dame was in South Bend, Indiana. However, when I got to ND I fell in love with the place. Actually, one of the guys I met on that recruitment weekend ended up being my roommate (Drew Lawrence). We met at Grace Hall, and then when we got our roommate assignments and talked on the phone prior to heading to ND in the fall, we figured out we had already met! We hit it off so well we roomed together all four years in Carroll Hall (Vermin Unite!)."*

"*The Naval Academy was quite interested in me, and their offer included me doing a post-graduate year instead of going directly in, and I wasn't interested in that. Amherst made a good offer as well. And then Notre Dame came, and they made me a great offer. Notre Dame's offer was academic-based, and that was the most appealing to me. I told my dad, 'I think I'm going to Notre Dame.' And he said, 'No you're not. The Naval Academy is offering you some serious money, you're going there.' We fought like cats and dogs about it, and finally, I went behind his back and signed the papers to attend Notre Dame without him. He was so upset with me. On the day of my last summer baseball game, he picked me up and had all of my stuff packed. He told me, 'If you are adult enough to make this kind of decision and not go to the Naval Academy, you're on your own.' He handed me two duffle bags, $200, a plane ticket to my mom's house and stuck me in a cab. I was still in my baseball uniform, and off to the airport I went. My mother met me at the airport in Detroit, Michigan, and I walked up to her and said, 'Hey.' And she said, 'Hey nothing. Who do you think you are signing papers behind your father's back?' She took me straight to Notre Dame 10 days before the official move in date, dropped me off at the gravel road at Carroll Hall, gave me another $200 and drove back to Michigan. She never even came in. Other than about one week after I got cut by the Giants, I never went back home. I've been on my own ever since that day.*"

After being alone in Carroll Hall with Father Sullivan for 10 days, people started to arrive and school eventually started. Eddie, who had committed to being at Notre Dame on a strictly academic quest, quickly realized he needed a bit more out of his college experience than just academics.

The Notre Dame Years

"I was on campus for just a few short days freshman year when realized I was completely bored. Classes finished each day around 2 or 3 pm and I had nothing to do. My roommate thought it was awesome. And it was pretty sweet for the first couple of days, and then after that I thought, 'This is not going to f-cking work. I'm gonna kill myself without more than just academics. I'm bored out of my mind. HOW ARE YOU PEOPLE NOT LOOKING FOR SOMETHING MORE?' As a high school student-athlete, I was always busy, and I traveled some playing baseball. I needed something more. Then, on the Saturday of that first week, I saw a sign on the wall in South Dining Hall which read: BASEBALL TRYOUTS. I looked at it and thought, 'Huh.' I had my glove with me, because my old man had packed up and given me all of my belongings. So, what the hell. The sign said meet at Loftus, and when I got there, there was a guy sitting next to the water fountain. He asked me, 'Are you here for baseball?' And I replied, 'Yes.' And he said, 'Head on down the hall.'"

"If you're ever late, you're done. Don't even bother to come back."
- Coach Pat Murphy

"I walked down the hall and there were 300-400 guys down there waiting for tryouts to start. We sat there for a good hour, hour and a half, and some of the guys eventually started to leave. I'd guess maybe 50-60 guys had left by the time Coach Pat Murphy ('Murph') arrived, who was, by-the-way, the guy who was sitting at the water fountain when I came in. Murph walked in and said, 'Well, now that those guys are gone, we can start.' And then he proceeded to curse us out for a good hour. He called us everything but a child of God. He told us that we had our heads so far up our asses, thinking that we could walk-on to the Notre Dame Men's Baseball team. It was blistering. The guy in front of me turned around and looked at me and said, 'Man, I am so far out of my league.' Along with another 100 or so guys who also left. Rico Lozano and I were the only two walk-ons out of that whole group who made the team. Murph even made current players, for example Tom Gulka, try out in order to keep their spots. And he made me try out again my sophomore year. Tom, by the way, works for Nike now (Absolutely brilliant guy. He was a Math major at Notre Dame). Tryouts went on for about a week.

After each tryout, you got a call in the evening telling you to come back the next day. And Murph told us at the very beginning, 'If you're ever late, you're done. Don't even bother to come back.' And so I wasn't late for a solid week or in the next four years."

"On the second day, there were probably 180 kids remaining after the first round of cuts. In the middle of the second day of tryouts, Murph proceeds to call the name of every single kid still at the workout, at every position. It was one of the most impressive things I have ever seen to this day. On the last day of tryouts, which was the next Sunday, Murph was throwing batting practice and said to me, 'Hartwell, come over here.' At that point there were only 15-20 guys left and he said to me, 'You're going to make the team, but don't say anything to anybody. Just keep doing everything you've been doing up to this point. You may not play, but you're going to make the team.' On the last day, he told me to come back on Monday and that I had a locker. I showed up on Monday, and everybody was there, and I remember thinking, 'This is too cool!!' My name was in tape on my locker, but I didn't care. I thought to myself, 'THIS IS SWEET!' I saw Irv and he said, 'YOU MADE IT!' And I said, 'YEAH!!' And then at that point I'm thinking, what the hell just happened? <laughs> I called my father and told him I made the team, and his response was, 'You made it? Is that it?' and he hung up on me. He didn't have much to say to me during my first two years at Notre Dame."

When you come from a rigorous college prep high school background, such as Eddie's at Country Day in Fort Worth, you expect to be able to handle the transition to college pretty smoothly, but even the most capable of student-athletes encounter some pitfalls when making the transition to college. That's where the Notre Dame student-athletes discover the *Notre Dame Value Stream*. She is always there to pick them up when they fall, offer them a little course correction to get them back on the right path, and keep them moving forward in the most optimal direction.

"It was tough. I was ready for class and the work. My college prep high school was quite rigorous, but doing both school and baseball? It was a lot. That first year we started working out in October and November, swung around in December and January (I lost 25-30 pounds and got in great shape), and then when our season truly started, Lord help us. Things shifted into another gear all together. I looked at Coach Murphy and thought he was insane. He was even nuttier in the regular season than he had been in the fall. He would leave us in the practice facility running for hours. He would even fall asleep in his office while we were out there running or practicing. We got up

> at crazy hours in the morning in order to have time in the gym to workout. I'd be up at 4 am, and would be at Loftus at 4:35 am running. I'd have my workout in before 8 am, and be back at my dorm where people would be just getting up. Then I'd go to class, go to practice in the afternoon, until 7 pm sometimes. Your teachers didn't care about your crazy schedule. My Comp and Lit teacher, after recognizing I could write, (thank you Fort Worth Country Day), made me tutor two other guys. Meanwhile all I want to say to her is, 'Lady, I'm struggling. I just made the baseball team. I'm just trying to survive here.' And she said to me, 'Do I care? You have an A/A- in my class, help those two guys.' I remember having a series of games in Hawaii my freshman year. We left on a Wednesday, and I had a paper due on Thursday. I explained my situation to her and her reply? 'I guess your paper better be in before you leave on Wednesday.' What? And so I had to have my paper done before we left. Most of college is a blur to me. I remember some really great moments, but it's all of the details that I miss. It was a constant go, go, go. One minute I was a freshman, then sophomore year you declare your major, junior year I played summer ball, senior year I was voted Captain, and then the next minute I'm graduating. Life just kind of happened."

Eddie was a competitive student-athlete both on and off the field in high school, but making the jump to college athletics was still quite a challenge.

> "Adjusting to the better pitching you see at the college level is a physical thing. Either you can do it or you cannot. But learning to come to the field, to play every day at a higher level was difficult. In high school, you are one of the better players. But in college and professional baseball, it's the mental game of baseball that sets players apart. Notre Dame was tough academically, but I felt more prepared than some of the other guys were, coming from Fort Worth Country Day."

The dynamic between scholarship and walk-on players can sometimes be complicated, but for Eddie, it was pretty straightforward.

> "On the baseball team, there really was no difference between the scholarship players and the walk-ons. No, Murph treated us all like shit. I never felt a difference among my teammates either. Baseball is different because you never know who is going to become the breakout or star player on the team. Football isn't like that. It's rare that a talented guy (like Rick Mirer) comes to college and doesn't play well. It happens. But in baseball, that is always a possibility. (Hal Morris was a walk-on at the University of Michigan and went on to play 15 years in the big leagues.) A lot of the guys were like me. They weren't star players or first round draft picks. They were just a bunch of smart guys

> *who could play ball. We were a bunch of average guys that Coach Murphy beat the shit out of until we didn't know that we were average anymore. We didn't know if we were good or bad, we just knew we were players, and that we played for Notre Dame. It never was about going to the big leagues, it was about getting a great education and playing some baseball along the way."*

Eddie was moving nicely through his academic and athletic career at Notre Dame when the unthinkable happened; he got "the thing."

> *"One day it happened. I got 'the thing.' I'm not sure what brought it on, but one day after my junior year I couldn't throw to hit anything. I had it bad. Craig Counsell completely had my back that summer, and took batting practice with me every day until I was able to shake 'the thing.' He told me, 'We're gonna take batting practice, you and me, and we're gonna do it until you get right.' I'd throw the ball 12 feet in front of the plate, and he'd tell me, 'Don't worry about it. Just keeping throwing.' And he wasn't the only one, all of the guys helped me. There would be days when I'd throw eight or nine balls over the fence, but Craig and my teammates hung in there with me, and low and behold I came through it. It was ugly. . . but I worked myself through it."*

The experience of being a student-athlete is different depending on what school you attend. But at Notre Dame, it's an experience like no other. Eddie talks about what it was like to manage being a walk-on for the baseball team and a marketing major.

> *"Being a student-athlete is one of the hardest things I have ever done and the most satisfying. At the same time, I would never want to do it again. There just were not any shortcuts; at least I didn't find any. It was a ball-breaking experience, to put it bluntly. I mean Notre Dame gave no quarter. She was an unrelenting bitch. And today I love Her for it. With that being said, I had some really good professors including Pat Murphy in Marketing and Ward in accounting. Both guys understood what I was trying to do by playing baseball as a walk-on, but neither ever let me take the easy way out."*

Coaches come in all shapes, sizes and levels of intensity. Coach Murphy had a larger than life personality and demanded all he could get out of you, and then he demanded just a little bit more.

> *"Coach Murphy's coaching style was very similar to my Notre Dame educational experience. He was a ball-breaking, unrelenting taskmaster, and just like ND, I will love him forever for teaching me to be a professional before I ever knew what was happening. Back then we were a bunch of borderline guys who could play a little. We were molded after Coach Murphy. He had*

some talent but plenty of toughness. You find out later that his type of makeup comprises most of the people you deal with in life. Most of us are not that talented, but the ones willing to put in the work always seem to move to the next level. There are no shortcuts. The advantage I had coming into pro ball was that I knew there were no days off, and was prepared to meet that head-on. Coach Murphy and Notre Dame had prepared all of us for that scenario."

> **Most of us are not that talented, but the ones willing to put in the work always seem to move to the next level.**

"To be completely honest, Coach Murphy was crazy. This one time we were playing in San Antonio against St. Mary's, and in one of my at bats I struck out. He followed me up the left field line just cursing me out the whole time. There was another time when he took out an umpire, who he thought made a bad call. Murph was running towards the umpire at home plate and it was wet from raining. Murph tried to stop but couldn't and absolutely took out the umpire. He hit him about waist high, and all we could hear was 'uugggghh.' It completely looked like a WWF wrestling move. He was nuts. Another time, Mike Coss was playing shortstop. He booted two or three balls in a row and Murph literally threw all of the catching gear out there, and told him to put it on. This was during a game!"

"But on the flip side, he absolutely had you ready to play baseball at the next level. You understood that you had to work from Sunday to Saturday. He didn't care about what else was going on in your life, you had to figure out how to manage your time on your own. His job was to teach us baseball. Don't get me wrong, Murph was really good at supporting us in our academics. We had a great study hall, and it really worked for us. The majority of our guys were eligible every season. But it was hard to play for Coach Murphy. If you couldn't take the harsh comments and cruelty, it could crush you. It didn't bother me, but my dad was also a very tough guy, so I was used to it. I still thought Coach Murphy was crazy, but it didn't crush me. It wasn't anything I couldn't handle."

"Coach Murphy was terrified of flying. He'd be all white knuckles, every time we got on a plane. He's now the bench coach with Manager Craig Counsell and the Milwaukee Brewers. After Notre Dame, Murph coached at Arizona State for a while, and then went to the Padres. He moved around a bit and then two years ago he was reunited with Counsell."

Any athletic career is filled with an assortment of magical moments, where the heavens aligned, and everything played out just as they were supposed to. Picking just one is all but impossible, but for Eddie, one memory quickly stood out from the rest.

> "My favorite on the field memory? That's easy. We had a series of games against Dayton my senior year where I hit three home runs one game and I think five or six home runs over the two days. They just kept coming. Every time I swung, the ball left the yard, or so it seemed. It was just perfection every time I stepped up to the plate. One of the homeruns was a grand slam and one was a three run homer. I don't remember all of it, because that series against Dayton was kind of a blur. I do remember, after my third or fourth homerun, I was running around the bases and our hitting instructor, Gary Tuck, said to me, 'Don't ever do that again, or I'll kick your ass!' And I said, 'What did I do?' And he yelled back, 'you just swung your arms in the air.' I didn't even know I had done it. 'My bad.'" <laughs>

> "That whole year, it seemed like I squared up everything. I hit a .447 that year, and was second in the country. I beat Peltier that year, I think he had a .446. I still hold the record for a single season best average with that .447. I had 13 home runs that year and drove in 65 runs. But that stretch against Dayton in particular, that was crazy. Coming up with my best off the field memory is also pretty easy for me. I won the Outstanding Student Award in 1993. Like I said, that year was a crazy good year. It also was a giant blur. I was working so hard on the field and in the classroom. It was a dream come true, being at the top like that. I squared up balls against guys that were incredible, throwing 97 and 98 mile per hour balls at me and I just spun them. It was just my time. I was totally lucky and got in a good zone. Oh, and the brawl against Butler was pretty awesome, too." (Edwin Hartwell, his classmate Eric Danapilis and Dan Peltier remain the only ND players ever to post a slugging pct. above .700 and on-base pct. above .500 in the same season.)[3]

> "The funniest thing about playing baseball at Notre Dame? People could not believe how bad our field was. When we played at the University of Texas, their baseball field was a cathedral. My friends who played at Texas, when they saw pictures of our field would comment to me, 'Man, you guys have a shitty field.' Here's another funny one. We traveled to play a series at UT. All of my friends and former teachers from Fort Worth Country Day, came to see me play. I get a hit. I get on second and steal third, and I'm feeling pretty good about myself right about then, in front of my peeps. I'm on third, and

---

ND Baseball Statistics from: http://grfx.cstv.com/photos/schools/nd/sports/m-basebl/auto_pdf/mg06-basebl-history2.pdf

> *I get a little too far off the base, forgetting I'm playing college ball and not high school ball. This guy throws a bullet at me and I go diving back to third and I'm safe. I don't know whether I was really safe or not. Some people said I was, some people said I wasn't. I get up . . . and I'm covered in chalk. In fact, my whole face, ears, neck, is all covered in chalk, and all of my friends in the stands are just rolling. They literally have to wash me down because there isn't an inch of black on me anymore."*

For a young man like Eddie who came to Notre Dame to get a top education, and ended up playing baseball only by chance, the opportunity to play baseball at the next level was an exceptionally great added bonus.

> *"We played our last tournament of my senior year in Florida and lost to Long Beach State. While talking to Coach Murphy he told me that I might get a chance as a free agent to play at the next level. Murph helped me get signed with the San Francisco Giants while we were still in Florida. In fact, it happened the same day that we lost to Long Beach State. I flew back to Notre Dame, packed up my things and got on a plane to Washington where I played Single A baseball for the Everett Giants. It had only been a mere 36 hours since we had graduated and I was on my way. The transition from Notre Dame to the pro level was not that hard for me for two reasons: first, I was ready mentally to play after 4 years at Notre Dame under Coach Murphy; and second, I had no choice. College was over and it was time for me to move on."*

The Professional Years

> *"A lot of guys were lost when they got to the pros because they hadn't quite realized that it was a job. You learn very quickly that there is a whole another level to this game that we were playing. In addition to that, I figured out pretty quickly that I was not a big league player. Billy Mueller was on my Single A team, and he went on to win a batting title and a World Series with the Red Sox. I saw those guys out there playing and just knew they were big league players, and at the same time I also knew I wasn't there. Within about six months I knew I had gone as far as I was going to go. I looked around at some of the guys I was playing with and thought, holy cow. One day I hit this ball and the outfielder climbed the wall and pulled it back in like nothing at all. I thought to myself, 'One, that's all I've got as far as hitting the ball. And two, I'm never going to climb the wall like that. I'm a pretty good baseball player, but I'm not that good.'"*

> *"I played every day and gave it everything I had, but I just wasn't good enough. I got shuffled around for a bit and was released in July of 1994. When I got*

released I went home to Michigan to my mom's, and while I was there I got a call from Brian Sabean in the front office of the San Francisco Giants. They told me, 'We really appreciate you and we know that you gave it all you had.' Meanwhile, in my mind I'm thinking, 'And all I got was a coke, a smile, and a plane ticket.' What I didn't realize is that when most minor league careers end, those phone calls don't happen. They were really looking for me to ask if there was a place somewhere else within the Giants organization, but I didn't see that at the time. I didn't see it because I didn't need them. I had my degree, and had already made some networking phone calls. They asked me if I had a job yet, and I said, 'No, I'm good.' At the end of the day, in order to play pro baseball you have to be both talented and mentally tough. But sometimes, you just aren't the guy, for one reason or another, to move to the next level. But I enjoyed my time in pro ball."

Today

"After being released I spent some time with my mother. I had not had that chance since my parents were divorced when I was young. I made some phone calls and reconnected with a dear friend, Korey Wrobleski, who had a sales job in Strongsville, OH as a sales rep in corporate relocation, and he put a good word in for me. Within two months I was in an 18 wheeler heading to Ohio to work for Mills Van Lines. It was a great business. You can make a ton of money in sales if you hustle and put in the time. I was with Korey for about a year and Coach Murphy called and said there was an opportunity with the Arizona Diamondbacks. I spoke with Joe Garagiola Jr (ND '72) the newly minted GM. I interviewed with Don Mitchell, a dear friend to this day, the Scouting Director on Thursday and left the next Tuesday to become the Assistant Director of Scouting for the Arizona Diamondbacks in October of 1995. It was a significant pay cut for me, but I was excited to be getting back into baseball, and I was fortunate that I had built up a good savings in my year doing sales."

"I slept in my Jeep for two days before I found a place to stay in Arizona. I arrived and hit the ground running. We were having winter meetings and things needed to be done, so I started working as soon as I arrived, and just forgot I needed a place to sleep. Working until midnight the first night, and 1 am the second night didn't help either, and I didn't have a credit card or a bank account set up yet in Arizona. I eventually found a hotel, crashed and then found an apartment in Scottsdale. As I am a Spanish speaker, I worked a lot with the Spanish speaking scouts. We helped build an academy in the Dominican Republic which was awesome. I worked there until 1998. In

> 1998 I was engaged to be married, and my soon-to-be wife (Adanna Fails, now Hartwell) was completing her MBA from Duke and got a huge offer from Anderson. I enjoyed my work with the Diamondbacks, and she had talked to Dial in Phoenix, but the offer she got from Anderson was huge, and way out performed what I was making. At the end of the day it was just a job and I was ready to move on to the next adventure. And so I packed up and moved to Atlanta. My dad thought I was crazy! 'You're the assistant director of scouting and you're only 25 years old!'"
>
> "When I got to Atlanta, I wasn't sure what I wanted to do next. I did some substitute teaching for a year - my whole family were teachers, and then I decided to start my own recruiting service company. I recruited for positions such as sales, technology, and CFOs. I did that for a couple of years at which point I found out that my friend Don Mitchell had left the Arizona Diamondbacks, and he and I decided to open a sport agency. We had six or seven first-round picks that we represented. I did that for seven or eight years until that kind of ran its course. At that fork in the road, I decided to veer off and try real estate. When I was working at the sport agency, I had recruited a young second baseman whose dad was a big time real estate agent in Atlanta, and he offered me a job to come and be a broker with his firm, Newmark Knight Frank. I never even showed him a resume. He knew a Notre Dame grad who knew me, and I got the job. I worked at Newmark for six years, and then in 2012 I joined a small investment bank, DPG Investments, and we raised money for real estate. In 2015 I joined Sinnott & Company, a law firm that specializes in real estate investment banking. I have been here three years as the head of business development."

Two of the best bi-products of a Notre Dame education are one, becoming a lifelong learner, and two, being agile and comfortable with change in your life. The *Notre Dame Value Stream* teaches you that life is filled with forks in the road, and each journey is often better than the one before! Not only does Notre Dame prepare you for a life filled with adventures, Our Lady's University also teachers Her students and student-athletes to give back to their communities, and leave them better than how they found them.

> "A dear friend of mine, CJ Stewart, runs a program called LEAD: Launch Expose Advice Direct. I don't do nearly as much as I did in the past, but LEAD takes the inner city youth in Atlanta and uses baseball as a tool to promote self-confidence, awareness and a staging platform to send young African America males to college. Their vision is: to develop ambassadors who will lead their City of Atlanta to lead the world; to launch student athletes

> *towards educational opportunities after converting raw talent into the skills required for entry into college athletic programs; to expose teens to service and local enrichment activities in order to instill a sense of responsibility, belonging and investment, key requirements for building a civically engaged individual; advise players, coaches and parents on the process of effectively supporting dreams of playing baseball on the college level; direct young men towards their promise by using the historical journey of past African American legends as the road map. If you live in the Atlanta area and are interested in helping out, please visit:* **www.lead2legacy.org**.*"*

Your teenage years may be a few years in the rear view mirror, as mine are, but I'm sure you can remember what it was like to be young, free, and have the feeling that you're invincible. So many young student-athletes head off to college feeling pretty invincible and thinking they know exactly what is in store for them when they arrive at college. Eddie shared with me his words of wisdom from his experience as a student-athlete and gives his recommendations for success.

> *"Well it's a lot different today than when I came out. The scrutiny of young high school players is insane. The one piece of advice I would give is to choose a school for you. I found Notre Dame, not ND football or baseball, just Notre Dame. If I never played a sport I would still love that place the same. You should pick a place that makes you happy. It is such a grind. I didn't know that in August of 1989. If you plan on playing a sport, you must be totally committed. I remember the first day of tryouts and Murph had the walk-on players sit in a large conference room (in Loftus) while he was sitting near the water fountain. He watched players come in and some leave as time went on. After about an hour of waiting, Coach Murphy comes into the room and said the guys who left were not committed, and we could begin the tryout. Then he absolutely tore into those of us that stayed and finished with if you think you have what it takes, go out that door and meet me on the field. I'm not sure exactly how many, but there were a lot less that went to the field than went home. You must be committed."*

Eddie currently lives in Atlanta, GA, with his lovely wife Adanna, to whom he's been married for twenty years, and they have two children: Justin (14) and Taylor (9).

Eddie Hartwell, his wife Adanna, and their children: Justin and Taylor.

Eddie Hartwell's Lessons from the Notre Dame Value Stream:

- When choosing a college, make sure you choose a school that is a good fit for you. I found Notre Dame, not ND football or baseball, just Notre Dame. If I never played a sport I would still love that place the same. You should pick a place that makes you happy.

- If you plan on playing a sport in college, you must be totally committed. I remember the first day of tryouts and Coach Murphy had the walk-on players sit in a large conference room (in Loftus) while he was sitting near the water fountain. He watched players come in and some leave as time went on. After about an hour of waiting, Coach Murphy comes into the room and said the guys who left were not committed, and we could begin the tryout. You must be committed.

- Make sure your education is always your priority. Sports will not last forever, but what you learn academically in college will carry you through the rest of your life.

Portrait of men's basketball player Charles Thomas Jr., October 2001.
(Photo courtesy of Notre Dame Archives.)

CHAPTER FIVE

The Concerned Citizen
Dr. Charles Thomas Jr.
(Notre Dame Basketball – Class of 2002)

In the iconic words of former Notre Dame Coach Lou Holtz, *"I can't believe God put us on this earth to be ordinary."* I don't think I've ever met anyone who walks through life in such a way that he proves the validity of this quote over and over again like Dr. Charles Thomas Jr. does. Charles is a man who challenges the thought processes of others in his daily encounters, who provides those who cross his path with a sense of hope in moments where all hope seems to be lost, whose selfless acts of community service help to mold and shape those who so very much need a sense of purpose and direction, and who strives to not only enrich his own life, but the lives of others as well. How does a kid from Flint, MI, end up playing Division I basketball under the hue of the Golden Dome at Our Lady's University, and go on to become a pillar not only in his career path but in his community as well? This is Dr. Charles Thomas Jr.'s story.

> "My journey to Notre Dame is actually pretty interesting. At least it is to me. I knew nothing about Notre Dame until my senior year of high school. I grew up in Flint, MI, surrounded by ambitious and intelligent young black men. Although we had big dreams, many of us lacked exposure to the realm of probable. Many of us didn't know anything about Ivy League schools, or schools such as Notre Dame. . . at least I didn't. I only really knew about the schools I could 'see,' such as Michigan, Michigan State, Central Michigan; I certainly never thought, 'I want to be a Golden Domer.'"

> "I went to this summer basketball camp and met some coaches from several different schools, one of which was Notre Dame; so I put ND on my list. I literally thought Notre Dame was located in California. My counselor called me into his office one day and said,

>> 'Have you ever thought about applying to Notre Dame and Princeton?'
>> 'I don't know where Princeton is, and I don't want to go to California.'
>> 'Notre Dame is in South Bend!'
>> 'South Bend what?!'
>> 'Indiana!!'

> "During my senior year of high school I got the itch; I just had to go to Notre Dame. When Mr. Reynolds planted the bug in my ear, my entire focus shifted to getting into Notre Dame. And then, once I got accepted, the only thing on my mind was playing basketball at Notre Dame. I knew academically I would be okay, but athletically I was so small. There was no reason I should have thought I had any chance to play basketball at that Division I school, with players of that caliber."

> "When I arrived at Notre Dame, I went to the basketball office, Coach MacLeod was the head coach at the time, and I introduced myself. 'Hey, I'm Charles Thomas, and I'm from Flint, Michigan. I want to speak with someone regarding the process one must go through to play basketball here.' One of the coaches came out to meet me, and the coach looked at me and he asked, 'Charles Thomas, how do I know that name?' And I answered, 'I'm from Flint, Michigan.' And he emphatically replied, 'You're not 6'1" tall!' My coach, Ray Jones, had made me out to be much bigger than I actually was!"

> "My AAU (Amateur Athletic Union of Boys Basketball) Coach, Ray Jones, had written letters about me, and filmed me working out in the gym, and

had bombarded the Notre Dame Basketball office with information about me. He told me if I 'work, work, work, work, work,' we'll figure out a way to get you to Notre Dame."

"One of the coaches at Notre Dame's basketball's office told me the process that I needed to follow in order to try out for the basketball team. He told me I couldn't 'officially' practice with the team, but informed me that I could work out at 'The Rock' (the workout facility and basketball gym for students on campus) in order to get ready for tryouts. He also told me that I could play pick-up games with the guys on the team, if they decided to pick me. 'You just have to keep showing up,' he said. With the stringent NCAA rules, as a prospective walk-on, you aren't allowed to practice with the team before tryouts, and so I would go sit in the gym and watch them practice. I would keep going, day after day. I wanted them to see my commitment, and know how much I wanted to play with the team."

> **Unbeknownst to them, I'm not afraid of the sharks,
> and I'm not afraid of living in the jungle,
> because I'm quite used to living in that space.**

"One day as I sat and watched them practice, one of the guards twisted his ankle, and so they called over to me, 'Hey Chuck, you want to play?' What kind of question was that? Of course I wanted to play. And from that day on, every day they picked me to play with the team. It was such a challenge for me, because I was little, compared to the rest of the guys. Many people told me I was too small, not strong enough, not fast enough; unbeknownst to them, I'm not afraid of the sharks, and I'm not afraid of living in the jungle, because I'm quite used to living in that space."

"I practiced every single day . . . 1,000 shots a day. I wasn't going to give up on my dream."

"At this point, I'm practicing with the team every day. When fall break rolls around, Coach Billy Taylor tells me, 'Go home for break and we'll call you and let you know when tryouts are.' When the call came during fall break, that epic phone call, that moment of joy on the phone; at first, I thought the call was a joke. Coach Taylor called and said, 'There's no need for you to try out, the fellas love you, come on back.'

Me: 'Is this a joke?? Are you serious??'

I handed the phone to my mom, and then she said, 'It's no joke!! They are serious!!'"

"We drove back to campus the next day, and when I walked into the gym, the lights felt like they were so much brighter. The team was standing there in the middle of the court, clapping for me."

"Academically, classes at Notre Dame were so hard. I knew it was going to be hard, but I wasn't doing as well as I thought I was going to do. The conversations were just so different from what I was used to hearing. We never talked about economics or any of these topics at home. But my parents had instilled this tremendous work ethic in me, and told me that even though I didn't have all of the resources that many of my peers had, if I worked hard I could make it happen. I called home and told my parents that I did not belong at Notre Dame, and my mother quickly told me that I needed to stop my 'woe is me' act. My mom sold her car so that I could stay in school. I may not have believed in myself, but she absolutely did."

"My teammates, however, were so cool. They told me to keep coming to practice. The focus that I had from my senior year of high school, straight through to October of my freshman year at ND, it was a singular focus to play basketball at Notre Dame. Months and months of the same routine every day, run, workout, shoot, eat, study, sleep, repeat, had finally paid off with that moment in the gym when my teammates were applauding me as I walked in. Easily the most memorable moment I had during my time at Notre Dame."

"I wasn't one of those kids who had always wanted to be an Irishman, but once the opportunity presented itself to me, I knew it was where I wanted to be. Before Notre Dame came onto my radar I looked at Michigan, Michigan State, Ohio State, Princeton, UNC – Chapel Hill, Hawaii, and some smaller schools such as Akron and Grand Valley. I went to a private high school in Flint, MI, but many of my classmates were looking at schools local to Michigan and Ohio. Only one of my classmates came to Notre Dame with me. Schools like Yale, Cal Berkeley, Vanderbilt, Duke, and Brown . . . none of those schools were on my radar because I didn't know about them."

Every student arrives at Notre Dame with visions of grandeur. The sky is the limit, the dreams are endless, and the confidence to reach the summit fills each and every cup. But then life happens. The journey along the *Notre Dame Value Stream* is not an easy one, and every student and student-athlete who roams the halls of Our Lady's University will have his (or her) ups and downs during the years spent under the Golden Dome. But the beauty of the *Notre Dame Value Stream* is this; She knows the journey will not be without strife, and She is always there to show you the way, so that when you come out on the other side, you are a stronger person than you were when you went in. Charles' journey was no different.

The Notre Dame Years

> "When I arrived at Notre Dame, I decided to study both science and business in the collegiate sequence program they offered, which was pretty new at the time. I liked science because of the process nature of it, but I also enjoyed business. Paul Rainey, one of my teammates, told me to check it out. He told me, 'You get the best of both worlds!' So I went and talked to my counselor and he told me it was a great program. I completed all of my major classes in three-and-a-half years, so during my last semester I was able to expand my horizons and take classes outside of my major."

> "I was absolutely the definition of a 'student-athlete.' I studied, studied, studied and then played sports. I didn't have the luxury of playing sports first and then studying as an afterthought. I wanted to be ready to play, but I knew academics was my focus. Initially, I thought the NBA was in my future. As college progressed and my game time experiences were limited, my NBA aspirations also decreased. This change in thought did not occur because I lost confidence in myself and my abilities. I simply began to accept the nature of my situation. At the point in which my focus started to shift, I knew that I was not an NBA caliber player. Maybe overseas, but not NBA level. My focus and desire shifted. My goal was to leverage sports to acquire the skills and education necessary to prepare myself for life after college."

Playing under a single head coach during your collegiate career is challenging enough, but playing under three different head coaches in four years; the thought seems inconceivable. But that is exactly what Charles experienced during his time playing Division I basketball at the University of Notre Dame.

> "The experiences were so extremely different. I arrived at Notre Dame under head coach John MacLeod, who offered me the opportunity to be a part of the team. I didn't travel my freshman year, but I would go to practice mostly every day, and Coach MacLeod and his assistant coaches were very helpful to me because I worked very hard. I wasn't the biggest guy on the team, but I worked hard and the coaches pushed me even harder. I played one game my freshman year, had one rebound, and that one game meant the absolute world to me. I wasn't even supposed to be there. It was super exciting. You would have thought I scored 47 points that game with as thrilled as I was to get the opportunity to be out there on the court. Even if I never played another second for the next three years, people would still say, 'Oh yea, that kid played on the team.' Now there was proof I existed!"

"We went 14-16 my freshman year. We didn't even make the NIT that year. I was at the Rolfs Sports Recreation Center when I heard that Coach MacLeod was leaving. My initial reaction. . . ugh. He was my connection to the program. I immediately got off the treadmill and went to talk to the other coaches. They reassured me that I'd be fine, and that they would make sure the new coach would know who I was and how hard I had worked my freshman year. But all I could think was, I had put in all of this hard work and now it's about to be gone. I did not want to be a one hit wonder. The consistency of having the same coach for four years is a big part of what makes you successful. I re-resolved in my mind to work even harder than I had before."

"And then it was announced. Our new coach was Matt Doherty. He had played at North Carolina in the early 1980s, and had been an assistant at Davidson and Kansas before becoming the head coach at Notre Dame. When Doherty arrived at Notre Dame, I went in right away and talked to him. I explained to him how hard I had worked my freshman year, and asked him if I would need to try out again. He told me that my 'tryout' would be my performance at practice. He explained that the team would work out over the summer, and whoever worked the hardest will get the opportunity to play. And so that's what we did, we gave it our all at each and every practice, and then one day I got the call from Coach D. 'You're good, you're a part of the team. You don't have to do anything else.'"

"Coach MacLeod was an old school coach with a raspy voice. He was more fatherly and soft spoken. He would get angry, of course, but his style was very different from Coach Doherty. Coach D was a fire starter. Young, energetic, had just come off a great opportunity at Kansas, and it was his way or the highway. You had to have a very strong personality to handle Coach Doherty. He was very X's and O's, and he was very clearly on an upward trajectory in his career. As a 19-year-old, I would sometimes get very upset as a result of his personality and coaching style. As I've gotten older, I've come to appreciate Coach Doherty more; at the time I thought, 'This dude is crazy!' He was go, go, go, all the time."

> **Coach Doherty called me into his office to tell me he was putting me on an athletic scholarship.**

"In the second semester of my sophomore year, Coach Doherty called me into his office to tell me he was putting me on an athletic scholarship. He said, 'We see that you've been working very hard. I know I've been tough on you, but you are tough on yourself as well. You've earned your place here, and I no longer consider you a walk-on. Here is your scholarship. We'll reevaluate it next year."

"Summer rolled around, and the buzz is swirling around that Doherty is applying for the head coach position at North Carolina. Doherty had played at North Carolina with Michael Jordan in the early 1980s, so you couldn't blame him for wanting to go back. And then the announcement came that Doherty was leaving to coach at his Alma Mater, North Carolina. I felt like the air had been knocked out of me all over again. With Coach Doherty I knew that if I worked hard enough, I would get the opportunity to play. Here I was, the walk-on kid who had proven himself to a second coach, and now I had to start over, again! I had to reprove myself, my heart, my athletic ability, my skillset, my ability to work with my teammates, all over again."

"Coach Doherty called us in and told us, 'I've decided to take this job at North Carolina.' The reaction was some good, some not so good. I couldn't believe this was happening again! I told my parents, you know what, I'm tired. I'm putting in all of this effort for something that is clearly not in the cards. Their response? Stop complaining and figure it out."

"Then we hear we're getting this guy who coached with Coach Krzyzewski. We're getting Mike Brey."

"Coach Brey accepted the job over the summer between my sophomore and junior year. I picked up the phone and called him. His first words were, 'You don't have to worry about a thing. There are no tryouts for you. You are a Notre Dame Basketball player. Period.' I felt this immediate weight fall off my shoulders. From the word 'go,' he was always honest with me. He told me that I did not have to worry about my place on this team, but he also told me that he was bringing in some of his own players and coaches. He told me, 'I'm not saying you're going to play a lot, but at the same time you don't have to worry. If you work hard, you may get some minutes here and there but I can't promise you a lot of playing time. Everyone attests to how hard you work on the court, how smart you are in the classroom, and how you study on road trips; you have nothing to worry about. You will be on this team. I can't promise you how many minutes, but I can promise you are good on this team.'"

"To be very honest, I was looking into transferring to another school before this conversation with Coach Brey. I had looked at Toledo, Marquette, and Akron, because at this point in my basketball career, I knew I was good enough to play, and I wanted to go somewhere that I would actually play. At this point, I was a Division I basketball player. But, at the end of the day, I wanted to do it at Notre Dame, I was an Irishman. I could have transferred and possibly have played more, but my parents told me not to. They told me, 'Don't throw away your Notre Dame degree just because you want to go somewhere and toss a ball through a hoop.' My mom told me, 'You're going to do it a different way. Basketball isn't the only way you can put a Rolls Royce in the driveway. Academics is what got you to Notre Dame. You think about and do the right things, you speak well, and you will have the opportunity to do great things in the business space. Don't get heartbroken just because you are not going to get a lot of playing time at Notre Dame or go pro. You need to stay at Notre Dame.' I went back and told Coach Brey what I was thinking, and he told me my mom was right. 'You have a bigger place in this world that you may not be able to accomplish through sports, but you will be able to accomplish based on your academic achievements.' Yes, I heard what Coach Brey was saying, but I was still so frustrated. He kept telling me all of this, and at the same time wanted me to sit on that stupid bench. Coach Brey was my coach for my junior and senior years at Notre Dame. By my senior year, I was okay with everything. I had accepted my role, and was going to stay on the team and enjoy it. I made the decision that I'm going to be okay with this. And, if the day comes when he wants me to play a lot, I'm ready for it. Even though it never came, he knew I was ready. Now, looking back, I know that sports is a business, and he had to play the kids the donors/sponsors wanted to see. And if I'm being honest with myself, they were probably just better than me."

"Coach Brey was hard on us, a highly energetic coach, but he was always straight with me. I'm not sure how he was with the other guys, but he always was honest with me. At a personal level, I could call him right now and if he didn't answer the phone right away, he'd call me back within a day. The three coaches I played for had very different personalities and coaching styles, and they each brought out very different emotions in me. By the end of my junior year I thought, if we have one more coaching change, I'm done. Thankfully we did not."

"Some of the guys I played with, such as Troy Murphy, David Graves, and Harold Swanagan, had much different journeys at Notre Dame than I did, as they knew they were going to be starters coming in. Maybe mentally it still bothered them when we had coaching changes, but they didn't have to worry about their jobs like I did. At least, that was my perception. Mentally and emotionally it was so tough for me to have to continually prove myself to new coaches. Being a student-athlete at Notre Dame was tough. Some professors were lenient on athletes who traveled, and some were not. But I made sure to have good relationships with my professors, and to show them that I was willing to put in the work. After games, I would go back to my room and study. I was a student first, and an athlete second. My teammates would want to go out and party, but I would go back and study. It was a blessing in disguise for me to not be tired after games, and to be able to go back to my room and study. Games were much easier for me than practices. Practices were my games, I would be exhausted after practice, but games were much easier for me."

"In my senior year, when we lost to Duke in our last game, my heart just broke. I looked around at my teammates and they were all crying. I knew that some of them would go pro and would continue to play, but for me, it was over. From the age of 7 until I was 21, basketball and books were all I knew; that day basketball effectively ended for me. We were in the second round of the NCAA Tournament, playing against Duke, and they went on an absolute tear. It was like Coach K had told them to not miss another shot, and they just went on fire. When that buzzer sounded, we went to the locker room and I just looked around at the guys on the team; it was over. For the previous 15 years, there was one thing I did every day, and that was take a ball and shoot it at a hoop. It was my entire focus. We all sat down after that game and tried to figure out what was next. I went to a bunch of different camps and got some baby offers to play ball post-college. I tried to do that for a few years, but I also took a job with the Federal Government, as I knew basketball would not last forever."

"I won several awards my senior year, and was selected to speak on our Senior Day. In totality, for a kid who wasn't even supposed to be there, I did pretty well for myself. There was no reason I should have made that team all four years except that God said at some point, this story is going to provide some value to someone. I would not trade the experience for anything. I played in the NIT, the NCAA tournament, and at Madison Square Garden. At the end, when I realized how many people knew me, I was shocked. When I received all of the awards and recognition – Dean's List, Sankofa Scholar, NAACP Senior of the Year, Knute Rockne Scholar Athlete of the Year, two-time Big East Academic All-Star team, two-time Notre Dame Monogram winner, Arthur Ashe Scholar Athlete Award winner; I didn't believe in me at the time. I was getting A's and B's in school, but it didn't matter, because all I wanted to do was play on that team."

**That four year experience at Notre Dame
has prepared me for the next 50 years.**

> "I haven't found anything that has replaced basketball for me. The teamwork, commitment, absolute pursuit of excellence, the crowd cheering you on; nothing else in life has replicated that for me. Not at that same level. However, I take that same focus and hustle mentality into my daily life. That four year experience at Notre Dame has prepared me for the next 50 years."

If you played a sport growing up, at one point or another you probably entertained the idea of playing one day for a big college program. The odds are so often stacked against you though, as the numbers dwindle from the large masses of kids who play sports at a young age, to the smaller number of kids who continue to play sports through their teen years and on to college. And then if you don't get a scholarship offer, you have to make the tough decision of either passing on your dream, or digging in and pursuing that walk-on spot. When Charles arrived at Notre Dame, he knew he was not the biggest, or the strongest, or the fastest, but he was by no means ready to give up on his dream, and he was ready to put in the work to secure that walk-on spot. But what does that really mean? Charles spoke with me about what it's like to be a walk-on at a big Division I program.

> "As a freshman and sophomore, I felt different. I felt the difference between the walk-ons and the scholarship players. That I sometimes didn't count because I was a walk-on player. It was more prevalent from certain players. And maybe I felt it more my sophomore year because I was sensitive to it, but I mostly felt it from certain members of the team, and a few of the coaches, but definitely not from everyone. In my sophomore year I was given an athletic scholarship, in my junior year it was part athletic and part academic, and then in my senior year Coach Brey put me back on a full athletic scholarship. I definitely remember moments during my sophomore year in which coaches and players still talked to me and treated me as if I was inferior, even though I was on an athletic scholarship for the latter half of my second year. One of the coaches said to one of my teammates, 'He's a walk-on. Are you going to let him score on you?' Hey, just because I don't have a scholarship doesn't mean I'm a bum. The term 'walk-on' bothered me back then because it was often used to reduce a person. To reduce me. It doesn't bother me now though. I embrace it. I know what it took to climb that mountain."

> "It only happened a few times, and actually I think people did it to see how I would respond. You can say what you want to me, but I always worked hard for my spot on the team, and I deserved it. I could see there were differences between the walk-ons and the scholarship players, but I tried my best not to let it bother me. I think it was just the pecking order of the team. For example, I never got jerseys or shoes first, but that was because I wasn't a starter or

> *a major game time contributor. It wasn't malicious, it was just the pecking order. By my junior and senior years, the disagreements that were had were purely competitive. There was no more treating me like a walk-on, instead the coaches would push me to become the best player I could possibly be."*

> *"There were clear differences in skill levels amongst the players on the team. I wasn't going to argue with the fact that Troy Murphy was going to play more than I was; I wasn't that egotistical. It wasn't scholarship guys versus non-scholarship guys; it was skill-level based. I knew that I was part of the team. In my sophomore year, before I was a scholarship player, we lost in an exhibition game. Coach Doherty made us all come in and run the next day. He told the other four walk-ons that they didn't have to come run, but he made me run. At that point, the guys really embraced me as one of them. I went through the same turmoil and terror that they went through after that game. We deserved it, we should not have lost that game. That was on us. It was awful, but we deserved it. My sophomore year was the only year that I felt any real negative tension regarding walk-on vs. scholarship athlete. I was so excited to be there my freshman year, I didn't really see it; by my junior year I had earned my place."*

When you play a sport at a school like the University of Notre Dame, without a doubt your career is filled with memorable moments both on and off the court. To pick one or two favorites is all but impossible, and yet more often than not, one or two shining moments rise to the top. Charles shared with me some of his favorite memories of his years spent under the Dome.

> *"My favorite basketball memory is the day I walked onto campus my freshman year, and walked onto the court for the first time. There's not even a close second to that moment. That day, it will always ring as one of the most powerful, emotional moments, from a positive standpoint, that I've ever experienced. Here I am, this little 18-year-old kid from Flint, Michigan, not even six feet tall at the time. Receiving my jersey, that said THOMAS 5, on it. Nothing compares to that. From a sports standpoint, no Notre Dame Basketball memory compares to that moment, that day. Not winning the Big East Championship my junior year, not speaking in front of the crowd of people when Coach Brey asked me to talk, but walking onto the court that day with my jersey on. That was the best moment ever."*

> *"'Introducing Charles Thomas Jr, from Flint, Michigan, number 5.' Do you know how many times I had played that out in my mind?? And to have them announce it like that. Some people take those moments for granted, but for me, that was unforgettable. For an 18-year-old kid who didn't have the faith*

> to believe that I was destined to play at Notre Dame; my mom, she had it. She had the faith in me. When I'm feeling bad, that I'm not progressing at the rate I should be, I go back to that moment. You are programmed to succeed."

Just when it seems that you are starting to get comfortable with what it takes to be successful both on and off the court at a big time Division I college program, your journey draws to a close, and your next adventure is about to begin. That first step on a new path may be scary and somewhat intimidating, but this is exactly where the *Notre Dame Value Stream*s shines. It is where She lifts you up, and sends you out into the world prepared with everything you need to face the challenges ahead.

Today

> "After my academic and athletic career at Notre Dame, I was recruited to work within the Intelligence Community. Working in that community was an awesome experience. To know that my academic background from Notre Dame set me up for such a prestigious job was incredible. I was just a kid from Flint, MI. Opportunities like that didn't exist for kids from Flint, MI. . . or at least I thought."

> "Then I changed course and got a job in the corporate space doing organizational dynamics and IT. I also went back to graduate school and earned my MBA at UTSA, and then went on to Creighton University to earn my Master of Science and Doctoral degrees. I'm back working in the intelligence community, as CEO of Clear Cloud, a technology company. When I was in school, I had always talked about being a forensic scientist, but then I decided to try something else. We all have to decide where our aptitude and abilities are going to take us."

> "The interdisciplinary training that I acquired at Notre Dame prepared me for interdisciplinary aspects of life. The success that I've achieved so far, it's not because of pure talent; it's because I put in significant effort. No one can ever say that I don't work hard. That will never be on my tombstone. You don't have to be the most analytical or the most intelligent, but you do have to put in effort. I know so many people who may not be the smartest one in the bunch, but they work extremely hard. Take your aptitude and abilities and align that with your future."

> "The adversity I felt in my dark days, when I wasn't playing on the team, wondering if I was ever going to be able to do this became, I'm going to turn this into what I want it to be. I am going to stop being mad and start working harder, to study harder, and to keep at it. You're going to have adversity in

your life, you need to be able to figure out how to solve it. Coach Brey told me, 'if you can shoot, you can play anywhere in the country. Now I'm not telling you to leave, but I am telling you no matter where you are, if you can produce, you can play.' I used this philosophy in the work force as well; if you can create, produce, and perform, you can work anywhere. You need to be able to take nothing, and turn it into something. Be an artist and create."

"The people in life who are the most successful are the ones who are able to produce something. They are no longer purely consumers of knowledge, but are producing something worthwhile. The sports journey that I traveled allowed me to become confident in telling stories. Not only in the books I've written, but even in my executive work I have to tell stories. We have a business objective we're going after, and we need to be able to explain why we want it, how it fits with us, how our employees fit with it. It's all story telling."

In addition to his work in the government and corporate space, and his collegiate level teaching activities, Charles also writes. He is a soon-to-be four-time published author. I asked Charles to tell me what prompted him to become an author, and what the writing experience has been like for him.

I didn't want to be an author, but I needed to release my demons, and writing was my way of releasing them.

"For starters, I don't consider myself an author. I just consider myself someone who wrote something and got it published. I also don't consider myself an academic, I just consider myself someone who likes to learn. I didn't want to be an author, but I needed to release my demons, and writing was my way of releasing them. I was in shambles internally, and the only way I knew how to get rid of the negativity was to write about it. Kind of like that song from Hamilton, I wrote my way out. I had to deal with my demons one way or another, and so I started writing to get them out. I sent the manuscript (for 'Scars, Exile & Vindication: My Life as an Experiment') to one of my graduate school professors, who told me I had a strong voice and that I needed to get it published. And that's what I did. Now, I have published a second book, 'Breakthrough: Stories of Resilience, Tragedy, and Triumph,' and a third book as well, 'Leading Through Difficulty: The Darker Side of Workplace Behavior.' My fourth book is on the way. It's about the walk-on journey."

"My grandmother always told me, 'Don't die with the stories inside of you.' I have so much inside of my head, and I need to get it out. There are so many of us going through things in our life, and we feel like we are alone. I hope that through my writing and speaking I can be a voice in the ensemble of

choices that can resonate with someone. One of my philosophies is to try to be the best I can, while I can. I don't necessarily think it was me deciding that I wanted to be an author. I wanted to tell stories, and to be of value, rather than to be an author, per se."

"After I wrote my first book, I let it sit for two years. I happened to send it to a friend, and he said, 'This is a real book! You actually made it flow and it tells a story!' I've always been able to tell a story, but I had no idea I could write a book. My desire to let my negativity go was my first desire. I was in a bad headspace. Before I started, my coping mechanism to deal with my negativity was to reach for the bottle. Even though I was drinking a tremendous amount of alcohol, I was still functioning well and performing at a high level in graduate school. It was pure intellect and instinct that carried me through those dark moments."

"I was in a downward spiral internally for several years, but externally you would have never known. I was still wearing three-piece suits, and going to the gym; at night I'd drink a bottle of tequila and read a book. It all seemed to be working for me until I walked into the liquor store one day and the guy said to me, 'Seriously? You were just here yesterday.' But I didn't feel anything was wrong. After I would drink a bottle, I should have felt something, but I didn't. I'd drink, write, work out, and feel perfectly fine. Get up the next day, go to class, and repeat the whole process the next night. I wrote my way out of a very dark place."

"In elementary school and high school, sports kept the negativity out of me, but as an adult, writing helped me deal with the negative situations I was facing in life. Something bad would happen and I would go home, write about it, get it out of my system, delete it, and feel better."

As the saying goes, hindsight is 20/20, and so for that exact reason, I love to ask former student-athletes to share some of their words of wisdom for junior high and high school athletes looking to improve their game and succeed at the Division I level. I think it is priceless to hear from someone who has been there and knows what it takes to succeed, what the "thrill of victory and agony of defeat" *(coined by Jim McKay, ABC's Wide World of Sports)* really look like, and the effort that it actually takes to get there and stay there.

"I would tell student-athletes, know who you are. Being a student-athlete is very hard, and as you go through your sports journey in college, know that there is a bigger story out there waiting for you. Sports is only one chapter in your book of life. You have to think about how you want that story to end,

how it's going to fit in the remainder of the chapters of your book. At some point, college will be over. You may go pro, but the vast majority of you will not. Only approximately 1-2% of high school students play college sports at a varsity level, and even a smaller percentage play at a pro level. Allow your college chapter to play out, but don't allow it to define you."

"While you are in college, do the absolute best that you can. Know that it will offer significant value to you after sports are over. I know, it's a basic piece of advice, but it's so important. If someone would have told me that, it would have made my time playing sports so much better. Those four years go by so fast. You have to write that chapter to the best of your ability and leverage it to propel you forward into the next chapter of your life. Don't take it for granted, because when it's done, it's done. Enjoy it, and elevate your mind to say, 'hey, I'm going to take advantage of each and every one of these opportunities.'"

"Work unlike you've worked before. Be hyper focused on whatever sport you want to play, while simultaneously keeping balance in the rest of your life. Don't let anyone outwork you physically or mentally. The fact of the matter is, most people don't make it because the mental and emotional grind drags them down, not the physical grind. The constant day-to-day mental grind is the hardest part of being a student-athlete. Your body can handle the physical part, but in order to handle the mental and emotional part, you need to sharpen your mind to have the focus of an assassin. Tell yourself, I am going to get to that goal, and once I'm there, I am going to maintain that level of mental and physical focus. That's the blueprint. Everyone knows it, but it is difficult to put it into action."

You might think that a successful government consulting career, along with writing books, would be enough to keep one more than busy; not so for Charles. He is also a keynote speaker, a co-host of the Divergent Thought radio show, and an educator. Charles is an Adjunct Professor of Leadership, Civility, and Personal Responsibility, Organizational Behavior, and Organizational Development and Transformation at the Undergraduate level. He also serves as an Adjunct Professor of Leadership Theory & Practice and Consulting Management & Practice at the Doctorate level. And within the local jail system, Charles teaches Life Skills: Communication, Financial Literacy, Decision Making, and Mental Health to men who are incarcerated and preparing for societal re-entry, and has committed himself to service before self through his many community service endeavors. How did Charles get involved in so many different things?

"When you learn, teach, when you get, give." - Maya Angelou

"I'm not the most profound person in the world, but I do things because I think they can get done. I stand on the shoulders of giants. I strive to meet and exceed the ideals and standards of the best of those that came before me. I teach at the county jail in Northern Virginia, I teach students at the University level, I work with the homeless, I have a radio show in which we talk about social justice; I believe that education and community engagement are so very important. Growing up in Flint, Michigan was a magnificent upbringing. As a teenager, I became very aware of the power of community. I didn't understand the magnitude of how much value people were offering, however, until I became older and more self-reflective. Although there were plenty of role models, external to my parents and some relatives, I mainly looked up to athletes and entertainers. Now, that I am older and have the opportunity to do so, I want to represent a different narrative for kids growing up in situations like I did."

"I was giving a speech not too long ago, and a young black man came up to me after I was done. He told me, 'I've seen President Obama speak and that's cool, but you, I know you. I've seen what you have done, and I know that I can do it too.' President Obama did just that for me. To see an educated black man achieve that level of success shows me that opportunities like that exist for me, and that maybe I can become something like that one day. I am constantly in a state of self-exploration, asking, can I do it myself? And who can I bring with me if I can't. As a demonstration of human potential, I want to show people something that they may not otherwise see."

"We do intellectual, mental, and spiritual rehabilitation at the county jail to give men and women the tools they need to successfully re-integrate into society. How do I respond to this situation? Not react to the situation, but respond. Not everyone is going to like me, but I'm out there shooting and catching arrows. You can't be afraid of success, failure, or of what people think of you. 'When you learn, teach, when you get, give.' Maya Angelou"

"At the very least, I'm trying. I want everyone to know I did my best. I want me to know that I did and am doing my best. You can't do that if you just sit at home. You have to offer value to other people. I want to use whatever talents, gifts, wisdom that I have. In order to get in the game, you need to be near the game. That pattern of life has propelled me, even into the community. If I want to share and/or solve a leadership problem, or a mass incarceration problem, I have to be involved."

"As an adult, I've won two Leader of the Year awards, an Outstanding Service to the community award, two 40 under 40 awards, a Rising Star award, and several other accolades. Those awards were bestowed upon me based on

the dealings I've had with people, and the impact I've had on people at the micro level (jail, community, and university work). Those acts of service are just as important to me as my corporate work."

"I try to be involved and offer insights to others based on my experiences and the lessons learned from other people. When you talk to so many people, you get so much insight on how to better live your own life. When you capture the life experiences of others, it gives you real insight as to whether or not you are living your life well. In the process, you learn that there are things that are an option that you never knew were a possibility before."

"I try to at least offer something of value, so that someone who is listening to me can take something away with them, one thing at the very least. They may not take everything away with them, but I want them to at least take one thing away with them. On our radio show, we try to offer something to counteract all the negativity that is in the world."

Charles currently lives in the Washington D.C. area with his wife, Manthanee, and their two children.

Charles Thomas Jr. and his family: his wife Manthanee, their two children, and his parents.

Dr. Charles Thomas Jr.'s Lessons from the Notre Dame Value Stream:

- I would tell student-athletes, know who you are. Being a student-athlete is very hard, and as you go through your sports journey in college, know that there is a bigger story out there waiting for you. Sports is only one chapter in your book of life. You have to think about how you want that story to end, how it's going to fit in the remainder of the chapters of your book.

- While you are in college, do the absolute best that you can. Know that it will offer significant value to you after sports are over. I know, it's a basic piece of advice, but it's so important.
- Work unlike you've worked before. Be hyper-focused on whatever sport you want to play, while simultaneously keeping balance in the rest of your life. Don't let anyone outwork you physically or mentally.
- Take the focus and hustle mentality you learn in college into your daily life. I haven't found anything that has replaced basketball for me. The teamwork, commitment, absolute pursuit of excellence, the crowd cheering you on; nothing else in life has replicated that for me. Not at that same level. However, I take that same focus and hustle mentality into my daily life. That four year experience at Notre Dame has prepared me for the next 50 years.

Portrait of women's soccer player Shannon Boxx, 1997.
(Photo courtesy of Notre Dame Archives.)

CHAPTER SIX

The World Champion

Shannon Boxx

(Notre Dame Soccer – Class of 1999)

When you grow up in the golden sunshine of Southern California, you can all but bet that your parents, at one point or another, signed you up to play a sport. The weather is gorgeous pretty much all year round, and what better way to keep your children active and out of trouble than to sign them up for a team sport. Shannon Boxx and her sister were no exceptions to this rule. And the first sport their mother signed them up for was one that so many Southern California kids play: soccer. At the young age of four, Shannon had no idea how much that soccer ball would become a part of her life, through her youth and well into adulthood; it certainly has taken her on adventures well beyond her wildest imagination. This is Shannon Boxx's story.

"I was born in Fontana, CA, but the majority of my childhood was spent in Torrance, CA. I grew up in a single parent household, with my mother, and my older sister who is four years older than me. My mom put my sister in sports at a very early age, and that's how I got interested in playing sports, starting with soccer. Soccer was very popular in Southern California, probably the number one sport that kids played, and so it was a very easy sport for my mom to throw us into. She loves to tell me how I couldn't wait to start doing what my sister was doing. I drove her so crazy wanting to play soccer that she went to registration and lied about my age. My sister and I played so many sports growing up. We played basketball, soccer, baseball to start (until about middle school) and eventually softball, flag football, ice hockey, and volleyball. My mom wanted us to try everything that we wanted to try. I think that's what is different today from when I was a kid. Today you cannot have your kids play everything. It's just not possible, and it's way too competitive, too early."

"When I was 10 years old my mom and I decided I needed more of a challenge from soccer and I joined a club soccer team. By the time I got to high school I played volleyball, soccer, and softball, until my senior year when I swapped out high school soccer for high school basketball, as I was playing soccer on a club team. When I was a freshman in high school, my sister headed off to college with a full ride to play softball at the University of California – Berkley. At that point my mom told me, 'I can't afford to pay for you to go to college so you're going to have to do what your sister did. You're going to have to either get an athletic full ride to a University, or start out at a Community College.' There weren't many soccer scholarships for women, so she suggested that maybe I should switch and play on a club softball team instead. And so for nine months I played club soccer and club softball, but at the end of the day I loved soccer, and I decided to make soccer my priority and go for it. While club soccer was my priority, I continued to play softball, volleyball and basketball for my high school teams."

"The dad who coached my club soccer team was really great in that he understood that many of us played other sports, and he tried to make our schedule so that we could do everything. There may have been fewer scholarships available back when I was in high school, but the recruiting process also started much later, which allowed us to play multiple sports. As far as my recruiting process went, schools came looking at me, I didn't really actively seek out any schools. And then during my senior year I went on several recruiting trips. By the time

I was a senior in high school, I knew that playing high school soccer wasn't going to prepare me for playing soccer at the collegiate level, so I focused on my club team and played on an adult women's team. I also played on my school's basketball team, as basketball was my other true love, and on the volleyball team as well. I had to switch to a different club soccer team my senior year as the girls on the previous team had all graduated, and my new team was pretty far away in Thousand Oaks, CA. Playing on this new team required me to travel quite a bit, and it made it challenging for me to make some of my volleyball practices and games. I was contemplating dropping volleyball, but my teammates and coaches were so great. I explained to them that this was basically my job, and I was going to get a scholarship to play soccer in college, and they told me it was totally okay if I had to miss some practices or leave games early. They told me they'd rather have me play as much as I could rather than lose me all together. Having that kind of support meant so much to me. I'd play in as many of the games as I could, and then I'd leave and go to soccer. It was the worst to have to leave, but at the same time it was great that I was able to be a part of both teams."

My first trip took me to the University of Notre Dame and I instantly fell in love.

"The University of Notre Dame was the furthest school that was recruiting me. I was also being recruited by Stanford, Santa Clara, UCLA, USC, and the University of Washington. Primarily west coast schools. There were some great schools in the mix for sure. I was really interested in Stanford, especially because my sister was already up north at Cal Berkley, but that changed once I made my first recruiting trip. My first trip took me to the University of Notre Dame and I instantly fell in love. The campus was beautiful. I loved the tradition of the school. I loved the soccer team. And not only was the team good (they had made it to the final four the year before), their style seemed like something that I would fit into perfectly and could really make a difference. I also knew that once I graduated from a school like Notre Dame that I would have a community of people there to support me and figure out my next steps. My official visit to Notre Dame was incredible. My host that weekend was Stacia Masters, and we got to attend the football game and be on the field. It was so fun to see all of the people there, all of the motor homes parked out in the parking lot with their big screen TVs. The whole weekend completely blew me away."

And just like that Shannon took the opportunity that was in front of her and traveled 2,000 miles across the United States to follow her collegiate soccer dream.

This might seem scary, and like a big leap, but the *Notre Dame Value Stream* always knows exactly what her student-athletes need to navigate the rough waters that may be waiting for them on their journey, and teach them how to not only survive, but thrive.

The Notre Dame Years

"I arrived at Notre Dame and I was lucky in the fact that I got to start right away, which in hindsight was pretty crazy. I certainly didn't expect to start my freshman year, but it was really fun to get thrown in right from the beginning. I knew it would be more challenging than high school soccer, but the speed and physicality was so much different. You had to figure out how to deal with that pretty quickly in order to not only be able to compete, but to survive. Academically, it took me at least a semester to really get up to speed. First semester freshman year was hard for me because it was soccer season. In addition to trying to get used to being away from home, you also had to try and figure out how to juggle your classes along with practices, games, and travel. It was a lot to acclimate to all at once. That first semester my grades weren't too good. I came from having straight A's in high school, and then all of the sudden I was struggling. Second semester I started to figure things out and was able to turn my grades around. By my senior year, things were pretty much smooth sailing. But after that first semester, I had a fair amount of catching up to do in order to get my grades where I wanted them to be. Freshman year is a transition, no matter how prepared you think you are, especially when you play a fall sport. You arrive at school early for fall camp, and then you jump right into school and games. It's a lot for an 18-year-old to have to figure out, and figure out quickly."

"When I was a student at Notre Dame I studied psychology. I knew, heading off to college, that psychology was what I was interested in pursuing, so that wasn't a difficult decision for me. Along the way, as I was picking electives, I took a lot of African-American Studies classes, and thought I was on track to earn a minor. As it turned out, I picked up so many African-American Studies classes, that I earned a double major. It just sort of happened that way. They were both subjects that I was interested in and passionate about, and so it wasn't much trouble to get a major in both."

"Where I grew up in Southern California, there were not many African-Americans living in our community. My mom is white and my dad is black, so when I got to Notre Dame and discovered the African-American Studies degree program, I was very excited to have the opportunity to learn more about my heritage. And my mom was very supportive of me as well. I

was also very happy to be at a school that was much more diverse than where I grew up, but even when I was at Notre Dame in the mid 1990s, it was still very segregated. As an athlete, my teammates and I didn't see each other as black or white. You were a team, and you saw each other as teammates."

A head coach in any sport, at any level, is a person who must wear many hats. Yes, they must teach, train, and guide their players on how to play the game. But the job is much more than that. It also includes teaching your players camaraderie, and how to play as a team, not just as individuals. It includes developing your players both on and off the field. And it often includes being a parental figure to players who are far away from their own moms and dads.

"Chris Petrucelli was an awesome coach. I joined the team with a couple other freshmen and had previously played club soccer with Monica Gerardo in California; but unlike some of my teammates I was very shy and reserved. I always respected Coach Petrucelli and looked up to him. I thought he was great with our team. But I couldn't banter with him like Monica and some of the other girls could. I was much more businesslike in my interactions with my coaches. Not too long ago I was at a wedding with a bunch of my former teammates from the 1995 team, and Coach Petrucelli was there as well. It was so great to see everyone. As former teammates we are still very connected to each other, as well as to Coach Petrucelli. He truly was the conduit that connected all of us together."

He set me up with the right people on campus to help me deal with my eating disorder, and he made sure I was okay.

"He was the perfect coach for our freshmen team. He pushed the starters to open their eyes, to be able to see when they were playing well and when they were not, and he was there to help us when we were not. He believed in me so much from the start. When Cindy Daws was injured early in the season, he without question put me in there and had the confidence that I could step into the role and succeed. And he definitely looked after me. I had an eating problem my freshman year. He noticed it before I even arrived at Notre Dame, and got me the help I needed once I got to school. I am so thankful for him that he was able to reach me and get me the help that I needed. He set me up with the right people on campus to help me deal with my eating disorder, and he made sure I was okay. That is an extraordinary coach. Coach Petrucelli and his staff kept an eye on our academics as well. That's a big part of the reason why I wanted to go to Notre Dame. Athletes didn't get special treatment. They had to work hard in their classes just like every other student there. I knew I needed to have a good education to be successful in the rest of my life, and I appreciated being at a school which demanded that from you."

I went into Coach Petrucelli's office and told him that I really wanted to study abroad in Australia in the spring semester.

"I went abroad during the second semester of my junior year which was unheard of for full ride student-athletes. I went into Coach Petrucelli's office and told him that I really wanted to study abroad in Australia in the spring semester. He told me that I couldn't, that he needed me at Notre Dame for the spring season; 'You're a full ride student-athlete.' And I said to him, 'I really want to do this, and I am a student-athlete. Which means I'm a student first, and an athlete second.' You could just see the look on his face. . . dang it. He thought about it, and at the next practice he announced, 'We're going to miss Shannon next semester.' And I just stood there. 'Wait, I'm going?!' I know how hard that decision was for him to say yes to that. I played a lot of soccer while I was in Australia, but when I came back I didn't pass the fitness test. <Oops. . . laughs> I ended up being fine by the time the season started, though. I appreciate that he heard me out and allowed me to go."

Each college athlete crafts a tapestry full of memories from their time in college, both on and off the field. While each and every one is meaningful and memorable, oftentimes a few stand out above the rest. For Shannon, winning the national championship in their green jerseys was that one shining moment that stands out from the rest.

"When we walked into the pre-game meal room before the semi-final game and our green jerseys were hanging on the back of our chairs, immediately we knew this game was going to be something special. And then, winning the championship game in double overtime - which doesn't even exist anymore - and flying home to see the number one sign lit up on top of Grace Hall; the whole experience from start to finish was just incredible. The group of women that we had on that team played so well together. The other thing that stands out for me from my time at Notre Dame are the countless hours spent with my teammates. There isn't a whole lot of things do to in South Bend, and so you have to figure out things to do on campus. I have very fond memories of time spent with my teammates and classmates. I remember playing soccer on the quad with friends, and exploring campus on a weekday night during a much needed study break. I mean, what else were we going to do? And of course, going to football games with my friends. I also remember walking to practice in the days leading up to a football weekend, and walking through all of the fans, and motor homes, and the marching band practicing. All of those everyday moments are just as meaningful to me as the big wins on the field."

Every athlete who plays in college or at the professional level has one primary goal, to win a championship. And though they all share the same common goal, very few actually reach that pinnacle of success. Shannon did just that at Notre Dame and beyond. Shannon shared with me what it was like to be a member of the first Notre Dame women's soccer team to win a NCAA Championship.

> "It's hard to put into words what the experience was like. We had so much talent on that team, and such great leaders. I was very lucky that this was the time when I came on to the team, and that we had the veterans we did, such as Cindy Daws and Jen Renola. They were such great leaders, and I loved the fact that they were our veterans when I came on to the team. And then we had so many quiet players that just did their job and were so amazing. The big turning point of that season was when we went to play in a tournament in Texas against UNC and Duke. It was around the midseason point, and we didn't do very well. Coach Petrucelli sat us down and asked us, 'Do you want to win a national championship? Because if you do, this is not how you're going to get it done.'"

Wow, we have to do this as a team, or it doesn't happen.

> "At that very moment we came up with a term that any of us could say, and it would make us all refocus and keep our eyes on the prize, and that word was 'focus.' Any one of us could say it on the field and it would instantly focus the team. That was a big turning point for us in that season. In another game, the starters were having a terrible day, and so Coach Petrucelli sat all of the starters and put in the second string. They came in and not only played awesome, but played together as a team. He looked at the starters and said, 'They are playing for each other, and they want to prove that they are worthy of starting, and you guys are just out there.' I remember hearing that and thinking, 'Wow, we have to do this as a team, or it doesn't happen. If everyone does their job, and fulfills their role, we win.' That was another big turning point in that season. Going into the semifinal and final games our coaches told us, 'If you do this like we've practiced it, you will win.' And we stuck to our game plan and it worked."

> "As I became more of the veteran player, our senior year was such a bummer. We felt we could have won it my junior year, and to lose in the semis of the Final Four was devastating. After I played on the national team, I came to realize that it was during my time at Notre Dame where I learned that I am playing for more than just myself. I'm playing for my team, for my University, for the fans, and for all of the students that go there; you can be successful if you all play together and are good teammates. Those are all things I left

> *Notre Dame with, and they helped me be really successful on all of the teams I played for after college. Luckily I was able to win at every level of the game."*

So many athletes achieve success at the collegiate level, and then when they reach the professional level, that success eludes them. Not so for Shannon. She was able to take the success and adversity she experienced at Notre Dame along the *Notre Dame Value Stream* and translate it into a successful professional soccer career. Yes, she was only one player and you have to have a little bit of luck in addition to a team full of extraordinary athletes to succeed at the next level; Shannon had just that. The luck of the Irish.

The Professional Years

> *"Being able to play in four World Cups and in the Olympics three times was absolutely outstanding. I don't think I ever thought I would actually play at that level. I was a late bloomer. I didn't even make the national team until I was 26 years old. I was beginning to think that it wasn't going to happen. And then it did. The first time I put on the national team jersey and sang the national anthem was in my home town Los Angeles, at the Home Depot Center, in front of all of my friends and family, and I really had to pinch myself at that moment. It was a big memory for me. When I played my first World Cup, I was a late addition to the team, and I was pretty much in awe the whole time. I kept thinking, 'Oh my gosh, I can't believe I'm here.' I was pinching myself. Seeing as it was my first time, my first experience playing in a World Cup game, I was 100% focused and invested in the games. I wasn't thinking, I was just playing. I was completely in the zone, and not one bit nervous. And then after it was over I thought to myself, 'Oh my goodness, I was just in a World Cup game.' I had even bought tickets to the game to attend as a fan, because I, in no way, shape or form, thought I was going to be playing on the team."*

> ### *As I watched her play, I knew that was what I wanted to do; I wanted to play in the Olympics.*

> *"My sister played on the Olympic softball team in 1996, and I had just finished my freshman year at Notre Dame. As I watched her play, I knew that was what I wanted to do; I wanted to play in the Olympics. When the Olympics came around in 2004, I thought that was going to be my one and only shot at playing at that level. Being able to play in the Olympics in Greece, where it all started, was amazing. And it was even more amazing knowing that my sister was in the stands for me, just like I was for her in Atlanta, and we won! After the game, when they played our National Anthem, I remember*

standing up on the podium and we sang at the top of our lungs. I'm sure we sounded terrible, but we didn't care. And then I ended up being on the National team for 12 years, and a starter for a good amount of that time, which was such an absolute privilege for me. Playing on the National team for 12 years was a lot of hard work on my end, but it was an absolute blessing to be able to stay healthy for the majority of the time, and to play for so long. I played in three Olympics and four World Cups; that is a blessing indeed. At this point in my life it's difficult to find a passion that equals my time on the soccer field. That passion is what drove me to keep playing. I always told myself when it wasn't fun, I would stop playing. I hit a couple of down times throughout the years, but something always came along and lit up the passion again. I've been out of soccer for three years now, and I'm still trying to figure out what the next passion in my life will be. I have found things that I like. I've done some coaching, and yes, I like it, but it's just not the same. I'm looking for the next passion that will drive me through this next chapter of my life."

To look at Shannon, you'd see a woman who is the vision of health. But that wasn't always the case for Shannon. And even if you knew Shannon when she was struggling to find out why she wasn't feeling well, you may not have even known she was sick. Shannon shared her heath struggles with me, and how soccer kept her moving forward, even on the hardest days.

"In 2002 I was playing in the WUSA, women's professional league, in San Diego, CA. I was so tired, all the time, and I just could not figure out what was going on. I couldn't even make it through practice most days. I was scrimmaging with the team one day and my legs felt like they were in quick sand. It was so bad I had to ask my coach to substitute me out, I just couldn't play. At that point I went to the doctor, and went through some testing that lasted a couple of weeks. They diagnosed me with Sjogren's syndrome which is an autoimmune disease. But the way they explained it to me it was as if it wasn't a big deal at all. They told me that I'd have some fatigue, and that I'd have dry skin, dry eyes, dry mouth, but nothing terrible. And yes, I felt a little better in that at least I knew what it was. But I still wasn't feeling well."

"We got a new coach, and I told him what I had just found out. He asked me if I could control it, and I told him no, but I also told him that I was feeling much better, and at least now I know what it is. But he must not have been convinced because he never started me again. Who knows if my telling him about my disease had anything to do with that, maybe he just didn't like the way I played. But I blamed my not playing on the fact that I told him about it, and from that point forward, I was very cautious about

whom I shared my disease with; I never talked about it with anyone. Plus I still didn't understand the disease completely either. When I joined a new team in New York the next year, I mentioned it to the coach, only because I trusted him and had known him previously. I told him about the disease, and that I was still learning how to control, and he agreed to keep my secret. He was very understanding on those days when I just couldn't make it to practice because I felt too bad. My role on that team was different from the previous team I was on. I had a bigger role on this team in New York as there weren't as many National team players on the team. I was so blessed to have a coach that was willing to work with me. He gave me the flexibility that I needed, which in turn boosted my confidence; my play that year was what lead me to making the National team."

"Once I made the National team, I kept my health issues very quiet. My symptoms were very stable at the time, so I appeared healthy. I was still going to see different doctors, though, and at that point they were telling me that I might have something more than just Sjogren's syndrome. It wasn't until 2008 that I was properly diagnosed with Lupus. I spent a lot of years suffering, and saw at least seven different doctors along the way, in several cities including San Diego, Los Angeles (at UCLA), and New York. It took me six years to find out what I was really dealing with. That was very difficult for me. In 2007, at a team physical, my numbers came back really bad and my coaches weren't going to let me play. They told me, 'We can't have you play until we look into this more,' and I told them, 'it's fine. I have Sjogren's syndrome.' They ran more tests and finally let me play. At that point I could definitely tell my teammates and people around were beginning to think that maybe something was wrong with me, but I was very nonchalant about everything. But in 2007, my symptoms were getting worse and more frequent. It was getting harder and harder to perform, and harder and harder to keep it quiet."

"In 2007 I had to go on steroids during the World Cup, to be able to manage my symptoms, so that it wouldn't affect my organs, and in order to be able to perform. I had to go through FIFA to be able to play while taking steroids. And then in 2008 I was finally diagnosed with Lupus. Now I've been on medicine since 2010, after two years of testing medications to see what worked for me. The symptoms come and go in flares, and they are quite unpredictable, so you never really know when symptoms will come. And the symptoms are different for each person, so there isn't one set of medications that work for everyone. I had a lot of triggers, though, that would let me know when a flare was coming. My wrists would swell and get sore, my legs would get easily fatigued, and then I'd have to rest in between sessions. I used compression pants. The disease is different for everyone. It could affect your organs, but for me fatigue, joint pain and rashes were my symptoms. Extreme fatigue and joint pain were my worst symptoms."

"I retired in 2015 after we played and won the World Cup, and at that point I had been on a combination of medications for five years. Sometimes the meds made me feel better, but sometimes they made me feel worse. And as the years went on the symptoms became a lot worse. Before the 2011 World Cup they took me off all of the meds I was taking. And then in 2012 we found the right combination of medications that work for me, and I've been doing that ever since. The medications I take help with not having as many flares, but flares still happen. In 2011 we trained in Florida, and the heat was very bad for me. It caused a lot of flares. That was the year I told my coaches and my teammates that I had Lupus. I was feeling very alone with my disease and I needed their support. My silence and dealing with the disease on my own was starting to take its toll on me physically on the field, but also mentally off the field. I had one friend who knew early on, and she could just look at me and say, 'You're not having a good day, are you? I've got your back.' Once I told my teammates, their support was what enabled me to play for four more years."

> *I'm just trying to figure out where my passion is, and where my next chapter is going to take me.*

Today

"Now I've been retired for three years, and I have two beautiful kids. I had my first child while I was still playing, and she traveled with us to the World Cup. In 2016 I had my second child. I've been enjoying my time as a stay-at-home mom. I'm also doing some coaching, and running camps with Abby Wambach and Christie Rampone: **www.fullpitchsocceracademy.com**. We do a couple camps a year, all over the United States, and it's been really fun. It has been a great way for us to stay in the mix of the community, and to work with the next generation of soccer players. And it gives me a chance to stay in touch with my former teammates. It's a win-win. I'm also coaching soccer here in Portland. I'm just trying to figure out where my passion is, and where my next chapter is going to take me."

"One thing that is a passion for me is working with the Lupus Foundation. I started working with them during the end of my career and I'm still working with them today. When I was being diagnosed, I had no idea what Lupus was, and most people that I tell I have Lupus say the same thing. Over the years

> *it is becoming better well known, and people are starting to recognize it, but that is a byproduct of what the foundation has done in educating people about the disease. I work with the education and awareness side of the foundation. The medicine I'm on is medicine made for other diseases, however it works for me. But there isn't one medicine, or one set of medications that works for every Lupus patient. We need more research to find out how and why people get Lupus, why the symptoms are different from patient to patient, and the best ways to treat it. The foundation holds walks all over the country to educate, increase awareness and raise money to fund more research."*

Shannon's collegiate and professional soccer experience, and her work with the next generation of soccer players made it easy for her to share her words of wisdom for current student-athletes looking to make the jump to a collegiate sport career.

> *"First I would explain to them that success at the college level is not easy. They will have to work really hard to be a top player and they will have to make sacrifices at times. I would also tell them to enjoy it. And to make sure they pick a school that fits all of their needs, not just their athletic requirements: academically, socially, the coaching staff, everything. Especially for women. They may not have a chance to play past their college career and so they need to make sure they are setting themselves up for success in more than just sports."*

Shannon currently lives in Portland, OR, with her husband Aaron Spearman, and their two children, Zoe and Jaden.

Shannon Boxx's Lessons from the Notre Dame Value Stream:

- I would tell all students and student-athletes, work hard in your classes and get a good education. Both your education and your work ethic will set you up for success in the rest of your life.

- As far as sports go, success at the college level is not easy. If you want to play sports at the Division I level you will have to work really hard to be a top player and you will have to make sacrifices at times. This also translates into life after college. In order to be successful at any job, you will also have to work hard and make sacrifices.

- Make sure you pick a school that fits all of you needs, not just your athletic requirements: academically, socially, the coaching staff, everything. Especially for women. You may not have a chance to play past your college career and so you will need to make sure you are setting yourself up for success in more than just sports.

- And finally, I would tell them to enjoy it.

Shannon Boxx, her husband Aaron Spearman, and their two children: Zoe and Jaden.

Portrait of hockey player Brett Bruininks, fall 1995.
(Photo courtesy of Notre Dame Archives.)

CHAPTER SEVEN

The Lifelong Learner

Brett Bruininks, Ph.D.

(Notre Dame Hockey – Class of 1996)

When you think of Minnesota, the first thing that comes to mind may be the popular nickname, the "Land of 10,000 Lakes." But for others, it's what happens on those lakes and ponds in the winter that is more closely associated with Minnesota; that is hockey. And if you're a kid growing up in Minnesota, you can all but guarantee that at one point or another during your childhood, you will play hockey. This certainly was the case for Brett Bruininks. The child of a Latvian immigrant, Brett's mom fell in love with the sport after moving to the United States, and signed all of her kids up to play the game. Which is not hard to do in the state of Minnesota, as no community is without an ice rink and a youth hockey league, or at the very least a pickup game on a lake or pond. How did a young man who grew up on the ice rink end up playing hockey at the University of Notre Dame? This is Brett Bruininks' story.

"Growing up in Minneapolis, MN, my parents and siblings were a huge influence on my becoming interested in playing hockey. My mother specifically, originally from Latvia, came over to the United States during the war, and was adopted over here. The story is, she fell in love with hockey after watching it for the first couple of times... so all of us played hockey. In the 70s, most of the hockey in Minneapolis was played on the lake or with a 'park-board' team; not like today where there is an organized association, school-sponsored teams, or elite travel teams. So, in my case, when I wasn't playing organized hockey, it was the lake. Obviously, there are a ton of lakes in Minnesota, and there is always a rink on a lake where you can skate and play hockey. We always joke around that hockey was our babysitter back in the day. She'd drop you off at the rink, give you five dollars, and pick you up eight hours later, and you'd spend the day at the park playing hockey."

"My dad was a basketball player who grew up in Michigan. He will admit in the beginning he didn't know too much about the game of hockey, but learned to very much appreciate the game; often commenting on the similarities between the sports. He really wanted one of us to be a basketball player, but that didn't work out. The way I look at it is, you have to be able to jump and shoot in order to play basketball, and none of us could do any of that effectively. My oldest brother played hockey until high school. My middle brother went on to Colorado College and played hockey there, and also played in Europe professionally for a few years. Being close in age and a very good athlete in his own right, I would say he was my primary hockey influence. He and I were always in each other's face and competing against each other. We would wreak havoc on the downstairs, putting stick marks in the wall, having fights, and all of that other good stuff. Growing up with two older brothers contributed greatly to my competitive nature and, perhaps, my appreciation of the physical side of hockey. The only bad part about being the youngest of three hockey playing boys... getting all of the hand me down equipment."

This is where I want to go to school and play hockey.

"After I was done with high school, I played two years of Junior A Ice Hockey. Notre Dame actually contacted me right after high school. I wanted to test out all of my options, and since I grew considerably during my $10^{th}/11^{th}$ grade years, I needed a little more time to develop. So I went and played two years in the United States Hockey League. Throughout my time in Juniors, Notre

Dame and I stayed in contact. Tom Carroll, the assistant coach, was always really good to me. And so when it came time to take recruiting visits, I went to Ohio State, Notre Dame, and talked with Alaska Fairbanks, Denver, and Miami of Ohio. On my visit to ND, before I even met with Coach Schafer or saw the training facilities or anything like that, when I stepped foot on campus, immediately I got a good feeling that Notre Dame was the place for me. Later that day, I called my dad (even before I met with the coaches or had any scholarship offers), and let him know, 'This is where I want to go to school and play hockey.' As the son of a mother who was a special education teacher and a dad who was a professor at the time, he (and I suppose I have to admit he was right) told me, 'You have to think about your long term future. An education from Notre Dame will help set you up for later in your life.' Hence, given the reputation of Notre Dame, he was pretty excited about my desire to play hockey at a school like Notre Dame."

"That feeling I had when I visited Notre Dame, it's the same idea I use when students come and visit my current university. I tell them, 'Your parents aren't living with you. You have to make the decision for yourself. You have to be comfortable.' If they're a student-athlete, I tell them to completely take away the athletics side of it. I ask them, 'If you weren't playing your respective sport, could you be here for four years?' That's how I felt about it when I was looking at schools, and I still take that philosophy with me whether it's looking for a job or a new opportunity. Am I going to be happy here? Am I going to be comfortable here?"

"Notre Dame was the place for me, even before I saw the rink. Having the opportunity to play in the CCHA was a big deal for me. With my being a bigger (and less fleet of foot) player, the CCHA had the reputation at the time of being a more physical league, and that was perfect for me. And with Notre Dame being a brand new team in the CCHA and in the process of rebuilding, it gave me the opportunity to compete for a position and contribute immediately to the team. Everybody wants playing time, and I'm a big fan of you've got to earn your playing time; Notre Dame gave me every opportunity to try and secure a spot in the lineup. That was a big factor for me as I was deciding on a university. When I saw ten freshmen come in that year with me, I knew the school was committed to building the program. It was a little bit of a risk going into a new program, but I kind of liked being a part of something you can build."

The Notre Dame Years

"I remember my first inter-squad captains practice, I was coming off two national championships in Junior Hockey, one with the St. Paul Vulcans *and the other with the Des Moines Buccaneers; so I was used to some success. A couple of the upperclassmen players said to me, 'Well, get used to losing.' A little tough to hear, to say the least, and that's not my typical mentality. I believe you've got to do everything you can to get rid of that kind of mentality; it can be destructive. And I think we did, as a group, bring in a little bit more life to that program. Some of my best experiences at Notre Dame were during my freshman year. Maybe it was because I was a 21-year-old freshman. All of the guys that I hung out with were the juniors/seniors that year: Dan Sawyer, Eric Gregoire, Tom Arkell, David Bankoske and Matt Osiecki to name a few. And so for me, when those guys left, while I missed them, they also had a huge impact on my loving the school. Just by those guys taking me under their wings and showing me the ropes, I think I appreciated the school more. I think hanging out with the older guys first, as opposed to hanging out with the 17-18 year old roommates that I had, gave me a better perspective of ND. The bad thing about being a 21-year-old freshman and a student-athlete that hadn't really seen a book in two years? The school had me in every time management class and tutoring session because there was a thought I was going to struggle in school. I remember the first conversation in which they told me I at least had to have a 2.2 GPA to play hockey, and I told them, 'If I bring home a 2.2 GPA, they (my parents) are not going to let me come back.' Even though at the time I'm sure I was somewhat resistant to the support, I look back now and I can appreciate ND's efforts to give me every opportunity to be successful in the classroom."*

In sports such as football and basketball, there definitely is a significant transition from playing at the high school level to playing at the college level. But in a sport like hockey, where some players play Junior Hockey in between high school and college, the transition has an additional level of complexity. In Juniors you are able to devote 100% of your time to hockey. And then when you move from Juniors to playing at the collegiate level, you have to factor back in the academic part of the equation, and figure out how to balance the time commitment required to be successful both on and off the ice. Thankfully, the *Notre Dame Value Stream* is there to help make this transition a little bit smoother.

> **It's also no secret that we played frustrated at times. You could see the talent was there, and that the guys cared; for some reason, we just couldn't seem to put it together consistently.**

"What was the transition to ND like? I use the idea of environment versus culture to describe it; we weren't 'old enough' as a team to have a culture. A culture takes years and perhaps decades to create. I (along with likely everyone

on the team) wasn't used to a less successful environment. There were some really good players on the team, from top to bottom. It's no secret we heard the 'whispers' during the losing streaks that we appeared to lose motivation, that drive to succeed. It's also no secret that we played frustrated at times. You could see the talent was there, and that the guys cared; for some reason, we just couldn't seem to put it together consistently. I'm sure I wasn't the only one; that was a transition for me. I can't remember phone numbers, but for some reason I can remember a record of 36-96-12; I believe that was our 4-year record. It's hard to pinpoint why we weren't as successful as other sports or teams. Oftentimes, it's easy to point the finger at the coach or lack of leadership at the top. But it is a team sport and we all had a role. Realistically, we could have scored more goals <laughs>, taken less penalties <mainly me>, played better defense and blocked more shots, made better passes, and I could have been a better captain. In fact, if I could go back and do it again, the latter is one of the main areas I would change. Whatever the reasons, the CCHA was a tough league; probably the best overall league in the country at that time (my opinion, of course), and you had to earn wins. Did we lose motivation or drive to succeed? I think if you asked everyone that played from 1992-1996, they would say no; it's Notre Dame, and there is that tradition of winning and success; you can't help but stay motivated to do bigger and better things."

"For me personally, I just loved the game (and still do); I loved the competition, and of course in hindsight I think I/we could have done things differently and better. We had a good group of guys and we never complained about getting less attention or support than other more established teams like football or basketball teams (hard not to recognize their successes and they deserved the attention). We were just a group of guys who loved the game. But when you're missing a few key elements, especially in a competitive world like the CCHA, you're not going to be as successful. Don't get me wrong, at times we were successful. We knocked off teams like Michigan and Denver; there were times we were on the edge of consistent success, which was the most frustrating part of the experience. The other part of the problem was, when you have that stigma of losing, and you come up against a Michigan (top 5 team in the country), you can't help but hear that tiny doubting voice in your head saying, 'Well, we're just going to lose here.' I share the following with athletes oftentimes to get them to think about how hard you have to work to be successful."

"The first time we faced Michigan, we played back-to-back games, and we lost them both 13-2. We just got lit up. And I'm sitting there thinking, 'Wow, I just won a national championship (in Junior Hockey), and we just got *outscored 26-4.' Even the team I was on in high school was successful, so the entire experience at Notre Dame was a whole new world to me. If the team had been a bunch of ill-tempered jerks, it would have been a tougher pill to swallow, but these guys were genuine; good people who were willing to work and compete every day. Some teams would have imploded, but we kept at it. I played with a lot of incredible competitors during my four years there. Win or lose, I was confident that we had each other's back; that goes a long way in hard times. I take a lot of principles that I learned from those guys into my classroom, my coaching, and into my family life. We had each other's back; a common message I convey to all teams/players I work with. We focused on school and hockey, but we made time to have a little fun as well. When you're immersed in it, you don't realize how genuine the guys truly were until you are removed from it; at which point you can truly appreciate it."*

Being a student-athlete at a school like Notre Dame is filled with challenges. It is difficult enough just to be a student at Notre Dame, let alone add on the demands of being a top tier, Division I athlete. But amidst all of the pressures and challenges that come with it, comes a set of experiences that one will not soon forget, and that may very well change your point of view forever.

"I don't think you appreciate the student-athlete experience until you're done. We all wore our blue and gold letter jackets, and maybe you got a little recognition because of it; but you don't truly appreciate what it means to be a student-athlete at a place like ND until you're out in the world. When you see the looks on people's faces when you say you went to Notre Dame. Whoa. That's when you realize what Notre Dame means to people (even if they don't like Notre Dame, they have respect for it). Notre Dame is invested in the success of its students and student-athletes. It amazes me how they afforded us the many (academic) services that the other students and/or other programs may not have had. We had people available if we had questions, we had tutors, professors and/or TA's were always available, and (not to mention) a great training staff. We also were lucky to have the support of the University."

"When Dave Poulin came in and saw the dingy locker room we were using, his first response was, 'Nope, we're not doing that.' He got us our own locker room with the Notre Dame symbol on the floor and our own wood stalls. We thought it was the greatest thing ever, and we never for one second took it for granted. I think that was just one of many things Coach Poulin did to push the program forward. Obviously he made a huge impact as a player at ND; not to mention in his professional career. However, his commitment to our program was more than commendable. I'd like to believe his work (along with

other coaches in the history of the program) has influenced today's success. With Coach Jackson, that's where ND Hockey belongs. . . competing for National Championships. Of course, I'd also like to think (there is a small hope), that what we did, and others before us, during our time at Notre Dame helped lead the program on to bigger and better things."

"I don't think you'll find an ND student-athlete who doesn't feel the way I do about their experience at Notre Dame; it was a great experience. I wasn't as skilled as other players like Jaime Ling, Jay Matushak, and Jamie Morshead; but my size and more physical style hopefully added to the team; I'm paying for it these days. . . aches and pains that weren't there 10 years ago. But then again, that's what I signed on to do. <laughs> The other thing that happened when you were a student-athlete at Notre Dame was that you all supported each other, even outside of your sport. It was cool to see some of the minor sports achieving some success. When I was there, the women's soccer team was unbelievable, and lacrosse did extremely well. We used to go watch other sports when we weren't playing. I had a chance to throw around a football with Demetrius DeBose, Charles Stafford, and some guys in the summertime, which was really cool. One time when we were out there playing a pickup game, an assistant football coach came up and asked me (I weighed 240 pounds at the time), 'Hey, have you ever thought about being on the scout team for football?' And I said, 'No! Not a job I want. You guys run too fast and hit too hard; I'll stick with hockey.'"

"Those are the kind of moments that I really appreciate now. Spending the summers at Notre Dame were some of the best experiences I had as a student at ND. That was when you really got a chance to get to know your fellow teammates, other student-athletes, and students. I got to know Demetrius DuBose (football), Shannon Tuttle (volleyball), and a number of other student-athletes during my time fairly well, as we spent a lot of time together in the training room. On occasion, you'd look up and see Demetrius and other student-athletes sitting there in the stands at our games. I remember seeing him and some of the other guys sitting there in the stands and I couldn't help but think, 'Wow, you guys are going to go to the NFL, and here you are at our game.' He and I were talking after one of my games and he told me, 'You guys are nuts.' Which is pretty much what I thought about them. 'What do you mean we're nuts?' <laughs>. He thought balancing on ¼ inch steel, chasing a puck around a frozen lake, all while avoiding contact from the other team was fascinating. There was a special unity amongst student-athletes at Notre Dame. There really wasn't much division or separation. From hanging out

together in the weight room, to playing with student-athletes from other sports on a Bookstore Basketball team (I got to play on a team with the Ross brothers and Matt Osiecki), there was great camaraderie between all of us at Notre Dame. We really felt like members of a larger family."

"One of my claims to fame during my time at Notre Dame was that I almost took out Coach Holtz. One of my teammates and I were late to practice one day, and we were hurrying through the parking lot to get to the rink. And then just like that, Coach Holtz came around the corner in his golf cart, and we came head to head with each other. . .as we came to a screeching halt. I thought he was going to shoot us a look (or perhaps another gesture) <laughs> for driving too fast, and all he did was wave. Man, if we had hurt Lou Holtz that would have been an interesting remainder of our stay at ND."

It is difficult to get used to playing for one head coach during your college career, master his style, develop a relationship, and adopt his philosophies. But during his time at Notre Dame, Brett had the opportunity to play under two very different coaches. This created an added layer of complexity to the transitions he faced during his time at Notre Dame. Brett shared with me what it was like to play for his first head coach Ric Schafer, as compared with second head coach Dave Poulin.

"As far as things with Ric Schafer went, compared to other coaches I had played for, he was a good guy and he treated everyone fairly. I believe he had knowledge of the game, but what we were looking for him to give to us, perhaps, was more leadership and guidance. Without knowing all of the circumstances, he just wasn't at that point in his coaching career to be the leader to drastically change the program. Some of the guys I played with through the years shared stories about the crazy coaches that they played for, who could flip the 'psycho' switch at any minute. Schafer wasn't like that. I remember one of the coaches I played for kicked the Gatorade® table on the team in between the first and second periods. The poor backup goalie had to go to the locker room and change all of his equipment because the table fell on him. Schafer may not have been the leader we needed, but he was a decent guy. I have to mention that I was fortunate to have good assistant coaches during my time with the Fighting Irish. Coach (Tom) Carroll, Coach (Jimmy) Johnson, and Coach (Andy) Slaggert (who is still there). They did a great job as a support staff for Coach Schafer."

He taught me that it was better to play quality minutes than to play quantity minutes.

"And then Coach Poulin came in. He had the credentials and made an immediate impact to the program. He brought a different vibe and different expectations. Poulin inherited a team my senior year that had experienced a lot of losses, and he came in with the expectation that this was going to change. I think the one big thing he brought in was hope and drive. He told us, 'If you're not going to try and make this program better, you're not going to be here;' and I think that was a good message. Personally, one experience sticks out in my mind that will help illustrate this idea. Up until my senior year, I had played every single game, and I was looking at the potential of playing every single game of my career at Notre Dame, not missing one. There came a point in my senior season where I wasn't playing well, and Coach Poulin made me sit out of a weekend series at Western Michigan. I will admit, I was so pissed at the time and let's say I somewhat destroyed a locker room. My whole family (my middle brother, step-mother, and father - who went to Western), had flown in to see me play, and he sat me the entire weekend. I was the captain of the team at the time so when the decision was finalized, needless-to-say, I was mad and embarrassed. But here's the thing, I wasn't playing well, and as a designated leader on the team, he expected more from me. He never straight out told me why he sat me, but I figured it out pretty quickly. After that I went on an eight or nine goal streak, and I stayed out of the penalty box. He taught me that it was better to play quality minutes than to play quantity minutes. . . pretty powerful message. More importantly, the message I got was. . . just because you have a uniform and you're out there playing, doesn't mean you're doing your job. I would have absolutely benefited from having a few more years with him."

"With Poulin, it was the start of a new era for Notre Dame Hockey. We learned a lot about how to play winning hockey that year, and, I think, he learned a lot about coaching. It's not easy to step in somewhere you didn't recruit any of the players (even though you are a hall of famer, and have All-Star experience), and change things around right away; he made some great changes in a very short time. Coach Poulin definitely revived the passion and competitive spirit within the program. At the end of my senior year, I got a call from Coach and he informed me that he had called the Philadelphia Flyers organization on my behalf. I was looking at graduate schools, and not necessarily thinking about the potential of playing professional hockey; didn't think it was actually an option. Needless-to-say, his phone call was pivotal for my hockey life and my life beyond ND. I appreciate him for going out on a limb for me, especially at a time when very few college kids went on to play professional hockey. When I left, I knew the program was *going to be good, and look at them now. I would be remiss if I didn't share one of the most important and influential experiences I had during my four years at Notre Dame; the time I got to spend with Lefty Smith. To be honest, what can you really say to do it justice? He is a legend. He didn't have to, but he took the time to talk with me after most, if not all of the home games he attended. He shared his knowledge and his ideas about the game. Most importantly, he would critique my play. I'd like to think we got along because we were basically cut from the same cloth, a blue-collar coach and a blue collar player; he appreciated hard work and physical play. Despite his 'gruff' nature, he cared greatly for Notre Dame and Fighting Irish Hockey. I'm fortunate to have had that time with him. I'm confident he would be thrilled and just so proud to see where the program is now. It's been such a long time coming."*

It's my favorite question to ask, and probably the most difficult question to answer: What's your favorite hockey memory during your time at Notre Dame? But it didn't take Brett long to put his finger on some of the electric moments he experienced at Notre Dame.

You're not an athlete that leaves Notre Dame, but you are a student-athlete who now becomes a part of the Notre Dame history, Notre Dame Legend.

"You can always talk about your individual moments, but I would say my favorite on-ice Notre Dame Hockey memory would be our victory against Michigan at the Joyce. The stands were filled with both ND and Michigan fans. They were ranked high that year... top 3 at least. I remember a back-and-forth game and Jeremy Coe scoring a huge goal at a pivotal time. Great win for the program. Another one of my favorite memories was the end of the year banquet my senior year. We had all of the guys together one last time, they talked about and recognized each one of the seniors, and they presented each senior with their home game jersey. I think the best way to sum it up is, you're not an athlete who leaves Notre Dame, but you are a student-athlete who now becomes a part of the Notre Dame history. I could try to sit here and reminisce about each game and each goal (and each misconduct...) <laughs>, but I don't really remember too many games. I do remember being part of a great team, with great teammates... those are the best memories, hanging out after a game or after a workout."

And then it happens, four years have gone by in a flash, and it's time to head out into the world, with a degree in one hand and a dream in your sights. You've put in the work, you've filled your tool box with the necessary skills needed to take that first step towards your future, and you know that the *Notre Dame Value Stream* is always by your side to support you as you need it along the countless adventures ahead. Yes, you know there will be ups and downs along the way, but you also know you are not alone, and that no mountain is too high for you to climb.

The Professional Years

> "My first experience (towards pursing a professional hockey career) was being connected with Coach Poulin's former agent, Steve Mountain. Upon his advice, from Notre Dame, I headed off to Los Angeles after graduation to train with ProCamp® and trainer, T.R. Goodman. ProCamp® was a group of NHL and aspiring professional hockey players, living in LA for three months, and training 4 hours a day. The experience with T.R. basically remapped my entire physiology and psychology. It was intense and eye opening. I got the chance to train alongside hall of famers, and got to step out on the ice with phenoms like Kevin Stevens, Alexander Mogilny, Rich Tocchet, and Wayne Gretzky."

> "When I went out to Philadelphia for a tryout, I was still just this 'college kid' in many eyes. Not going to lie, it was a big transition from college hockey. It was a different game. So they guaranteed me a three or four day tryout. The practice facility had three levels. The bottom level was for the guys on the existing team, the second level was for all of the draft picks, and the third level was for all of the free agents and guys who had gotten in basically on a coin flip. I was on the third level. The organization was willing to give me a three or four day tryout. On day two, I went up the two flights of stairs to get my gear on and all of my stuff was gone. . .I had been cut already. Unbeknownst to me, they had moved my stuff down a level. Whew!" And then, after four days of competing with his peers, all of the hard work paid off and Brett was signed.

> "After a few days, I was brought into the assistant general manager's office in Philadelphia. He told me, 'We like your size and we like what you can do. . . here is your role. Your job will be to create space for people.' (pause. . .) 'Wait, you're going to pay me to do that? I can do that!' It was the job of the blue collar players I had always tried to emulate. That was now officially my role. It was the first time I had been given a role and told, 'This is what we want you to do. We don't expect you to do A, we don't expect you to do B, this is the role you are going to play on this team.' And it was great. In my mind I was thinking, 'Just tell me what you want me to do and I'll do it.' Despite what some think about the Flyers organization (misconceptions), it is an organization built from grit and hard work and you have to respect that. The lessons learned from playing for that organization (although short), in

many ways helped me succeed in my professional life after leaving hockey. I would have gone through a brick wall for them (teammates, coaches, etc.)."

"It was a different game. Everyone was trying to make it to the top, and stay there, so the intensity was high every single day; at practice and off-ice training. It was an environment I loved being in, but at the same time it was a pressure cooker for sure. When you make it to any of the levels (minors, NHL), any given day a guy could step in and take your spot. In college, you weren't necessarily used to having six guys behind you waiting for your job. You didn't ever want to be the worst person on the ice. That was something that served me well."

"I think when I got to the professional level, I didn't know the game as well as some of my peers did. And when they gave me my role I thought, fantastic! I learned a lot my first year in the AHL. I learned how to play the game a different way. I relearned how to play hockey, how to read plays and position and strategy. It was a huge learning curve for me, as it was a different style of play. I think as the years went on I got better and faster and stronger. If I could do it over I would do some things differently. It was pretty cool, but it was definitely a different game from what we played in college. No masks on the helmet. (I liked that part.) You played three games in three nights. You were in one city one day, and a different city the next day. We spent a lot of time on buses traveling. I think we spent more time sitting on buses than we did playing on the ice. But on the flip side, you didn't have to study and go to class like you did in college, you just had to practice, workout and watch video. It was pretty awesome."

"I played for two and a half years, and as I was getting ready for my third year of camp I tore something in my lower back. . . and just like that my career was pretty much over. I split my time between Minnesota and Philadelphia trying to rehab. About 4 months after the injury, I got a call from a team in the East Coast League. One of my former coaches (who coached me in Juniors) asked me if I would think about coming back. Not having too many other options, I went to Florida and tried to play myself back into shape. By the end of the season I was basically at the point where I was crawling to the bathroom. My back was so torn apart. And with me being the physical player that I was, I knew it was time to hang up my skates."

And then it happens. Yes, you know it is inevitable, but it's also unthinkable at the same time. Thank goodness the *Notre Dame Value Stream* is there to carry you on its back, and show you which path to take when you hit that daunting fork in the road.

Today

"Once you realize that it truly is time to hang up your skates, you go through a period of depression and you think, 'Wow, what am I going to do next?' I had the support of my family, but I kept thinking, 'I was in the best shape of my life. How did I get injured?' My dad told me if I really wanted to figure out how I got hurt, I should go back to school and get a masters in a related area; I said okay. I didn't know what direction I wanted to go in so I moved back to Minneapolis, got un-engaged, went back to school as an adult student at the University of Minnesota, and started, basically a new life. I took my first exercise physiology class and absolutely loved it. I got my Masters and then went on to get my PhD in Kinesiology, with an emphasis in Exercise Physiology. I never imagined myself as a professor, but I absolutely love it. I enjoy being in the classroom, and doing research and developing things."

"One of the best things that Notre Dame ever did for me was turn me into a lifelong learner. When I was in high school, as soon as I made the varsity squad, I found myself putting too much of my time into hockey and not enough time into my grades. As my grades started to slide, Notre Dame told me that I needed to have certain grades and a certain SAT score in order to get in, and so I had to start applying myself once again. I believe myself and Jamie Morshead were two of the first hockey players who had been admitted to Notre Dame after playing Junior Hockey. Notre Dame took a chance on me, but they also gave me all of the resources I needed to be successful. Most importantly, ND taught me how to really engage the material and critically think. Those skills have served me well my entire life. I consider myself what I call a very independent learner. I was the kid who was going to try and do it myself, and if I failed, it was on me. When it got to the point where I asked for help, it was because I had already tried three or four other things and none of them had worked. I remember one day Pete Bercich and I were talking while we were playing NHL '94, and he told me, 'You just need to learn how to study.' It was more than just going to class. You had to figure out what the professor wanted, and think about how the material can be applied. . . active learning."

> **One of the best things that Notre Dame ever did for me was turn me into a lifelong learner.**

"One of the reasons I like physiology so much is because it shows how we are all different. We may all be built similarly, but we respond differently. For example: You may encounter an ACL injury, but in order to treat it effectively, the doctor or therapist not only needs to look at the injury, but you also have to address the emotional/mental state, and the goals of the patient. You have to look at who they are in order to treat it. Are they an 80-year-old man who simply wants to be able to walk again, or are they an elite athlete who will drive you crazy because they want to get back out on the field and compete? It makes a difference in how you treat them, and if you recognize that, it will make you a better professional. My students may all get sick and tired of me saying it in class right now, but we all respond to situations differently. Put down the iPhones and have a conversation."

"My first job out of graduate school was at a small Lutheran college in northwest Minnesota, Concordia College (Moorhead, MN). Great job, great people. My main responsibility was to help revamp the exercise science program. A lot of work in the beginning (e.g. changing the curriculum), but we saw significant growth in a very short time. As I said, the job was great, but I was missing the hockey side. One day I was talking with the Men's Hockey coach at Concordia. We discussed hockey and training and eventually I ended up volunteering with the team. To be honest, at first I fought the idea of being a hockey coach. I had worked so hard to get my PhD, and my thought was, I'm just going to be an academic now. I didn't want to be the cliché... he was a hockey player and now is a coach. But it's hard to completely walk away from something you've done your whole life. Chris Howe, the head coach of Concordia, let me join the staff as a volunteer... the start of something."

"In my second year at Concordia, I was in France on a trip with some friends when I got a call from my athletic director, who had a proposal for me. He said, 'You can say no if you want to, but we had an incident happen with the coach of our women's hockey team, and we would like to know if you'd be interested in being our interim head coach until we find somebody?' I paused to think a while to make it look like I was really thinking about the offer. However, inside, I was jumping at the chance to get back into hockey. I told him, as long as I can continue to do my academic work, I would be interested. So I was a professor and a hockey coach. When I took over the program, the team was in 7th or 8th place in the league. However, we (myself and my assistant Joe Vannett) were convinced they were underachieving. I will admit it was a struggle at first. The team was skeptical of a new coach, especially one from the academic side, wondering if I could actually coach. It wasn't a simple process. Although I was committed to building this team with the existing players, we did need to make some changes to the training, systems, and player roles. Eventually, they bought into our system, and this group of athletes worked harder than any team I coached... and we had some success. The first season we finished in 5th and lost in the semi-finals of the *league playoffs. In my second season, we finished second in the league and went to a national tournament. Then, after my third season of coaching, Minnesota State University-Mankato contacted me and asked if I would be interested in coaching at the Division I level. It was a tough decision since I would be leaving a great college and a group of outstanding student-athletes. However, I tend to live by the idea. . . if you are going to regret it in the morning, you need to do it. I went down there and looked at the school, and talked to some of the coaches and players. On the ride home, I was convinced if I didn't take the job, or at least give it a try, I'd kick myself. I left a tenured track faculty position, one year away from applying for tenure, and took the job at Minnesota State serving as an assistant coach with their Women's Hockey team. I took a pay cut, but absolutely loved it. I got to work with a great coaching staff (Eric Means and Shari Dickerman) and some pretty amazing student-athletes. Certainly a lot around me thought it was crazy, but it was a new adventure, and I didn't want to have any future regrets by not taking it. I blame all of my success over the years on my athletes. Without them, I would not have achieved the coaching successes that I have. I've had the chance to work with some fantastic student-athletes."*

"I loved Concordia, and I had a great group of student-athletes. I had some awesome recruits coming in (10 players actually), so I did regret leaving the school and the program. I regretted leaving a group of players that really put me on the map. But it was an opportunity I just couldn't pass up. One consequence, I went from a winning environment at Concordia to a losing environment at Minnesota State. Maybe I'm a glutton for punishment. They had only won 8 to 10 games the year before I came, and the team definitely needed more energy, and I was happy to give that to them. I told them, 'You've been underachieving the last few years, and that's going to change. Enter my experience at Notre Dame. If you don't want to do the work, then you're not going to play here.'"

"Minnesota State gave me the chance to have some amazing experiences. I had a really good couple of years there, but our head coach decided to step down. Sports are risky. And anyone who has coached understands that records mean everything. I knew there was the potential for our head coach to step away from the game, and a potential change in that position doesn't necessarily guarantee you will still have a job. There was some talk about me being in line for the head coaching position, but in sports there are risks and no guarantees."

"During the middle of my second season at MSU, a friend of mine alerted me to a potential job opening at the University of St. Thomas. As much as I loved coaching, I did miss the classroom. So, I had to make a very difficult decision to leave Minnesota State, leave the game, and go back into the classroom as a

professor. I love my job as a professor. And I still have the opportunity to work with some phenomenal athletes. I get to work with the football team and I also am connected with the hockey team (e.g. writing off-season programs). I have a lot of student-athletes in my classes, and I watch a lot of my school's sporting teams. In the summertime I do some coaching with some of the local hockey teams around here."

"It's kind of interesting looking back on it. To be honest, I didn't watch any hockey for two years after I retired from playing professional hockey. I went through about a two-year span where I almost had an aversion to the sport. Likely, it was because I was trying to come to grips with losing the one thing that I had always wanted to do. I'm fairly good at compartmentalizing things so I just put it somewhere. While I was in graduate school at the University of Minnesota, I ran into an old family friend whose son was about 10 or 11 years old and was getting into pee-wee hockey. He asked me if I wouldn't mind coming out and being a guest coach. They had some fathers coaching who really didn't know much about the game. At first I said no, I didn't have any interest. But he kept bothering me and finally I said yes. I went to one practice, and the dads who were coaching were not creating a very positive environment for these kids. After about five minutes of my being on the ice coaching with these dads, I told all of them to 'get off the ice.' They looked at me and said, 'What?' and I said, 'Get. Off. I'm taking over the team.' The team was a group of blue collar, south of the city pee-wees; every kid had mostly used mismatched equipment. We even had one girl on the team; who I must mention was the toughest hockey player I ever coached. This group played for the love of the game and it brought back the thrill of hockey for me."

"The reason why I mention having a girl on the team is that after the kids moved on to the older age group teams, I kept in touch with some of my players and their families, including Grace Olson who was the only female on that pee-wee team. Several years later, her mother called and told me about an assistant coach opening at Grace's high school, and she asked me if I would be willing to move up and coach girl's high school hockey. At first I didn't want to. . . I was comfortable coaching at the lower levels. However, I decided to at least take a meeting with the head coach, Jaime Grossman. Jaime is one of the most successful coaches in Minnesota girl's hockey. We talked extensively about our philosophies and coaching methods; we jelled instantly and, by the end of the meeting or a short time after he asked me to join his staff."

> **I am convinced coaching girls and women has made me a better coach.**

> *"I am convinced coaching girls and women has made me a better coach and professor. Mainly because of one simple question: Why? In my experience, women are more apt to ask you the 'why' questions. Why and what is your thinking behind that strategy? These discussions have improved my communication skills and ability to relate to different types of learners. It really is all about communication. And once the athletes know the why, they will go through a brick wall for you. I have found over the years, simply asking/answering one question 'why' can make you a better coach, professor, etc.*

> *"Everyone I have met or encountered along the way has helped to build my coaching and teaching philosophy. It all goes back to my hockey background, because I want to teach kids the things I wish I would have known back then. It's been fun. And it's great that my current job allows me to do some creative things both in and out of the classroom."*

The beauty of being a former student-athlete, professor, and active member of the hockey community as a coach, is that Brett has a unique perspective on what it takes to be successful as a student-athlete and beyond. He can look at it from the athlete's perspective, from the perspective of what the professors actually expect from their student-athletes, and from the coach's point of view as well.

Champions do things that others find uncomfortable.

> *"First, you have to put in the work. In addition to that, I think you have to develop a plan as to where you want to go and what you want to accomplish athletically. Very few student-athletes go on to play at the Division I level, and in order to get there, you are going to have to do some things and make some sacrifices that other people don't want to do. Champions do things that others find uncomfortable. It takes huge sacrifices to be a Division I athlete. You really have to be okay with having to give up some things in order to be successful. At times, it can be a pressure cooker and expectations are great."*

> *"I have a philosophy on what to do and how to train. Don't do it because someone else wants you to do it, do it because it's your passion. It may be a grind, but when it's your passion, it is totally worth it. You can tell very quickly who has the drive and commitment to be a Division I athlete. Some do not understand the sacrifices... the time spent on the road, at practice, studying... necessary to be successful at that level. If you want to go to a school and be a member of the community at large, that's probably not going to happen. That's one of the sacrifices you're going to have to make if you want to play a Division I sport. Don't let anyone feel bad for you, though, because there are a lot of perks. However, it definitely is a sacrifice... but worth it.*

To be honest, I didn't even know who my dorm next door neighbors were because I never hung out in my dorm. I was always in the library, at practice, traveling, or with the team."

"*The reason why my teammates and I bonded so tightly together was because we were experiencing the same things. If you didn't do the work in regard to your classes, you ran the risk of losing your scholarship. If you didn't do the work in regard to practice, you ran the risk of not starting in a game or even playing. These were challenges that, perhaps, your non-athlete peers didn't quite fully understand. You really have to want it, and have to do the work, because even at the college level it's basically a year-to-year contract. If you don't do the work on and off the ice, you don't get to return. At the end of the day, if you are fortunate enough to get a scholarship to play at the university level, give everything you have for the school and your teammates. I was taught at a young age to always try to be the first player on the ice and the last player to leave. Careers can end at any time, from one hit, or one torn ACL. Appreciate it once you get there. . . it's a great accomplishment, but you're not done yet. There is a lot to be done not only in sports, but in the rest of your life as well. Whether it's in the pros, or in graduate school, or your intended profession. And always leave things better than how you found them."*

And always leave things better than how you found them.

"*As far as finding a school that's the right fit, during the recruiting process, ask a lot of questions. If something seems too good to be true, it probably is. Everyone who is coming out of high school and being recruited is going to be just as good as you are. If a coach is promising you big things for your freshman year, I would be leery of that. There are a lot of talented players already there, who have more experience than you, and who are going to compete with you for playing time. In order to be successful at the next level (in the classroom or on the field), it's got to be the right fit, so ask lots of questions and be confident in your decision. And finally, have some fun with the process. Yes, ask the right questions, but enjoy it. You are in that less than 1% who are being sought after to advance to the next level; enjoy it."*

"*And when you're ready to move on to the next stage of your life post-college, don't forget to lean on your school's alumni. They are so knowledgeable about life after college and are excited to speak to you. Call on them and ask for their advice."*

Looking back on it all, Brett did mention one thing he'd do differently if he had the chance to do it over again.

> *"I was so focused on my academics and on hockey that I really didn't extend myself to meet people outside of my immediate circle. I guess you could say I was pretty self-centered back then. If I had to do it over again, I would definitely make more of an effort to extend myself to other people and spend more time supporting those who supported me."*

Yes, we all know that hockey, or any sport for that matter, is comprised of the daily activities, the grind, and the work that you need to put in, in order to be successful. But it isn't all work, there were some fun moments mixed in there as well.

> *"One of the funnier memories I have about Coach Schafer was how frugal he was as a head coach. They had these boards that they would bring out in between periods during games, and have fans come out on the ice and shoot for prizes. He got the brilliant idea one day to bring the boards out and set them up in front of the net. He told us that we'd each get a shot from center ice, and if we made a goal from center ice, he'd buy each goal scorer a pizza. I think the first five or six guys who tried the shot, made it. I was tenth or eleventh in line, and as I'm watching each guy step up there, shoot and score, I'm also watching his face and you could see the anxiety building. . . this was costing him some money. When the seventh guy scored, he said, 'That's it. We're done.' Meanwhile the rest of us are standing there going, 'Are you kidding me?!' It could not have been scripted any better, to have all seven of those guys score from center ice and watch him stand there and do the 'number crunching' in his head. I'm not sure whether or not any of those guys actually got their pizzas. It was all in fun."*

Brett currently lives in St. Paul, MN, where he is an Assistant Professor in the Department of Health & Exercise Science at the University of St. Thomas, and his current research interests primarily focus on external loading mechanics and their effects on musculoskeletal health and development in children and young adults and fall prevention strategies with older populations. He is the co-author of the Bruininks-Oseretsky Test of Motor Proficiency (BOT-2) and the Bruininks Motor Ability Test for Adults (BMAT).

Brett Bruininks

Brett Bruininks' Lessons from the Notre Dame Value Stream:

- Student-athletes should find a college that is the right fit for them. During the recruiting process, ask a lot of questions. If something seems too good to be true, it probably is. Everyone who is coming out of high school and being recruited is going to be just as good as you are. If a coach is promising you big things for your freshman year, I would be leery of that. In order to be successful at the next level, it's got to be the right fit, so ask lots of questions and be confident in your decision.

- Be sure to always put in the work. In addition to that, I think you have to develop a plan as to where you want to go and what you want to accomplish athletically. Very few student-athletes go on to play at the Division I level, and in order to get there, you are going to have to do some things and make some sacrifices that other people don't want to do. Champions do things that others find uncomfortable. It takes huge sacrifices to be a Division I athlete.

- While focusing on your academics and athletics is important, also try and meet people outside of your immediate circle. This is where the networking process begins. Start to build your network early.
- When you're ready to move on to the next stage of your life post-college, don't forget to lean on your school's alumni. They are so knowledgeable about life after college and are excited to speak to you. Call on them and ask for their advice. And continue to use them throughout your career. They are a valuable resource, use them!
- And always leave things better than how you found them.

Portrait of football player Billy Hackett in uniform inside Notre Dame Stadium, 1987.
Media Day proof photo by Bradley Photographers.
(Photo courtesy of Notre Dame Archives.)

CHAPTER EIGHT

The Family Man
Bill Hackett

(Notre Dame Football – Class of 1992)

*W*hen you ask a child, "What do you want to be when you grow up?" there are a list of answers that pretty much every child will have on their list. You know the answers: police officer, fireman, doctor, nurse, veterinarian, baseball player, football player. But how many of those kids actually hold on to one of those dreams, follow it, and make it come to fruition? Probably not many. Most of us start out with at least one idealistic childhood dream, and somewhere along the way either figure out we don't have the skillset for that dream, or come to the reality that the dream isn't quite what we thought it was; then, through that realization find another, more achievable dream to seek. For

Bill Hackett, playing football wasn't on his original list, but he eventually found out it was a dream within his grasp, and a dream worth chasing. How did Bill become a kicker on the famed 1988 National Championship football team at the University of Notre Dame? This is Bill Hackett's story.

Bill was born in Boston, MA, where he spent the first half of his childhood and where his love of sports began. As a child, Bill's life was all about sports.

"My mom and dad were both coaches, and I played on the tennis and soccer teams. My dad coached the boys soccer team, and my mom coached the girls team. When I was going into middle school, my father decided he was ready to leave the financial industry in Boston and embark upon a new career, and so he relocated the family to Sarasota, FL. We arrived in Sarasota and I got involved in sports right away, but I hated it there. I had a great group of friends back in Boston and I did not want to leave them. But, once we got settled in Florida, I made new friends, got involved in soccer, and continued to excel in sports. As a freshman in high school, I was picked to play on the varsity soccer team. I played on the varsity team my first two years of high school. While I was out on the practice field with the soccer team, the football team was practicing on a nearby field, and the football coaches began to notice me. One day, John Sprague, the Riverview High School football coach, came over and said,

'Hackett, can you kick a football?'
And I responded, 'I don't know, but I guess I can.'

"So, after practice, I went over to the football field and kicked a few balls. Not being a football player/kicker, I asked the coaches, 'Do you want me to kick with my right foot or left foot?' and they replied, 'Which ever you are most comfortable with.' The next thing I knew, I was a place kicker on the football team. My junior year they moved me up to the varsity football team, and I started making some pretty big field goals and getting some recognition in the state of Florida. Our coach, Coach Sprague, took really good care of his players. He wanted each and every one of us to get into a good college so that we could continue our education, and as a result he made sure we were taking high school seriously and kept us in line. After I started to receive recognition in Florida, I also started getting noticed by colleges. I was getting looks from Boston College, Clemson, Florida State, and Miami; the letters started to roll in. The recruiting process is a very difficult time for a family, and it was the first time my family had ever been through it."

"Penn State and Joe Paterno were recruiting me exceptionally hard. I even went up to Penn State for a visit, and had a one-on-one meeting with Coach

Paterno, and I was very impressed. I had a great visit, and was pretty fired up about going to Penn State, but decided I didn't want to commit right there on the spot. My dad and I were still looking at other schools, and we wanted to keep my options open, even though I was strongly leaning towards Penn State. After I returned to Florida, I received a letter from Coach Paterno which said they had given away my scholarship to another student, but if I decided I did want to attend Penn State they would still honor their original offer. Penn State went on to play for the national championship that year against Miami. One of the Penn State coaches kept calling me from the sideline to ask me, 'We're going to kick a field goal here, do you think you could make it?' That was absolutely crazy."

"Even with all of the schools that were interested in me, in the back of my mind, Notre Dame was calling me. I made a VCR tape of my highlights and sent it to Notre Dame, and a week later they invited me to come up for a visit. We planned a trip north during my Christmas break, and scheduled visits to Notre Dame and Michigan. When we arrived at Notre Dame, we met with Vinnie Cerrato. We were there over Christmas break and there wasn't a single student on campus. It was snowing, and we met with Vinnie at the Morris Inn. After our meeting, he took us on a tour around campus, to the Joyce ACC, and the stadium. Notre Dame absolutely blew me away. I was ready to commit to ND right there, and it was going to be the end of my college search. The coaches at Notre Dame were so professional. They never spoke negatively about any of the other schools. They told me, 'We'd love to have you, but if you don't choose us, that's okay. We wish you the best of luck in your decision process.'"

"And of course, the whole idea of being on television every week was absolutely awesome. I was raised in an Irish Catholic family, but I didn't have any Notre Dame alums within my family. My dad went to Boston College and my mom was a stay-at-home mom. Going to Notre Dame was one of the best decisions I ever made. Don't get me wrong. . . my trip to the University of Miami sure was tempting. They take you out on boats, and have sorority girls sending you letters, but Notre Dame completely won me over. After seeing the Grotto, the church, visiting a few dorms; there was just something about Notre Dame, this indescribable connection, which drew me to commit to Notre Dame. I had no idea how lucky I was as I embarked on my journey to Notre Dame."

And just like that, Bill's journey along the *Notre Dame Value Stream* had begun. He went from going to Happy Valley to South Bend, and knew deep down inside that Our Lady wouldn't lead him astray. Bill, like so many of us, already felt "at home" long before he actually moved in to his dorm and started classes. Little did he know how much the Notre Dame family would become a part of his life, and support him over the years. When coaches like head coach Lou Holtz tell you, "Give me four years and I'll give you 40," they're 100% serious about the offer. When you join the Notre Dame family, as either a student or a student-athlete, you are a family member for life. And as the Eagles sang, it's kind of like the Hotel California, "you can check out any time you like, but you can never leave."

The Notre Dame Years

"While I had no idea how lucky I was as I headed off to Notre Dame, I also really had no idea what I had gotten myself into. When you go on your college visits, they show you the best of the best, but then you get to college and the work begins. They even sent you home with a workout plan that you needed to follow before you reported for summer ball. Notre Dame was quite a culture shock for me. My mom and dad dropped me off at Cavanaugh Hall, and after summer ball I was already homesick. The stress of trying to compete for a position on the team with all of these All-American football players, and then when school started, add on trying to keep your grades up alongside peers who were tops of their classes. Quite intimidating. There were nights when I'd call home and beg my parents to come get me, that it was too hard. Eventually, I figured out how to balance the stresses of academics and football. I'm not sure it got much easier, but I did get less homesick."

"Sometimes it was hard to wrap your head around what the non-student-athletes did all day. I'd come back to Cavanaugh and ask them, 'What did you guys do all day? You went to two classes and then what?' What did they do? We had class, practice, special teams meetings, film, weight room, and then had to go study. There was very little free time, especially during football season. In high school, you were a big fish in a little pond, but when you get to a place like Notre Dame, everyone is a big fish, everyone is good at what they do. I was there with the likes of Todd Lyght and Ricky Watters, who truly were the best-of-the-best. Looking back, obviously I loved it, and I'm glad I stuck it out. My dad kept telling me that I would be fine, but those decisions were tough at 18-years-old. It was tough just to get acquainted with everything."

"Even though Notre Dame didn't have fraternities and sororities, your dorm community was very similar to Greek life at other schools. Coach Holtz told us, 'Become friends with the guys in your dorm, those guys will employ you someday.' I'm glad Notre Dame didn't have 'football dorms.' I was fortunate to be at a place where they had athletes and non-athletes in dorms together. My freshman year I lived with non-athletes, and then after that I lived with

Stan Smagala and some hockey players. What was nice about rooming with fellow athletes is that you were on the same schedule. You could vent to them about what had happened at practice. It was tough to do that when you had roommates that weren't going through what you were going through. I wouldn't have changed my experience, though. It was a good mix to be a part of Cavanaugh Hall."

For guys who played football under head coach Lou Holtz, they had a love/hate relationship with the man. Sometimes they felt like he was this crazy little tyrant, whose expectations far exceeded anything they could accomplish or attain. But then at other times, they felt the fatherly love and unconditional support which he gave them, and knew that he was only looking out for their best interest. What was without question, though, was that Coach Holtz and the *Notre Dame Value Stream* would always be there to lift them up on the good days, pick them up on the bad days, and carry them through to the prize at the end; graduation.

"I was in Coach Holtz's first recruiting class. It was tough playing for Coach Holtz. He was strong in his ways, and he didn't accept anything except making sure you were the best you could be. He had an agenda, and he knew exactly where he wanted to be. And if you played for him, he demanded your respect. As a special teams player, we practiced special teams an hour before the main practice every day, and usually Coach Holtz didn't arrive until the beginning of the actual practice. Then, when it was time for practice to start for the entire team, Coach Holtz would arrive. You'd see the gates open up, then you'd see his golf cart driving towards the practice field. He'd have his two towels, his strawberry shake, and his pipe going. I think he liked starting every practice by yelling at someone. The cart wouldn't even stop and he'd already be jumping out of the cart and laying into someone. Sometimes it was me, sometimes it was (John) Foley. The intensity at practice was already high, but as soon as he got there it went right through the roof."

He preached the fundamentals and doing the little things right. He was a stickler for that. He didn't just preach it, he practiced it.

"We would practice special teams for an hour, the kickers would kick for a bit, and then we'd have time on our own; we just had to be back at the end of practice to run with the team. It would be getting dark by the time practice was wrapping up. You'd know how practice was going, and whether or not he (Coach Holtz) was happy, based on if the lights came on. The following was a pretty typical occurrence at practice. A play would be called out of huddle, they'd walk to the line, and Coach Holtz would get upset because there was no walking to the line. He expected you to hustle to the line. So to teach them

a lesson, he'd have them call the play, come out of the huddle, run to the line, and Coach would blow the whistle and have them do it again, over and over. Never run the actual play, just keep running to the line over and over to prove his point. That was Coach Holtz. He preached the fundamentals and doing the little things right. He was a stickler for that. He didn't just preach it, he practiced it."

"The psychology that Coach Holtz used in his coaching strategy was most definitely what took him from being a good coach to being a great coach. A good coach will pull 70% out of you, but a great coach will pull 90% out of you. It's up to the head coach to pull that talent out of you. Not once did I go into a game thinking that the other team would beat us. I always thought we were going to go in there and win. We believed in Coach, 100%. We were in the Joyce ACC when I introduced my parents to Coach Holtz. He walked up to me and said, 'Bill, how are you?' And I said, 'Coach, I'd like you to meet my mom and dad.' But when I said mom I pointed to my dad, and when I said dad I pointed to my mom. Coach looked right at me and said, 'Bill, let's do that again.' <laughs>"

"Coach Holtz may not have been tall, but when he grabbed your face mask, dragged you off of the field and yelled at you with that lisp he most definitely demanded respect. That demand for respect, that's what made him who he was. He was easy to follow. He was a good man, he loved us, and he cared deeply for us. Before we would cross the road from our football life back into our student life, he would tell us, 'Remember that I love you and care for you.' And he honestly meant it. In 1988, the season in which we went to the national championship, we may not have had the best talent that year, but we sure did have the chemistry, and that's what got us there. It brought us together, and we 100% believed in Coach Holtz and what he told us. We also had the luck of the Irish that year, the balls just bounced our way. At our 25th reunion, one of the student managers was talking about how everything just went right that year. All of the guys made every play, no one forgot their helmet; thank goodness for the student managers. They really ran the show."

"Pressure is when you have to do something you aren't prepared to do." – Coach Lou Holtz

"Coach Holtz would come to practice every day and tell us what he was going to do, and then he'd do it. He never veered from his plan. If you got a C in a class, you were sent to study hall after training table. Then they'd check you into study hall every day, and they'd check you into every class every day until your grades went up. He wasn't going to let you sway. He had a lot of control over us as a team. A lot of great coaches have a good handle on their players. They are admirals and they run a very tight ship."

"Speaking of funny Coach Holtz stories. . . I was kicking off at practice one day, and I was supposed to put it high, have a decent hang time, and drop it inside of the 20 yard line so that the guys could stop it inside of the 20. Apparently I didn't put it quite where he wanted it, and he was so pissed. He was yelling and screaming at me. And then what did he do? He put an ad in the Observer early the next week, 'Looking for a kicker,' and at the next practice there were 15 to 20 guys there to try out. And then he kept two punters and one kicker! He said to me, 'I don't care if we're paying your whole tuition or not. If you don't put the ball where I tell you to put it, I'm going to have some backups around here.' I didn't want to let him down, and after that I knew I needed to concentrate and do better. He sure did capture my attention."

"After our special teams practice was over, we'd have some time to kill until we had to be back out on the field for the end of the regular practice. We spent a lot of time in the Joyce ACC, or in Coach's office eating his Zag Nut candy bars (his favorite candy). When we'd go out for the end of practice, he'd put us out there for three final kicks. If we made three kicks in a row, the offense wouldn't have to run. Everyone would be yelling and cheering for us. Then there'd be someone throwing pencils at the holder, trying to put more pressure on him. And if you made all three kicks, you'd get a tap on the head. And even if you didn't, you'd still get the tap on the head because it was expected. At the end of practice, he'd tell us he loved us. That was the best part. He wasn't a warm person to us, even though he was a warm person on the inside. He needed to put on the dictator front to garner the respect that he expected from us."

"Have you ever heard of Lou Holtz time? It absolutely was a thing. If you had a team meeting at 10 am on a Sunday, your butt had better be there at 9:45 am, because if you were there after 9:45 am the doors would be locked. And if the doors were locked you could guarantee that you were going to be doing bear crawls at 6 am for the next three days. He would tell us, 'You may never be in the military, but this is going to be the closest thing to being in a military installation.' And you had better have your eyes on him at all times. If he moved to the left of the podium, your eyes had better follow him, and if not, he'd kick you out of the meeting."

> **Do you want to know what the difference is from the current Notre Dame team and our Notre Dame team? Discipline.**

> "He would always have a couple of razors with him at meetings, and if you weren't clean shaven, he'd have one of the managers give you a razor and you had to dry shave right then and there. Do you want to know what the difference is from the current Notre Dame team and our Notre Dame team? Discipline. They are never going to win another national championship unless they 'tuck their shirts in.' They need more discipline. More discipline on grades, on being a team player, on doing their job, on being a Notre Dame man and doing what's expected of them. It all goes back to doing the little things right. Coach Holtz was a champion at doing the little things right, and we followed him without flinching one bit."

> "I love Coach Holtz so much. He is a big part of what has made me into the man I am today. How I run my family, that's because of him and what he taught us. My passion for Notre Dame, that comes from Coach Holtz, too. My wife isn't a big sports fan, but she has been blown away by the overwhelming support we've received since my heart attack (in January of 2017). The support from the Notre Dame Alumni, and subway alumni, it's been very humbling. The support and good thoughts are greatly appreciated. Notre Dame is so much more than just football. The feeling I get when I'm on campus, when I hear the fight song, when I'm at the grotto; it's just unexplainable."

Being at a place like the University of Notre Dame is magical, even on an ordinary day. But when part of your journey along the *Notre Dame Value Streams* involves you being on a team that wins a national championship, that magic is amplified into something that is difficult to believe, and impossible to forget. Bill spoke with me about that magical 1988 season, and how Coach Holtz was able to transform the talent he was given into champions.

> "The '88 season was different. It's only different, though, when looking back on it. In our eyes it was just another season, where we kept on winning week after week. It was a special season for sure. One of the things that was different was the chemistry we had that year. There seemed to be more togetherness that year than we had the previous year. And everyone was going the extra mile, such as staying after practice to do more drills. And then there was the building momentum. After beating Michigan the way we did, and then Miami. Coach Holtz kept telling us, 'You don't have to be the best team in the country on Saturday, you just have to be the best team in the stadium.' He had a vision and he was telling it to us week after week."

> "My friend and fellow teammate John Foley wasn't able to play that year, due to a neck injury he had sustained earlier in his football career at Notre Dame. But he still had an active recruiting role with the team, and was with us in the

> locker room for every game. He had such an intense personality. Even though he wasn't able to get out on the field with us, just having him in the locker room, with tears in his eyes, was magic. Especially as we kept winning games."

> "To kick a field goal in the national championship game, and have it go through like it did, that was a magical moment as well."

> "There's a time in the huddle, at the end of practice, when Coach Holtz was in the middle of everything. I don't know if everyone was out of breath from running drills, but there was this quiet hum. There was a level of intensity in that huddle. I can still feel it. It wasn't like that the year before, or the year after. There was a happiness, a contentment, a chemistry on that team that only came together that year. There was something in that huddle that brought us together, I could feel it. Coach Holtz told us, 'You don't win a national championship, you wake up to one.' It took us years to figure that out, but he was totally right."

As if winning the national championship wasn't amazing enough in itself, what happened next was equally as memorable.

> "We had to wait until the spring to get our national championship rings. It was just a small, simple ceremony at the Loftus practice facility, but it was the perfect way to wrap up the togetherness we had experienced through the season. And then we got to go to the White House! I snuck up and stood with the seniors, so I'm in all of the photos with President Reagan and the presentation of the Gipper's sweater."

> "We had already met another President, George Bush Sr. when he came to one of our practices. All of the political reporters who were there kept asking us who our coach was, and a helicopter flew over the field with snipers and rifles. When the President was in the huddle with us, it was the first time that a President wasn't in the line of site of his secret service agents."

> **"His 45-yard field goal opened the scoring in the Irish's Fiesta Bowl matchup with West Virginia. Hackett wasn't needed the rest of the game, as the Irish did what they had done 11 times before that 1988 season." – Doug Fernandes, the Herald Tribune**[4]

> "When I made the kick I made in the Fiesta Bowl, right at the point of impact I actually slid on my butt, but I was still able to watch it go right through the middle. Thank goodness I made that field goal. And thank goodness we

---

Doug Fernandes, the Herald Tribune: http://www.heraldtribune.com/sports/20130106/riverview-grad-was-part-of-last-irish-title

> were able to beat Miami during the regular season. . . because my field goal in that game was blocked."

Student life at Notre Dame is challenging, and the peer competition is incredibly difficult, as each and every student was the best-of-the-best from their respective high school. And then for the student-athletes you have to add the time commitment which is required to succeed in Division I athletics. It is no walk in the park to thrive both on and off the field, but fortunately Her Lady's student-athletes have the *Notre Dame Value Stream* to keep them afloat, and on the right path.

> "Being a student-athlete at Notre Dame taught me many things. It made me realize that when you get knocked down, you need to brush yourself off, get up and keep going. Always learn from your mistakes. And even though you have no control of your past or your future, keep moving forward. To go through the challenges, the ups and downs that we went through during our four years at Notre Dame; that helped me handle the ups and downs that I've encountered in the rest of my life. It's helped me get through the big successes and challenges in my life, but also through the little things, like being able to shake off a bad mood. To be able to recognize when you aren't where you want to be, and to be able to make the necessary changes to get where you want to be. If you are a spiritual being, it's all about living consciously. Notre Dame helped me evolve into that way of life. Coach Holtz told us, 'If you give me four years, I'll give you 40.' But that was bigger than just Coach Holtz, that was how Notre Dame was set up. Notre Dame is pure love. Love of school, love of God, love of Mary, love of each other. That's what it is, and that love carries you through the rest of your life."

When you arrive on campus to begin your college career, graduation seems like a lifetime away. But then, before you know it, you are turning the tassel on your cap at graduation, gathering your freshly amassed toolbox of knowledge from your journey along the *Notre Dame Value Stream*, and heading out into the world on your next adventure. No one is ever 100% sure as to where their life's journey will take them, but there's one thing for sure if you are a graduate of the University of Notre Dame. What is that you ask? The answer is that your Notre Dame family will always be there for you along the twists and turns that are life. Always.

Today

> "Since I graduated from Notre Dame in 1992 with a Bachelor of Arts in American Studies, life has lead me on a winding path. I have spent most of my career working in the insurance industry, and have found a lot of satisfaction in my work, but it's what I do, not who I am. Most importantly,

> *I'm a spiritual being on a journey of discovery and fulfillment. This journey has lead me to the loves of my life; my wife (Pam) and children (daughters Sarah and Mae, and step-son Elijah). It is through my family, and our love for each other that I've found the greatest sense of meaning and purpose. I am so pleased with who I am and where I am today, and I know that I would not be who I am without my experience as a student-athlete at Notre Dame. There's not a day that goes by that I don't think of the time I spent there, the lessons I learned, and the people I came to love."*

As Bill has traveled along this journey that we call life, he has had time to reflect upon his time at Notre Dame, and the impact that it left on his life. He has also had time to reflect upon his experience as a student-athlete, and shared with me the words of wisdom that he would like to pass along to the youth of today who are not only hoping to be academically successful in college, but are also hoping to thrive on the field while playing a Division I sport.

> *"Enjoy yourself. Whatever you're worrying about, it doesn't really mean that much. When you're in the middle of it, it's hard to see that. Concentrate on your grades and the friendships you make in college. Sports are great, but very few student-athletes go on to do it at a professional level. Have fun. It's all about having fun. When you have fun you breathe better, your life goes better, everything around you goes more smoothly if you have fun while you're doing it. Go to school and enjoy it. Enjoy your teammates and the relationships you make. I wish I had made more relationships with people in college, but I just wasn't ready for it. In your 18-year-old mind, do the absolute best you can do."*

> *"Remember to always do the little things right. Work on the fundamentals. Have a good handshake and look people in the eye. That will take you far. Don't let life get in the way of your happiness. Be like a child. . . the closer you can stay to that the better you are. Kids have nothing but fun."*

Bill and his wife Pam currently live in Nashville, TN, with their daughter Mae.

Bill Hackett's Lessons from the Notre Dame Value Stream:

- Enjoy yourself. Whatever you're worrying about, it doesn't really mean that much. When you're in the middle of it, it's hard to see that. When you have fun you breathe better, your life goes better, everything around you goes more smoothly if you have fun while you're doing it.

- When you get knocked down, you need to brush yourself off, get up and keep going. Always learn from your mistakes. And even though you have no control of your past or your future, keep moving forward. To go through the challenges, the ups and downs that we went through during our four years at Notre Dame, that helped me handle the ups and downs that I've encountered in the rest of my life. It's helped me get through the big successes and challenges in my life, but also through the little things, like being able to shake off a bad mood.

- Concentrate on your grades and the friendships you make in college. Sports are great, but very few student-athletes go on to do it at a professional level.
- Remember to always do the little things right. Work on the fundamentals. Have a good handshake and look people in the eye. That will take you far.
- Don't let life get in the way of your happiness.

Bill Hackett and his daughters Sarah and Mae

Football player Richard Thomann, in uniform, 1969.
(Photo courtesy of Notre Dame Archives.)

CHAPTER NINE

The Medical Salesmen
Rich Thomann
(Notre Dame Football – Class of 1972)

Rich Thomann grew up in Akron, Ohio, a northeastern Ohio town settled in 1825 and named from the Greek word "high place," as it sat at the highest point of the not-yet-built Ohio and Erie Canal. If you happen to be a Notre Dame fan, as I am, you might be familiar with another gentleman who hailed from this Ohio town, Ara Parseghian. They may not have crossed paths on the streets of their home town, but they certainly did at the University of Notre Dame, and that Akron connection was a strong one. And not just a geographical connection, but a family one as well. How does a young man who was a better baseball player than football player, follow his first love and go on to play football at the University of Notre Dame? This is Rich Thomann's story.

> "The two boys who lived next to me, John and Bob Neidert, were four years and one year older than me, respectively. Bob signed with Notre Dame the year before me, in 1967, after making the All-Ohio team as a tight end, and that was my first real taste of Fighting Irish football, as he and I were best friends. I was a better baseball player than I was a football player. Our baseball team had played together for many, many years, and had won several state championships, but I was always a football player at heart. It was my first love. When I entered my senior year of high school, the recruiting process began. I was being recruited by Ohio State and Penn State pretty heavily, and Notre Dame came on the scene quite late in the recruiting cycle. I had a phone conversation with Tom Pagna on Christmas Eve of 1967, and that was the first contact I had with Notre Dame. I knew, prior to that, Notre Dame was interested, but that was my first official contact with anyone from the school. I told Coach Pagna I was going to be his easiest recruit; if you offer, I'll accept. Coach Pagna told me that he had already spoken with Coach Parseghian about me, and that Coach Parseghian remarked that he had gone to high school with two of my aunts. It was incredible to know the University of Notre Dame was interested in me."

> "Eddie Niam, who was Coach Parseghian's best friend at South High School in Akron, Ohio, gave me the first indication that Notre Dame was interested in me. He owned a restaurant in Akron, the Parkside Diner, and whenever my family and I would go there for dinner, he'd never let us pay. The walls of the restaurant were decorated with countless pieces of Notre Dame memorabilia. It got to the point that we stopped going there because we felt bad that he'd never let us pay, and we didn't want him to think we were expecting a free meal every time we came in."

College shouldn't be easy, right? It's a time for young men and women to learn the skills that they will need not only to thrive and excel in their future careers, but in their lives in general as well. But sometimes when kids reach college, it is quite a culture shock to make that adjustment from the amount of work needed to be successful at the high school level, to what is required of you to make it at the college level. Not so for Rich. The rigors of his high school in Akron, Ohio, ran by the same Holy Cross Brothers who run the University of Notre Dame, more than adequately prepared him for the rigors he would face both on and off the field at Our Lady's University. No, it wasn't easy, but he wasn't afraid of hard work, and he also had the *Notre Dame Value Stream* to guide him through the rough waters, and keep him moving towards the summit of success.

The Notre Dame Years

> *"It was an absolute dream come true. I went to Archbishop Hoban High School in Akron, Ohio, with 1,500 boys. It was a Holy Cross school, and it was pretty intense in terms of academics. Quite a few of the brothers who taught there had gone to Notre Dame, so they put us through the paces. It was a great upbringing, and it definitely set the tone for me. Notre Dame wasn't as much of a shock for me as it was for some of my teammates. Despite the initial shock that some of my peers experienced, we did have some highly intelligent guys on the team like John Raterman and John Cieszkowski who went on to medical school after football and became doctors. Being a student-athlete at Notre Dame required a tremendous amount of work, don't get me wrong, but you had help readily available, which meant there was nothing you couldn't do. But it was hard, no question about it."*
>
> *"When I was at Notre Dame, freshmen student-athletes were not on the varsity team. We would scrimmage and practice with the varsity team, but other than that they'd keep us apart. It was challenging to be tucked away like that. Many of us were used to being in the limelight, and then to all of the sudden be tucked away like that; it was quite an adjustment. As freshmen, we would sit in the stands and watch the games on Saturdays. There were 35 of us in the freshmen class, maybe 15 walk-ons, and every Saturday we would sit together and watch what we hoped to be a part of the next year. It was hard, but it was great fun."*
>
> *"When you're there with friends and people you really like, it makes it all worthwhile. When you play a sport at the collegiate level, you get so close to the guys you play with, and they become an incredible support system for you."*

Twice I had the opportunity to spend some one-on-one time with legendary Notre Dame head coach, Ara Parseghian. And both times I walked away feeling so incredibly blessed to have had the opportunity to spend time with such an amazing human being. I feel the same way every time I am able to spend time with former Notre Dame head coach Lou Holtz as well. Both men have left such an impression on me, but I know I am not the only one who feels that way about these two men. As I have talked to the men who played for both of these coaches, you can see in the way their faces light up, how these coaches were such a big influence on who these men would become as they traveled through their lives. Rich talked to me about what it was like to play for Coach Ara Parseghian, and how he coached them not only in the game of football, but the game of life as well.

"I am not sure there is an adequate way to describe it. I can tell you that playing for Coach Parseghian is probably as good of an experience as you can have in college football. He was so unique. He was so well thought of and respected, but at the same time you feared him. You didn't want to disappoint him, and you certainly didn't want to be on his bad side. Whatever you did, whether it was on or off the field, you constantly asked yourself, 'How is this going to affect Coach Parseghian? What is he going to say?' Even though he wasn't around you most of the time, the thought of him guided almost each and every decision you made. If you got a bad grade in class, you thought, 'What is Coach going to say?'"

"You lived in fear of what the ramifications were going to be. The last thing you wanted to do was upset Coach. When you played for Ara Parseghian, you gave him and your teammates everything you had, because you knew he was going to see the film later, and you didn't want him to be unhappy with your play. As far as discipline went, Ara didn't have to scream at you. All he had to do was look at you, and you knew you had screwed up. The assistant coach would come over and set you straight, meanwhile Ara was already on to the next play. That is how Ara was able to develop his players and make them better and better."

"What made Ara Parseghian such a good coach? For starters, his success. When I arrived at Notre Dame Coach Parseghian had won a national championship in 1966, had come incredibly close in 1964, and Notre Dame had been a Top 10, if not number one team, for five or six consecutive years. He was one of the top coaches in the country along with Woody Hayes and Joe Paterno. When you stepped foot onto Notre Dame's campus, you recognized he was at the top of his profession. The aura of being around the top guy, who had his photo on the cover of Time Magazine, it was like being around the President of the United States. It was really something."

"Any time I was in his presence, all through the years, I was nervous around him. You know when you're around someone important when they affect your life like that without even knowing it. Just like former head coach Lou Holtz, who also wasn't 'just another guy.' They were the ultimate when it came to coaches, the real deal. Notre Dame Basketball Coach, Mike Brey, also has qualities that remind me of Parseghian and Holtz. He has such great command of the game, and his players love playing for him. He knows how to get the best out of his players."

"With Ara and his staff coaching us, we rarely lost a game in which we were highly favored. Notre Dame may not have won every big game, but he made *absolutely sure we were prepared, maintained our focus, and got as many wins as we could. Oftentimes it seem we worked harder during the weeks in which we were heavily favored, as opposed to the rivalry game weeks (such as USC, Purdue, and Michigan State). During those rivalry game weeks the coaches seemed to be in better moods, and even though we worked just as hard, practices seemed to be more fun."*

"When I was being recruited by Penn State head coach Joe Paterno, my great friend and high school teammate, Chuck Mesko, was their number one target. I did get to know Coach Paterno quiet well, though, during visits and phone calls, even though I was just one of thousands of recruits he met over the years. I ran into him at a coaching convention 25 years later. He was coming out of the hotel across the street from the University of Florida, and I said, 'Hello, Coach Paterno!' And he replied, 'Richie Thomann! It's so great to see you! How's your mom doing?' I didn't even play for him, and I only knew him for a brief period of time, and all of those years later he still remembered me. He was so much like Ara. What made coaches like Parseghian, Paterno and Hayes so great was that they had these amazing memories and incredible people skills; they never forgot you."

You can't diminish the importance of the game of football. Universities use football as a tool to develop young men both intellectually and physically, but they also want to win games.

"As a football player playing for an elite coach, such as Coach Parseghian, you were like a little bird in their hands. If they squeezed you hard enough, they could end your career; of course, they never went that far. They had total control of you, in a good way. You can't diminish the importance of the game of football. Universities use football as a tool to develop young men both intellectually and physically, but they also want to win games. At the end of the day, it all comes down to winning and pushing the program forward. Beating that other team on the field that Saturday."

Coach Parseghian could just look at you and melt you. You never wanted to cross him.

Coach Ara Parseghian did a great job at developing the young men whom he coached into leaders both on and off the field. He guided them to be able to make decisions under pressure, and to be able to work together towards their common goal: winning. But, he also knew they were still kids, and that at times he needed to step in and make decisions for them. Or at least guide them towards the proper decision. At the time they may not have seen what he was doing, but that's exactly what Coach Parseghian did as he spoke with the team about their bowl game opportunities heading into January of 1971.

> "As a team, we were so committed to go to Miami and play in the Orange Bowl. We did not want to go to Dallas and play Texas in the Cotton Bowl. We thought Miami would be a much better trip. The year before when we played in Dallas it had snowed, and the weather was a chilly 40 degrees; it was anything but warm. We all had our eyes set on playing a bowl game in balmy Miami, FL. Ara was going to let us vote, but before we did he gave this great presentation to us about why we should play Texas, and how important it was for us to beat them right there in their backyard of Dallas. When we went to vote, he first asked, 'if you want to go to the Orange Bowl, please stand up,' and not a single person stood up. We were going to the Cotton Bowl whether we liked it or not, and Ara made sure we liked it!"

> "We really thought we deserved to be the number one team that season. The same night we played Texas, LSU played Nebraska, and late in the game Nebraska made the go ahead score, and so they were named National Champions with a record of 10-1, the same record that we had. It was a close vote, but they chose Nebraska over Notre Dame. It didn't bother us too much then. We had achieved our goal of beating Texas in the Cotton Bowl. Later on in life, however, it did begin to bother us; we came to realize how important it would have been to have had a national championship that year. Had we beaten Southern Cal in our last game of the season, we could have gone down in history as one of the best teams at Notre Dame."

> "That team still holds the record for most number of offensive plays per game. We rushed/passed for over 250 yards per game. We shut out three opponents (Purdue, Michigan State and LSU). And we only allowed (on average) 10 points per game. Our peers included players such as Joe Theisman and Tom Gatewood; it was a pretty special team."

> "Coach Parseghian recruited guys who reminded him of himself. He always said he saw himself in us. He was a smaller guy when he played professional ball. He didn't recruit you because you were big, he recruited you because you were good. He recruited the size of your will. Coaches like Parseghian and Holtz, they had this special ability to find the 'Notre Dame' type of football players. And both of these coaches had the ability to move players into new positions in order to set them up to achieve their biggest success possible. Ara loved to recruit quarterbacks because he knew they were good athletes, and then he'd move them around. He loved the shorter, thicker build of running

backs. He wanted all-around guys who could block, catch, and run. His players may not have been really big or really fast, but they were really good."

The best part of these interviews is listening to each athlete reminisce about their time at Notre Dame. Some of their favorite memories occurred on the field, and some of their favorite memories occurred off the field. As they share their stories, and walk down memory lane, you can hear it in their voices. Their time spent, and memories created, traveling on the *Notre Dame Value Stream* is something they will never forget, and something they carry with them every day. It's a place they look forward to returning to, and is a place that they ever so fondly call home. Home under the Dome.

"My favorite play at Notre Dame was in the 1970 season. In our game against LSU, late in the game, LSU had driven down to around the 25 yard line, and was going to attempt a field goal to tie the game. I was supposed to rush from the outside (as the outside linebacker), and I was playing on the line with my neighbor, Bob, who was the defensive end. If they had made the field goal, the game would have ended in a 3-3 tie and we would not have gone to the Cotton Bowl. As we were in the huddle, I was afraid I was not going to be able to get there in time. So I told Bob, I can pull the wing back out of position, and you cut up underneath him and try to block the kick. When we did the play, it worked out perfectly. I made the wing back think he had to block me. Bob cut underneath (a shorter straighter path to the ball), laid out and blocked the kick. Final score: ND 3 - LSU 0! When I caught Ara's eyes coming off the field, he knew exactly what I had done. It was such a great feeling of satisfaction to get his approval."

"Then, in my sophomore year, in our game against Air Force, I had another memorable moment. It was the last game of the 1969 season, and Notre Dame had accepted a bid to the Cotton Bowl (the first accepted bowl game bid in 45 years) during the build up to the game, which made losing to Air Force not an option. We scored the go ahead touchdown to go up 14-7, and Air Force came roaring back. On the kickoff, the running back got to the outside and was headed up the field. I was the outside contain guy but I was on the other side of the field. I cut all the way across the field and as he broke by I had an angle on him and tackled him at about the 50 yard line. That play was such a great thrill for me, to think I had a part in securing the victory for Notre Dame."

There is no better satisfaction than to know you did something to help your team win.

> "So many of us on the team excelled at the little things which all added up to the big wins, but oftentimes recognition on the team was scarce. Only a few guys sucked up most of the oxygen, so when someone recognized you for an excellent play, that was such a great feeling. If someone noticed you or came up to you after a game and congratulated you on a great tackle, that meant so much. Very few people noticed the little things that were going on, on the field. A lot of the plays we made that truly made a difference in the win or loss column weren't noticed. The coaches noticed, but the media didn't always see that all of those things added up to winning a football game. I was fast at 215 pounds, ran a 4.5 40 yard dash many times (starting in high school preseason practice), and was remembered for being able to run with the best of them. Bobby Washington, a freshman wide receiver in 1971, told me during a practice, as we were running man-to-man coverage, that I was the fastest 'white boy' he had ever seen! <laughs> During my freshman year they took us to the old field house (where they played basketball in those days) and we ran 40 yard dashes for time. Thom Gatewood ran a 4.6 and I followed him with a 4.5. He stared at me and said, 'who are you?' I told him, 'just another linebacker!'"

After four incredible years at Our Lady's University, it was time for Rich to take all that he had been taught and set out to see where life would take him next. For most of us, our path is never straight. It's a winding road, filled with twists and turns along the *Notre Dame Value Stream*, a road that creates for us a lifetime of memories experienced with friends and family.

The Professional Years

> "Playing football at Notre Dame was akin to reaching the pinnacle of your career. When you got there, you worked so hard to get the chance to play as there were a lot of great athletes on the team with you. A lot of your teammates were the best from their respective city, state, or school, as well as possibly being the best in the entire country at their position. When you were a starter, a lot went into that. You had to be gifted and you also had to stay healthy. A lot of gifted guys didn't get the chance to play because they couldn't stay healthy. I was so lucky. Once I got into the starting spot as a sophomore, I never changed positions and I never dropped out of the number one spot; that was so rare. I was pretty fast, and good sized; everyone remembered me for my speed. And additionally, I was healthy and I stayed healthy. A lot of guys could play, but it was of utmost importance to stay healthy. When it came time to play professional football, it was almost a letdown. I signed with the Calgary Stampeders, as I knew at my size (5'11", 199 lbs.) I probably didn't have

a chance to play in the NFL. I signed to play football in Canada because I figured it was my best shot to play football professionally, and it didn't hurt that Joe Theisman had gone up the year before."

"In order for me to make the team I had to be a starter, and there were only 13 Americans allowed to be on each Canadian football team. The only way I thought I could be one of those 13 starters was to be a center, and I didn't really want to play center. Granville Liggins, who went to OU (and weighed 270 lbs.), was the nose tackle at the time. He hit me so hard one day in practice, he split my helmet in two, and the only thing that was holding it together was my facemask. At this point I thought there was no way I could play center across from guys like him. I was in Calgary for two weeks before I came to this realization."

"I left Calgary, drove home to Ohio to get my wife, and we relocated to Stuart, Florida, where we both got into teaching. My wife had a degree in education, and I taught book keeping and was an assistant football coach for our first two years in Stuart. My contract to play Canadian football was $15K, and when we got to Florida our combined income teaching was $15K, so there was no great financial reason to play professional football back in those days. It's not like I was missing out on millions of dollars."

"Then, when the World Football League started, I went to Jacksonville, Florida, to try out, and ended up signing a football contract to play with them for two years. 300 guys tried out for that additional team, a lot of whom already had some professional football experience. Those 300 guys were trying out for 40 spots, and there were 37 linebackers trying out for 5 spots; one of which I was lucky to get. Our very first game was the Jacksonville Sharks versus the New York Stars. What a thrill it was to run out on the field, but it never really approached how it felt to run out of the tunnel and onto the field at Notre Dame Stadium. Mike Townsend was on the team with me (who we nicknamed Kip Keino, after the great barefoot Ethiopian runner), and Bob Thomas was on the team as well."

Today

"I played in the World Football League in 1974 and 1975 for Jacksonville and then Memphis, and at that point the WFL folded. The next stop in my career would be coaching high school football, and then college football in Shelby, North Carolina, where we had our first daughter. The coach I was working for in Shelby decided to take a job in Wyoming and when they brought the new coach in, I decided to take a year off and we moved back to

> *Jacksonville, Fla. And I got into medical sales. I loved coaching, but I didn't want to have to move my family every two years, which is the reality when you are coaching college football. In 1998 I returned to coaching when I was offered an assistant coaching position at the Bolles School. I coached under legendary head coach, Corky Rodgers, who retired in 2017 as the third most winningest high school football coach, behind John T. Curtis of Louisiana (in second) and G.A. Moore of Texas (in first). I coached under Rodgers for 18 years, and I have been privileged to be a part of seven state championship titles. I loved playing high school football, and for me, have the opportunity to be around high school kids whom you can still mold, shape, and have a great deal of influence on, was the perfect place to be."*

Rich was truly blessed to be able to coach some wonderful young men, which often opened doors for them and led to future opportunities.

> *"Lloyd Regas was one of our backup quarterbacks, and he was a pretty good athlete. The assistant head coach at Navy at the time was Sammy Steinmark, who was recruiting Regas, and during that process, Sammy and I became friends. He came to Florida on a recruiting trip, along with Navy's head coach, and they made some time to have dinner at my house. I just happened to have the film with me of a kid who was interested in going to Navy, and we sat down to watch the film. Our backup quarterback was the holder, and in the film, the team we were playing blocked a kick, picked up the ball and started running down the field. Our backup quarterback tackled him, recovered the ball and took off down the field, which was pretty much the only big play that kid made all year. The Navy coach watched that play and said, 'Who's that kid??' And that young man ended up playing football at Navy, having an outstanding career as a Navy wide receiver. Had they not been to dinner at my house, had I not pulled out that particular film, that kid probably would not have gone on to play football at Navy. It's just one of many examples of the difference we made the lives of these kids, all because you 'knew a guy, who knew a guy'. . . and you were in the right place at the right time."*

> *"It's crazy the stuff that has happened, that I've been a part of, over the last 18 years. My being a Notre Dame alum has helped a lot when it comes to recruiting guys to play football at Bolles. When the recruits come down to talk to us, they respect me because they understand that I know how to get them to the next level."*

> *"There is nothing that has happened in my life that Notre Dame didn't affect in a positive way. The 'Give me four, I'll give you 40' mantra is so true. Notre Dame has followed me, and has been a part of me, everywhere I've gone. I met*

> my wife my senior year at Notre Dame. She was a student at the University of Akron, and she got to meet the guys and go through my senior year with me. From my first job as a teacher in Stuart, FL. (which I got because the hiring manager was a huge Notre Dame fan), to the jobs I have today at Medacta USA, and a linebackers coach at the Bolles School; Notre Dame is as much a part of me as the clothes I wear. Notre Dame is a part of me, inside and out. When Ara passed, I got so many messages of condolence. When friends of mine hear Notre Dame, they think of me."

> "To have been a Notre Dame Football player, it means as much when you're 66 years old as it does when you're 18. I think it gets more intense as time goes by. Everyone makes you out to be better than you really were, and no one remembers whether or not you played in the NFL; it's all about your time at ND. 'You played football at Notre Dame?!' That stays with you for the rest of your life. I can't think of a single successful thing I have done that didn't somehow relate back to Notre Dame. Even in my sales career, I hear it all the time, 'You played football at ND?!' And immediately we're connected."

> "I have a doctor that I call, and he looks up to me because I played football at Notre Dame, and he's a huge ND fan. How great is it for me to know that when people hear Notre Dame they think of me. It means so much to people when they find out you went to Notre Dame. The school has such an aura about it, and it becomes part of your being."

Looking back on your life shows you two things. It shows you the things you did right, and it also shows you the things you did wrong. What it also allows you to do is share your experiences with the next generation, and give them some guidance on how to navigate the rough waters they may someday encounter, and give them tips on how to weather the storm. Rich shared with me what advice he would give to young men and women who want to play sports at the collegiate level.

> "You have to be realistic. Size today is so important. Some kids are going to be eliminated by their height and weight. It didn't used to be important, but today it is, absolutely. Some colleges even have height and weight restrictions. It's so difficult to get a college scholarship at a major school, but if a young man wants to play football, there is a school for them. It may not be a big time school, but there are opportunities out there."

> **Also, by playing multiple sports, you are developing the whole body, which oftentimes leads to fewer injuries. You take all of the skills you learn from each sport, and you'll turn yourself into an even better athlete.**

"As a student-athlete, not only is a great work ethic important, but grades are extremely important as well. Always stay focused, and make sure you are making the sacrifices needed to be a great teammate and a great athlete. Play more than one sport. The athlete who focuses on one sport rarely goes on to play that sport in college. If you play several sports, your opportunities open up to so many more options. Also, by playing multiple sports, you are developing the whole body, which oftentimes leads to fewer injuries. You take all of the skills you learn from each sport, and you'll turn yourself into an even better athlete. Guys who can move, run, who are agile, have body control; all of those things turn you into a great football player."

You can still find Rich and his wife Linda in Jacksonville, FL, soaking up the Florida sun and enjoying time with their three children, Kaley, Shawn and Erin, and 10 (soon to be 11) grandchildren.

Rich Thomann and his beautiful family. From left to right: Margaret, (daughter) Erin, Ruby and Penny, Kevin, Waylon (in the hoody, being held by Rich), Lucy, Andrew, Grant, (daughter) Kaley, Quade, Duncan, (daughter) Shawn, and (wife) Linda.

Rich Thomann's Lessons from the Notre Dame Value Stream:

- As a student-athlete, not only is a great work ethic important, but grades are extremely important as well.
- Play more than one sport. The athlete who focuses on one sport rarely goes on to play that sport in college. If you play several sports, your opportunities open up to so many more options. Also, by playing

multiple sports, you are developing the whole body, which oftentimes leads to fewer injuries. You take all of the skills you learn from each sport, and you'll turn yourself into an even better athlete. Guys who can move, run, who are agile, have body control; all of those things turn you into a great football player.

- Always stay focused, be prepared, and make sure you are making the sacrifices needed to be a great teammate and a great athlete. These skills will also serve you well for the rest of your life.

Portrait of women's soccer player Elizabeth Wagner, 1998.
(Photo courtesy of Notre Dame Archives.)

CHAPTER TEN

The Great Adventurer

Elizabeth Wagner

(Notre Dame Soccer – Class of 2002)

If there is one thing that is pretty much guaranteed in this crazy thing we call life, it's that no one can truly predict where their life will go, and life will almost definitely throw a curveball or two at you that you never saw coming. But, if you're able to keep an open mind, and enjoy the ride, your potential in life is endless. This is pretty much the mantra of former Notre Dame soccer player, Elizabeth Wagner. From the age of five, Elizabeth was positive that she wanted to become a doctor when she grew up, but after completing her pre-medicine degree at Notre Dame, she discovered that her career aspirations may have changed, and little did she know, her life adventure was just getting started. This is Elizabeth Wagner's story.

"I grew up outside of Houston in Spring, Texas, and started playing soccer at the age of five. I have an older brother and a younger sister and we all played soccer. It was just something we all did as kids. I think soccer is a wonderful sport for the majority of kids, and I think it is a sport that most kids at least try at one point in their childhood. I don't remember too much of my early days of playing soccer, but I must have enjoyed it because I continued to play every year. When I got a little older, around nine or ten years old, I have distinct memories of playing the game. At that age, the coaches rotated us around to the different positions, including goalkeeper. I really had a knack for the goalkeeping position, and I very much enjoyed it, and so the coaches put me back there for tournament games. This really built up my confidence, which made me like goalkeeping even more. I tried out for a select soccer team when I was ten years old (Challenge Soccer Club), and during the tryout I was asked where I wanted to play. I told them I wanted to be a goalkeeper with some occasional time on the field. I made the team and they had an excellent program."

"But soccer wasn't the only sport I played growing up. I also played softball for a year, tennis for a few years, basketball in junior high, and volleyball in junior high and high school. Volleyball and soccer were the two sports that I played all the way through high school. When I got into high school I had the opportunity to try out for a travel volleyball team, but I really liked soccer more. I had a great relationship with my teammates, and our soccer team had achieved a lot of success and had a winning program, so I decided that I only had time to do one competitive club/travel team. I stuck with playing volleyball on the high school team and played soccer for the club team as it was more competitive."

"The club soccer team that I played on hosts a big tournament (Texas Shootout) in the Houston area at the end of May, beginning of June, on the very same fields that I played on growing up. Back when it started, they brought in all of the top club soccer teams from around the country, and college coaches would come and use it as a big recruiting weekend. They also held a big golf tournament that weekend as a fundraiser for the tournament. The best part of having all of these college coaches at our tournament every year was that I already knew many of them before they started to actively recruit me. I knew I wanted to attend a college which had strong academics in addition to a strong athletic program. I had gotten to know Coach Chris Petrucelli and how well he and Notre Dame had done in checking all of the boxes that I was interested in, both on and off the field. My club team was invited to attend the NCAA Women's Soccer Final Four during several of *my later years of high school. Adidas hosted a tournament that took place the same weekend as the Final Four, which brought in the top four club soccer teams to play each other. This gave me additional exposure to Notre Dame, watching them play in the Final Four. I really liked Coach Petrucelli as a person and a coach, and while that wasn't the main reason I decided to play soccer at Notre Dame, it definitely helped."*

Seeing the tradition, seeing how tight knit the team was, and how they really felt like a family unit: that's what really sold Notre Dame for me.

"When I began my college search, I looked at a number of schools. Being a goalkeeper makes the recruiting search a bit more challenging, because there are fewer goalkeepers on each team, and timing makes a big difference. I was interested in Stanford, but they had just brought in a girl who would be just one year ahead of me, which would significantly limit my opportunity to play. I took recruiting trips to the University of Florida, Texas A&M, Vanderbilt and Notre Dame. I decided not to take a fifth visit because at that point I had already made my decision. Monica Gonzalez, who was also from Texas (I knew her from back home), was who I stayed with during my official visit to Notre Dame. I think if you know someone who is already there, they try and have you stay with them. I was there the third weekend in September, and it was an absolutely fantastic weekend. There were a ton of recruits there from all sports, not just soccer, and it was cool to speak to and hang out with other recruits, and to hear what they thought about the Notre Dame experience."

"There was also a soccer tournament that weekend hosted by Notre Dame Women's soccer (they played the University of North Carolina and Duke). That game against North Carolina on a Friday night under the lights gave me a lasting impression of what it would be like to attend Notre Dame. They tied 2-2 after a hard fought regular time and overtime, but the support the Notre Dame community gave to the women's team and the camaraderie of the team members made me realize that this was a special place. The Notre Dame football team, unfortunately, got beaten pretty badly by Michigan State University, but being able to see the campus, experience the atmosphere, and see what Notre Dame was really like absolutely sold me on the school. I'm not Catholic, and I'm not Irish, and so Notre Dame probably would not have been on my radar had they not had such a successful soccer program. That weekend at Notre Dame, seeing the tradition, seeing how tight knit the team was, and how they really felt like a family unit, that's what really sold it for me: along with all of the other wonderful things about Notre Dame, which is quite a long list."

And then your dream becomes a reality. You step foot on campus at the University of Notre Dame, you are on your own for the first time, and the world is your canvas. Now is your time to begin the transformation from who you are, to who you will be, along your journey on the *Notre Dame Value Stream*. But as a student-athlete, there is a little more to figure out than how to not oversleep and miss class, how to manage your time, and how to keep up with the rigors that are Notre Dame academics. You also have to figure out how to be an athlete on top of all of that. What did that transition look like for Elizabeth?

The Notre Dame Years

> *"For me it wasn't too bad. The training itself at the collegiate level is more difficult, and more intense. You train every day at the collegiate level, as opposed to three or four days a week at the high school level. The hardest part of the transition for me was learning how to be an adult - living on my own, making my own decisions, managing my time, and taking care of myself. Those things were more of a challenge for me. Soccer wise, you had so much support from the University, and your coaches, and your teammates; transition wasn't bad at all. The one soccer transition that was tough for me was playing time. I went from starting and playing all of the time in high school, to sitting on the bench once I got to Notre Dame. I knew this would be the case, and so I used it as an opportunity to learn from the amazing person (LaKeysia Beene) who was ahead of me. It still was a challenge, having to work equally as hard as the starters, knowing you would be riding the bench. You always want to be able to be out there, playing, and helping the team. But even though I didn't play as much my freshman and sophomore years, I still had opportunities to gain valuable experience in several games."*

> *"That first year of being on your own, taking responsibility for yourself, and adjusting to the academic rigors of Notre Dame wasn't too bad for me, but as school progressed it definitely got harder. I had taken advanced placement calculus and chemistry in high school. I didn't take the AP tests, which you need in order to get college credits for the classes, and so I had to take them over again freshman year. Being that I'd already seen the material before, freshman year academics wasn't too difficult, even with adjusting to the rigors of college soccer. I still had to study, but it was helpful for me that I had taken the classes before. By the time my classes got really hard (I was pre-med), I was used to college life, and had figured out how to manage my time."*

As a student-athlete in any college athletic program, your coach plays a significant role in your collegiate experience. The job of a head coach is multi-faceted. He must develop individual players, and mold them into a cohesive team unit. He must provide them with the tools they need to be successful on the field. And he must also be invested in their off the field lives, to make sure they are receiving the proper personal and academic development in order to be successful in life beyond sports. The two coaches that Elizabeth played under at Notre Dame did a great job at coaching Elizabeth and her teammates in all aspects of their collegiate lives.

> **It's a challenge when you're accustomed to one kind of training and practices, and then you have to start over with a different coach.**

> "I was recruited to play soccer at Notre Dame by Coach Chris Petrucelli, and he was my coach for my first year at Notre Dame. In the spring of my freshman year it was announced that Coach Petrucelli was leaving and Coach Randy Waldrum was taking over as head coach. Coach Waldrum wasn't any better or worse than Coach Petrucelli, he was just very different. It's a challenge when you're accustomed to one kind of training and practices, and then you have to start over with a different coach. Coach Waldrum had built a great soccer program at Baylor, and he came to Notre Dame with some success under his belt. But he came in with a different philosophy than the one that Coach Petrucelli coached under. However, he didn't force it on us right away, and that made the transition much easier."

> "I think he did a really great job of gradually converting us from Coach Petrucelli's coaching style to his coaching style, and earned the respect of the players along the way. It also helped that we were very successful that year. I'm not sure if that was because of the coach, or the leadership on the team; he did a great job of coming in and shifting us to his playing style. Some of the upperclassmen might have had a tougher time with the transition, but I never felt any tension with him because he did what he needed to do. He spoke with each one of us individually to see what our goals were, and made sure we were doing okay in our classes. You could tell he really cared about his players. He wanted each and every one of us to be successful, and he wanted us to win as a team; he also saw the big picture, and saw that it was more than just the win/loss column. He wanted to make sure that we were prepared for life beyond sports, and that we were good people. Notre Dame does a fantastic job of hiring the type of coaches who think that way, who see the big picture, and who realize that we are students before we are athletes. That is the Notre Dame philosophy in general. Academics is a priority for every student."

A collegiate athletic career is filled with countless memories, both on and off the field. As an observer, you might assume that the on the field memories hold the most shine as the years go by, but that may not necessarily be the case. Elizabeth shared with me her favorite memories from her time at Notre Dame as she traveled along the *Notre Dame Value Stream*: memories that took place both on and off the field.

> "I have so many great memories from Notre Dame, both on and off the field. A lot of the things that I remember from my time at Notre Dame took place off the field, and there were quite a few memorable ones. After practice, we would go to our weight training, and we wouldn't get out of the Loftus weight room until around 6:45 pm or 6:50 pm. This was kind of a problem as dinner at North Dining Hall closed at 7 pm. Our solution? We'd throw ice on someone's leg, pile into one or two cars, try to convince the security guard to let us drive onto campus, park right by North Dining Hall (I don't know how many tickets I got at Notre Dame. <laughs> I can't believe they didn't tow my car!), and then run to get there right before it closed. It's memories like that which are some of my favorites. Oh sure, we could have gone to South Dining Hall, which was open later, but it was so much fun trying to get on campus as a team like that. Our 'trying to get on campus' shenanigans happened about twice a week, on the nights we'd lift after practice. And the fun wasn't limited to the challenge of getting on campus, but also the team bonding which occurred around the table while eating dinner. We had some fantastic personalities on the team."

> "My favorite on the field memory would have to be from my sophomore year. I wasn't even playing much that year because senior All-American LaKeysia Beene was still starting, but in the semi-finals against Santa Clara (in the Final Four), we ended up winning in an upset. They were ranked number 1 going into the tournament (we were number 6, and we scored with 15 minutes to go in the game to win 1-0). The joy that we all felt as that final whistle blew, and we all ran out onto the field and over to the stands where our parents were sitting. Truly incredible. To see the success that we were achieving as a team, it is a memory I won't ever forget. We didn't win in the finals, but it didn't matter. That victory in the semi-finals, and the pursuit of victory that got us there, was pure joy. I have so many fond memories from that year. Going into four overtimes and a shoot out to win against Nebraska in the quarterfinal game, is another one. Every time we found ourselves in an overtime situation, we'd be so thankful for all of the time that we spent in strength and conditioning. Whenever we did fitness after practice, if we'd have to do ten reps, we'd always say, 'one more for overtime!' And after that one, we'd say once more, 'one more for overtime!'. . . and boy did that pay off for us. We knew that if we'd ever get ourselves into overtime situations, we'd need

> to be a fit team, and when we went into four overtimes in that quarterfinal game, we knew we were the most fit team on the field."

> "For me on an individual level, playing in the Final Four of my junior season was a personal high, and a personal achievement for me. I played extremely well, and even though we lost in the semifinal game, it was something I had never done before: playing in front of fifteen thousand people."

And then the next phase of the student-athletes journey begins. The transformation along the *Notre Dame Value Stream* from college student to college graduate has completed. It is now time to take the building blocks that you have collected, and to make a decision as to what you are going to construct with them. Is it the dream you've held on to since you were five years old? Or do the building blocks you've collected along the way alter your vision and alter your path ever so slightly? For so many college students, the vision they come out of school with looks nothing like the vision they came into school with, and that is totally okay. That is part of the developmental process, and part of what makes life fun.

Today

> "When I was graduating from Notre Dame, there were opportunities to play soccer professionally in the Women's United Soccer Association (WUSA). Upon graduation, a couple of my teammates were already playing in the league. I received a call from the team in Philadelphia the December after my senior season. They said they were going to draft me and wanted to know when I could report. I had to some extent thought about playing soccer professionally, but. . . we didn't have as much success my senior year as I would have liked, and we lost in the round of 16. It was a very frustrating year for me, and as I had been talking to some of my friends who were already playing in the WUSA, they weren't making a lot of money. It just didn't seem like the type of lifestyle I wanted to pursue either, and so I decided not to play. The main driver of why I chose not to pursue soccer professionally was the frustrations I was still feeling from my senior season. Had we done better that year as a team, or had it been a more personally rewarding year for me on the field, I might have made a different decision; but that just wasn't the case. And of course, everything that has happened to me since then has worked out, so I have no regrets whatsoever."

> "Upon graduation, I thought I wanted to go to medical school. From the time I was five years old I wanted to be a doctor. After graduation, I went to Houston for one year and worked in a laboratory at the MD Anderson Cancer Center while I studied for and took the MCAT. I applied to medical

school, and talked to some doctors, and eventually decided that I did not want to be a doctor. I liked science, but what I wanted to do with science did not include being a doctor. I also discovered that it didn't include working in a lab. And so I decided to try my hand at biotech. It was the early 2000s, and biotech had recently grown out of its infancy. Seeing as I didn't know anyone or have any connections in Boston, I decided to move there (as it was one of the hubs of the biotech industry) and go to graduate school; I would figure it out while I was taking classes."

"I found a one year graduate program at Boston University in clinical research, and after I completed my master's degree, I got an internship at Genzyme Corporation. Genzyme was one of the bigger biotech companies in Boston, and the internship was in their clinical research department, which was a really great experience. As I was finishing up my internship a position opened up at Genzyme, within the group I was working in, and I applied for it and got the job. I worked there for four and a half years doing clinical research and drug development. I learned what it takes to get a drug through the process from development to commercialization. But I was becoming frustrated with some of the decisions that were being made by the business unit, because they didn't seem to make a lot of sense to me. I decided to continue my graduate education and go to business school to further figure out why those business units were making the decisions that they were. I searched for a healthcare focused business school and decided to go to MIT to earn their dual degree in biomedical enterprise. The program was a three year dual degree program which combined an MBA degree with a master's in science degree. The master's in science degree was basically a third of the classes that one would take in medical school, so I guess I ended up in medical school after all. <laughs> The Biomedical Enterprise Program was an outstanding experience. I made a ton of great connections and had some amazing mentors. Plus it gave me a few summers to do different internships and figure out what I wanted to do after I completed my degrees."

"I did one internship at Amgen in Thousand Oaks, CA, in their commercial group, and then I did another internship at Genentech in South San Francisco, in their pipeline and portfolio planning group. When I was finishing up my thesis for my master's in science degree I did an internship in Lexington, MA, for Cubist Pharmaceuticals in their business development group. After working at Amgen, I realized I didn't like the commercial side of the business, and that I liked the development side better. I liked the work at Genentech, but I also realized that I didn't want to work at that big of a company. Cubist

was great because it was more of a mid-sized company. The problem was, there weren't a lot of opportunities for people coming out of business school if you didn't want to work on the commercial side of the business. Before long I would need to decide where I wanted to go next: business development, program management, or something in the venture capital realm."

"The head of the business development group at Cubist (Mary) was at a conference with the gentleman I now work with (Rick). He was working by himself and was ready to hire someone to help with his business; Mary said, 'I know someone who would be a great fit for you. We don't have the budget to hire her, but she's great!' Mary came back from the conference, gave me his contact information, and I reached out to him to inquire about the job. He offered me the job and for the past seven years I've been working with him on a couple of different startups. I went from working at a big company, like Amgen and Genentech, to working at a very small company (we only have 3 people); I love it. Working at a startup gives you exposure to all sides of the business. I literally do everything. This means you get exposure to many different experiences and have a great deal of responsibility. I also have the flexibility to work remotely, which I love because it means I can travel and work from wherever."

"I also went back and taught at MIT for about four years (from 2014-2018) which was an incredible opportunity. Teaching was something I had always thought about doing, I just thought it would happen much later in my career; but when the opportunity presented itself, I took it. A friend of mine who did the same post-graduate program at MIT that I did had taken over the class from her boss, who had brought her in to help out. She then asked me to come in and help her teach the class. It was a seminar course for PhD students, and I learned as much from them as they did from me. I think teaching is such a rewarding experience, as well as a great personal learning opportunity. I think that anyone who gets the opportunity to teach should do it."

"The startup that I am currently working for is raising money to open a location in Australia. The Australian government has a program that will give companies who make under a certain amount in revenue a 41% rebate on their research and development costs, in order to bring more businesses to Australia. Healthcare and biotech are two of the industries they are trying to grow. It would allow us to run a clinical trial in Australia, and some other work that we want to do, and save millions of dollars. We've created a subsidiary to go and do that, and the plan is for me to move to Australia and spearhead the project. I love seeing the world and traveling, so I am very *much looking forward to moving to Melbourne and being able to travel that part of the world."*

"The direction my career path has taken definitely wasn't in my 'plan.' I have merely followed the opportunities presented to me as they have popped up. I thought working in the startup arena sounded like something I might want to do, but I also knew if for some reason it didn't work out, I could simply choose a new direction. I was very fortunate that the timing of my current opportunity was perfect, and the pieces just fell into place. There's always a tradeoff. I could be making more money if I was working at a bigger company, but I wouldn't have the flexibility that I have right now. This lifestyle fits me really well, and it has been a fantastic opportunity for me."

The direction my career path has taken definitely wasn't in my 'plan.' I have merely followed the opportunities presented to me as they have popped up.

"When I stopped playing soccer, and began focusing on developing my career, I needed something to fill the athletic void that it left in my life. When I first moved to Boston, there was a semi-pro soccer league down in Providence, RI, and I played with them for a season. The problem with playing at the semi-professional level is that people aren't as committed as they may be at the professional level. It's oftentimes difficult to get everyone together for practice and games as they have real jobs and families that take precedent. So then I transitioned from that into doing individual sports such as triathlons and marathons to fill the void. I've run seven marathons, an Ironman, and ten Half Ironman, including competing in 2 different Half Ironman World Championships. These endeavors really helped me challenge myself and keep my competitive spirit alive and fulfilled."

As a student-athlete, your days are filled from sun up to sun down: filled with athletic and academic rigor, time with friends, causing you to making efficient use of every moment of your day. For individuals who are used to effectively using every second of their day, sometimes the transition from collegiate life to the "real world" can be at minimum an adjustment, or even a disappointment. The key is to figure out how to translate that intensity into the next chapter of your life, and keep yourself challenged, both mentally and physically.

"The biggest thing I missed when I made the transition from being a student-athlete at Notre Dame to life after was time with my teammates and my friends. I worked for a year before I went back to graduate school, and when you have a job to go to every day, you do fall into a routine. You

get up and go to work for nine hours, which replaces the time you used to spend in class and at practice with your friends and teammates. It's kind of a shock to the system when you don't have the rigors of athletics, and so that first year out of college I started running right away. I started by training for my first marathon, and I had a healthy fear of what it was going to be like to run a marathon, which made me stick to my training plan. That helped fill the void of the missing athletic rigor in my life."

"You spend four years with your friends and teammates, and I think for most people, your college friends are the friends you keep your whole life. Even if you don't live in the same city, you keep in touch over the years, because the four years you spent together in college were such important developmental years of your life, as you all transitioned into adulthood; you spent so much quality time together. My friend group from Notre Dame goes back to games and has reunions every year. We made it a point our senior year that we'd do our best to see each other at least once a year. But at the end of the day, losing that daily friend support system that you had in college, and making new friends in a new city, in your chosen career or in graduate school, is hard. Over the years I've gotten pretty good at making friends and finding people who have similar interests, whether its soccer, running groups, or science. One of the most difficult things you will face in your life is creating a support system, wherever you are."

College athletes are part of a somewhat elite club. In order to be successful at the Division I level, you not only have to be dedicated in all areas of your life (both on and off the field), but you also have to follow the guidance of parents, teachers and upperclassmen who can help you along your journey. As someone who has survived the journey, Elizabeth shares her words of wisdom for student-athletes looking to play collegiate sports, and looking to be successful in life beyond sports.

> **You have to have the confidence to make a change in your life and to feel like you don't have to be stuck in one place forever if you aren't happy with it.**

"When I mentor people, whether it's about career advice, or its advice about playing athletics at the collegiate level, I tell them a lot of what it takes to be successful has to do with your personality. And that a positive outlook is important. If you are the type of person who needs to have everything planned out, to ease your mind, then that's fine. But I'm very much a go with the flow type of person, and I believe that none of us really knows what life has in store for us, and so you need to keep an open mind in order to see opportunities as they are presented to you. You never know when a really cool opportunity

is going to come along, and you don't want to miss it. You also need to have the confidence in yourself to try new things, and also to know that if you try them and don't like them, you can always try something else. So many people are afraid to make a change, or take a chance. You're educated, you've accomplished so much already. You have to have the confidence to make a change in your life and to feel like you don't have to be stuck in one place forever if you aren't happy with it. It's so easy to become complacent, or to be afraid to take that next step. Be open, and have confidence."

One of the more important thing that Our Lady's students and student-athletes learn along the *Notre Dame Value Stream* is the importance of giving back. Elizabeth learned this lesson and took it to heart as she remains active in philanthropic efforts in the Boston area, and enjoys giving of her time and talents to those in need in her community. So much joy can be gained in helping others, and oftentimes we find our own strength to adapt to adversity, through helping others find theirs.

*"In Boston I am involved with three charities. One is Life Science Cares (**www.lifesciencecares.org**), and I'm on their board of advisors. It's an organization that my mentor at MIT (Rob Perez) got me involved in. He's always been a very philanthropic person, and he saw an opportunity within the life science community to unite the industry and to help with some of the issues here in Boston in regard to income inequality and poverty. He created this organization to bring together the life science community in order to raise money to help the existing non-profits who are doing the hands on work, and also to provide volunteers from the life science community to help the non-profits actually do the hands on work. There are so many smaller and mid-sized companies that just don't have the infrastructure in-house to be able to coordinate these efforts, the way large companies do. So Life Science Cares provides hands-on help. I've been involved for three years and have been able to help them in both fundraising and volunteer hours. It's been great to be involved with such a wonderful organization."*

*"The second organization I am involved in is called Lovin' Spoonfuls (**www.lovinspoonfulsinc.org**). A friend of mine started Lovin' Spoonfuls, which is a food rescue program. They go around with refrigerated trucks and collect bruised or day-old produce and other food items from grocery stores and food facilities and distribute them to homeless shelters, community centers and food pantries which are so often underserved of fresh food sources. I am on one of their advisory boards as well. We are trying to come up with new ideas to get more trucks on the road, and how to more efficiently rescue food*

and get it to the people in need. They just had their big fundraiser a few weeks ago, and they had a woman who receives some of the fresh produce tell her story. She told us how having good healthy food, and not having to worry about how she was going to get it for her family, has completely changed her life. It gave her the confidence and the ability to go back to school and get her nursing degree. It's such a little thing that many people don't have to worry about, but it has made such a big difference in her life, and in so many people's lives who receive support from Lovin' Spoonfuls."

*"Finally, I am involved in the Junior League of Boston (****www.jlboston.org****), which is part of The Association of Junior Leagues International, Inc. They are a women's volunteer organization that has been around for over a hundred years. My mom was also involved in the Junior League, so it's something I always wanted to become involved in. I've been volunteering with them for eight years and have held a number of leadership roles. They provide volunteer support for other organizations and charities, and they also have some programs of their own, including teaching school aged girls leadership skills, healthy eating, and the arts. The Junior League also provides internal trainings to develop strong women leaders within the community and promote diversity and inclusion efforts. They offer financial planning courses, career guidance, and provide classes for the development of communication skills; all to help develop strong women leaders in addition to serving the community. I was on the board for one year, and now I'm back to being a volunteer, which is very rewarding."*

As Elizabeth gets ready to embark on the next chapter of her journey and begin her new role in Australia, she is looking forward to learning about a new culture, exploring a new part of the globe, and finding ways to be a force for good in her newly adopted community. True to her mantra, she has embraced yet another new opportunity placed in front of her, and sets off with an open mind as to the potential that awaits her.

Elizabeth Wagner's Lessons from the Notre Dame Value Stream:

- When I mentor people, whether it's about career advice, or its advice about playing athletics at the collegiate level, I tell them a lot of what it takes to be successful has to do with your personality. And having a positive outlook, which is also so important.

- I also like to tell people to keep an open mind in order to see opportunities as they are presented to you. You never know when a really cool opportunity is going to come along, and you don't want to miss it.

- You also need to have the confidence in yourself to try new things, and to know that if you try them and don't like them, you can always try something else. So many people are afraid to make a change, or take a chance. You're educated, you've accomplished so much already. You have to have the confidence to make a change in your life and to feel like you don't have to be stuck in one place for ever if you aren't happy with it. It's so easy to become complacent, or to be afraid to take that next step. Be open, and have confidence.

Elizabeth Wagner with her mother.

Notre Dame vs. Pittsburgh, 2003. Torrian Jones finishes off a nice dish from Thomas. Photo by Tim Kacmar. (Photo courtesy of Notre Dame Archives.)

CHAPTER ELEVEN

The Shaper of Men
Torrian Jones
(Notre Dame Basketball – Class of 2004)

Oftentimes, people who move around during their childhood years have one particular place that they relate to, or call home. This was the case for former Notre Dame basketball player Torrian Jones, who may have had several stops along the way in his childhood, but will always call Pennsylvania home. What, you ask, could have drawn Torrian away from his tight knit family and home in Philadelphia, PA, to play college basketball at the University of Notre Dame, his new "home under the dome?" This is Torrian Jones's story.

"I was originally born in New Bern, NC. My mom's side of the family is from New Bern, and my dad's side of the family is from Trenton, NJ. My parents met at Fayetteville State College in Fayetteville, NC and we lived there until I was six years old. When I was six years old we moved to Washington D.C. briefly, and from there we moved to Morrisville, PA, with my dad's job (Morrisville is 25 minutes from downtown Philadelphia). This is where I spent the majority of my youth. I definitely associate with Morrisville and that northeast area. As far as playing basketball goes, I never really had a choice but to love basketball. I had three uncles who played basketball in college, two at the Division I level, and one at Fayetteville State with my father; I grew up surrounded by it. Even though my mom's side of the family doesn't have any college athletes, they all love sports as well. My mom is a big sports fan and loves the Pittsburgh Steelers. She was also a big fan of Michael Jordan when he played at UNC. I was always drawn towards basketball, and I got to see two of my uncles play basketball from a very young age (one played at LaSalle, and the other played at Rutgers). At the beginning, I was too young to know what was going on. But when my second uncle was at Rutgers, I was a bit older (around 10 years old). I got to go visit him at his dorm and bring him care packages, and I got to go to a lot of his games. I completely fell in love with the atmosphere there and was very proud to see my family successful at a very high level."

"Since my uncle was at Rutgers when I was at a very conscious age, I really wanted to go to Rutgers and they recruited me pretty hard. I visited Rutgers unofficially. I also visited Seton Hall, Penn, Princeton, (all three of those were also unofficial visits), and my only two official visits were to James Madison and Notre Dame. I suffered some injuries the summer going into my senior year, at which point I had been rated pretty high. Even with my injury, I had time to do some good things, and so I was going to wait until later in the season to commit. As I was going through that fall, one of the AAU (Amateur Athletic Union of Boys Basketball) teams I was on randomly asked me if I would ever be interested in playing basketball at Notre Dame and I said, 'Yeah, I guess;' even though I didn't really think anything of it. Notre Dame's new coach at the time, Matt Doherty, had recruited me as a sophomore when he was still at Kansas and that's how he knew who I was. Now that he was at Notre Dame, I was still on his radar."

I always thought, 'Why would they go to Notre Dame, it's a football school?'

"When I visited Notre Dame, I had already taken a few unofficial visits at that point, but when I got to Notre Dame (which was my last visit) I was *completely blown away. I was familiar with Notre Dame because of the football team and the movie Rudy, but basketball wise, I wasn't very conscious of it even though a few people from my area had gone there (Matt Carroll and Martin Ingelsby). I always thought, 'Why would they go to Notre Dame, it's a football school?' They were the biggest deal in basketball, where I came from, and yet they went to play basketball at a football school. At that point I was unaware of the rich basketball history at Notre Dame. When I went to Notre Dame for my official visit, Matt Carroll was my host, who, by-the-way, is one of the coolest, smoothest dudes you'll ever meet. You could not (and still cannot) find one single person who didn't like Matt. I had played against him in high school and ironically he was one of the reasons I got recruited on a high level. A lot of AAU teams were at our games recruiting him, and so I got looks as a result of the scouts being at our games. When I visited James Madison I enjoyed it, but they were obviously nervous about me going to Notre Dame the next weekend. They kept telling me, 'Remember you're going to Notre Dame next weekend, and ND is a football school,' trying to temper my excitement. But once I went to ND, and hung with the guys, and experienced that football game, it wasn't even a thought. I committed before I even left Notre Dame. It was a no brainer for me. And the rest, as they say, is history."*

Without even knowing it, the *Notre Dame Value Stream* had entered Torrian's life and swept him towards a path that would change his life forever.

The Notre Dame Years

"After I had committed, Doherty came and watched one of my high school games and did an in-home visit at my house to meet my family. I was asking him the normal questions, and one thing I asked him was, 'How long do you see yourself at Notre Dame?' To which he replied, 'This is honestly a dream job and the only way I'd ever leave is if (my alma mater) North Carolina called.' We laughed about it because Bill Guthridge had just gotten the job at UNC and we didn't see him going anywhere any time soon. Shortly after that he retired unexpectedly and, no surprise, Doherty got the call. He was a hot young coach that had almost gotten Notre Dame to the tournament in his first year, a team that hadn't been there in 10 or 11 years. He was very good and gracious about it. He called me and he actually cried on the phone to me, he felt that bad about leaving us behind. He's a very emotional guy in general, and he had spent a lot of time building relationships with each of us. He had told me on many occasions that he couldn't wait for me to get there. I felt it was cool that he reached out like that. And, in a roundabout way, without overstepping any bounds, he suggested that I come with him

> to UNC. But obviously I was all in on Notre Dame. Coach Brey made it a point to come and visit me (and also Martin Ingelsby) pretty quickly during the off season. Then he actually came back and visited me a second time. When Coach Brey made that quick connection, that was very important and it meant a lot to me. And after meeting him the first time, I felt very reassured that I was making the right decision."

As a top-rated, successful high school basketball player, you are used to playing under pressure, and in front of packed houses and rambunctious crowds. But the transition from the high school scene to a Division I school is something that is extremely difficult to prepare for. This is when the Notre Dame student-athlete is fortunate to have the *Notre Dame Value Stream* at their side to guide them through the rocky waters of the transition, and settle them into a place of peace and calm.

> The transition for Torrian *"was a mixture of different things. Overall, it was great to be in the family environment that naturally happens really quickly when you're on any sort of college team. I inherited a group of guys who became like brothers to me. It was tough making the transition from high school to a school like Notre Dame. I worked harder at Notre Dame than I ever had to work before. It was frustrating at times because we all came from being the big fish in a small pond, to being the small fish in a big pond. There were a lot of very talented players ahead of me in my position, and I had to work extremely hard to get a starting job. My hope was that I would arrive at Notre Dame and make a big splash right from the beginning, but that wasn't my path. It was challenging at times just trying to remain confident and to continue to work and know that you're making an investment. I worked very hard, but yet I didn't play much my freshman year. It really killed me, feeling that I could do more for the team than what I was able to show the coaches, and that made the transition quite difficult for me. But with everything involved, from the social experience, to the teammates and friends (with whom I became close very quickly), to the environment playing on that huge stage that was Big East basketball; the transition did get easier. I was used to playing to sellout crowds when I was in high school, but it was nothing like playing in the Big East conference, and playing teams like Kentucky on the road. Or playing at the basketball mecca, Madison Square Garden, and to look up in the rafters and see all of the names hanging up there."*

The transition from playing high school basketball to playing at the Division I level may have gotten easier for Torrian, but the struggles continued for him during his journey at Notre Dame. Struggles, however, don't have to be a negative thing. They can do a tremendous amount in building our character, and shaping us into who we are supposed to be. Torrian talked about the challenges he faced as a result of not being able to play and showcase his skills on a consistent basis until his senior year.

> *"That was definitely tough. It was the constant challenge of battling what you had felt for the longest time. You had the utmost confidence in yourself, and yet your coaches weren't rewarding you for all of your efforts and hard work. At practice I had my good days where I thought my performance was going to earn me in game playing minutes, and then it wasn't happening. It seemed like my playing time wasn't based on my production during practice. It was either based on guys ahead of me playing poorly or guys ahead of me getting injured, in order for me to get minutes on the court. Dealing with that situation at that age was hard. It was difficult for me to wrap my mind around what I needed to do to prove myself. I had always been used to getting playing time based on my production and the merits of my talent, and my frustration and immaturity with the situation then lead me to not wanting to put in the work outside of practice. My immature mind's reaction was, 'What's the point? Why should I continue to work on my skills outside of practice?' That first year was definitely the toughest for me."*

> *"And then, after that first year, I leaned on my family to help me figure out how to crack the rotation. As a sophomore, there were still a bunch of guys ahead of me, and so I started playing outside of my position as a backup point guard, and then Notre Dame recruited Chris Thomas, a big point guard who slid right in there into a starting spot. But I continued to do what I did well, paying attention to what only I could bring to the table, instead of trying to fit in and do what everyone else was doing. By the second or third game of conference play I ended up starting. At the beginning, I tried to assimilate what other guys were doing, instead of bringing the unique skills that only I could bring to the team. When I began to shift my focus on what I could do that others couldn't do, for example my defensive ability, Coach Brey rewarded me with more playing time. I still didn't have the opportunities I thought I should have to showcase my skills freely, but at least I had a role and could get in there. And then as I grew with the team, finally as a senior, I started every game that year. I had more opportunities to play and showcase my talents within the system, and had more confidence as to where I fit in to the team."*

Everyone knows it is difficult to be a student at Notre Dame, but to survive as a student-athlete at a school where both academics and athletes are quite rigorous; you have to be willing to put in the work and make the necessary sacrifices. Thankfully you have the *Notre Dame Value Stream* there with you to show you why the work is necessary, and how to do it.

"It's cool to be able to do both things (student and athlete) and travel, and participate in the athlete experience, but it's pretty difficult as you can image. Being a student at Notre Dame is difficult in itself. When you add the time demands of being an athlete, and then the physical and mental demands, it is tough to balance all of that and still put the time and energy necessary into academics. My freshman year was solid, and overall my entire academic career was solid, but I had my ups and downs. Maintaining my ability to prioritize things was challenging. I had to learn to not allow whatever was going on during the season to affect how I managed my time as it pertained to academics. Some semesters were harder than others depending on what classes you had and your specific major."

"When I first got to Notre Dame I wanted to be a computer science major, based on a couple of classes I had taken in high school. This was before I realized that at Notre Dame, computer science was in the school of engineering, and I was not a science person at all. I realized early on that computer science was not a good fit for me. Martin Ingelsby was a senior when I was a freshman and he was a marketing major. He had mentioned to me that he liked it a lot because it involved a lot of group projects and presentations, and it focused on how you speak and present in front of a group. He also told me that it was a very manageable major when combined with playing a sport like basketball. What I didn't realize at the time was that being a marketing major would help me learn how to speak well in front of a group, which I now use every day as a college coach. I decided to switch and became a marketing major, maybe for the wrong reasons (merely because Martin told me it was manageable along with playing basketball). However, at the end of the day it was the perfect degree for me and it prepared me for everything I've done in life since Notre Dame, in both my business career and my current basketball career. It matured me and it helped me strengthen my weakness, which at the time was being able to confidently speak in front of a group, as I was quite shy. I went into the financial industry after college, and so the economics, accounting and finance classes that I took really helped springboard me into my career outside of basketball."

Let's be honest, while academics and athletics are the primary focus of a student-athlete at any Division I school, a student's social life does enter into the mix. The peers you meet and friends you make in college often carry on into the rest of your life, and provide future opportunities that you may not have otherwise had without those social interactions in college. Torrian spoke with me about what it was like to balance a social life along with the demands of academics and basketball.

"It was a delicate balance, which I had to figure out as I got older and moved along in my college career. My fellow teammate Charles Thomas Jr. and I always joke about it. One of the reasons I look up to Charles so much is that he's one of the most driven, accomplished people that I know; he was exactly the same way in college. When I got to Indiana, just a kid from the Northeast, moving that far from home and being away from my family was really difficult for me. I was very homesick. I became good friends with Charles and Harold Swanagan, and sometimes I would hang out with them after practice until it was time to go to bed. I really wasn't out in social situations trying to meet people who weren't on the team. I didn't go to the freshman social. I wasn't a partier in high school. I was a pretty shy person, and trying to fit into the social scene at ND was tough for me. Charles and Harold made it easy for me to eventually get out there and meet people."

Seeing the example that Charles set really made me buckle down, especially when I got in to the core classes for my major. I found a way to incorporate those influences into how I dialed in and approached my academics.

"I wasn't dialed into my academics at first, I merely did what I had to do. I am a relatively intelligent person, so when I buckle down, I can do what I need to do to get it done; my true investment wasn't where it needed to be. Here's a great example of what Charles did for me. Charles would call me on a school night at 9:07 pm, and he would tell me, 'Hey, what's up T? I have a three minute study break, what's going on?' And then at exactly 9:10 pm he would say, 'Okay, I've gotta go!' Seeing the example that Charles set really made me buckle down, especially when I got in to the core classes for my major. I found a way to incorporate those influences into how I dialed in and approached my academics. On the flip side, I was the one who got Charles into the social scene. I kept thinking, 'Who comes to college to do work all the time?' He had such laser focus when it came to school and he didn't really let his hair down. He was very success driven, and I was the stereotypical procrastinator, but the good thing was we were able to help balance each other out! Together we were able to enjoy the total experience that was Notre Dame. ND was not a big party school, but you could still have some fun if you had a good group of friends. It was an appropriate balance for me to not have too many things distracting me. I'm not sure if I'd be sitting here talking to you if there had been too many distractions for me at Notre Dame, if I'm being totally honest. I think I had a good social and academic experience at Notre Dame, and made a lot of good connections with people that I would not

have met anywhere else. Notre Dame does such a great job of supporting their student-athletes. The fan interactions I had at Notre Dame were awesome, too. I was a fan favorite because my athleticism allowed me to make athletic plays likes dunks or high flying blocks. Their support really helped me cope when I was struggling to find consistency, or production, or even minutes on the court. It really helped me create a sense of pride in what I was doing, and in my contribution, because I knew that people cared about me."

Motivate yourself to realize how important your academic experience really is to you.

"When you are a student-athlete at a place like Notre Dame, time management is the key to success. As difficult and taxing as it can be, there are still enough hours in the day to do both (sports and academics) if you prioritize correctly, and you don't let yourself get distracted by things that aren't your priority. You are going to find the time to do the things that matter to you. Motivate yourself to realize how important your academic experience really is to you. My academic counselor Pat Holmes, who later on became my boss when I came back and worked at Notre Dame, was a person who made a long lasting impression on me. One, for the care he showed me in regards to my being a successful student-athlete, and then with the good work ethic and ideologies he instilled with me that I've utilized in my professional life both in the financial industry and as a coach."

Coaches come in all shapes, sizes and personalities. Some are larger than life, some you can hear coming long before they enter the room, and some are the "be seen but not heard" variety. Torrian described his beloved coach, Mike Brey, and shared what it was like to play basketball for him for four years at Notre Dame.

"If you act like a man, I'll treat you like a man." - Coach Mike Brey

"It was a non-stop fun experience. I came into a situation where it was his first year at Notre Dame, as well as my first year at Notre Dame. The team had a hot start, and we won a bunch of games. Coach Brey is such a cool and calm customer. He shows it more naturally now, and that was the great thing about being a part of it back then; now you can see his growth both as a person and as a coach. Coach Brey and I didn't always see eye to eye, and I struggled at times to figure out what he wanted from me and to find a way to produce at a level where he felt comfortable in giving me playing minutes. Even though he was hard to figure out, he was always easy to communicate with, and really funny. At any given moment he had a one liner locked and loaded in his chamber, ready to spring it on you. He's a player's coach and

> *very laid back. He's not much of a yeller or screamer. He's not one to kill you with long practices. He always treated us like men."*

> *"That was one of his staple lines, 'If you act like a man, I'll treat you like a man.' We didn't have curfew on the road, we didn't have bed check when we traveled. He didn't get into your personal life, about what you were doing off the court. As long as we didn't do anything stupid, didn't do anything to embarrass ourselves, our family, the program or the University, he'd give us the freedom to come and go as we pleased. I think he does a great job of recruiting players who fit well into his culture as opposed to players who have a particular skill set. He isn't full of himself, and he isn't the kind of coach who needs all of the glory. He doesn't over coach, but empowers you to make decisions on your own. It could be a two point game with 11 seconds to go, or you could be up by 30, and you would never know the difference based on how he was coaching you. He always had a certain demeanor that was contagious and that always made you feel calm, even in the heat of battle; and made you feel confident that regardless of the scenario you were going to find a way to win. He had us well prepared for game situations, so that we always felt we knew what we needed to do to win, and he put his trust in us. He manipulated the team, and I don't mean that in a bad way, to believe that they knew exactly what they needed to know. Coaching the way he does, it's an art form. If you're not really paying attention to it, you don't even realize he's doing it."*

The collegiate career of a student-athlete is comprised of hundreds, maybe thousands, of memories both on and off the field. To pick just one favorite memory is practically impossible, but Torrian very eloquently described to me what made his time as a student-athlete at Notre Dame an experience he will cherish forever.

> *"My best individual memory, in terms of one specific moment, would have to be getting to the Sweet 16 my junior year, and knowing that we had accomplished something that a Notre Dame team hadn't done in so long. That was really huge. It was a great accomplishment for us. In addition to that, we were one of the only teams to beat three top 10 teams in one week that year. We beat No. 10 Marquette (and D. Wade) at home by 30 points, we went to Washington D.C. and beat No. 5 Texas in the BB&T Classic, and then we beat No. 3 Maryland who were the reigning national champs. We went from unranked to No. 10 in one week. That was such a huge deal for us, and it was an incredible experience. And then later in that year we played Arizona (and Luke Walton, Andre Iguodala, and Channing Frye) in the Sweet 16."*

> *"Team memories stick with me longer than the individual moments as a player. All of those times we were clowning around on the bus trips and flights,*

> *and in the locker room. That's what you miss the most after you graduate. You miss the big crowds, the crazy stages, and the big wins; more than that you miss the camaraderie and celebrating the big wins with your teammates. You miss those moments way more than you miss accomplishing them. You miss the brotherhood that you developed with your teammates, and the time off the court and away from the cameras. I still find myself thinking back to those days as being some of the best times of my life. Those moments are what give me the passion to be a coach. I want my players to soak it up for the experience that it is and to not take it for granted."*

Eventually the lights do fade, the noise of the crowd silences, and you cross the grand stage on graduation day and receive your diploma. And then, with the *Notre Dame Value Stream* in your back pocket, it's time to set out into the world and embark upon your next journey. Notre Dame wasn't easy, but pretty much nothing in life worth doing is easy, is it? What happened to Torrian after graduation?

The Professional Years

> *"It was pretty interesting because my Notre Dame career, from the perspective of my personal achievements, was not exactly what I had envisioned it to be. I think I made the best of the situation given the fact that I played for a coach (Brey) whose coaching style was very different from the style of the coach (Doherty) who had recruited me. Even though I had an integral part on the team, my specific skill set, in particular offense, never quite translated there. When I went to play professionally, I experienced more success there than what I experienced or was able to achieve in college, which you don't typically see. You typically have a great college player who then is maybe a good NBA player if things go well for them, or maybe being a great college player gets them to a higher level of play in the NBA. I was a solid college player that became a pretty good pro in the short time that I played after college."*

> *"My first experience was in the CBA, and I ended up getting cut because they didn't have enough roster spots for the rookies, because they brought back so many regular guys. That was quite a jarring experience for me as I'd never been cut from anything in my entire life. To have to go home and tell people that you had been cut from the team was pretty tough and quite humbling. That really hurt, but it also instilled a burning desire in me to continue to work on my game and go harder. In the spring of 2005, I played for a semi-pro team in the USBL, the Westchester Wildfire (owned and coached by John Stark), and played well enough to springboard me into getting drafted into the D league where I played really well initially, only to get injured. Then in the next spring (2006), I also played in the USBL, but didn't do as well*

being that I was still struggling with my injury. I only played for a year and a half after college, and quickly recognized the business side of basketball; I realized it was time to move on. Being on that CBL team for one week, and then being cut the next week, all because a veteran player came back from Europe and they wanted to go with him instead of an unproven rookie was quite a rude awakening for me. Not only was it a rude awakening, but the experience of being cut began to affect my love for the game and I started to get really bitter, given how things weren't working out. At that point, I knew it was time for me to step back and move forward to take on that next challenge."

"The transition from college basketball to the pros was tough at first, and then once I experienced some successes I became reassured and confident in my ability to be able to compete against the best. Then, once I had the confidence in my ability, I had to deal with the business side of the game. I became aware that I either needed to be willing to deal with it for as long as it took to get to the glory I wanted, or I had to take a step into that next stage of my life; that's what I decided to do. I put my degree to use and found the next mountain to climb."

Today

"Acknowledging that I was done playing basketball, something that had defined me for so long, was really tough. I had a minor bout with depression, and my confidence was down because I didn't really know who I was, and that was tough for me. And although I developed some really good personal skills from being a marketing major, I never really thought about what my career path would look like based on my marketing degree. One of my uncles who had played Division I basketball at LaSalle in the early 80s, his son (who was like a little brother to me) was just getting old enough to begin playing organized basketball (he was about 10 or 11), and so I started helping my uncle coach, and run skills camps as my primary source of income. Then I went to a temp agency and found some work through them, the first of which was a data entry job. And then I finally (around the end of 2007) got a job with Enterprise Rent-A-Car in their sales department, where one of my friends also worked. I did sales for a while and then finally realized that I hated it. One night, I ran into an old buddy who was a supervisor at Merrill Lynch (at one of the home offices out of New Jersey), and I told him that I was looking for a job. He immediately told me, 'Send me your resume.' I had an interview within a week and got the job within 10 days."

"I worked there from 2008 until 2014 at which point I went back to Notre Dame. While I was at Merrill Lynch, I worked in a couple different capacities

within a risk management and compliance department. At first I was taking phone calls, and then I moved on to monitoring money movement within accounts; I learned a lot which was great for me. It became my new basketball as it was something to learn and master. Then I became a specialist in the high net worth department, and then moved back to my old department as a supervisor. All the while I was still doing some coaching and skills training, and volunteered at my old high school with both the junior varsity and varsity teams. Little did I know I was inching closer and closer towards getting back into basketball. Then I became the assistant head coach at Bryn Athyn College in Northeast Philadelphia. All of those things lead me to having the opportunity to go back to Notre Dame and work in the academic services department, working with student-athletes specifically, and working for my old academic-counselor Pat Holmes. It was really fun how all of that evolved because I still had a little bitterness about basketball. It was hard for me to even follow basketball in general, let alone follow Notre Dame. I kept thinking, 'Dang, I could have been that dude.' I was always trying to relive that coulda-woulda-shoulda."

And just when you think your life is moving on, just as you had planned, you are faced with something that turns your life completely upside down. It's at that very moment that you remember all that you learned along the *Notre Dame Value Stream*, and put it into action.

"From when I graduated from Notre Dame in 2004, until around 2010, I still played basketball pretty regularly in order to stay in shape and just have fun with it. One day I got really tired, and was completely out of breath. I thought maybe I was just out of shape, because I wasn't very consistent with it. After feeling bad for a couple of days I went to the doctor and found out I had a collapsed lung and was going to have to have surgery. I had emergency surgery and was in the hospital for a week. Previously I had thought it was just asthma, but as it turned out I had a birth defect which was preventing my lungs from sending oxygen to my brain. On the same day I found that out, I got the call from Notre Dame to see if I wanted to come back and work there. In hindsight, had I truly pursued my basketball career at the professional level longer than the 18 months in which I did, I could have put my life in danger."

"I believe that everything happens for a reason. One of my favorite books is 'The Alchemist.' The book talks about your personal legend, and how when you are doing things that you were put on this earth to accomplish and using your God given ability, that the universe becomes liquid. You are still going to have obstacles, but if you stay the course, they will move out of your way

> *basically. I really believe in that, and this experience showed me how each chapter of your life directly leads you to the next chapter. It helped me give a different perspective on my path and journey to the student-athletes that I supported when I was working at Notre Dame, and to my players now in my current role as an assistant coach at the University of Delaware (alongside former teammate and current head coach, Martin Ingelsby). I'm constantly reiterating to my players that they should follow their dreams and not ever choose a major because they think it will help them find a job quicker. You have to follow your passions, and if you do, life has a funny way of working out for you when you stay the course."*

What better question to ask a college basketball coach than for him to share his advice for young adults who want to become student-athletes at the collegiate level.

> *"Put everything you have into it. Don't allow your own personal successes or lack thereof stop you from working as hard as you can on perfecting your craft. I think I could have done a better job at that. I had a solid impact on my team, but because things didn't go a certain way for me, I didn't invest in myself as much as I could have and I limited myself. Work on your skills and always continue to grow. Ask questions of your coaches. Don't be shy, initiate meetings and conversations, and ask questions so that you can be absolutely clear as to what you can do in order to better your opportunities. At the University of Delaware, Martin Ingelsby (our head coach) and I take great pride in having an open door policy. I don't think traditionally it was always that way in coaching. Oftentimes you only talked to your coach when he asked you to come in and see him. I think all coaches should be open to a player who is coming in, asking questions and trying to learn. That's critical. And finally, make sure to always focus on what you can bring to the team, in your own unique way, that helps them win. So often we measure success on tangible statistics (which does help), but now being a coach there is nothing I respect more than players who fully buy into a role. I struggled with that concept as a player, which led to a lot of frustration on my part, but looking back I can appreciate what I contributed so much more. Ironicially, that unselfish committment to winning is what has positioned me to be a coach today."*

> ### *Invest in yourself and take a true interest in finding out what it is you do well besides your respective sport.*

> *"On the academic side, invest in yourself and take a true interest in finding out what it is you do well besides your respective sport. To be an upper level student-athlete, you are conditioned to look at it as if you have to be a*

professional athlete or bust; you also have to maximize your academic experience and try to figure out what you are passionate about besides your sport. At some point, the ball is going to stop bouncing, and you're going to have a large chunk of your life still left to figure out. If you do not have that transition in place it can be drastic and dramatic. The student-athletes who have a plan regarding what they want to do after sports, typically are more successful at it because they have that direction early. Take pride in figuring out what makes you tick as a person. Take personality tests and go and talk to your counselor and try to figure out the best way to maximize your academic experience."

"My last piece of advice would be to take the time to really network while you are in school, by meeting people and stepping outside of your comfort zone. That's how you make it in life, and that's how you get your opportunities in life. Networking helps you set yourself up for long term success and it will open up doors for you in the future. Your opportunities come from who you know, not necessarily what you know. You will be able to stay in those opportunities and positions based on what you know, but who you know will get your foot in the door in the first place. Fake it 'til you make it. I pretended that I liked marketing and speaking publicly, but I really didn't like it at the beginning. Coach Brey would always send me to speak at these banquets or youth organizations in the inner city, and these opportunities made me more introspective than I normally would have been as a young man. This is because in order to speak at these types of events, you had to know what you stood for, and what made you tick. Those opportunities directly shaped the successes I've had as an adult because now I have a great passion for speaking to kids and young adults, and paying it forward. That's what inspired me to become a coach, and what attracted Martin to bring me along with him when he got this opportunity to coach at Delaware. I wasn't getting paid any money to work guys out at Notre Dame, or spend time on the weekend training players on the team; I did it because I knew they valued my input and that meant something to me. I think it is important to be able to find the value in selfless things, and to define who you are and what you stand for moving forward."

Not every moment with a coach is a serious teaching moment, and from what I've heard about Coach Brey, he seems to have his fair share of non-serious moments. I asked Torrian to share one of his favorite "light hearted" moments with Coach Brey.

"When you see Coach Brey walking your way, and he has this sheepish grin on his face, you already know he's got something locked and loaded in the chamber, ready to destroy you with. Just the anxiety that you felt when you saw Coach

Brey walking towards you, having no idea what he had in his mind, kept you on your toes. It could have been a joke directly regarding your performance, or a joke about something going on in your personal life. He was the king of dropping these one liners and walking away before you even had a chance to defend yourself. Let's face it, as players, we always had an excuse as to why we didn't do what he told us to do. I think that's another part of what made him such a good coach, being able to think of things on the fly, things that are witty and of substance, and then getting away from you before you even had a chance to respond. He is the ultimate 'mic dropper' that I have ever met. He's a master with his words: so witty. A smooth operator. It's no coincidence that he's the winningest coach at Notre Dame. No matter what his roster looks like, he finds a way to be successful and show a level of consistency. He is strong in his foundation, and what he believes, he believes. He's unwavering, and more than anything he empowers his players. He takes pride in not only coaching that way, but making sure his players know that he's empowering them, so that they can take advantage of the opportunity. He's quite a character."

Coach Torrian Jones (Photograph courtesy of Mark Campbell – UD Athletics)

Torrian Jones's Lessons from the Notre Dame Value Stream:

- In college, and in life, I think you should put everything you have into it. Don't allow your own personal successes or lack thereof stop you from working as hard as you can on perfecting your craft.

- Work on your skills and always continue to grow. Ask questions of your coaches, and later on in life, ask questions of your bosses. Don't be shy, initiate meetings and conversations, and ask questions so that you can be absolutely clear as to what you can do in order to better your opportunities.

- On the academic side, invest in yourself and take a true interest in finding out what it is you do well besides your respective sport. To be an upper level student-athlete, you are conditioned to look at it as if you have to be a professional athlete or bust; you also have to maximize your academic experience and try to figure out what you are passionate about besides your sport. At some point, the ball is going to stop bouncing, and you're going to have a large chunk of your life still left to figure out. Take pride in figuring out what makes you tick as a person.

- My last piece of advice would be to take the time to really network while you are in school, by meeting people and stepping outside of your comfort zone. That's how you make it in life, and that's how you get your opportunities in life. Networking helps you set yourself up for long term success and it will open up doors for you in the future. Your opportunities come from who you know, not necessarily what you know. You will be able to stay in those opportunities and positions based on what you know, but who you know will get your foot in the door in the first place.

Women's soccer team photo outdoors - MCC Champions, 1992. Denise Chabot: front row, third from right. (Photo courtesy of Notre Dame Archives.)

CHAPTER TWELVE

The Chief Marketing Officer
Denise (Chabot) Karkos

(Notre Dame Soccer – Class of 1993)

*I*f you take a moment to pause and look back on your life, there is often one single moment that you can put your finger on when a defining event happened, altering the course of your life forever. Without that moment, you may not have gotten to where you are today or have chosen the path you traveled down, but as a result of that one single moment your life's course was chartered. Denise Karkos has one such moment for sure. And although it may not have completely defined her as a person, it definitely defined her identity and pushed her forward toward many great successes in her life. What was that moment you ask? Stay tuned. This is Denise (Chabot) Karkos' story.

"I grew up in Winchester, MA, about ten minutes north of Boston. I started playing two sports when I was three years old, one of which was soccer. The women's soccer program at Winchester High school and in town was very popular in the mid-70s (which was kind of crazy in 1974), and all of the little girls in town aspired to one day play soccer for their team. And as a result, the town had a great youth soccer program. I also took ballet, which was my true first love. I thought ballet was going to be my future, and that one day I would be dancing in the Nutcracker Ballet. I did both ballet and soccer for 13 years, until I was 16 years old, and at that point I had to pick one of them, as they were both so demanding and time consuming. It was a critical decision for me, and a very difficult one for me to make. But when it came down to it, the fun team sport (soccer) won over the lonely individual sport (ballet)."

"From very early on, I wanted to go to Bowdoin College, a small liberal arts school in Brunswick, Maine. They had a soccer program (Division III), and I definitely wanted to play soccer in college. There wasn't a question about that. But, I was open to looking at other schools. I took visits and looked at the soccer programs at Harvard, Dartmouth, Yale, Boston College, and Bates College. There was a Notre Dame alum who lived in town who kept sending me the Notre Dame application. I didn't grow up in a Notre Dame family, and so going to ND was not on my radar at all. But as a result of his persistence, I finally applied to Notre Dame. Every time someone would ask me where I got in to college, and I'd say Bowdoin, they'd smile and be happy for me. But when I told them I had also gotten in to Notre Dame, their reaction was so much more enthusiastic. 'Notre Dame?! Oh my goodness!!' This reaction to Notre Dame that I kept getting from adults over and over again prompted me to make a visit to Notre Dame in the spring of my senior year (on a Bookstore Basketball weekend); once I stepped foot on campus at Notre Dame I was sold. They had a Division I soccer program, and I knew Susie Zilvitis from back home (she was from Sudbury, MA), who was the captain of the women's soccer team the year before me. She was who I stayed with when I visited campus, and she gave me quite the indoctrination to Notre Dame that weekend: which included hanging out with Tony Rice and Dean Brown. After that weekend, there was no question in my mind that Notre Dame was where I was supposed to be."

It's a big leap of faith when you leave home and head off to college. You and your parents collect the necessary information, visit schools, and make a decision about where you are going to spend the next four years of your life; are you really ever

100% confident that you've made the right decision? Maybe, but maybe not. But the best part of going to a school like Notre Dame is that the *Notre Dame Value Stream* not only welcomes you home with open arms, but carries and supports you on your journey until you yourself completely realize that you are indeed home.

The Notre Dame Years

"I attended Notre Dame on a partial soccer scholarship, as they didn't offer full scholarships for women soccer players at that time. I played soccer growing up in a fairly small town against the same finite pool of competition from 8th grade on. I remember when my parents dropped me off at Notre Dame for double sessions in August of 1989, I instantly knew things were so very different. Walking onto the field and not knowing a single person, it was the first time that my confidence really came into question. Do I deserve to be here, on this team of young women who were the best of the best from around the country? It was such a carefully curated group of elite soccer players, and it was a huge transition for me as far as confidence went. I didn't anticipate the jump in competition that happened when I walked away from Winchester, MA, and stepped onto the field at Notre Dame with 22 of the best women's soccer players from across the United States. That was one of the biggest adjustments for me."

> **Being accomplished, checking things off my list,**
> **and getting stuff done: that's what drives and motivates me.**

"I earned my BA at Notre Dame with a concentration in Marketing, and the biggest skill that I developed during my time at Notre Dame was discipline. As a student-athlete, you had to have an incredible amount of discipline. Non-student-athletes oftentimes have the luxury of time that many student-athletes don't have. I was up early taking morning classes, followed by no nap, and then I headed off to practice, never missing a beat. Not a single moment was left unused in my day, which suited my personality very well. All four years that I was at Notre Dame, and I'm sure it happens still today, 100% of the team's grades were better in season than out of season, because you had to be so completely disciplined during the season. Being accomplished, checking things off my list, and getting stuff done: that's what drives and motivates me."

One thing that student-athletes have that the general student body does not have is the benefit of having a parent at school, in the form of their coach. Being in such a rigorous academic and athletic environment, it is helpful to have a mentor to guide you both on and off the field. And a good head coach will do just that.

"When I arrived at Notre Dame, my head coach was Dennis Grace. He was who recruited me to play soccer at Notre Dame, and he was our coach for my freshman year. But at the end of my freshman year, we were told that Coach Grace was leaving, and Chris Petrucelli was going to be our new head coach. When you are recruited on a partial scholarship to play a Division I sport, you arrive on campus that first fall and go through double and triple sessions and work your tail off to make the team; it is a little disheartening to be told that a new coach is coming in and that you'll have to do it all over again. We knew everyone's job was at stake, and we all had to re-tryout for our positions again sophomore year. When Coach Petrucelli arrived, he had a great deal of swag. He sat in the grandstands for three straight days watching us play full game scrimmages, and didn't say one word. It was the most stressful and intimidating experience I had ever been through up to that point in my life; but he got exactly what he needed out of his observations."

"He also incorporated the Cooper Test to our fall tryouts.[5] He wanted everyone on the women's team to be able to run 7 laps in 12 minutes, and everyone on the men's team to be able to run 8 laps in 12 minutes by the end of fall camp. Every day we had triple sessions, and the first session was always the Cooper Test. The good news was Coach Petrucelli was very upfront as to what he was going to test us on, he had a plan set up for us, and we knew what we had to deliver in August. It was just a question of whether or not we put the work in. If you did, you knew you'd be able to attain the goals. He definitely raised the bar and pushed us to move ourselves to the next level. And at the end of the tryouts, some people lost their starting roles. I remembered there was one girl who showed up freshman year with 'ND Soccer' on her license plate, and then sophomore year she didn't make the team. That was absolutely crushing, for all of us. For me, Coach Petrucelli's 'test' made me work doubly hard to make sure that I earned my spot again, and that I would never lose it."

> **I had never been pushed that hard in
> my entire life, and it taught me a huge lesson.
> It taught me that even if you think your boundaries
> and limits are in one place, they are so not.**

The Cooper Test was designed by Kenneth H. Cooper in 1968 for US military use, and in its original form was used to test how far you can run in 12 minutes. The test is meant to measure the condition of the person taking it and therefore is supposed to be run at a steady pace instead of sprints and fast running.

> "Coach Petrucelli was an amazing coach, and he brought the women's soccer team a national title just five years after arriving at Notre Dame (two years after I graduated). He had never coached women before, so he didn't see a distinction between how he coached the men and how he coached the women. This also meant he worked us harder than we had ever worked before. Practices were grueling. I remember running 30 minutes of all out sprints, with barely any stops, half field and back. I had never been pushed that hard in my entire life, and it taught me a huge lesson. It taught me that even if you think your boundaries and limits are in one place, they are so not. I couldn't believe what we were all able to accomplish in those practices; it was just remarkable. I loved that he treated us this way. He was constantly moving the bar on us, and that was a great lesson for us. It's just like anything else in life, we could have complained about what he was making us do, or we could take lessons from the good and the bad, and use them as learning opportunities, which was what we decided to do. Today I use that point of view in the work place. Challenges should be viewed as lessons and learning opportunities, not frustrations to be complained about. You can always push harder."

> "I think every great leader should push those under them to their limit. As a leader, I don't think I do that enough, but I do feel it is very effective to push people to do more, to give you more. And I am grateful I had the experience that I did at Notre Dame and that it was a physical experience, because I can vividly remember it like it was yesterday. One other notable thing about Coach Petrucelli was that he was pretty much hands-off. If we had a conflict, or had too much on our plate, and were having a tough time balancing the team and our academic work, he would say to us, 'Those are real issues, but I am not going to make a decision for you. Maybe you shouldn't travel with the team this weekend to focus on your studies, or maybe you should ask your professor if you can postpone the test, but ultimately you have to make those decisions yourself. You are in control, you are an adult, and you need to figure it out. I expect you to get good grades, and I also expect you to play well on the field. And if you have a conflict, you need to prioritize how to get that done.' He was not at all an enabler. He encouraged us to make our own decisions, and to own them."

I think every great leader should push those under them to their limit.

Four years on any Division I athletic team are filled with ups and downs. They are filled with moments of victory, of team bonding and camaraderie, of strength and of adversity, and of heartbreaks as well. But as Denise traveled along the *Notre Dame Value Stream*, a few of those moments stood out from the rest.

"I remember our very first game on the road at the University of Massachusetts. We went into the locker room and our uniforms were all laid out for us. For me, putting on the Notre Dame uniform that very first time was such an emotional moment. All I wanted to do was call my mom. It was incredible, and completely unforgettable. And then there is the companion part to that moment: the great sense of pride that I feel for the University of Notre Dame, for the achievements that I was able to accomplish while I was there, and then ultimately seeing my name displayed on the wall in Heritage Hall. The cutest thing about that is all of the people who take the time to find my name in Heritage Hall and take a picture of it to send to me; that has been so overwhelming to me, and gives me such a sense of pride. One of my high school friend's father was at Notre Dame and found my name in Heritage Hall and sent it to me; just that simple act meant so much to me. People are so supportive of me, even all of these years later, and I never forget that or take it for granted. I love it. Those are some of the most emotional memories for me."

It showed me that no amount of adversity could keep me down.

"I do have one other memorable Notre Dame experience, but it happened two years after I graduated from school. But there's a little back story that I have to tell to set up the moment back at Notre Dame. A year and a half after I graduated from Notre Dame, I was living in Detroit and was working at an advertising firm with Frank Loftus, who is another Notre Dame alum. (Fun fact: Frank has ND etched into one of his molars! Anyways, I digress.) He and I were on the way to a business dinner one night, and as we got in the car to head to the restaurant, he told everyone to put on their seatbelts. The next night, I was in the car with one of my coworkers from the night before, and I told him, 'Put on your seatbelt or Frank will be mad.' Five minutes later we were in a horrific accident. Our car was hit head on by someone who ran a red light, and everyone involved walked away from the accident but me. The seatbelt saved my life, because without it I would have gone through the windshield, but I also broke countless bones in my body. I was pronounced dead at the scene, but the paramedics were able to resuscitate me in the ambulance on the way to the hospital, and I was then put in a coma. They called my mom and told her they didn't think I would make it through the night. I'm not sure she has ever recovered from that phone call. My seatbelt saved my life, but I also broke almost every bone in my body. I was in the hospital for three months between in-patient treatments, out-patient treatments, and rehab (which included learning to walk again), and dealing with a huge amount of memory loss caused by the traumatic brain injury I

> *suffered. The accident occurred in October of 1994, and remarkably I was back to work in February of 1995."*

> *"After I recovered from the accident, I was asked to come back to Notre Dame and speak to the Notre Dame's Women Soccer team (in the locker room) before they played in the semi-final game of the NCAA Tournament (on their way to winning the national championship in 1995). It was such an incredible honor for me, to be invited back to speak to them at that incredible moment. I talked to them about the fitness level of my body, and how it significantly shortened how long it took me to recover. I had broken so many bones; I broke my pelvis in three places, all of my ribs, my shoulder, dislocated my hip, punctured a lung, and had a traumatic brain injury. There were so many things that had to be rehabilitated during my recovery, but because I was in such good physical shape prior to the accident, my recovery went very well. In fact, my recovery had gone so well, they couldn't put me on the stand in my trial because I looked too healthy, as crazy as that sounds. Yes, the accident was a detour in my life, but it showed me that no amount of adversity could keep me down."*

> **You only have one go at this, give it a chance.**

> *"I told the team about my near death experience and how everything, even something as awful as what I went through, should be looked at as an opportunity. I told them, look at the opportunities that you've been handed, or that you've earned. How do you excel to the highest degree? I encouraged them all to recognize the stage that they were on. You're at the University of Notre Dame playing Division I soccer. You've worked your ass off to get here. If you're not a starter, why not? You've got the opportunity to be one. If you're not scoring as many goals as you want to be, ask yourself the tough questions. Do you need to work harder? Do you need more coaching? You have the ability to achieve greatness and you are on a stage that is allowing that. Recognize the opportunities that are in front of you, and take full advantage of them. So many people talk themselves out of opportunities, and out of the potential to achieve greatness before they even give it a try. You only have one go at this, give it a chance."*

Denise graduated from Notre Dame with a Marketing degree, and developed all of the skills that she would need for the next chapter of her life as she traveled along the *Notre Dame Value Stream*. With her degree in hand, she headed out into the world to pursue the career set before her, and to leave her mark on the world.

Today

> *"When I graduated from Notre Dame in 1993 there really weren't options for women to play soccer at the professional level. I got a junior level marketing*

job right out of college, and ended up back in Boston in late 1995, early 1996. The WUSA (Women's United Soccer Association) was formed in 2000, with women like Mia Hamm and Brandi Chastain joining teams. I was still playing in recreational soccer leagues and on fun club teams, and I felt that my skills were still pretty good, so I sent away for an application. I was working at Digitas in Boston, and it was a pretty high pressure job. As I sat there looking at the application it was very intimidating. The application included questions like, 'What European teams have you played on?' Me: 'None.' I sat there looking at it, I finally thought to myself, no way. I decided to keep moving forward with my 'day job' and I threw the application away. That application did a great job of weeding out the people who weren't totally committed, and who were not at the highest caliber of soccer. I did, however, continue to play recreational soccer until I was 42 years old."

"One of the coolest things about having a Notre Dame degree, and having been a Division I athlete at Notre Dame, is that it becomes a huge part of your personal brand. I never thought I was a big deal when I was in school, compared to the other programs and athletes, or even other players on our team. But once you graduate from Notre Dame, the doors which that degree opens and the brand that being a Notre Dame athlete gives you, it just surprised me. Even now, my bosses will present me as, 'She played soccer at Notre Dame.' And the chairman of my board introduces me as 'The former captain of the Notre Dame women's soccer team.' Meanwhile I'm thinking, 'That was 25 years ago and you're supposed to be introducing me as the Chief Marketing Officer,' but I don't really mind. They are so proud of me, and I think it's the cutest thing. I've chosen to embrace it as opposed to defending it with my academic/professional pedigree. My being in a male dominated industry (financial services), sports is what makes me relatable to the men I work with; it's a common ground that we all share. I like that it's how they want to introduce me."

"I spend a lot of time talking to student-athletes, and students in general. There is so much learning to be had as an athlete, which is completely translatable in the business world. There are three things I like to talk about when I speak to young people in regard to how the things you learn in sports apply in business. The first one is defining a win. On the field in a game, it's super clear as to what a win is and what a loss is. But in business, wins and losses need to be more clearly defined. After a meeting, you may be asked how something went, and it's very subjective. One thing I've done to help myself is to define for me and my team what a win looks like. If they are going in to meet with the

CEO, and they are expecting to get an 'atta boy,' they're probably not going to get it from the CEO. I explain to them, in certain meetings, a win is to get in and get out unscathed. That is success. These CEOs are so busy running their companies, they are not going to take the time to say good job to people, and so if I can go in and get my point across and not have any changes from them, that is a win in my book. There is so much more grey area and subjectivity in business; you must set expectations and define what a win looks like before you go into a meeting or project."

"The second thing is getting past a loss. In soccer, or sports in general, you have to get past a loss pretty quickly. You have practice the next day and then on to the next game, so the quicker you can let it go, the better. In business, we tend to get in our own way, and we get hung up if we don't perform well on a project, or when metrics are not met; this can cause us to ruminate and propel us onto a downward spiral. The problem is, oftentimes there is no 'next game' to force us to let go and move our focus forward. I typically give myself 24 hours to get over it. I think it through, digest it, figure out how I can do it better next time, and then I move on. Personally, I can move on rationally long before I can emotionally. Emotionally I know I'm not going to feel 100% better until I get my next win. And so that propels me forward to put another win on the board professionally, and makes me do bigger things. But so many times people undermine their own careers when they can't get past a loss."

"And the third thing I like to talk about is how sports gives you accountability, and doesn't allow you to make excuses. In sports, you have to own your own performance, and you understand the role you play in a win and in a loss. In business, there are a lot of complexities that come into play as to whether or not something goes right or wrong. Ultimately, if something goes wrong the most mature and productive thing you can do is to be accountable and accept it, and make no excuses for it. Excuses in business sound so weak, and they never work. Fessing up to something that didn't work or a mistake you made, and giving a clear rational as to why, and then moving on is always going to be a stronger approach than giving excuses for failures."

"I've been in the marketing field since I graduated from Notre Dame, and I began in the agency world for the first half of my career. I worked at advertising agencies in Chicago, Detroit, and Boston; took larger roles with every move I made. And then I took a job with LL Bean and moved over to the brand side. I was the advertising manager at LL Bean, and reported to the Chief Marketing Officer (CMO). From there I moved to TD Bank, where I also reported to the CMO. Most recently (nine years ago) I moved to New

> *York City to work for TD Ameritrade, reporting to the CMO, and five years ago I became the CMO. I am a member of the senior operating committee (and one of the top ten people in the company). I manage 250 people, with a 300 million dollar marketing budget, and I love it. I live in an apartment in New York City during the week, and I spend the weekends with my husband at our home in Portland, ME, where he runs a small business with his father."*

When seeking out a mentor, or asking for advice, it is always best to consult with someone who has already been in the situation you are about to embark upon. Denise shared with me, as a former Division I athlete, her words of wisdom for young men and women who want to pursue athletics at the collegiate level.

> *"The first thing is, do not talk yourself out of it before you even get there. Yes, the competition is going to be harder, but at least give it a try or you'll never know whether it's worth it or not. In terms of time management, this is a problem you will have for the rest of your life. There will never be more time in the day, it's all about how you use the time you have; I think that collegiate sports is a great use of your time. The second thing I'd say is recognize that the skills you will gain as a collegiate athlete will be invaluable in the workplace. Things like leadership, followership, dedication, prioritization, and the ability to take feedback; these will all occur both on and off the field, as well as later on in the business world. The ability to take feedback is so important; from a team member or coach in college, as well as later on from a boss in the workplace. And the last thing is, how many times in your life will you be handed an opportunity to achieve greatness. It is really easy to understand how you are performing in sports, and that is a great opportunity for you to seize. Why not try to take advantage of the position you are in and see how far you can take it."*

> *"I am so grateful to Notre Dame, for everything they taught me and the experiences I had while I was there. To express my gratitude, I have just given a ten year endowment to the University to be put towards the thing that is closest to me, which is the upkeep of the lakes and trails. I ran those lakes from day one, and they mean so much to me. If I didn't have a good game, I'd go back to the dorm and then run the lakes and get all of my adrenaline out. If I didn't get enough playing time in a game, I'd go run the lakes. And now, 25 years later, I go back every year with my best college roommates, and we run the lakes and get caught up. The lakes have been, and still are, an integral part of me, my friends, and my Notre Dame experience. I love them so much. And so I have set up this endowment to make sure they are kept pristine, and are well lit so that they can be safely used by all."*

Denise and her husband currently split their time between Portland, ME, where he runs a small business with his father, and New York City, where she works with TD Ameritrade.

Denise Karkos

Denise Karkos' Lessons from the Notre Dame Value Stream:

- There is so much learning to be had as an athlete, which is completely translatable in the business world. The first one is defining a win. On the field in a game, it's super clear as to what a win is and what a loss is. But in business, wins and losses need to be more clearly defined. After a meeting, you may be asked how something went, and it's very subjective. One thing I've done to help myself is to define for me and my team what a win looks like. There is so much more grey area and subjectivity in business; you must set expectations and define what a win looks like before you go into a meeting or project.

- The second thing is getting past a loss. In soccer, or sports in general, you have to get past a loss pretty quickly. You have practice the next day and then on to the next game, so the quicker you can let it go, the better. In business, we tend to get in our own way, and we get hung up if we don't perform well on a project, and this can cause us to ruminate and propel us onto a downward spiral. The problem is, oftentimes there is no "next game" to force us to let go and move our focus forward. I typically give myself 24 hours to get over it. I think it through, digest it, figure out how I can do it better next time, and then I move on.

- The third thing I like to talk about is how sports gives you accountability, and doesn't allow you to make excuses. In sports, you have to own your own performance, and you understand the role you play in a win and in a loss. In business, there are a lot of complexities that come into play as to whether or not something goes right or wrong. Ultimately, if something goes wrong the most mature and productive thing you can do is to be accountable and accept it, and make no excuses for it. Excuses in business sound so weak, and they never work. Fessing up to something that didn't work or a mistake you made, and giving a clear rational as to why, and then moving on is always going to be a stronger approach than giving excuses for failures.

Notre Dame vs. Ferris State, 1990. Player: Eric Gregoire (#29).
Photo by Katey Charles. (Photo courtesy of Notre Dame Archives.)

CHAPTER THIRTEEN

The US Marshal

Eric Gregoire

(Notre Dame Hockey – Class of 1993)

*E*ric Gregoire grew up in Ithaca, NY, home to Cornell University. He attended school in Ithaca through his junior year of high school, and then finished his final year at Northwood (Prep) School in Lake Placid, New York. The boys hockey team at Northwood school had a long tradition of outstanding achievement, including players and coaches who have gone on to renowned careers in college, international and professional ice hockey, which drew Eric to their school. Their hockey program was built on developing each individual player and giving them the tools and coaching needed to reach their full potential. How did Eric make the leap from playing hockey at Northwood (Prep) School in Lake

Placid, New York, to playing for the Fighting Irish of Notre Dame? This is Eric Gregoire's story.

"I grew up in Ithaca, NY, in the shadow of Cornell University, which has a very popular hockey program. I grew up playing hockey at their rink, and as a result of that exposure I was very familiar with college hockey and looked up to the college hockey players. For me, playing college hockey was the only avenue I wanted to pursue. I did have some opportunities to play Juniors, but I never really gave it much thought. I knew I wanted to play college hockey. When it came time to look at colleges, the first school I looked at was Cornell, based on its close proximity. Realistically, I was willing to go anywhere as long as I was going to play, but of course I had my preferences."

"As a high school hockey player in Ithaca, I was not at all familiar with Notre Dame Hockey. I distinctly remember going to a college fair during my junior year at Ithaca High School, and I came across the Notre Dame table and it captivated me for some reason. The Notre Dame representative who was working the table was the father of a boy I played baseball with, and was a member of the Central New York Notre Dame Alumni Club. The way he talked about Notre Dame was so different from how the other reps talked about their schools. You could just feel the passion he had for Notre Dame, and that conversation really peaked my interest. Speaking with Mr. Sullivan that day triggered an old memory from when I was 10 years old."

"No one in my family was a Notre Dame fan, but one Saturday my dad was watching college football and he said to me, 'Hey Eric, you see this team? This school (Notre Dame)? That's where you should go to college.' And he never said anything about Notre Dame before that, or after that. So on that day, visiting the Notre Dame table at the college fair, and remembering that moment with my dad, it all clicked for me. I reached out to the hockey coaches at Notre Dame and expressed my interest in playing hockey for them. From that point on they became one of the teams I really wanted to play for, one of the schools I wanted to get into. They came to Boston to scout me when my Northwood team played against the Harvard JV team. Soon after watching me play, Notre Dame made me an offer. And that is how I became interested in playing hockey at Notre Dame. It was a lightning strike the way it all played out. I was also recruited by Rensselaer Polytechnic Institute in Troy, NY, Colgate University, the Air Force Academy, and Merrimack College in Boston."

**I wasn't able to make a visit to Notre Dame
during my senior year of high school,**

> *but I was confident in making my decision based on everything I had been told, and the feeling in my gut that it was the right place for me.*

> "From there it was an easy decision for me to go to Notre Dame. I did pause slightly looking at Colgate, as they regularly played Cornell University, which was in my hometown, my home rink, and that was of interest to me; I knew there was something special about Notre Dame, and that drew me there. Even though I had never been there, and I had not grown up a Notre Dame fan; something about Notre Dame just captivated me, and I knew that was where I wanted to go. All through my high school years I didn't even consider going to Notre Dame to play hockey until that day I went to the college recruitment fair. Then I started seeing all of the media attention around Notre Dame when they won the National Title in 1988, but what truly moved me was when I saw how passionate people were when it came to Notre Dame. I knew I wanted to go there. I wasn't able to make a visit to Notre Dame during my senior year of high school, but I was confident in making my decision based on everything I had been told, and the feeling in my gut that it was the right place for me. It just clicked."

> "When the Compton Family Ice Arena opened in 2011, I had the opportunity to go and see the first game and sit with a group of former Notre Dame Hockey players. When I walked into the new arena, it literally took my breath away. It was a very emotional experience. To be a part of that first game, and to understand where the program came from and to see where it is today, it was just incredible. It's a top notch program, playing in an equally impressive facility with players who are competing with the very best teams in college hockey. The entire program is operating at such a high level. I am glad the program finally got the rink that it deserved, and I could not be more proud."

Making the jump from high school to college life can be an overwhelming undertaking, not only for student-athletes, but for students as well. Moving away from home, having new-found freedoms, and developing the responsibility to shy away from temptations and make good decisions have created bumps in the road even for the smartest of kids. But Eric was one of the few who accepted the challenges that Notre Dame gave to him and tackled them head on.

The Notre Dame Years

> "Since I spent my final year of high school at Northwood Prep school, the transition wasn't that hard for me, to be honest with you. At the time, Northwood Prep school had 120 students and three hockey teams: Varsity A, Varsity

> B, and a Junior Varsity team. I played on the Varsity A team and we played almost exclusively against College Junior Varsity teams. To be playing teams of that caliber when I was still in high school was an incredible recruiting tool for me. We played the JV teams at schools like Yale, Dartmouth, and Harvard, in their home arenas. Oftentimes their varsity coach would come out of his office and scout our players. Then, if they were interested in one of us in particular, they'd pull a freshman varsity player down to play on their JV team in order to get an apples-to-apples comparison versus somebody who's a known quantity on their varsity team, and suddenly you'd be on a coach's short list."

> "Playing hockey at Notre Dame was still the next level up, of course, but it wasn't as difficult of a transition for me based on the competition I was facing at Northwood Prep. In my freshman year at Notre Dame we played Wisconsin, who ended up winning the national championship that season, defeating Colgate in the finals, and teams like Boston College and University of Minnesota – Duluth. That experience, playing those caliber of teams, was a huge jump. We went to a Christmas tournament in Milwaukee, Wisconsin, and played in their AHL team's arena, which was quite impressive compared to Notre Dame's rink at that time. That experience was quite a shock to the system. We opened against Wisconsin, and the attendance was 18,000 strong, all of whom were wearing Wisconsin red. That was where the adjustment was for me, getting used to playing on that big of a stage. Even though at Northwood I had played against College Junior Varsity teams, the rinks were almost always empty; you could hear an echo while you were playing. That definitely didn't prepare me for playing in a packed arena of screaming fans. And when Notre Dame traveled, they were always a huge draw; people wanted to see the Fighting Irish."

For students and student-athletes alike, trying to decide at the age of 18 what you want to study and what career you want to pursue can be quite daunting. Thankfully, as a Notre Dame student, you have the *Notre Dame Value Stream* there to guide you along your journey, and help you discover your talents, ability and passions.

> "I can't really say how my experience as a student-athlete at Notre Dame was different from those who didn't play a sport at Notre Dame because being a student-athlete was all that I knew. From the day I stepped on campus, hockey was a part of my student experience. That first day of freshman orientation also had hockey meetings. Hockey was a part of daily life for me, so I can't compare it to anything else. It was just my reality, my routine. Everything

revolved around hockey. You had to schedule your classes in the morning so that you could make it to strength training and practice in the afternoon. If practice ran late, you'd have dinner at training table instead of going to the dining hall, even though back then training table just meant they kept part of South Dining Hall open late for us. It's not like what the guys have now."

"I can't say that the transition to Notre Dame was overwhelming for me, it was all about creating a routine and finding a way to make sure your academics got done. To me, hockey didn't feel like anything 'extra.' Being that I had played multiple sports in high school, having to juggle school and sports felt normal to me. It also meant that only playing one sport at Notre Dame was great for me because I could really focus on hockey and give an adequate amount of time to my academics. I will say, in some of my classes at Notre Dame it was the first time for me academically that I was truly challenged. I had never encountered that in high school. I would get my work done, study, do well on a test, and move on. There were definitely some classes at Notre Dame that required me to seek tutoring and put in the extra work in order for me to successfully get through them. I did change majors a couple of times, but that was more of me trying to figure out what I wanted to do than anything else."

At moments like these, Notre Dame student-athletes are grateful to have the *Notre Dame Value Stream* there for them, ready to support them and guide them through the challenges so carefully placed in front of them.

Notre Dame does a tremendous job at making sure their students have all of the resources that they need to succeed.

"One of the things that Notre Dame does quite well is providing academic support for their students and student-athletes. Mike McNeill's dad was my advisor freshman year through the Freshman Year of Studies department (Mike McNeill played hockey at Notre Dame from 1984-1988, and his father, Tim, was a hockey coach at Notre Dame in the late 1960s), and then my next three years I had a priest as my advisor. As freshmen, we had to go in on a regular basis and check in with our advisor, which was a big part of why I never felt overwhelmed balancing academics and sports at Notre Dame. They provided us with such a great support system, and they were there for us whenever we needed them. It was their job to make sure we were staying on track. I could go in there at any time and tell them I was having trouble with a class and they would make sure I had the right level of support. Notre Dame does a tremendous job at making sure their students have all of the resources that they need to succeed."

During Eric's time at Notre Dame he witnessed some big changes in the hockey program, changes that were at the forefront of what has propelled Notre Dame Hockey to where it is today. In his first two years at Notre Dame, the hockey program was Division I, but they were still an Independent, and so the schedule may not have been as rigorous as it could have been had they been in a conference. In the fall of 1991, Notre Dame Hockey joined the CCHA as an affiliate member, playing a partial schedule of CCHA teams, and by the fall of 1992 they were a full time member in the CCHA conference.

"Being in the CCHA was definitely more competitive. As a Division I Independent team, we played a mix of teams, of varying levels of competitiveness. We did play some pretty big opponents (Boston College, University of Maine, University of New Hampshire, University of Wisconsin), and then we had some Independent teams that were maybe not as competitive as we would have liked. In the CCHA, all of the teams were dominate and every weekend was a big matchup. Once we moved into the CCHA we played teams like Michigan, Michigan State, and Lake Superior State, Ohio State, Western Michigan on a weekly basis. Every weekend we were facing a top Division I hockey program. It was definitely an upgrade in competition. Previously, when we played teams such as University of Alabama – Huntsville or University of Alaska - Anchorage, even though they were Division I teams, they didn't draw much of a crowd. Once we began playing teams like Michigan at home, all of the sudden our games were sold out. It was a much different environment once we became facing this new level of teams. And on the flip side, when we'd travel to play these teams on the road, their rinks would sell out because Notre Dame was in town."

"When I played hockey at Notre Dame, we had very few scholarship players on the team. We weren't even close to hitting the max on number of scholarships available. When I was a freshman, only me and a few other players were on scholarship. Each year a couple more would come in, but we just didn't have the depth that the Michigan's and Maine's had, as far as scholarship players went. When we moved into the CCHA and had to face those high caliber teams week in and week out, it was quite challenging for us, and our record reflected that. I think on many occasions we were good enough to win, we just did not know how to win yet. We found ourselves in many game situations where we'd be tied in the third period, but we didn't know how to win. Maybe it was because we didn't expect ourselves to win. Or maybe it was that we got too excited at the possibility of winning, being on the cusp of an upset, and we lost our focus. The first time we beat Western Michigan, we celebrated as

> *if we had won the Stanley Cup Finals. That first full year in the CCHA, in 1992-1993, that was the first year of the new era of Notre Dame Hockey. That year launched everything that you now see when you watch a hockey game at Notre Dame. And that incoming freshmen class in 1992-1993, was the first legitimate recruiting class of the modern era of Notre Dame Hockey. It took longer to come to fruition than any of us wanted or hoped, but even back then guys wanted to come to Notre Dame to play hockey because it was Notre Dame."*

If you've ever played a sport, at any level, you understand that coaches come in all shapes and sizes, skill levels, and possess a wide variety of techniques and philosophies. Some coaches you will love, and some coaches you simply won't connect with, but you still show up every day and put in your 110% for your team. The hope is, even when you're playing for a coach that you don't exactly see eye-to-eye with, that you'll have an assistant coach or senior leader on the team ready to step in and fill the gap.

> *"Unfortunately, playing for Coach Ric Schafer wasn't one of my better memories at Notre Dame. My first experience with Coach Schafer didn't exactly set us off on the right foot. Assistant Coach Tom Carroll had recruited me, not Coach Schafer, and at my first time meeting Coach Schafer he expressed that he didn't think I was worth a scholarship. Maybe he truly believed that, or maybe he was trying to challenge or motivate me to prove him wrong. I was much more comfortable with my relationship with Coach Carroll and preferred his coaching methods over Coach Schafer's."*

> *"In some ways my experience with the hockey team at Notre Dame was a disappointment. Northwood Prep had one of the top teams in the country when I was there with 11 of the 12 seniors from my class going on to play Division I hockey. At Notre Dame we went through a lot of growing pains being part of a new Division I program with a limited budget. But I will say, the overall experience, the camaraderie I developed with my teammates, playing on such a big stage, traveling to Europe, and playing in tournaments did outweigh the negatives, and made my time at Notre Dame truly unforgettable."*

Welcome to college hockey...

Picking one favorite moment is never easy, but Eric quickly had one that stood out from the rest.

> *"When we played the University of Wisconsin in the Badger Showdown in Milwaukee my freshman year, that is one of my best and most vivid memories from my hockey days at Notre Dame. We had played some other pretty big*

> *games up to that point, such as when we upset St. Cloud State, but this was our first huge Division I hockey matchup. Coming out onto the ice and seeing 18,000 screaming Wisconsin fans, all dressed in red, rooting against us, that was something else. Welcome to college hockey. That moment right there, that was what college hockey was all about, a big-time arena teeming with passionate fans. Even though all of those over exuberant fans were rooting against us, it was hands down one of my best hockey memories at Notre Dame."*

Most of us are told, when our parents drop us off at college, "Enjoy every moment they will fly by much too fast." And even though very few of us actually thought that would be the case, it did indeed fly by in the blink of an eye. It seemed like we had just been dropped off for freshmen orientation weekend, and then there we were in our black robes, ready to turn our tassels and head out into the world to face our next adventure. As Eric finished up his time at Notre Dame, he looked beyond the Golden Dome to see where the *Notre Dame Value Stream* would take him next.

The Professional Years

> *"All along I knew I was going to at least try to play hockey at a professional level. I was going to take a chance and see where it took me, and at the very least walk away with the experience of playing at the next level. Minor league teams started calling me right around graduation time. I never had any internships or gave much thought to how I was going to use my degree for post-college employment. I'm not even sure why I had that much confidence in my ability to play hockey after college, but I definitely did."*

> *"After graduation, several teams from the ECHL were showing interest in me, and I ended up signing with the Erie Panthers (who were shared by the New York Rangers and the Los Angeles Kings) as a free agent. Playing in the ECHL wasn't as fun as playing in college, or as fun as youth hockey growing up. The game of hockey at the professional level is quite different. In the 90s, hockey was becoming a game of 'goons,' and there wasn't another league that had more goons in it than the ECHL. It was a completely different game, and a completely different mindset. When you played hockey at the professional level, you were no longer representing your school and your friends, putting on that Notre Dame jersey which stood for something. At the professional level people were constantly being traded and cut, and there was a new person in the locker room every day, or so it seemed."*

> *"Being that the ECHL was such a 'goon' type league, coaching went like this. You'd come into the locker room at intermission and the coach would point*

out a player on the other team who was causing a lot of problems. Then he'd tape a $100 bill on the board and tell us, whoever can take him out of the game, as in have him medically removed from the game, would get the $100 bonus. That type of hockey was not fun for me. It wasn't the same atmosphere as college hockey where you had fellow classmates on the team. While you had friends on the team, it was different than playing at Notre Dame, where you hung out together in the dorms, ate together in the dining halls, and even went on double dates together. It was very different. And if you didn't have a passion for the game, a burning desire to keep playing, it was a difficult environment to exist in. I played the entire season for the Erie Panthers and at the end of the season I really wasn't sure what I wanted to do next. I started exploring other options, and even though I was offered a try-out the following season with the New York Rangers AHL affiliate, the Binghamton Rangers, I decided it was time to move on from hockey."

Today

"At that point I decided it was time for me to put that Notre Dame degree to use, and pursue a career in federal law enforcement. I decided the best path to achieve this goal was to combine my Notre Dame degree with military training, so I enlisted in the Army. My father was in the Army, and the Army reserves for over 40 years, and so I grew up watching him go to drills and go on mission trips in the summer. Growing up with his Army uniform and gear around made an impression on me, and definitely caught my attention and peeked my interest. He read a lot of military books and enjoyed watching war movies. . . a lot of John Wayne movies. I think my interest in the military was always there, and when it came time to make a decision about what career I was going to pursue post hockey, it was a no brainer for me to join the Army. The military training I would receive in the Army combined with my Notre Dame degree would give me a strong resume to get into Federal Law Enforcement after the military, (which had always been an interest of mine), in addition to satisfying this interest I had in the military. I realized the timing was right to join the military, as I needed to do it while I was still young. When I was at Notre Dame I had done some research into pursuing a career in federal law enforcement, and discovered that they (the FBI and Secret Service) didn't hire right out of college. They wanted people who had real world jobs or military experience. Joining the military was the perfect next step for me to increase my chances of getting hired in my desired career."

"My time in the Army provided me with some of the hardest and most challenging experiences I've ever had in my life. The Army made me a man if you

will. I had no choice but to mature with regard to responsibility, dedication and commitment. The Army is one of the branches that gives you options as to what role you want to perform when you enlist, as long as you score well enough on the entrance exams. And so when I enlisted, my choice was to become a Ranger, and because I scored high enough on my entrance exam, a Ranger contract is what I was offered. Now that didn't guarantee that I was going to be a Ranger, but it did give me the opportunity, as long as I passed all of the requirements along the way. Once I completed Basic Training I was sent to Airborne school. And then, upon completing Airborne school, I was sent to the Ranger Indoctrination Program (RIP), which consisted of three weeks of mental and physical torture in order to find out if you had the fortitude to make it into one of the Ranger Battalions. Every day the challenges got harder and harder until we made it. I became a member of the 75th Ranger Regiment, which along with the Navy SEALS and the 'Green Berets' is part of the Special Operations family. Once you make it into the Ranger Regiment the hard part isn't over; you exist and work at the highest level of intensity the whole time you are there."

The mental, physical and academic challenges placed in front of me were harder than I had ever seen before or since.

"My time in the Army as a Ranger was the most dedicated time of my life. The mental, physical and academic challenges placed in front of me were harder than I had ever seen before or since. You may think that the most challenging part of being in the Army is the physical aspect of the job, but that wasn't the case for me. In the Ranger Regiment, one of my collateral duties, if you will, was that of a sniper. There is a great deal of math and science that goes behind hitting a moving target that's 800 meters away, and subject to a 20 mile per hour wind. There is a science behind it. It's much more than just aiming a rifle and pulling the trigger. And then when you're dealing with explosives or jumping from an airplane, there is a right way and a wrong way to do it. Which, as an Army Ranger, means there is only the right way. Developing the skills and competency to be a Ranger in the Special Operations Forces is intense to say the least. You either do your job right or you're gone. 'Almost' doesn't count, and it certainly isn't good enough. Either you can do it, or they find someone else who can. Being in that kind of environment, and understanding the consequences of there not being a second chance, matured me tremendously. It's what made me a man. My Ranger training and experiences took me from a boy to a responsible, dedicated man."

"When your time in the Army is through, all you can see is life on the other side. You've had enough and you are ready to move on. But now, looking back, the pain is gone and the memories are fond. The two things in my life that I am most proud of besides my family are being a graduate of Notre Dame, and my time and experiences in the Army as a Ranger. Being in the Army was a very important time for me. I met some amazing people in both of those places. Notre Dame is a special place amongst colleges and universities, but the 75th Ranger Regiment was a special place as well. In order to get to the Ranger Regiment you have to be a three-time volunteer. You go through Basic training, Airborne training and then the Ranger assessment and selection process in order to make it into one of the three Ranger Battalions within the 75th Ranger Regiment. Even with a college degree under my belt, I chose to enlist (rather than to become an officer) in order to have the opportunity to get to the Ranger Regiment. People are often surprised to learn that a significant percentage of the enlisted Special Operations soldiers are actually college educated. In my platoon alone we had graduates from Notre Dame, Harvard, West Virginia, Baylor, New Hampshire, and Ferrum College."

"Following my time in the Army, I spent approximately 10 years with the U.S. Secret Service as a Special Agent. The job of a Special Agent is to protect select members of the Executive Branch, such as the President and Vice President. When not assigned to protection details, Special Agents conduct criminal investigations for various financial and electronic crimes. The first nine years I worked in the Syracuse, NY office, and in my 10th year I was in the process of moving from New York to Washington DC to do full-time protection detail when an opening in the U.S. Marshals Service became available in Syracuse. It was very similar to the job I had previously been doing for the Secret Service (physical protection and criminal investigative work), just for a different division of the United States government. While doing full-time protection detail in Washington D.C. would have been a new adventure for me, not having to move my family, and staying in Syracuse where the living was much more affordable was the better choice for all of us. My new role with the Marshals Service has become my latest adventure. I have been tracking fugitives and protecting Federal Judges with the U.S. Marshals Service for eight years. It's definitely challenging. Some days I absolutely love my job and am so fortunate to do the work I do, and then the next day I can't wait to retire; I'm sure most people feel that way about their job. I'm happy with the work I do within the Marshals Service, as each position has its own set of subtleties. My current assignment is pursing non-compliant sex offenders. If a sex-offender fails to register with the appropriate sex offender registry, they are considered a fugitive and will be pursued by the U.S. Marshals Service."

> "For example, if an individual is convicted of a sex offense, after they serve their time and are released back into society, they have to register with their community's sex offender registry. It's their responsibility and obligation to make sure they are properly registered, and if they move to a new town or new state and don't register, they become non-compliant and are in violation of federal laws. Not all sex offenders are predatory, but some of them do pose a threat to their communities and move to avoid detection, to avoid the scrutiny of always having law enforcement looking over their shoulder. Those are the people that I am most concerned with, and it is my job to track them down. At times the job is disturbing, and at times the job is quite satisfying, knowing you are protecting the people in your own community as well as across the United States. Oftentimes we use our federal resources to help out local law enforcement officers do compliance checks. They send out their officers to check on their local sex offenders to make sure they are living at the address reflected on the registry, and then we help the local law enforcement agencies find the offenders who have left the area without updating their registration information. If I learn an offender no longer resides at their registered address, I will conduct an investigation to locate the offender to either bring them into compliance or arrest them. If my investigation shows the offender has moved to another city or state, I will send an investigative lead to my counterpart in that area to have the offender located and arrested. It's great to be able to keep our communities safe and protect anyone else from being victimized. It brings me a great deal of satisfaction."

When embarking upon any new adventure in my life, I always find it helpful to find someone who has had a similar experience and ask for their advice This is why I ask each one of the former student-athletes whom I interview to give a few words of wisdom for today's young men and women who hope to pursue athletics in college.

> "These days, it is so difficult to become a Division I athlete; it is so much more competitive than when I played hockey at Notre Dame. It's what I've heard called the 'Tiger Woods effect.' Tiger was swinging a golf club at two years old, and that kind of early development is the norm in youth sports today. It's not just in golf. . . it's in hockey, baseball and football. . . in every sport. Youth sports today are also demanding year-round participation if you hope to excel and move on to play at the high school or college level. It is a very challenging environment for young athletes now to make it to the next level. If you look at youth hockey in the United States, it has grown tremendously. There are over 500K kids playing youth hockey today, but the number of Division I

schools has not changed, and so therein lies the disparity. And now, kids from other countries are coming to the United States to play for that same finite amount of Division I hockey spots, which makes it even more difficult to be able to make the cut."

Don't forget to enjoy the experiences along the way, and cherish your teammates and the friends you'll make.

"My advice to athletes who want to play at the Division I level is to understand how difficult the journey is going to be, and be willing to put in the time, effort, and work that is necessary to get to that level. It doesn't just happen on its own, as it may have in the past. It takes commitment, hard work and a great deal of drive and motivation to get there. But, on the flip side, playing sports at the Division I level is so much more than just the sport itself. Don't forget to enjoy the experiences along the way, and cherish your teammates and the friends you'll make. What do I remember most from my days playing hockey? Goofing around at the hotel, on a trip, at one o'clock in the morning. Of course, the big wins will count. But the friendship, camaraderie, experiences, traveling, car rides, bus trips. . . all of those things are equally as important as the wins and losses. Those experiences, those are what you will remember, and what you will take with you into the rest of your life."

One of the things that Notre Dame instilled in each and every one of us was an obligation to service, which Eric has had double exposure to after going to Notre Dame and serving in the Army. Eric serves his community outside of the work he does daily for the United States government through the Special Operations Warrior Foundation: **www.specialops.org** *"The foundation provides college scholarships to surviving children of special operators (Army Rangers, Navy Seals, Special Forces) who have lost their lives in the line of duty. Over the past 15 or 16 years of war and conflict, several of my friends have lost their lives in battle, so it's important to me to make sure their families and children receive the resources they need."* Eric also supports another organization, Hockey Saves, which ties his two passions together and brings hockey to military members as a stress outlet: **www.hockeysaves.us**.

Hockey Saves is a play on words which caught on to a project accidentally after discovering how helpful the game of ice hockey can be for people. "Saves" are a good thing in the hockey world. You know, "Nice save," or "Did you see that save?" In addition to that, the game itself can "save" people. Hockey, for some, is like chicken noodle soup for the soul, and from this a simple idea emerged. What better way to thank a soldier?

> "The organization started out donating hockey equipment to soldiers on military bases so that they could play hockey as a recreational activity, as most soldiers can't afford the cost of purchasing their own hockey equipment. From there it has grown to helping pay for ice time, the purchase of tickets to hockey games for military members, and sending care packages to hockey playing troops currently deployed. On January 24th and 25th in 2014, Notre Dame Hockey, spearheaded by their backup goalie Joe Rogers, paired up with Hockey Saves and did a special game to raise awareness and funding for the foundation. ND's hockey team wore special camo jerseys which were then auctioned off for the charity. They also brought in military service members to attend the game and scrimmage after the Notre Dame game."

Eric currently lives in Syracuse, NY, with his wife and two children, and makes the pilgrimage back to Notre Dame to catch ND Hockey as often as he can.

Eric Gregoire at the Compton Family Ice Arena with his wife and their two children.

Eric Gregoire's Lessons from the Notre Dame Value Stream:

- For student-athletes wanting to play at the Division I level, understand how difficult the journey is going to be, and be willing to put in the time, effort, and work that is necessary to get to that level. It doesn't just happen on its own, as it may have in the past. It takes commitment, hard work and a great deal of drive and motivation to get there.

- On the flip side of that, remember that playing sports at the Division I level is so much more than just the sport itself. Don't forget to enjoy the experiences along the way, and cherish your teammates and the friends you'll make.

- When you're playing days are over and you head out to find a career, find something you love. In doing so, that will get you through the tough days. Some days I absolutely love my job and am so fortunate to do the work I do, and then the next day I can't wait to retire; I'm sure most people feel that way about their job.

Portrait of football player Jeremy Sample, 1991. (Photo courtesy of Notre Dame Archives.)

CHAPTER FOURTEEN

The Harlem Stuntman

Jeremy Sample

(Notre Dame Football – Class of 1995)

In the immortal words of former Notre Dame head coach Lou Holtz, "For those who know Notre Dame, no explanation's necessary. For those who don't, no explanation will suffice." As so many of us know from personal experience, each person who passes through the hallowed halls of Notre Dame is touched by a special something that oftentimes cannot be explained, and most definitely cannot be taken away. As Our Lady's graduates travel through their lives, Notre Dame is much more than just a "network," it is a family. A family ready to celebrate with you in the good times, and comfort you in the bad times. For a young man who had no previous connections to the University of Notre Dame, what he experienced and heard on that first visit to ND was exactly what Jeremy and his parents were looking for as he was considering his options for college. Ultimately, what sold him on Notre Dame, you ask? Here's Jeremy Sample's story.

> "What made Notre Dame special was the fact they told you upfront, 'If you make it to the NFL, great; but if you don't, that's great, too.' It wasn't the be-all and end-all for a lot of us, and the opportunities in front of you did not end if you didn't move on to play in the NFL. My plan as I headed to Notre Dame was to be redshirted my freshman year, finish my undergraduate degree in 3.5 years, and complete my master's degree through my fifth year of eligibility. But plans don't always play out the way you want them to. The great thing about Notre Dame was that, first and foremost, your goal was to walk away with a degree and an outstanding chance to be successful in life. It was what Coach Holtz preached to us every day. Football is great, and togetherness with your team is great, but what is most important is to be set up for a lifetime of success."

> "As a kid, although I always wanted to play football, there was a time when I thought I would never be able to do it. I suffered a neck injury as a child, and my mom was not very receptive to the fact that I wanted to play organized football. Even though as kids we were already playing rough touch football of some kind, it wasn't until we started to put pads on that she realized, oh, you could get hurt doing this. But in reality, we were already playing full-speed tackle football with no pads, sandlot football. One of my best friends begged my mom to let me play, and even though she did eventually agree, she had one rule: I had to wear a neck guard or a neck roll. My mom finally let me play, and I got my feet wet in the game of organized football. Then we moved from Memphis, TN, where I was born, to Chicago, IL, as my dad's job transferred him, and I became immersed in football at this new high school, Downers Grove North – the Trojans. We were fairly successful during my time playing for the Trojans, and I started getting recruited by several Division I football programs: the Air Force Academy, Army, UCLA, Michigan, and Notre Dame. When I made my official visit to Notre Dame, I got to meet Jerome Bettis, Bryant Young, Anthony Peterson, Willie Clark, Oscar McBride, Irv Smith, and Dean Lytle. We had such an amazing group of guys at the school, who looked out for us after we arrived and during our time at Notre Dame. I can honestly say that Oscar McBride was a great mentor to me during my time at Notre Dame, and he really took me under his wing. We both sang and were performers, and I think that was one of the things that connected us."

*When people say that Notre Dame is a family,
and a close knit one, they are not lying.*

"When it came time for me to make my college decision, my parents stepped in and gave me their thoughts. Of course, your parents know more than you do. Let's face it, at 17 or 18 years old, what do you really know about life? You may know football, but you don't know life. My parents were always looking at the long-term goals of what should come out of college. They told me that while 'Football is great, you could get hurt or things could go south, and you will always need to rely on your education in anything that you do in your life.' They told me that my decision could not only be made based on football. So they nudged me in the direction of Notre Dame. When I visited, Coach Holtz told us, 'If you're looking to party while you're in college, this isn't the school for you.' Notre Dame had less than ten thousand students, compared to a lot of state schools that had forty or fifty thousand. There may not have been as much to do at Notre Dame as compared to a Michigan or a UCLA, but when people say that Notre Dame is a family, and a close knit one, they are not lying. Everyone pretty much knows everyone."

The Notre Dame Years

"On November 2nd (1991) of my freshman year, we played Navy at home. I think it was in the neighborhood of minus twenty degrees that day. It was the coldest weather I had ever played football in, and I remember telling my mom, 'Oh wow, it's so cold here mom.' My parents came to every home game because they were close enough that they could. I always felt that, while I was away at school, I was still close enough that if I got homesick, my parents could be there for me. It was the perfect combination for me. But back to the cold... people don't understand, there is a different kind of cold when you are at Notre Dame. Coming from Illinois, you have an idea of what cold is, and that brutal winters are not uncommon. But in Notre Dame Stadium, there is no place to hide from the elements. That Navy game was my rude awakening to the South Bend cold. Just brutal. There was no sun, it was all wind, and the temperature just kept falling. There were a bunch of guys from the incoming freshmen class who visited Notre Dame that weekend, and they commented, 'Man you looked so cold out there.' And we were! But as Coach Holtz always told us, 'Remember son, it is cold on both sides of the ball.'"

"I came back to Notre Dame a few years ago and went to the ND versus USC game, and it was great to experience Notre Dame Football from a fan's perspective. We never got to see the other side of a ND football weekend. We never really got a chance to see all of the pomp and circumstance that happened *on a football weekend. After the pep rally, we got carted off and did not return to campus until it was time for the pre-game Mass the next day. We missed out on all of the energy that was bubbling up around campus. Coming back as a fan and being a part of the electricity that is a Notre Dame Football game weekend, hanging out with the people in the crowd, that was amazing; it brought back these awesome flashbacks."*

Being a student at Notre Dame is a challenge in itself, but being a student-athlete at Notre Dame brings ups and downs that are incredibly difficult to prepare for. Most young men and women who accept the challenge of being a Notre Dame student-athlete stumble a time or two, but that is where the *Notre Dame Value Stream* provides the support needed to get you through those trying times and carry you to the next victory waiting for you just around the bend.

Notre Dame is not for everyone.

"I think being a student-athlete at a school like Notre Dame is much more difficult than most people realize. You are in the same classes, side-by-side with your peers. But when they get out of class and head out onto the quad to play a bit of Frisbee before diving into their studies, you have to head on over to workout, go to team meetings, practice, dinner, study hall, and then do all of your work that is due the next day. In the winter you have early morning conditioning and then you have to prep for spring football. It's a year-round endeavor, but that's exactly what you signed up for. You don't go to a school like Notre Dame because you think it's going to be easy, because if it was, everyone would go there. Notre Dame was not an easy place to be, and we were told going into it that we'd have to work at it or we wouldn't make it. Notre Dame is not for everyone."

"The other thing you realize as a student-athlete is that each and every moment is spoken for, and your time is not your own. The University is giving you this tremendous opportunity, but everything comes at a price. And the price you pay for this opportunity is your time, because your time is no longer yours. That is the sacrifice you make. At the end of the day, when it's all said and done, the experiences you encounter, the people you meet and you connect with, the journey and the appreciation of the journey which you endured, it is all worth it. I can't imagine the life I would have had if I didn't create the memories and connections I made at Notre Dame. It was the best decision that has ever been made for me. Coach Holtz says, 'Life is nothing more than a series of decisions.' When you think about it, Coach said a lot of things, and then at one point in your life they all click."

> *Coach said a lot of things, and then at one point in your life they all click.*

> "He talked about the preparation and the work, paying attention to the details, having every person be accountable, you focus on doing your job; and then you realize that all of those things are life's realities and it all makes sense. Life is nothing more than a series of decisions. One of the most important things that I took from Coach Holtz is, when you apply that simple phrase to the different aspects of your life, it all makes sense. When you think about some of the things you have done and the situations you've put yourself in, and you think about how Coach Holtz said that life is nothing more than a series of decisions. . . you see that your life doesn't have to be hard. When he says, 'Always do what's right,' yep. That's it. He was able to bring all of these kids together, from various backgrounds, various regions of the country, various upbringings, and unify them all under this golden helmet. It didn't matter where you were from or what your history was; nothing mattered. It was all about the team, the unity, and the togetherness."

Coach Holtz is such a legend at Notre Dame, and the years he spent coaching at Notre Dame are surrounded by such lore. Jeremy talks about what it was like to play Division I college football under such a storied head coach, and how the lessons Coach Holtz taught them both on and off the field are still a big part of his everyday life.

> "It was a lot of different things. And I don't know anyone who will tell you otherwise. It was hard, because he expected so much from you. His level of expectation was for you to be your very best, and you, in return, did not want to disappoint him. At the end of the day, you knew you'd have to sit in the film room and explain to him what you did. He taught you that you needed to step with this foot, and you needed to have your helmet in this location, and you needed to stay in this lane when you ran down the field, and if you didn't do that, you had to hold yourself accountable. Coach Holtz's whole philosophy was based around making sure you were prepared. And if he felt that he didn't prepare you properly, he would take the blame for that and tell you, 'That was on me. That was my fault.'"

> *If you are one of his guys, you are one of his guys forever. And that's such a beautiful thing.*

> "Yes it was hard, but it was fun, too. There were times when he was heavy on discipline and structure, but at the same time you could go to him with any issue you had, with anything that was troubling you, and he'd be there

for you. His door was always open and he was always available to us. He made us feel like his family. And he never forgets a player. If you are one of his guys, you are one of his guys forever. And that's such a beautiful thing."

One of the most popular conversations that people have in regard to Notre Dame Football is what makes a coach successful. Notre Dame has had several extremely successful coaches over the years, and Coach Holtz is definitely one of them. Jeremy talks about what made Coach Holtz such an excellent football coach.

"Coach Holtz had such a focus on discipline and accountability. He made sure that we all knew what our jobs were, and if everyone did their job, everything would be fine. He would go to his board and list out the reasons why we're going to win, and how we're going to win. He would write down his list. These are the things we need to do in order for us to be successful, and if each and every one of you does these things, you will win. We went over this chart every week, 'The Ways We Win.' And then after the game each week, we'd go back over the chart, and as we went through each thing, you could pinpoint exactly why we won or why we lost. If we did the things on the chart, we were successful. If we did not do the things on the chart, we were not successful. It was just that clear. And when you think about it, you say to yourself, 'Wow, did that really happen?'"

"The thing was, it was just a chart, but we went through the chart every week, and the chart was spot on. He would tell us we have to out-hit them and we have to have the best fundamentals. Then he'd go into each of our areas. Did we win turnovers? Did we give up the big plays? Did we make the big plays? Were there missed assignments? Third downs? Foolish penalties? How did we do on the goal line? The kicking game? And then he'd talk about togetherness, being together as a team, always having each other's back, always being positive, always believing we'd win, don't flinch, and in the moment where you need to make the play, make the play. And so he would go down this chart and tell us, this is how you're going to beat them. When you think about it, it's brilliant. If you follow the plan you will win, and if you don't follow the plan you will lose. There is no grey area there. He is a brilliant man, and anyone who plays for him walks away with something. You take a piece of all of that time with you. For me, one of the big things I took away from Coach Holtz was time, and being on time, and being a stickler for being on time. I'm always early, it's something that carried over into my regular life. It's tough, I make plans with friends, and I'm always early. My body is just programmed to the Notre Dame way. Time is the one thing you can never get back, and I am not here to waste anyone's time. When Coach Holtz called a meeting, he expected you not just to be on time, but to be early. He wasn't going to wait

> on you, you were going to wait on him. If Coach Holtz called a meeting for 4:30 pm, we showed up as early as 3:30 pm, because if Coach was early and you weren't there, you were late. The meeting started when he got there, and if you weren't in your seat, you were late."

> "It's funny, anybody who knows me knows I am someone who is always early. It's to the point where my friends lie to me about what time I need to be there, so that I'm not there so early. And working in my career as a stunt professional, that has become arriving an hour early. I'll show up at a location an hour early because sometimes a director or someone will want to do a walkthrough, or they'll move your call time up. Let's say your call time is 5 pm, and you happen to be there at 3:30 pm or 4 pm. They'll say, 'Hey, are there any stunt guys here? We'd like to do an early walk through or rehearsal.' Or, 'We'd like to help set up a shot and we need some stunt guys to set that up.' If people are there, they move your call time up. And if you're not there you miss out on an opportunity."

I happened to talk to Renaldo Wynn, a dear friend of Jeremy's, before speaking with him, and Renaldo prompted me to ask Jeremy, "What made the difference for you, to have a 'never give up' attitude and become a starter at Notre Dame?" Here's how Jeremy responded.

> "We all have goals and aspirations as players, and everyone on a Division I football team pretty much has been a starter or considered an elite athlete at whatever schools they came from. So one of my goals as a freshman was to one day be a starting player at the University of Notre Dame. First, you want to make the travel team as a freshman, get some special teams play, and work your way up during spring practice to become a backup player, and then eventually a starter. We had an amazing sophomore class in front of us, and so you had these fantastic guys in front of you to learn from who helped mentor you and who pushed you along to become a better athlete and a better football player. Attending summer school and putting in the extra time and the extra work paid off, and then one day you got the nod. You got opportunities as a backup player to go in and make plays. The more plays you made gave the coaches confidence that you could contribute as a starter, and you eventually made the first team."

> "I spent a lot of time with Renaldo Wynn, Oscar McBride, and Stephen Pope. We worked out together and we hung out in the same circles, and you built relationships with people; but you know, after school everyone goes their separate ways. But now, with social media, we've been able to reconnect, which is great."

Every single day at a place like Notre Dame is special, but there are always one or two memories that stick out above the rest, and for Jeremy, this would be the 1993 Notre Dame versus Florida State game. Number one versus number two.

> *"My favorite on-the-field memory would have to be the weekend we beat Florida State. That game trumps them all. That was an incredibly exciting game and we walked away with a victory. It was a battle for the number one spot in the country, we were facing Florida State at home, and it was a night game. All of the focus was on us and this game, and we were able to beat a highly ranked, amazing Florida State team at Notre Dame Stadium. It doesn't get any bigger than that."*

Like Coach Holtz, who always had a plan, Jeremy had a plan, but as we all know. . . not all of our plans are able to come to fruition. And although it didn't turn out exactly as he wanted it to, with a little guidance from the *Notre Dame Value Stream*, Jeremy was able to find a new path, and a journey that was even better than he could have dreamed of by himself.

> *"Coach Holtz pulled me aside after a team meeting and told me that he'd like to talk to me, to which I replied, 'yes sir.' He sat me down and explained to me that, unfortunately, I was not eligible to play for a fifth year at the University of Notre Dame. And just like that, the plan I had in my head kind of went up in smoke. I found out I played for three minutes and eighteen seconds during one game of my freshman year, and it cost me a year of my life. So instead of taking 15 credit hours first semester of my senior year and graduating in December, I dropped a class and took 12 credit hours the fall semester, and then 3 credit hours my spring semester so I could graduate with the rest of my class. You adapt."*

Today

> *"I graduated with a degree in Human Resources Management, and after graduation I moved to New York and accepted a job at a technology company. I started out working in their 401K Plan department, then moved to the Health Benefits department, and finally transitioned into the Human Resources/IT department as a project lead. I then came to a point in my life where I said to myself, 'This isn't something I want to do for the next 20 years.' At that fork in the road, an opportunity presented itself."*

What happened next may take you by surprise!

> *"One of my Notre Dame teammates, Stephen Pope, also lived in New York, and we kept in touch and periodically got together. I knew after graduation,*

Stephen (ND class of '94) had gone out to Los Angeles and gotten into film, and then became a stunt guy, and then a stunt coordinator, and relocated to the east coast. He knew I was working in the corporate world, but we never really talked about work when we kept in touch or hung out. When he found out that I was no longer working in the corporate space, he was coordinating a show in New York and was looking for some African American stunt guys, and he asked me, 'Hey, is this something you would be interested in trying? I know you are a physical/athletic person, and you'd be a great fit if you're interested.' And I said, 'SURE! That sounds like fun!'"

"It was the exact opposite of what I had been doing: not behind a desk, not going over forecasts and timelines for the deployment of applications, and I was ready to try something different. He hired me for the film he was working on, 'Freedomland,' which was shot in Yonkers. Looking back on it, I feel very fortunate to have had that experience. I was exposed to a lot of people who were stunt coordinators in New York, and it was basically a soft introduction to the New York stunt community as a whole. I did a good job that week, and I told myself this was my new career path: to become a stunt performer, eventually a stunt coordinator, and ultimately a second unit director. At this point in my career, I'm working more as a stunt coordinator, which has been great! I would not be in this situation had I not connected with Stephen Pope at Notre Dame. It's funny how that works. We just happened to be friends from ND, who worked out and played football together. Our connection lead to this incredible opportunity and a new career path for me. He helped me get my foot in the door, and everything else took care of itself."

"In addition to my career in the film and television world, I also support Help Us Adopt - **www.helpusadopt.org**. It's an organization that provides grants to families to help with the costs associated with adopting a child. I became involved in the organization through a friend of mine. She and her husband had tried everything possible to have a child and nothing worked, so they decided to move forward with the adoption process. During their adoption experience, they found the process to be so cumbersome and difficult and expensive, so they decided to do something about it. They started this organization in order to help other families, and they have been very successful in helping families navigate the adoption process. I support it every year. I believe any time you can help someone else within your means, you should do it."

Notre Dame is a special place, and once your time at ND is over and you head out into the world, you really begin to miss it.

> "In 2000, I had the opportunity to play in the 'Charity 2000' game in Volksparkstadium in Hamburg, Germany. The game was a team comprised of Notre Dame alumni football players playing against the Hamburg Blue Devils.[6] Tony Rice was my roommate over in Hamburg, and I was able to connect with a lot of former players who I had never met before. It was such a wonderful experience. We had players from the '88 National Championship team, and guys I had watched over the years, or heard of; now I was playing with them! We were all working professionals, and came back to the gridiron to put on the pads once again and run around and smash into people. It was a chance for us to represent the University of Notre Dame one more time. And we won, which was awesome. Notre Dame is a special place, and once your time at ND is over and you head out into the world, you really begin to miss it. Being able to put the pads on once more really gave you something to strive for, to work towards. The game was for charity, but it was also for friendship and for rekindling that Notre Dame spirit that we had all come to miss so very much. It's something I will always be proud of, and it was a very special experience for all of us."

When asked what advice he would give to current student-athletes working towards playing collegiate athletics at a school like Notre Dame, Jeremy had some words of wisdom to share with future generations of Domers.

> "Embrace the Notre Dame experience. It's going to be difficult, there are going to be moments when you will question yourself, but don't give up. Work hard. If Notre Dame teaches you anything, it will definitely teach you that there are no shortcuts. Anyone who has attended Notre Dame can attest to that. There are no easy routes. It will take dedication, hard work, discipline, and time management; those are definitely some things you will need to have if you are going to be successful at the University, as well as in life after school."

And to wrap everything up, Jeremy shared one of his favorite memories of head coach Lou Holtz.

> "One of my most memorable Coach Holtz moments was the day I got switched from a running back to a linebacker. We were scrimmaging out at Loftus. The quarterback had thrown an interception and the defensive back who caught the ball was just scurrying up the sideline, no one was near him to make a tackle. I'm thinking, 'Great, this guy is going to score on us.' So I ran over there and, in perfect form, left my feet, and boom. . . tackled him. Everyone was cheering. There was all of this excitement and energy. Coach Holtz came

---

Charity 2000 game: http://www.und.com/sports/m-footbl/spec-rel/071300aaa.html

running over and patted me on the helmet and said, 'Son, I'm moving you to defense. You need to be a linebacker.' And the very next week he switched me from running back to linebacker. Coach Holtz was a visionary. He had a knack for making sure everyone was in the position they needed to be in."

Currently, Jeremy, the "Harlem Stuntman," resides in New York City. Keep your eyes on the big screen for his next great role.

Jeremy Sample, the "Harlem Stuntman."

Jeremy Sample's Lessons from the Notre Dame Value Stream:

- For student-athletes at Notre Dame, embrace the Notre Dame experience. It's going to be difficult, there are going to be moments when you will question yourself, but don't give up. Work hard. If Notre Dame teaches you anything, it will definitely teach you that there are no shortcuts. Anyone who has attended Notre Dame can attest to that. There are no easy routes.

- Also, understand that the skills you learned playing a Division I sport in college, dedication, hard work, discipline, and time management; those are definitely some things you will need to have if you are going to be successful at the University, as well as in life after school.

- Make sure your priority as a student-athlete is to earn your degree. That is your best chance for a successful life. Football is great, and togetherness with your team is great, but what is most important is to be set up for a lifetime of success.

- Always be on time. I've come to learn the importance of time, and being on time. Time is the one thing you can never get back. It's incredibly valuable to not only be on time, but to be early. It creates a lasting first impression, not just in your career, but also with friends and family in your everyday life.

Portrait of football player Raki Nelson, 1996.
(Photo courtesy of Notre Dame Archives.)

CHAPTER FIFTEEN

The Skill Developer

Raki Nelson

(Notre Dame Football – Class of 2002)

When children are exposed to sports from a young age, they tend to try all of them in order to find the one or two that spark their passion; Raki Nelson was no different. Raki Dalas Nelson, born in Harrisburg, PA, was the second youngest of five children, and like most kids, loved to play sports. He dabbled at baseball, basketball and football, before he felt that "spark" with basketball and football. How did Raki decide to follow the spark that he felt for football and pursue a collegiate career at the University of Notre Dame? This is Raki Nelson's story.

"I played little league baseball as a kid, but baseball felt way too slow for me; I needed something with more action, more excitement. As I hit the teenage years, basketball and football definitely ignited my passion." Raki played both basketball and football at Bishop McDevitt High School, home of another Notre Dame Football player you may remember, Ricky Watters. Raki shared with me one win that his basketball team had in a high school tournament, over another player you may have heard of - Kobe Bryant; a win that now seems like a much bigger deal than it did back then.

"I remember playing in this tournament against Lower Merion High School, and they had this guy on their team, Kobe Bryant. We really didn't know who Kobe was, but after watching him play, Kobe seemed like he was really going to be something. We beat them that day and I probably scored about 27 points, but in comparison, Kobe had about 40 points. He also cried foul a lot in that game <laughs>, but we ended up coming out on top. I remember when I heard Kobe was going into the NBA draft thinking, 'Hey, we beat that guy!'"

As the time grew closer for Raki to figure out where his post high school path was going to take him, he was confident that football was his ticket to the next level. As he did his homework on the various colleges he was interested in, toured campuses, and talked to coaches, he may not have noticed what was happening, but the *Notre Dame Value Stream* was already making its way towards him.

"I was very interested in the University of Florida, North Carolina and Pitt; Syracuse was interested in me as well, though I wasn't very interested in them. However, when I made my visit to Syracuse, my host was Donovan McNabb, which was pretty cool. Pitt was pursuing me very hard, and then Notre Dame came into the picture a bit late in the recruiting process. When you play football at a Catholic high school, ND was always in the back of your mind, but when Coach Holtz and Coach Mosley started to pursue me, Notre Dame rose to the top of the pile. Eric Chappell (quarterback from Carver High School in Montgomery, AL) and I had both been at UF and Notre Dame at the same time for our official visits, and we had exchanged numbers at Notre Dame. We were talking on the phone, comparing Florida and Notre Dame, and the more we talked, the more we both liked what we saw at ND. I really liked the atmosphere at Notre Dame. Everything I saw during my visit was very appealing, and that's where I decided my football career would continue."

As a young man playing football at a Catholic High School, Raki experienced the rigors of what it's like to be a student-athlete. The expectations placed on him both on and off the field were high, and it wasn't an option to only be successful in one area, and merely be getting by in the other; success in both was required. But that jump from high school to college is still quite a shock to the system, and nothing at the high school level can truly prepare you for what's about to happen. This is when Notre Dame student-athletes become very thankful to have the *Notre Dame Value Stream* there to help keep them afloat.

The Notre Dame Years

> *"For me, the transition from high school to Notre Dame was very tough. My classes required a great deal of work outside of the classroom. Then you had to add in time on the practice field, games, and travel. You not only had to take care of your school work, but you had to take care of your body, too, which I did not do too well. Surviving as a student-athlete at a school like Notre Dame requires a lot of time management, and that was something I wasn't very good at in the beginning. You have to take everything seriously, not just football. If you didn't take care of your classwork first and foremost, you were gone; so that had to be your top priority. But at the same time, you had to take care of football, and your health as well. And if anything was out of balance, you would suffer."*

> *"One of the best parts of being a student-athlete at Notre Dame was that the coaching staff and professors knew it wasn't going to be easy for us, and so they had measures in place to help us out. The Freshman Year of Studies office got you off to a good start, but your coaches, professors, and tutors helped you get through the day-to-day grind that you were trying to survive. It was an eye opening experience for sure. You get to college, you're on your own with your own vices, and anything can happen. The experience definitely made me a better person, as I quickly learned you had to get things done."*

> *"Can I trust you? Are you committed? Do you care?"*
> *- Coach Lou Holtz*

Every coach that a player encounters during their athletic career has their own style. They all want to reach the pinnacle of their craft, whether that is a national championship or an undefeated season; how an individual coach gets there can be similar to and different from their peers. During his time at Notre Dame, Raki had the opportunity to be coached by two different head coaches: first Lou Holtz and then Bob Davie. While both men were chasing that elusive championship title, how they pursued their goals were very different.

> *"For me, Coach Holtz was much more of a disciplinarian than Coach Davie was. Holtz was more profound, more serious; he was like a father-figure to each and every one of us. When he walked into the meeting room you felt*

like your dad just walked in, and you were scared to death. You wanted to be at the top of your game, you certainly didn't want to disappoint him, and you would absolutely go to war for him. That's what he brought out of you. The way he treated me, day in and day out, truly made me feel like he cared for me. And when you watched how the assistant coaches reacted to him, it wasn't any different. They also wanted to be at the top of their game, they didn't want to disappoint him, and they would absolutely go to war for him. He instilled this loyalty in each and every person in the organization, from the bottom all the way to the top. You could just see the coaches stand a little taller when Coach Holtz walked into the room."

Pretty much every player who has played for Coach Holtz has had that moment at which they realize exactly what is expected of them. Raki had his moment early-on in his Notre Dame Football career.

"It was '96, my freshman year, we were just wrapping up practice and Coach Holtz was making his final remarks about practice. I was goofing off a little bit, telling my friends something, and while Coach was still talking I said something funny and burst out laughing. Everyone froze. 'Who was that??' And then the red sea parted, and there I was, exposed to Coach Holtz. Coach screamed, 'Raki, get your butt up here!' And he proceeded to chew me out, right there in front of everyone. He told me, as a result of my disturbance during his practice, I was not going to dress for the Boston College game. My stomach sank. My mom, dad, and my third grade teacher were all coming in for the game. What was I going to do? But coach took care of everything, they all got their tickets. But me? I didn't dress, and I watched the game from my dorm room. That was some lesson for me. When coach was talking, no one talked. It's all about respect."

"When Coach Davie came in, the atmosphere changed. It wasn't better or worse, it was just a very different experience. Something about Coach Davie just didn't seem as genuine as it did with Coach Holtz; something felt a little off. He wasn't quite as thorough with the day-to-day operations as Coach Holtz; he was not as organized. He didn't instill the fear in us that Coach Holtz had, and maybe we didn't quite respect him as much as we had Coach Holtz. He was a decent guy, and treated us well. He was a great defensive coordinator, but the leap to head coach is a big one, and maybe it was too big for him at that time. I thought about transferring, but Coach Davie talked me out of it. 'Would you rather get 25 catches here and be a Notre Dame Football player, or go to some place like Kentucky and get 50 catches.' At the end of the day, I'm glad I stayed at Notre Dame. I got

a top notch education, and experiences that made me into the man I have become today."

"Urban Meyer was my position coach, and he mirrored Coach Holtz's coaching style in so many ways. He was extremely thorough, meticulous, hard-nosed. He was a stickler for on the field discipline, and he made sure you not only put in the work on the field, but off the field as well. Coach Meyer was an excellent teacher, and excelled at his craft. He was all in: do or die. He made you want to be the best you could be, and to prove that to him. That's what he brought out of you. His practices were so much harder than games were. In fact, games were actually pretty easy because he had you prepared for anything you were going to face during a game. And if he thought of something, after practice was over and you were back in your room studying, it wasn't unusual for him to call you. He'd call, remind you of a certain situation that you had seen in practice or during a game, and give you his thoughts on how to do it differently. He wanted to make sure everything had been taken care of before the next day started. He just couldn't wait."

"All of the qualities that Urban Meyer had, and the skills he learned from Coach Holtz at Notre Dame, this all lead to him to go on to be a successful head coach. Meyer's success throughout doesn't surprise me one bit. He surrounded himself with good people. One thing in particular that I think Coach Meyer took from Coach Holtz's playbook was Holtz's attention to special teams. Coach Holtz took special teams very seriously. I had never played for a coach before who spent so much time focusing on special teams like Coach Holtz did. Coach Meyer did the same thing. That's one part of the game that coaches often overlook, but not the great ones. The great ones know that games can be easily won or lost on special teams."

A collegiate career for any college athlete is filled with memories: some good, some bad, and some that will never be forgotten. Raki had his own fair share of unforgettable moments as he traveled along the *Notre Dame Value Stream*, and he shared a few of the most memorable ones with me.

"The LSU game my junior year (in 1998), when LSU came to Notre Dame, has to be one of my most memorable games during my time at ND. We had beat them previously at LSU the year before, and then they came to ND the following year to play in South Bend under the lights. Mark Roman was the lights out free safety for the Tigers, but we had a lot of wide receivers who were hungry to play football. Our offense had been opening up all day long. I only had one pass in the first half, and had to wait until the fourth quarter before I saw more action. I had three catches in the final drive, concluding with a catch

> *that I took into the end zone and was followed by this huge hit. Somehow, I was able to hold onto the ball and that was the game winner. That was such an awesome experience for me, a huge win, under the lights at Notre Dame Stadium. I remember that moment as if it happened yesterday, the perfect pass from Jarious Jackson, the catch. . . boom. . . touchdown! Celebrating in the end zone with Autry Denson as he lifted me up in celebration. Incredible. My second favorite memory, the first time I was introduced as a starter at a pep rally. Hearing the hype song, and the roar of the crowd, those were the moments you lived for."*

All college football players have their favorite in-game moments, but for the Notre Dame guys who had the privilege of playing football under head coach Lou Holtz, they also have a few classic Holtz moments to share. On more than one occasion, Coach Holtz's players may have thought he was truly out of his mind. But as they learned the lessons Coach Holtz was trying to impart upon them, through his unique coaching style, they discovered that not only was he not crazy, but that he 100% cared about them, and was only trying to mold them into the best versions of themselves. This was Coach Holtz at his finest.

> *"I missed a block against Washington in my freshman year (1996), and at our next practice we ran drills involving the same situation. Once again, I didn't block the guy correctly, and then it happened. Coach Holtz comes over, takes off his hat, slams it on the ground, and puts his face right onto my cage. The next thing I know, I see that his face got cut on my cage and is bleeding. He's not just bleeding, he's bleeding everywhere, and he's screaming at me, 'HIT ME!! HIT ME!! HIT ME!!' I look back at him and say, 'Coach, I'm not going to hit you.' And he's still screaming at me, 'HIT ME! HIT ME!' And so I had to block him a little bit. He just wanted to prove to me how much he cared, and to make absolutely sure I did not miss that block again. And what happened after that? I became a pretty darn good blocker from there on out. He truly cared about each and every one of us, and he wanted us all to be the best we could be. He showed me that day he'd go to war for me, and he did during the Air Force game. I made a catch, which the refs said was not a catch. Holtz asked me if I caught it, and when I said yes, he fought the ref for me. Whenever he says he's going to do something, he does it. He's a great person."*

Every football player that passes through the halls of Notre Dame hopes to get the chance to showcase their skills at the next level, but they also know that the odds are stacked against them, along with the numbers. There are so many guys shooting for very few spots. Regardless of where their post-football path takes them, the *Notre Dame Value Stream* is always there to float them until they can swim on their own.

> "I only played four games my senior year, and my knee was torn up pretty badly by the end of the season, but I didn't have surgery. I still got picked up by the Philadelphia Eagles as a first tier free agent, and made it to the last day of camp, but at the end of the day my knee was just too torn up. I didn't communicate with my coaches at Notre Dame to let them know how bad my knee was, and how much pain I was in. I was scared. I was doing my best to get out on the field week-after-week, and onto the next level, and little did I know I was making it worse. After I got cut by the Eagles, I finally saw a doctor, and the news was not good. My ACL was so stretched and torn, and my MCL and PCL were torn as well. It was basically bone rubbing on bone. My knee had to be completely reconstructed. And while it feels great now, it was too late for me to get a second chance at the NFL."

> **Football is all about being healthy, survival of the fittest.**

"Injury is a part of football, I knew that; if I had been more communicative with my coaches and trainers, maybe I could've taken better care of my body and had the opportunity to play at the next level. My skill level was there, but the injury prohibited me from getting the chance to try my luck in the NFL. Football is all about being healthy, survival of the fittest. If you are fortunate enough to get a starting spot on a Division I team, all you have to do is stay healthy, and do what you do best at the NFL combine, and you'll get a chance to play at the next level. You almost hope that you don't play a lot in your senior year in order to try and ensure you'll be healthy going into the combine. As long as your coaches gave the NFL scouts a positive report, your chances were good."

> **Having a son was a turning point for me.**
> **I stopped being selfish and focusing on myself,**
> **and concentrated on him, on teaching him.**

"Following surgery, I rehabbed and continued to condition and work out in hopes I could get back into the NFL, but the scouts all labeled me as damaged goods, which made me feel even worse. Once I realized my football career was over, I was very upset. I couldn't watch football or the draft for years. My immature mind led me to make some bad decisions. I got busted for marijuana twice. I was in a very bad place. I wasn't ready for the transition from football to the next stage of my life, and I got myself into trouble. Having a son was a turning point for me. I stopped being selfish and focusing on myself, and concentrated on him, on teaching him."

Today

"Today I work with my three brothers in our family business, Dirty Dog Hauling: Junk and Trash Removal (**www.dirtydoghauling.com**). We are pretty big in the (Pennsylvania) mid-state area, and we offer franchise opportunities to entrepreneurs who want to offer professional junk removal services in their area. We provide the muscle and pride ourselves on customer service, and we base that on being courteous, efficient and punctual. We also believe it is our responsibility to give back to our community. From creating and sponsoring a local inner city baseball team to hosting children's holiday activities, we recognize the impact that we are able to have on the lives of others - not only by removing their unwanted junk - but by putting a smile on their face."

"I am also running a local football camp for kids, Skills Development Academy (**www.instagram.com/skillsdevelopmentacademy**). I love working with kids, to be able to teach them the things that I know and see them develop into better players. Right now I'm just focusing on football, but I plan on adding more sports (baseball, basketball, soccer) to our skills camp. In addition to helping kids develop their athletic skills, my second focus is to help make sure these kids get the guidance they need in the academic sphere of their lives. Giving them guidance as to what classes they need to be taking, how to prepare for and take the right tests to get into college, and filling out the proper paperwork such as the FAFSA. Sometimes these kids are getting this guidance from their school counselors, but not always. And even when they do, the information doesn't always make it home. I want to be there not only for the kids, but for their parents, too, to make sure they are checking all of the necessary boxes. I want to prevent these kids from falling through the cracks. I'm doing everything I can do to educate them, so they have the whole picture of what they need to do to get into college."

"And for those kids who aren't ready to move straight into a university or college, we help them network with junior colleges, and get them into a program that will set them up for success. Our goal is to develop all parts of the student-athlete, and to make sure they are still being taken care of even when they are done playing high school ball. So many kids can't break the cycle because they don't have mentors in their lives who can help them break the cycle. That's what I want to provide for the youth in my community. Someday our facility will be like a charter school for athletes, complete with after school programs, tutors, and mentors in addition to the athletic camps and development. We are going to do great things in this community."

It may seem strange or funny to some people, but the *Notre Dame Value Stream* truly does know how to take care of each and every student that comes to Our Lady's University, to show them how to be the best possible version of themselves. Raki is a perfect example of this. When asked what advice he would give to current student-athletes, this is what he shared.

> "There are several things I would pass along. My first piece of advice would be to make sure you choose a school that you really want to go to, a school where you get along with the coaching staff, and the atmosphere fits what you're looking for. And if you get there, and it's not what you want, talk to your parents and transfer. There is no need to stay somewhere if it is a bad fit. Second, make sure you take care of your grades or you will be out on the streets. Don't think you won't suffer the consequences. They will kick you out and you'll be back home where you started. And then, after school, stay clean and don't do anything stupid. If you do something stupid, they have a place for you, too: it's called jail. Look at all of the opportunities in front of you, and take advantage of the good things. No one is going to care if you played football 'back in the day.' Try and enhance your situation legally, not illegally. Be a good person and do the right thing."

Raki currently lives with his son Kari in Harrisburg, PA, and is looking forward to sharing more of his post-football life adventures in an autobiography that he will soon be working on.

Raki Nelson and his son Kari

Raki Nelson's Lessons from the Notre Dame Value Stream:

- Make sure you choose a school that you really want to go to, a school where you get along with the coaching staff, and the atmosphere fits what you're looking for. And if you get there, and it's not what you want, talk to your parents and transfer. There is no need to stay somewhere if it is a bad fit.

- Prioritize your schoolwork and make sure you take care of your grades or you will be out on the streets. Don't think you won't suffer the consequences. They will kick you out and you'll be back home where you started.

- After school, stay clean and don't do anything stupid. If you do something stupid, they have a place for you, too: it's called jail. Look at all of the opportunities in front of you, and take advantage of the good things. No one is going to care if you played football 'back in the day.' Try and enhance your situation legally, not illegally. Be a good person and do the right thing.

Mike O'Connell and his family (from left to right: his brother Chris, his dad Mike, his mom Jane, and himself) at the Ohio State Golf Tournament in the spring of 1991. (Photo courtesy of Mike O'Connell.)

CHAPTER SIXTEEN

The Sporting Event Curator
Mike O'Connell
(Notre Dame Golf – Class of 1992)

The University of Notre Dame isn't a place that you experience for four years and then leave behind. It's a place that becomes a part of you, a place that is a key piece of who you are at your very core, and its footprint grows within you as you travel through life along that elusive *Notre Dame Value Stream*. For Mike O'Connell, Notre Dame wasn't something that he gained knowledge of as he stepped foot on campus as a freshman. It was something that had been indoctrinated in him from birth, by his father who was a Notre Dame alum, and is such a huge part of his life to this very day that he cannot imagine his life without it. So much so, that when he went to the Notre Dame vs. Washington State game in 2003 at Notre Dame stadium, with his then girlfriend, Janelle, who was a Washington State alum, he got down on one knee after the game and proposed to her, further connecting his life with his beloved alma mater. How did Mike follow in his dad's footsteps and play golf at the University of Notre Dame? This is Mike O'Connell's story.

> "I played almost all sports when I was growing up: soccer, baseball, golf, and basketball. Ironically, the only sport I did not play was football, because it coincided with golf season in the Midwest. When I got into junior high and high school I narrowed my focus down to basketball and golf, knowing that I wanted to play golf professionally for a living one day if it was possible. My dad was a really good golfer in the Quincy, IL, area. He didn't play golf professionally, but from a very young age it was something I wanted to pursue at the professional level. I remember when I was in the fifth or sixth grade, my mom and dad took my brother Chris (meet Chris O'Connell in Chapter 17) and I out of school, and took us to Notre Dame for a football game. We would go every year and my dad would meet up with his college teammates and buddies. From that year on, we'd go back every year for a game, but I just remember falling in love with Notre Dame on that trip. We went into the bookstore, and my dad would give my brother and me each $50, and the two of us would strategically shop the bookstore. One of us would get as many things as we could with the Notre Dame logo on it, and the other one would get one or two nice things. The whole experience, it was just so much fun."

"I didn't know too much about Notre Dame, though, besides what I saw on those football weekends. I didn't know how tough it was to get in, or how rigorous the academics were. I just assumed that if I wanted to go there, I would get in. I was very naïve to that part of it until I got into high school. When I was a junior in high school, I started looking around at different schools, trying to narrow down where I wanted to go to college. I knew I wanted to go somewhere that I could play golf, and if that could be Notre Dame, and I could get accepted, I was in. In addition to looking at Notre Dame, I took recruiting trips to two schools. I visited Illinois State upon the recommendation of a good family friend who played on the PGA TOUR, D.A. Weibring. D.A. was also from Quincy, IL, was a good friend of my dad, and had played golf there. I also visited the University of Iowa. It was funny, my dad never pushed us to go to Notre Dame. He wanted our choice in school to be our decision, but that was where I wanted to go. The thing about Notre Dame is, you either love it, or you hate it. I lived in Dallas for a while after college, and now I've been living in the northwest for 20 years,

> *and the polarizing effect that Notre Dame has on people is such a cool thing. It elicits an opinion from someone instantly, and it's either great, or it brings on a conversation."*

> *"Golf, basketball and soccer were super competitive at my high school (Quincy Senior High School). From when I was a freshman in high school, all the way until today, there have been quite a few good golfers who have come out of the program at Quincy. When I was a senior in high school, my brother Chris was a freshman, and we took third at the State Championship that year. In his next three years they won state one year, and took second place one year; they were definitely dominating in high school golf. There was one public high school in Quincy, Quincy Senior High School, which is where I went. And then a private high school, Quincy Notre Dame. I remember getting made fun of, a lot, when I wore my University of Notre Dame sweatshirt to school. Even though I tried to explain to them that it was the University of Notre Dame, not the local high school. Getting made fun of didn't really matter to me, though, I was still wearing it."*

If you are even the slightest bit good at your sport in high school, and have the opportunity to play it at the next level, you probably make assumptions that the transition to college will be seamless. Part of this comes with the confidence you have in your ability to play said sport, but most student-athletes very quickly learn that there is a definite transition that takes place, and it takes a concerted effort to succeed at the next level.

The Notre Dame Years

> *"For starters, we played on tougher golf courses at the collegiate level. It was definitely a step up from playing in high school to playing in college. Even if you're facing an average college team, you're still playing with and against guys who were all state at their respective high schools. The top six or seven guys on my team were from California, Georgia, Arizona, Colorado, and Illinois, among other places, and that was pretty cool to me. The most difficult part of the transition from high school to college was being on your own. In high school, you had your parents to look out for you. My dad was an excellent player, and so if I got off track and needed a lesson, we could just go work it out on the range. In college, you're away at school, and I was still trying to do lessons with my dad over the phone in my dorm, or on a pay phone on the road. We didn't have FaceTime or video chats like you have today. But that was how I learned the game, and how I improved; I asked my dad for a lesson. Learning the game of golf was never forced upon me, it was just a fun experience. Not having him there with me was the biggest challenge for me*

when I got to Notre Dame. Having to figure things out on my own was also a huge adjustment. Everyone at Notre Dame was as good as I was, or better, and the golf courses were tougher. I called home once a week to go over things with my dad, and I'd call him from a payphone after every round of golf when we were on the road to let him know what I shot. It was fun to have a five minute conversation with him and get a few pointers before the next round. I shared everything with my parents when I was at Notre Dame. . . my brother Chris? He shared nothing."

Anyone who is or has been a student at Notre Dame, or who has tried to get in to Notre Dame, knows the academic rigors that accompany being a student there; adding athletics on top of that adds an additional challenge.

"No doubt, student life at Notre Dame is demanding. Obviously everyone who is there is a good student. As an athlete, you tried to have all of your classes in the morning, so that you could practice in the afternoon. We had some practices as a team/group, but a lot of it was on you to manage your own practices. If you needed to work on your game, you did that on your own. When you practiced, you did it on the Burke Memorial Golf Course on campus, behind The Rock. The golf course was a long way from my dorm, Stanford Hall, so I spent many afternoons carrying my golf bag across campus to practice. One of my best memories of practicing was, if you were out there on a Wednesday or Thursday night and it was close to football season, you'd be able to hear the marching band practicing as you were hitting balls; that was really cool. Being a student-athlete at Notre Dame was tremendously challenging, but I had every opportunity and tool that I needed to be successful. If I was having trouble with a class, there were tutors available to help me. Some subjects I could pretty much figure out on my own. Others, not so much. I had five years of Spanish between junior high and high school, and I mistakenly thought Spanish would be an easy elective. I could not have been more wrong."

"I ended up majoring in accounting. I was good with numbers, and my mom thought this would be a good career path for me. My goal, though, was to play professional golf, and so that was my priority, and that was what I was working towards, or at least I thought I was headed in that direction. One of the most important habits of a student-athlete, though, is that of time management. You need to be able to manage your time effectively, and you also need to have the humility to ask for help when you need it."

In any sport, the relationship between a coach and a player is a tight knit one. But in a sport like golf, it's a different kind of relationship, compared to a team sport such as football or basketball. In golf, the instruction is primarily one-on-one, and if you don't implement what your coach tells you or shows you, you will not get better.

"It's kind of a funny story. The coach who recruited me was a guy by the name of Noel O'Sullivan, and he had been a coach at Notre Dame for quite a while. I had only been on campus freshman year two or three days when we heard that he had been let go. I called him and met him at The Rock, and he was in tears. I didn't know him that well. And on top of that, I had just arrived on campus, had just met my roommate (who was from New York), and my coach gets fired. A gentleman by the name of George Thomas was named the new coach, and was brought in to help upgrade the program. Coach Thomas was the head golf pro at Elcona Country Club (in Elkhart, IN). He was a really good player, and had played in some senior tour level events. But up until this point, my dad had always been my coach. My dad was the one who gave me thoughts and ideas, and talked strategy and things like that. He was part psychologist, and part cheerleader. He was a great listener and taught me everything I knew about the game. The thing is, there are many different ways to play golf, and so it is very difficult to switch teachers mid-stream, as you're starting out your freshman year at Notre Dame."

> **Golf is such an individual sport (even though you're technically on a 'team'): it's more about the attitude and personality the coach brings to the experience.**

"Coach Thomas was a great guy, but the dynamic between him and the team was a little off my freshman year. We were all expecting to be working with Coach O'Sullivan, and now we had Coach Thomas. We were familiar with Coach O'Sullivan's style and what he expected from us after going through the recruiting process, and now we had to start learning all of that from scratch with the new coach. That was a definite shock to the system, but it ended up working out just fine. With golf, it's a little different than with other team sports. You don't practice as a team with your coach day in and day out. Golf is such an individual sport (even though you're technically on a 'team'): it's more about the attitude and personality the coach brings to the experience. He brought in two assistants with him, one of whom was his son. It was a good coaching staff, but it still took us a little while to get to know him, and know what his expectations were. All I knew was that I was going to practice as hard as I could, in order to make sure that I made it to the next level."

It's funny the things that come back to you when you're walking down memory lane. As Mike talked about his coaching challenges freshman year, he shared a touching moment with his dad.

> "When my dad would come to a tournament, he was big into photography and would take a ton of pictures. Then after the tournament he would go home and make a mini post card collage for me, with maybe five or six pictures in there, and write some notes on the back. Just some inspiration for me. I was going through some stuff a few years back and found about thirty of them, which brought back a flood of memories."

I love asking the "what is your favorite Notre Dame memory" question. Even though almost every person groans at the question, the process of them going down memory lane to pick out just the right one always takes them back to a place that looks even more perfect looking back, and puts a smile on their face.

> "One of my favorite golfing memories from my time at Notre Dame was playing at Ohio State University, where Jack Nicklaus played golf in college. Every year we'd play in a tournament there, and when you'd walk in their Pro Shop there was a plaque which read, 'The Ohio State University Golf Courses, Collegiate Home of Jack Nicklaus, the Greatest Golfer to Ever Play the Game.' His son, Gary Nicklaus, was also a golfer, and was playing in college at the same time. (I think he was a year or two older than me.) Every year that we'd go to the tournament at Ohio State, it seemed like we'd get paired with OSU, either in the first, second or third round. The one thing you didn't want, however, was to be ranked #1. This was because Gary Nicklaus would be ranked either 2, 3, or 4, and you were hoping to be paired with him as his dad would always be there to watch his son play. I had never met him before that, and being so close to Jack Nicklaus was such an incredible experience. One year we got a team picture with Jack, and that's a memory I'll never forget. Unfortunately, I never got paired with Gary, and so he and his dad were either behind me or in front of me. But it was still cool."

> "One of my favorite non-golfing Notre Dame memories was when the Notre Dame Football team played for the national championship in 1988, my freshman year. One of my teammates on the golf team (Paul Nolta) was from Phoenix, and he invited six or seven of us to stay at his house and go to the game. Even though we had only known each other for three or four months, we all made the trip out to Phoenix, and that weekend was fun beyond belief. I think my ticket cost around $35 for the national championship game, and my parents bought the ticket and my flight as my Christmas present. It was a once in a lifetime opportunity, for sure, and something I will never forget.

After we won the game, Sports Illustrated had Tony Rice on the cover. I went and bought three copies of the Sports Illustrated, and I was hoping that I could get Tony to sign one of them for my dad. I remember walking over to his dorm room (I had looked up his room number in the student directory), scared to death, not even sure that he'd be there, with the three issues of Sports Illustrated in my hand, and I knocked on his door. I think Ricky Watters was the one who answered the door, and I asked him, 'Is Tony Rice here?' The two of them could not have been any nicer. Ricky invited me in and Tony signed all three of them. And I ever so graciously said, 'Thanks a lot, guys.' I had one of them framed and gave it to my dad for Christmas the next year. I don't think I was in their room for more than two minutes, but it felt like an hour! He could not have been nicer."

As a Notre Dame student, you know that you are lucky to be at a place like Notre Dame, but you don't truly understand the blessings that it will bring to you over the course of your lifetime until you head out into the world and experience life a bit. Mike was thrilled to follow in his father's footsteps and attend the University of Notre Dame, but he never dreamed of the lifelong support that he would receive from Notre Dame and the *Notre Dame Value Stream*.

In between my junior and senior years at Notre Dame my father passed away unexpectedly.

"In between my junior and senior years at Notre Dame my father passed away unexpectedly. When I was 11 years old, my dad had taken us to the 1981 Notre Dame/Florida State game, and after the game he had a seizure at the Monogram Club gathering at the Joyce Athletic & Convocation Center. Following his seizure he learned that he had a malformation very close to his brain. They told him while operating was an option, there was around an 80% chance that he'd end up in a vegetative state, a 10% chance that they could not get the mass out, and maybe a 5% chance that everything would go okay. If they could go in now, they could probably take care of it and there would be no issue at all. The doctor also told my dad that there was a chance that it may never bother him, that he could live a long life and die of old age, or, that he could die tomorrow, if it bursts. My brother and I were never told about any of this. From that diagnosis, he lived for 10 years, and then passed away suddenly in June of 1991, which was the summer between my junior and senior year. Heading back to Notre Dame that fall for my senior year was pretty rough, and it was a bit of an off year for me. It was incredibly difficult for me to be around golf, and I played terribly. I didn't have the desire to practice, and even with my brother

there (he was a freshman that year, and was trying to get a spot on the golf team), it was a tough year for me. Well, for both of us for sure, although he probably has a different take on that year."

Today

"When I graduated from Notre Dame I took an accounting position in my hometown, just for something to do, and then D.A. Weibring (who at the time was playing on the PGA TOUR) asked me to caddy for him full-time (in 1993). I did that for a couple of years, and looking back, I am so grateful to him for that opportunity. D.A. and I talked a lot about my dad, and through that experience I was able to learn to love golf again. I didn't realize how closely connected I was to golf, Notre Dame, and my dad, as well as how interconnected those three things were in my life; it was very hard for me when my father was no longer there. When my brother Chris graduated from Notre Dame in 1995, he and I played together on the Lone Star Golf Tour for a couple of years in Dallas, but eventually I realized that I just wasn't good enough for that level of golf. I no longer had that undeniable will to play the game, and I no longer felt that need to run through a wall in order to play golf. My perspective on life changed, and I just wanted to enjoy life again. For a while I even had a tough time watching Notre Dame football. It just took me a while to figure out what life would look like without my dad."

"At that point, my brother was set up with Peter Jacobsen (through D.A. Weibring), and Peter asked Chris to caddy for him full-time, and then I eventually (after I caddied for D.A. Weibring a bit longer) went on to work for Peter in his sports management agency. What happened was, in 1998 I flew to New York City looking for my next opportunity. I thought I was interested in working on Wall Street, but then I spoke with Peter and he offered me a job at his sports management agency. So I flew to New York for one interview, with Bear Sterns, and then I flew to Portland, Oregon, to meet with Peter and his group. Following the two interviews, it was a very easy decision for me to go to work for him. I thought maybe I'd be a tournament director of PGA TOUR events, which sounded interesting, and it still involved golf; 20 years later I'm still with Peter Jacobsen. In hindsight, caddying on the PGA TOUR was kind of like my MBA. I got to see what professional golf was really like, and that was an education unto itself. Some of the caddies were quite the characters. Some guys were doing it for a living, and there were some well-educated guys out there caddying. Caddying for D.A. was the best thing I could have asked for after losing my dad. Thank

God I was at Notre Dame when my father passed. It was the best thing for me, and the best place I could have been, to be able to deal with his death. I cannot image going through it anywhere else."

"Taking the job with Peter Jacobsen Sports was such an incredible opportunity for me. He's such a unique guy. He always sees the positive side of things. He's a complete golf nut, and working with him and his business has been very eye opening for me. He's not a bottom line guy, he's a 'Let's create an experience and make it memorable' kind of guy. And if we leave a little on the table, that's completely okay, but let's do it right and not cut corners. If it's not fun, he does not want to be a part of it. He's a University of Oregon fan, and he absolutely loves college football. He and I have a lot in common, including that he also lost his dad at a young age. It's hard to talk to people about something like that, who haven't gone through it. He's been such a remarkable mentor for me. He's a great guy, and we've had some pretty cool opportunities and have had the chance to do so many outstanding things together."

"For example, Peter was good friends with Arnold Palmer (one of the greatest players ever), and Jim Rohr (also a Notre Dame graduate), the CEO of PNC Bank, was also good friends with Palmer. Our company was hired to help with Arnold Palmer's 80th birthday party which was sponsored by PNC Bank, and it was such an incredible experience. One that I'll never forget. Part of the party was at PNC Park, where the Pirates play, and the next night the party was at Laurel Valley Golf Club, where Arnold was a member. I also had the chance to play golf with Peter and Jim Rohr the day before the outing, and we talked Notre Dame. Another more recent memory I have of working with Peter Jacobsen Sports was being hired to run a junior event for Nick Faldo, another well-known professional golfer. He started an event called the Major Champions Invitational in Orlando. One of the sponsors of this event happened to bring in former Notre Dame head coach Lou Holtz to speak; I had never met Coach Holtz before."

"Coach Holtz was larger than life when I was in college, I remember listening to those pep rallies, and all I wanted to do was hear him speak. He was great. When he walked into the room at this junior golf event, to speak in front of these kids who are 15-19 years old, they had no earthly clue who Lou Holtz was. I kept telling them, 'You guys are going to like this: trust me.' He gets on stage and immediately goes into one of his classic Lou Holtz speeches, and I felt like I was a freshman in college all over again. The way he speaks, the way he talks, the way he makes fun of himself: incredible. He ended the night with his infamous newspaper magic trick, and the kids thought he was an

> absolute rock star. All of the kids were getting pictures with him afterwards. When he was done speaking I went over and introduced myself to him. I told him I was a freshman when they won the national championship in 1988. And he looked right up at me and said, 'Hold on, I've got something for you.' He reached into his backpack and pulled out a Notre Dame helmet keychain and gave it to me. I was speechless. That moment took me back to 1988 all over again, listening to every one of his speeches. The best part about working for Peter Jacobsen is that our business is different from year to year, event to event, experience to experience. We're never doing the same thing, and it's been awesome to meet Notre Dame people along our journey through the sports marketing world. I would have never had all of these experiences had I stuck with accounting."

> "I've also been able to get involved with some philanthropic efforts through my work with Peter Jacobsen. Our company does some big events for charities, such as the Fred Meyer Challenge, sponsored by Fred Meyer who owns the local supermarket chain. Over the span of about 20 years, the Fred Meyer Challenge (which was a professional golf team event) raised in the neighborhood of 15-20 million dollars for local charities in the area, and for a lot of them, the money they received was 100% of their operating budget. We also ran the CVS Health Charity Classic, which raised 20 million dollars over 20 years, benefitting such charities as the Brain Injury Association, the March of Dimes, Save the Bay, the Autism Project and the Arthritis Foundation. This work has been especially rewarding to me, to be able to use our network to do good."

Playing any sport at the Division I level is no walk in the park, but for those who are interested in heading that direction, there is nothing better than hearing some words of wisdom from those who have been there before.

> "My first piece of wisdom that I would share with anyone wanting to play a Division I sport is to enjoy the process. Yes, you're there to play a sport, but you may get injured, have a family emergency, or any number of things; even though it may feel like life or death at the time, it's not. Learn how to manage your time wisely. It will not only help you succeed in your sport, but in everything you do in life. I had a good friend that I played against when I played basketball in high school, LaPhonso Ellis, and LaPhonso then played basketball at Notre Dame. He was academically ineligible during part of his career at Notre Dame, and had to miss some games. He and I had some accounting classes together, and I knew exactly what he was going through because I, too, was worried that I would be academically ineligible at one point. LaPhonso didn't give up, he kept working not only on his school work but basketball as well, and he made

it through and got his degree. My time at Notre Dame went quick, everyone told me it would; it really did go by so fast. Looking back, you remember all of the good experiences, even though there were days in there where you might have failed a test or missed out on something. But overall, when you look back, all you can think is, 'Man, how great was that?'"

"As I look back on my experience at Notre Dame, I am so very glad that my mom didn't let me transfer from Notre Dame when things got rough, and when I didn't play as well as I wanted to. To think I've been out of ND for 26 years and I still feel that special connection to the place, it makes me feel extremely humbled that I was able to go to Notre Dame, play golf, and receive my degree from such an incredible place. As Coach Holtz always says, 'For those who know Notre Dame, no explanation is necessary. For those who don't, no explanation will suffice.'"

Mike currently lives in Portland, Oregon, with his wife Janelle, and their two children Campbell and Hudson, where he continues to work for Peter Jacobsen Sports.

Mike O'Connell, his wife Janelle, and their children Campbell and Hudson on the Oregon Coast.

Mike O'Connell's Lessons from the Notre Dame Value Stream:

- Enjoy the process. Yes, you're there to play a sport, but you may get injured, have a family emergency, or any number of things; even though it may feel like life or death at the time, it's not.

- Learn how to manage your time wisely. It will not only help you succeed in your sport, but in everything you do in life.

- Have the humility to ask for help when you need it. There is no need to struggle when there are resources there for you to use. Being able to ask for help will serve you well in your career as well.

Portrait of men's golfer Chris O'Connell, October 1992.
(Photo courtesy of Notre Dame Archives.)

CHAPTER SEVENTEEN

The Golf Pro
Chris O'Connell
(Notre Dame Golf – Class of 1995)

I know I am one of many "legacies" who followed in their parent's footsteps to attend the University of Notre Dame. But when you have both a father and a brother who have attended Notre Dame ahead of you, one of two things happens. You either run for the hills and go somewhere as far away from Notre Dame as humanly possible (University of Hawaii, anyone?), or you step in line and follow right along. For Chris O'Connell, Notre Dame was the only school he wanted to attend. There simply wasn't a second choice. And who could blame him? This is Chris O'Connell's story.

"I grew up in a sports family, and my dad also grew up playing sports. My mom didn't play a whole lot of sports, but they didn't have the opportunities for women to play sports back then, like they do now. My dad played basketball, football, baseball and golf growing up, and he went to the University of Notre Dame where he was an All-American on the golf team. Golf was a big part of my dad's life, but my brother and I grew up playing a little bit of everything: soccer, football, basketball, baseball, wrestling and golf. But, being that golf was such a big part of my father's life, our family was very much a golf family. My dad was very active in the golfing community and played a lot of tournament golf (at the amateur level), and my brother and I just followed along. Opportunities to golf were offered to us, but we never felt pressured to play golf. My brother (meet Mike O'Connell in Chapter 16) and I were encouraged to play any and all sports. We both played both basketball and golf all the way through high school. And, like my father, my brother and I were both captains on the golf team at the University of Notre Dame. One of the best things about golf is it's a sport for a lifetime; it's something you can play your entire life. Whether you're a professional or just a weekend warrior, anyone can play the game of golf and enjoy himself. The game of golf has a unique format in that you're not competing with anyone but yourself, and the golf course."

"When I was looking at colleges, I looked at Vanderbilt, Iowa, Michigan State and Notre Dame. Looking back on it now, I knew I was going to go to Notre Dame. I went ahead and looked around at other schools to make my parents and teachers happy. I think my parents were a little worried that I wasn't going to get in to Notre Dame, but in my teenage mind that's where I was going. When I got in, my brother was already there, and my dad was a graduate, so the decision was a no brainer for me. We grew up watching Notre Dame Football on Saturdays. Notre Dame was such a big part of our family, I simply could not imagine going to school anywhere else. From a golfing perspective, South Bend wasn't exactly the ideal golfing atmosphere, and most of the top golf programs were in the south or on the west coast, but I felt Notre Dame was where I was destined to go. And while I did go on an official visit to Notre Dame, that visit wasn't what sealed the deal for me. I had already been there quite a bit as my brother had been there for three years at that point, and my family had made multiple trips back to campus for football games, so my official visit was merely a formality in the process."

Making the transition from high school to college is never easy, but it does help when you go to a school where you've already spent a fair amount of time, and where your brother is an upperclassman and can show you the ropes.

The Notre Dame Years

"When I arrived at Notre Dame for my freshman year my brother was a senior, and he was the captain of the golf team. My high school team had been very successful. We had one guy go to the University of Missouri, and one to the University of Illinois, and I went to Notre Dame on a golf scholarship. We finished third at state my freshman year, second at state my junior year, and won state my senior year, so I had some great experiences with team golf. Many high school golf programs, when I played golf, were not very organized, and a lot of them had a volunteer as their coach."

"But at my high school, we had a coach who was very detail oriented. Our coach went so far as to schedule our practices for us to keep us organized. And so when I got to Notre Dame, I was already quite detail oriented, and had received some excellent coaching as far as 'team golf' went, but not so much in the way of mechanical individual instruction. Back then, Notre Dame's golf program was fairly mediocre in terms of being competitive, and I wanted to try and take what we had done with our high school team and elevate the program at Notre Dame. The transition from playing golf in high school to college was pretty seamless for me as I already knew most of the players on the team through my brother. In that respect, they were already like family to me, and I had a pretty good rapport with them going into it."

"What did make my freshman year difficult, was the loss I experienced that summer prior to attending Notre Dame. My father passed away the June after my senior year in high school, which made heading off to Notre Dame that fall bittersweet. Both Notre Dame and golf had been such a big part of my dad's life, and our lives with him, and so not being able to share my time at ND with him was tough for me. The academic rigor at Notre Dame was also a challenge for me. My high school golf coach, and my dad, had prepared me well to play golf at ND, but I did not feel as if my high school had prepared me for what I was going to face academically at Notre Dame."

The good thing about being a student-athlete at Notre Dame is that the coaches, professors, and counselors all really looked out for you.

"School came pretty easy for me in high school, but when I got to Notre Dame, I really had to work at my studies in order to survive. The good thing about being a student-athlete at Notre Dame is that the coaches, professors, and counselors all really looked out for you. Especially your freshman year, because it truly is a big adjustment from high school to a place like Notre Dame. But even with the academic challenges that I faced, Notre Dame really felt like

> *family to me. Notre Dame is so difficult to get into, but as long as you put in the work both academically and athletically, they will look after you. My GPA after fall break my freshman year was a pretty low number, and I really had to rally that second half of the semester (you had to have a 2.0 in order to be eligible to golf in the spring semester), but I felt if I could get my grades up, I was good enough to play on the team."*

A common theme in so many of these stories is time management. In hindsight, we all wish we would have been better at it going into college. But as each and every student and student-athlete makes their way through Notre Dame, it's one of the most important things they will learn on the *Notre Dame Value Stream*, and it's one of the tools they will use for the rest of their lives.

> *"When I got to Notre Dame, I had no clue how to study or how to manage my time. That's one of the things that almost everyone has to learn when they get to college, and if you're a student-athlete, you better figure it out pretty quickly. Notre Dame had an incredible support network for their student athletes from the counselors to the tutoring they provided. I'm sure at some schools students feel like they are just a number, or one of thousands of students and no one even knows you're there, but I did not feel that way at Notre Dame. I didn't have to search for help, they checked on us and made sure we were doing okay."*

When I interview former student-athletes, one of my go-to questions is to ask them about their experience with their coach. Whether an athlete is successful or not can be greatly affected by their coach or coaching staff. But golf is a little different.

> *"Golf is not really a 'team' sport, in the traditional sense of the word. You all play the game, and they add your scores together, but you are not really able to help your fellow teammates during the course of a tournament. It's not like you're passing the ball or blocking for someone. You play on your own, and they add your scores to get the team total. Even with golf, though, some teams have good chemistry and get along with each other, and some teams are good as a team but don't really have good chemistry. George Thomas was the golf coach at Notre Dame, and he was a highly touted golf instructor. He was the head pro at Elcona Country Club in Elkhart, IN, for many years, and was a very good player in his own right. When I got there, he was probably in his late 60s, but as he was a good player himself, you would pay attention to him."*

> *"He worked with everyone on their swing, and helped them improve their technique. Some guys weren't interested in changing their technique, though.*

They may have had a coach at home whom they liked to work with, so that was challenging for Coach Thomas. Some coaches are more administrative, and simply just schedule practices and travel. But Coach Thomas always wanted to help. He spent a lot of time with us, individually, working with us on our swing. He often split his time with different guys during practice, in order to give each one of us some advice. Golf is different than most sports. You're trying to play your best, and you're pulling for your teammates, but you can't truly help them as players like you can in other sports."

"The Notre Dame Golf team's schedule now is much more extensive than it was when I was there. We played a lot of midwest teams such as Purdue, Indiana, Ohio State, Michigan State when I was there; we mainly drove to most of our tournaments. In the spring we'd go down to Florida for a week for a big tournament, and that was always an interesting trip. It was usually in the middle of March, and at that point we more than likely hadn't even been outside yet to swing a club. There was always one guy from the team who would go on this trip to Florida who was never heard from again. The problem with going to play in this tournament with no outside practice under our belts was that the golf course was in the middle of this beautiful neighborhood, with out of bounds on both sides of the course. There would always be one guy on the team who would go out there and just have no control over his golf ball, and would be so scarred that he'd never recover; never play another tournament for the school. We'd fly down to Florida, have one practice round on the course, and then tee it up in the tournament. We couldn't wait to get down there, get in the warm weather, and play the game we loved. But at the same time you were nervous that you'd be that guy who was never to be seen again. Other than that big trip, most of the other tournaments we played in were within driving distance from South Bend. Once we did fly to Colorado Springs, CO, though, to play in a tournament at the Air Force Academy."

You can't go to a school like Notre Dame and not collect countless memories. The journey along the *Notre Dame Value Stream* brings us good times and bad times, victories and challenges, and all we can hope for is to walk away better than we were when we got there, and with a collection of memories that will make us smile for a lifetime.

Hands down, the best part of playing golf at Notre Dame was, for one year, playing alongside my brother, the team captain.

"Hands down, the best part of playing golf at Notre Dame was, for one year, playing alongside my brother, the team captain. I knew we only had one year together at ND, and there were a couple of tournaments that I didn't

qualify for as a freshman. But being able to play alongside him at the college level, at a school that we both held so near and dear to our hearts, that our dad had gone to: that was the best. I wish we had been able to play together for more than just one year. But the fact that we got one, was great. For me, even though my dad wasn't there to see me play golf at Notre Dame, I was so incredibly excited to be able to attend the same school that he did. There would be times in the winter, when everything was so hard, and all I wanted to be doing was playing golf and getting better, (and then you looked out your window at all of the snow)."

"My whole life, I dreamed of being a professional golfer. There were a few moments where I thought maybe Notre Dame wasn't the best place for me, in terms of developing my golf game, but those moments were fleeting. I never really seriously considered going anywhere but Notre Dame, because deep down inside I knew it was the right place for me. Even if I had been the number one player in the country, I still would have gone to Notre Dame. I simply cannot imagine what my life would have looked like had I gone to school anywhere but Notre Dame. Even if I would have gone to some amazing golf school, my life would not be what it is today. It means a great deal to me to be a graduate of the University of Notre Dame."

In the blink of an eye, it seems like you just arrived on the hallowed grounds that are the University of Notre Dame, and your four year journey on the *Notre Dame Value Stream* has flashed before your eyes, and it's time to set out on your next adventure.

The Professional Years

"I knew I wanted to try and play golf professionally. Looking back, I probably wasn't good enough to play golf at the next level. I didn't have enough success at the college level to warrant that kind of jump. Yes, I was one of the best players on the team at Notre Dame, but our team was a middle of the road team as far as being competitive. But, at that time in my life, nothing was going to stop my quest to play at the next level. You're not looking at things rationally, you're following your heart. I had a very strong will, and following my dream was exactly what I was going to do. After graduating from Notre Dame I spent the summer working at Bloomington Country Club, where my golf instructor Rick Sellers was the head pro, and I worked with him a lot that summer trying to improve my game. The situation allowed me to work on my game and provided opportunities to play in some amateur golf tournaments while preparing to turn pro. That winter, I moved to Dallas with my brother, and our close family friend PGA TOUR player D.A. Weibring looked after

us, getting us playing privileges at his home course Royal Oaks Country Club. In Texas we began competing on a mini tour called The Lone Star Tour that was comparable to AA baseball. We started out golfing in some pretty small, rural areas in Texas, Oklahoma and Louisiana, trying to improve our game, and hopefully eventually work our way up to getting to the PGA TOUR."

Without the two of them in my life, I'm not sure where I'd be today.

"I did that for about two and a half years. I put together a sponsorship group, which helped me stay afloat, because unless you play extremely well you're not going to make money playing on the small, mini tours. After that two and a half years, while I still wanted to keep playing, financially I didn't have the money to continue, and D.A. Weibring recommended that I try caddying on the PGA TOUR. Caddying would allow me to work 22 weeks a year, and still allow me time to work on my game and play smaller tournaments. It would also give me an inside look at the PGA TOUR, and allow me to see what it's really like to be on that level of a tour. He connected me with Peter Jacobsen, who was an established player on the PGA TOUR. Typically an established player wouldn't normally accept just any guy as his caddy, especially a guy like me who had no experience caddying. Yes, I had experience golfing, but none as a caddy. D.A. Weibring set it up as a onetime deal, but Peter and I got along so well that the one week deal turned into a three and a half year deal. D.A. Weibring has been such a mentor to me over the years, along with Peter Jacobsen. Without the two of them in my life, I'm not sure where I'd be today. Caddying for Jacobsen was quite an eye opening experience for me. I got to see where my game was competitive, and where my game did not stack up. It was the perfect opportunity for me as I was single, able to travel, and made some good money doing it."

"When I started caddying for Peter Jacobsen, he introduced me to his golf instructor, Jim Hardy. He was the first golf instructor who actually made golf make sense to me. There are a lot of myths about golf. Golf is kind of this magical thing, one day you have it, and one day you don't. My dad may have passed away when I was still a young golfer, but I had three amazing men who looked out for me: D.A. Weibring, Peter Jacobsen, and Jim Hardy. During the three and a half years that I caddied for Peter, I worked on my golf game with Jim, and one day Peter told me that he thought I had improved enough to get back to playing myself. Peter told me if I didn't go play full time that he'd fire me. So with Peter and D.A.'s help, I put together another sponsorship group, and played full time for three years. My personal goal was to be able to financially take care of myself through golf, and if I wasn't at that level in three years, then I was going to move on. I really had no idea what that meant, but I knew I'd figure it out one way or another."

Today

"At the end of three years I was better than I had ever been, but I also knew where my game needed to be, and I decided at that point I just wasn't good enough. I knew I didn't want to be 40 years old and still trying to make it. At that point, the question was, what am I going to do next? That question really scared me. I kept thinking, if I don't make it in professional golf, I'm not sure what type of career will really excite or fulfill me like golf did. All I ever planned on was playing professional golf. There was no plan B. In those seven and a half years that I spent caddying and playing professionally, I learned a lot about the mechanics of the golf swing, about what makes it work, and why some guys succeed while other guys fail. I really wanted to somehow stay involved in the game of golf, but I wasn't sure how to make that work. I had a curious mind in that I wasn't just looking for help with my game during that time, I had a desire to understand the totality of golf and how the pieces fit together. I felt that after my seven and a half years of experience in caddying and primarily my time with Jim Hardy, I had some great insight into the game, and that I may be able to help some people with their game; so I decided to become a golf instructor."

"Starting out as a golf instructor was the equivalent of starting any new job, you start from zero with no clients. The first year in any new business is tough. You work like crazy in order to build up your client base. I was told that it would take me three years to get to a point where I was making decent money, and 'If after three years you aren't as busy as you want to be, you're either not good enough or you're not trying hard enough.' Year one was slim. Year two I started to gain some notoriety. I never really marketed my business too much, I've mainly used word of mouth. I used my students as my marketing strategy, hoping that they'd share positive feedback about my instruction to others. But my big break was having the support of D.A. Weibring, Peter Jacobsen and Jim Hardy. At the time I was building my business, Matt Kuchar was playing on the Web.com Tour, which is one step below the PGA TOUR. He wanted to get back to the PGA TOUR, but knew he needed to improve his mechanics in order to do that, and Matt Weibring encouraged him to take some lessons from me. (Matt Kuchar and Matt Weibring had been teammates at Georgia Tech. Matt Weibring was already a student of mine, and was also playing on the Web.com Tour.) Matt Kuchar came to me knowing that he needed to get better, and he was the player who helped put me on the map as I helped *him get back onto the PGA TOUR. He now has some significant wins on his resume, and is one of the top players in the world. It's been an amazing elevation in both his career and mine, and we've become very close. I never really wanted to teach golf, or was ever interested in that part of the game. Rather than worry about my game I now worry about my students' games and helping them improve is very rewarding. I couldn't be happier, and I feel that I am exactly where I am supposed to be."*

And then it happens, your journey takes you somewhere you never expected, and you know you're exactly where you are supposed to be.

> **When you can help them either get their game back on track, or even elevate it to a place they never thought they were capable of, that is the most rewarding part of being an instructor.**

"When people come in for a golf lesson, they're pretty down on the game. They don't come to you when they're doing well, they come to you when they are down on their luck, even desperate, and are thinking about quitting the game for the 63rd time. For me, the best part of being a golf instructor is this: if I can be the one who can pinpoint what's causing their ball to misbehave, to not fly accordingly; if I can figure it out and get them to understand what they're doing incorrectly and show them how to make a change; if I can get them to feel the difference between what they are currently doing, and what they need to do; then at that point we can instantly change the flight of their golf ball. If they hit a couple of good shots, then all of the sudden their excitement for the game comes back, and they leave the lesson not only a better player, but with a better disposition than they had when they showed up. For so many of my students, golf is a big part of their life, and their identity. When you can help them either get their game back on track, or even elevate it to a place they never thought they were capable of, that is the most rewarding part of being an instructor."

What I've learned about most people who travel through Notre Dame on the *Notre Dame Value Stream*, is that overwhelmingly, they have a desire and feel an obligation to "pay it forward" once they make it to the other side. This is why when I ask the question, "What advice would you give a student-athlete interested in playing a sport at the Division I level," they jump at the chance to share some words of wisdom to the next generation.

"If you're going to play a Division I sport, you really have to be able to manage your time well, and you have to be able to stay on top of things. I'm sure it's easier now with all of the technology that's at a student's finger tips,

but I would say that time management is one of the most important things that you need to implement in order to be successful at the Division I level. I would also say, don't let your education get in the way of your education. You only go to college once, and those are going to be four of the best years of your life, so try and relish in that and enjoy it. Everyone says college goes by fast, and it really does."

"For me, the fact that both my brother and I and my father all went to Notre Dame, Notre Dame is a very special place to me. I don't get back to campus as often as I'd like, but even in watching Notre Dame Football on TV, the memories come flooding back. I love taking friends there who have never been to campus before, and sharing it with them. I am a proud graduate of the University of Notre Dame."

Chris and his wife Sara currently live in Plano, Texas, during the school year, and spend their summers on Long Island in New York, where Chris teaches at Friar's Head. They have two girls, ages eight and seven, Georgia and Emerson (who also love Notre Dame), and the family has two dogs.

Chris O'Connell, his wife Sara, and their two girls:
Georgia and Emerson.

Chris O'Connell's Lessons from the Notre Dame Value Stream:

- If you're going to play a Division I sport, you really have to be able to manage your time well, and you have to be able to stay on top of things. I'm sure it's easier now with all of the technology that is at a student's finger tips, but I would say that time management is one of the most important things that you need to implement in order to be successful at the Division I level.

- Don't let you education get in the way of your education. You only go to college once, and those are going to be four of the best years of your life, so try and relish and enjoy it. Everyone says college goes by fast, and it really does.

Notre Dame Women's Basketball player Karen Robinson.
(Photo courtesy of Notre Dame Athletics.)

CHAPTER EIGHTEEN

The Sideline Reporter and Coach

Karen (Robinson) Keyes

(Notre Dame Basketball – Class of 1991)

K aren (Robinson) Keyes grew up in Washington Township, NJ, and spent her childhood playing multiple sports. When she got to high school, however, the choices of sports for young women at that level were limited. She began her high school career playing three sports (field hockey, basketball and cross country), but after some inspiring words from an upperclassman on the basketball team, and a timely introduction, she focused her efforts solely on basketball with her sights set on playing at the next level. How did Karen become drawn to attend the University of Notre Dame and have the opportunity to play basketball for the legendary head coach Muffet McGraw? This is Karen (Robinson) Keyes' story.

"My brother and I were a year apart, and back then we pretty much played everything. We were even on some of the same teams together. In middle school I was on the swim team and played soccer, and when I became a freshman at Paul VI High School in Haddonfield, NJ, they didn't have a girl's soccer team. At that point I had to make a decision as to what sport(s) I was going to play. My dad said to me that fall, there are two sports you can choose from; field hockey and tennis. Since I had played soccer, and all of the positions were the same in both soccer and field hockey, I chose field hockey. I also played basketball and ran cross country. By the time I was a junior in high school I narrowed my focus and strictly played basketball. Our basketball team at Paul VI was really good, and one of the seniors who was on my team (Martina Attanasi), when I was a freshman, had a full scholarship to play basketball at Oregon State University. She was one of those girls who played basketball all year round. She introduced me to Mike Flynn, who was the head of the Philadelphia Belles in the AAU (Amateur Athletic Union of Girls Basketball) league. She was also the one who said to me, 'You could be really good. You should play with us all year.' In addition to being involved with the Philadelphia Belles, Mike Flynn also ran the national Blue Star camps (where all of the college recruiters went to scout high school basketball players). Between attending the Blue Star camps and playing in the AAU league, I was able to get a lot of exposure. Martina was the one, though, who pushed me to become more involved in basketball. She was our senior captain and was very dynamic. Once she introduced me to Mike Flynn, and I started working on my game, the recruiting letters started to come in. I knew, at that point, that if I kept growing as a player I could go on and be successful at the next level."

"When I started looking at colleges, I looked at Rutgers and Villanova on the east coast (which were pretty close to where I grew up), and I also looked at Duke, Notre Dame and North Carolina. As I went through the recruiting process, I narrowed my choices down to Duke and Notre Dame. I remember coming home from every recruiting trip and saying, 'Oh yes, I love this school. I definitely want to go here.' Of course every school shows you the absolute best they have to offer during your visit there. I wanted to commit early, (by October of my senior year), and on the North Carolina visit the UNC coaches told me they wanted to come and see me play once more, and so I eliminated them from my list. Once it came time to make a decision between Duke and Notre Dame, which are two great choices, I knew I couldn't go wrong with either one. But somehow I knew in my gut that Notre Dame was where I wanted to go."

> "When we traveled down to play Duke during my freshman season, I was a little apprehensive about making the trip. I knew a lot of their players, and we were all friends, but I couldn't help thinking; what if I get there and I wish I would have gone to Duke? What if I regret my decision? What if they beat us? <laughs> But we ended up beating them, and after the game we went out with their team and had a great time. I had no regrets in my choice to attend the University of Notre Dame."

> "It's kind of ironic, but I had known Mary Gavin (my host during my recruiting visit to Notre Dame) my whole life. My family had a house on the Jersey Shore, and it was one block from where Mary grew up. She went to Wildwood Catholic High School. Growing up we played pickup basketball, and I always watched her play because she was a really good point guard. In the summer between my senior year in high school and my freshman year at Notre Dame, the coaching change happened at Notre Dame. That's when head coach Mary DiStanislao left and head coach Muffet McGraw was hired. I picked up the phone and called Mary Gavin and said, 'What's going on? Is everything okay? Should I still come? Is this more than just a coaching change?' Now obviously I didn't choose Notre Dame only because of the coach, or the team, but I wanted to make sure nothing was seriously wrong with the program. She reassured me that it was just time for a coaching change, and despite the change, I still wanted to go to ND and play for them. Notre Dame even gave me the option to go somewhere else if I wanted to (because of the coaching change), but I didn't want to go anywhere else."

> "Prior to coaching at Notre Dame, Coach McGraw had coached at Lehigh. And while she was coaching at Lehigh she was recruiting a girl that I played basketball with, Sherri Androwlewicz, during my junior year in high school. This actually worked in my favor when I got to Notre Dame as Coach McGraw had been to a lot of my games, had seen me play, and we knew each other because of that."

Yes, it can be stressful being recruited by one coach, and then arriving to college to be coached by a brand new coach. But that situation can also have some advantages, and Karen shared a few of them with me.

The Notre Dame Years

> "My freshman year at Notre Dame was also Coach McGraw's first year at Notre Dame, and this worked in my favor (along with everyone else on the team) as Coach McGraw placed every single one of us on an even playing field. None of us were players she had recruited. This was great for me as I

> *ended up starting at point guard as a freshman along with (senior) Mary Gavin. Mary was the senior leader and a point guard, and I started in the backcourt with her at the number two guard position. This allowed me to have a pretty easy transition from high school to college. It really did benefit me a lot that Coach McGraw had seen me play so much in high school, and she knew what my game was like."*

When you play sports in high school, and you're good at what you do, you are a big fish in a pretty small pond. But once you reach the collegiate level, suddenly you realize you are no longer a big fish in a small pond, but rather a small fish in a fairly large pond. For some this transition is quite a challenge, and for others, they sail through the transition with grace and poise. Karen knew she was no longer a big fish in a small pond, but she also knew how to put in the work, and quickly developed good relationships with her coaches and teammates. The journey is never easy, even for those whose transition is smooth, but fortunately for Karen the *Notre Dame Value Stream* was with her every step of the way.

> *"It was a big jump. I had a lot of experience playing with older kids in the AAU circuit, and that definitely helped me have a smooth transition from high school to college. I started at Notre Dame from the very first game my freshman year, and it helped that I knew the other point guard, Mary Gavin. She was also from New Jersey, and we had very similar playing styles in the back court. I was a shooting point guard, she was a dynamic point guard, and we played very well together. We had two really good post players in Heidi Bunek and Sandy Botham (from Milwaukee and Madison, Wisconsin, respectively), and a great guard in Diondra Toney (from Chicago, Illinois). We had an impressive combination of guards and posts, and in Coach McGraw's first year, (my freshman year), we ended up winning 20 games, which was pretty good! I wasn't really homesick during the first semester of my freshman year until we got to Christmas break. All of the other kids got to go home and have a month off school, but that was when we did the bulk of our traveling, and so we only got to go home for two or three days. That's when the homesickness hit me hard. I remember we had to stay at the Jameson Inn during the Christmas break, as the dorms were closed, and I remember walking across the frozen field to go to the ACC to practice. . . it was brutally cold."*

Being a student at a school like Notre Dame is no easy task, but when you add being an athlete on top of that, it can be quite the uphill battle, especially as a freshman. Learning how to balance the academic rigors in the classroom along with the time constraints of being an athlete requires a lot of hard work and strong time management skills. However, the rewards of being a student-athlete last a lifetime, and often translate into a lifetime of success. Once again, the *Notre Dame Value Stream* gives Her students the skills to not only succeed during their time at Notre Dame, but in the many adventures they will encounter during the rest of their lives.

"I loved being a student-athlete, I thought it was the best thing. It's what I always wanted to do, from a very young age. I had always known that I wanted to play sports at the collegiate level, and I also knew what an honor and a privilege it was to play at a school like Notre Dame. I still cherish my memories of my time at Notre Dame. I was an American Studies major as a student at ND. I wanted to get a liberal arts degree, because I didn't know what I wanted to be when I grew up. I liked it because it gave me the chance to take a wide variety of classes. I also minored in Communications and Government. Some of my favorite Communications classes were in TV and Culture, because I knew at some point I wanted to try broadcasting. In addition, I knew I wanted to try coaching someday. And, I have been able to do both in my career. I coached at the college level for five years, before my husband and I had kids, and I worked as a journalist for the New York Jets, on Jets TV, during the tenure of Herm Edwards and Eric Mangini. It was a lot of fun to work for a team at the professional level. I did pre and post-game interviews on ESPN Radio, interviewed players and coaches on a weekly basis, celebrity interviews on the field on game day, and I also did some color analysis for the New York Liberty in the WNBA. I've definitely had the opportunity to put my communications classes into action."

Coach McGraw encouraged us to use our academic counselors and utilize all of the resources available to student-athletes at ND.

"I love the reaction I get when I tell people I played basketball at Notre Dame. When you tell people you went to Notre Dame, that stops them in their tracks; but when you tell them you were an athlete at ND, that really blows them away. People are always interested in hearing about it. As a student-athlete at Notre Dame, we had a crazy travel schedule, although it wasn't quite as busy as it is for student-athletes today. The furthest we would travel usually took place during Christmas break. Coach McGraw was from Philadelphia, and so that would usually be one of our destinations over Christmas break. We'd also travel to the west coast to play Stanford and UCLA, along with games in the mid-west and the south. Sometimes the travel was challenging, but we always managed. We had all the resources we needed at Notre Dame to help guide us through the demanding travel schedules and rigorous course work during our busy basketball season. Coach McGraw encouraged

> us to use our academic counselors and utilize all of the resources available to student-athletes at ND. I think travel is harder now with Notre Dame in the ACC. I remember what it was like trying to manage class, practice, games and travel. You were super stressed during exams, like every student was, but I would absolutely do it again. I wouldn't trade it for anything."

If you follow NCAA Women's Basketball, you definitely know the name Muffet McGraw. She's one of the elite coaches in the sport, and has built an impressive career for herself. Karen spoke with me about what it was like to be there for Coach McGraw's first four years at Notre Dame, and how her relationship with her beloved coach has continued and grown over the years.

> "I loved playing for Coach McGraw. She was intense, extremely competitive, and placed great importance on mastering the fundamentals. We were required to be fundamentally sound, and if you were not, she would stop in the middle of practice to work on it. It was of the utmost importance to her that we could do the basic things well. Little things like using the backboard on your layups instead of doing finger rolls were a priority for her. I have tried to carry on that philosophy in how I coach my players, but the game is a little bit different today than it was back then. Everybody wants to shoot threes and finger roll. Coach McGraw expected us to stick to the basics and fundamentals, and if you mastered those she'd encourage you to try other skills. She would challenge us with conditioning and pre-season workouts so we were battle tested mentally and physically. She was constantly giving us books to read, teaching us manners out of her etiquette books, or just leaving motivational notes in our lockers to help us improve ourselves. She definitely held us to a high standard in terms of what she expected, and she prepared us in the way she coached us. I loved playing for her."

She expected you to give her the absolute best that you had, at all times.

> "One time we were playing at Butler, and I had a really bad ankle sprain. It wasn't bad enough to keep me out for the season, or anything like that, but it did cause me to miss some games here and there. On this particular day my ankle was the size of a softball. I wrapped it up because Coach McGraw still wanted me to warm up. I wasn't sure whether or not I would be able to play, but I warmed up like she instructed. I didn't start the game, but the game was very close, and she ended up putting me in. I thought she was going to go easy on me seeing as I was hurt, but I messed up a play and she started screaming at me. She expected you to give her the absolute best that you had, at all times. And she definitely didn't like to lose. If we lost on the road, the trip home would be

pretty rough. She was intense and demanding, and she knew what she wanted out of her career as a women's basketball coach right from the beginning. When she began her coaching career at Notre Dame, she knew she wanted to go to a NCAA tournament, and she wanted to win a championship. And she started planting those seeds with us, her first team at Notre Dame."

"Here's a funny Coach McGraw story for you. A few years ago when we were back at Notre Dame for a football game we dropped in on one of Coach McGraw's basketball practices. I was trying to learn one of Coach McGraw's offenses to run with my high school team. Coach McGraw had me come out on the court and run the play called 'chin' with the team in my tailgating outfit (boots and jeans)!"

This is the question that makes each and every person pause, and rummage through their rolodex of college memories, but by the time they settle on the one or two they are going to share, it's magic. Even though I conduct most of my interviews over the phone, you can almost see their eyes light up, and you can most definitely hear the spark in their voice, as they share their favorite memories from their time traveling along the *Notre Dame Value Stream* at the University of Notre Dame. Here are Karen's.

"What was my favorite memory from my time at Notre Dame? There are so many of them! My freshman year I lived in Howard Hall, which had been a male dorm the year before, and there had been a lot of single rooms in Howard when the men lived there. Apparently our room had been a single the year before when it was a male dorm, and they had converted it into a double for the women. When we arrived the room had two desks stacked on top of each other, and two dressers stacked on top of each other, because there was so little floor space in the room. I remember moving furniture out of the room entirely because we simply had no place to put everything. It was basically a glorified closet. I have no idea how we lived like that, but now it's a great memory. Coleen Krachuk and I ended up rooming together my freshman year at ND. We went to Paul VI High School together, and we roomed together all four years at Notre Dame in Howard Hall. She and I are still good friends today."

"The bonds that I shared with my teammates and friends on the hoop squad are so special to me, along with all of the friends that I made at Notre Dame, and have still kept in touch with over the years. Coach McGraw gave birth to her son, Murph, while we were there, and it was incredible for us to go through that whole process with her. It's been an amazing journey, watching her coach throughout the years. I went to the St. Louis Final Four when they won the national championship in 2001, and I was also in Columbus last

year (2018) when they won the national championship yet again. I had such a sense of pride watching Beth Morgan break my scoring record, and then seeing her lead the Fighting Irish to the Final Four for the first time in Notre Dame Women's Basketball history. Even though they didn't win it all that year, she broke a barrier, and she helped to prove that Notre Dame could compete with the rest of the country. That definitely helped to boost them to the next level. And then when Notre Dame moved into the Big East Conference, and played the University of Connecticut several times a year, that really helped them get to the level they're at today. I have so many tremendous memories from my time on the Notre Dame Women's Basketball team. Playing with Mary Gavin, the girl I grew up with. Playing with Sara Liebscher and Krissi Davis. Sara, Krissi and I were all part of Coach McGraw's first four years at Notre Dame. We won 20 plus games during each season of Coach McGraw's first 4 years at ND. We like to claim we built the foundation! The three of us are still close today. Sara, Krissi and I were freshmen together, played all four years together, and were tri-captains together our senior year. Sara Liebscher still works at Notre Dame and we oversee the student-athlete advisory council together. It's great to have friends that you've known for thirty years."

For so many of us, college is a time when you really find out what you're made of, and a time when you learn to overcome adversity, quite possibly for the first time. The trials and tribulations that you go through in college set you up for a lifetime of success, because you've already had the experience of being knocked down, and you know how to pick yourself back up again. The *Notre Dame Value Stream* does a great job of supporting Her students and student-athletes at Notre Dame, and teaching them in a safe environment how to overcome just about anything that is placed in front of them. Karen shared with me how being a student-athlete at Notre Dame prepared her for life after college.

"It prepares you in so many ways. Being an athlete and playing at such a high level tests you. You are tested both mentally and physically, and you have to balance the demands of life both on and off the court. Today, when life gets tough, you can compare it to something that happened to you as a student-athlete. Whether it's something that is physically, mentally or emotionally challenging you know you can overcome anything. When you're making big life decisions, you have experiences to fall back on. Being challenged at that level, and being in the spotlight does prepare you for the demands you will face the rest of your life. It gives you the confidence that you can weather any storm, and get through anything life puts in front of you. The demanding schedule that you lived every day in college, the high pressure and high stress,

that's what happens when you head out into the real world. I wish I would have known how fast college was going to fly by, maybe I would have appreciated it more, and maybe I could have done more when I was there. I feel like college has changed a lot for student-athletes today. It's turned into a job for them. I never felt that way when I was a student-athlete."

I feel like college has changed a lot for student-athletes today. It's turned into a job for them. I never felt that way when I was a student-athlete.

"Yes, our preseason workouts started at 5 am, and we had to be at the track at 5:30 am. Even the things that were hard or challenging, I wouldn't trade any of it. Today, they don't have much downtime in the offseason. We actually had a month or so to be regular students, which was very nice. Student-athletes now have very little down time because the collegiate landscape is so hyper-competitive. When I was a student-athlete, it wasn't presented to us as a job, and I never felt like it was a duty. I loved it, and I worked hard because I loved it."

And just like Karen said, in the blink of an eye your four years of college are over, and it's time to move beyond the shadow of the Golden Dome and out into the world. Some of us know exactly what those next steps will look like, and others have a laundry list of things they want to try in the months and years that follow college. Karen knew two things for sure. She wanted to try her hand at coaching, and she wanted to try her hand at broadcasting, and as fate would have it she'd have the chance to try them both.

The Professional Years

"I played in Switzerland for a year after I graduated from Notre Dame (in 1991) for a club team. I absolutely loved it. They had a high standard of living in Switzerland. I learned to speak French while I was there, coached a youth team, and worked in a ski shop which was an hour away from Geneva. The town we were in was a small Swiss Mountain town called Monthey (populations 15,000). The team gave me a flat to live in and a car, and the Swiss girls would take me out on the slopes and try and teach me to become a better skier. I also had a chance to travel around Europe while I was there. I made a bunch of friends that year, a lot of whom came to our wedding in 1995. It was such an incredible experience."

"Following my year in Switzerland, I was an assistant women's basketball coach at Manhattan College for one year. Then I went back to Notre Dame where I served as a Graduate Assistant for Coach McGraw while

simultaneously earning my MSA. I worked in the basketball office all day, and then I took classes from 6 – 9 pm at night. It was a two-year program, which was perfect because it allowed me see if I wanted to coach someday, and it also allowed me to earn a Master's Degree from Notre Dame. I had the opportunity to coach some really great players, including Beth Morgan, who ended up leading Notre Dame to the Final Four for the very first time. I graduated with my MSA in May of 1995. Then in the fall of 1995 my husband and I got married at the Basilica on campus on a glorious, sunny September day. Shortly after I graduated in May, Coach McGraw offered me an assistant job, but I was getting married in September, my husband already had a job in New York City, and there was no way I could do both things. . . and so I got married and moved to New York!"

Today

"Once we got to New York, I coached at Fordham, and that was the year that Beth Morgan led Notre Dame to the Final Four. I remember watching the game, and watching Beth score 40 points in the Elite Eight game. I was jumping up and down, screaming at the game, and my husband Kevin was sitting there thinking to himself, 'Oh my gosh, she's going to kill me, she could be working there right now!' But it was one of those things where a sacrifice had to be made, and I was happy to make it. I coached for a few years, and then my husband and I decided it was time for us to start having kids. At that point I got a lead on a job opening with the New York Jets."

"We were living in New York when I started interviewing for the job with the Jets in July. In September of that year, my husband and I were moving out to Ridgewood, New Jersey, and on the exact day that we moved I received the call that I got the job with the Jets. This meant that I had to get up extra early in order to commute from New Jersey to Hempstead, New York to do the job, but it was totally worth it. I did broadcasting for Jets TV, and pre and post-game work on ESPN Radio. For Jets TV, I interviewed coaches and players, and the interviews would get posted onto their website. This was ground breaking at the time, as it was before everyone did everything online. I got to cover a lot of great players, had access to interview players both down on the field and in the locker room. But once my third child was born, I decided it was time to put my reporting career on the back burner."

"Then I got involved in youth coaching, which lead to me coaching at the local high school. It wasn't what I thought I'd be doing, but it has been very rewarding to be able to help young women build their confidence through sports. I've had the opportunity to coach both of my twin girls. They are seniors *this year (2019). One of them is running track, and the other one is playing basketball. I have coached them since they were in the 5th grade. To be able to give back to the young women in my community has been such a blessing to me. And high school girls are so funny!" <laughs>*

My husband and I decided our gift would be given as an endowment to Coach McGraw (in 2015), which made her the first coach at Notre Dame to be endowed.

"A few years ago my husband and I decided we wanted to do something to give back to the University of Notre Dame. It took us a while to figure out exactly what we wanted to do. We knew we wanted to make a gift to the University, but we also wanted to make sure we could do it in a personal way, and make the gift impactful. Sara Liebscher, who was a four-year teammate of mine and now works in athletic advancement and development at Notre Dame, helped Kevin and I figure out the best way for us to help the University. She was in the process of initiating endowments for coaches at Notre Dame, and had been studying how Stanford endows their coaches. Stanford is the gold standard and has been extremely successful in getting all of their coaches endowed, and that is the direction Notre Dame is trying to head. In speaking with Sara, we were able to figure out how to do it at Notre Dame, and my husband and I decided our gift would be given as an endowment to Coach McGraw (in 2015), which made her the first coach at Notre Dame to be endowed. Since Sara began this initiative, they've endowed seven or eight more coaches, but Coach McGraw is the only female coach who has been endowed. So now we're working toward not only getting more women coaches at Notre Dame endowed, but getting all of the Notre Dame coaches endowed."

"It was special for my husband and I to be able to set up the endowment for Coach McGraw. With all of the accolades she's accomplished over the years, including being enshrined in the Naismith Basketball Hall of Fame, she deserves it. The head coaches for football, basketball, lacrosse, tennis, and the athletic director all have been endowed, along with several of the assistant football coaches. Now we're trying to get all of the coaches endowed."

"It meant a lot to me that my husband, Kevin, wanted to set up the endowment for Coach McGraw. He grew up with six sisters so he has a lot of strong women in his life. His dad went to Notre Dame, and he grew up loving Notre Dame. He listened to Tony Roberts on the radio, and traveled to ND with his family to attend football games every year. Five of his six sisters went to St. Mary's, and he went to Notre Dame. Today he's the CEO of his company, Annaly Capital Management, and 40% of his employees are women; which

is a lot compared to many companies on Wall Street. He's very conscientious in giving women opportunities, and the accolades which they deserve. He and Sara came up with the endowment idea all on their own."

I love asking the former athletes that I interview to share some words of wisdom for aspiring high school student-athletes looking to play sports at the next level. With Karen a former student-athlete and a current high school coach, she has a unique perspective on what kids today need to be successful at the next level.

"For starters, I would tell them when they get to college to enjoy every minute of wearing their college uniform because it truly goes so fast. The dynamic of being a student-athlete has changed since I was in school. The current crop of student-athletes have access to so much information, right at their fingertips. Everything they do, every big play they make, they can immediately see on their phones. We really didn't care. We played for the love of the game. I coach our high school basketball team, and I watch what they go through in the recruiting process. It is unique and special to be a recruited athlete. The pressure placed on them starts earlier and earlier. I wish high school players got more enjoyment out of the game, and out of the recruiting process; so often it's not very much fun for them. Maybe the parents are partly to blame, too. I coach in a town that is a big lacrosse town, and as freshmen they were trying to make collegiate decisions, as that is when it happens for the lacrosse players. Recently they've changed this rule, which I think is so much better for the kids. How can a freshman possibly know where they want to go to college? So much happens in four years of high school as far as the maturation process goes. By the time they get to college they are so pressurized. I wish high school student-athletes could get more enjoyment out of both the process and the game."

"In both high school and college, the student-athlete's schedules are so demanding. They need to find a balance between academics and athletics, and so often they don't find it. And then what happens is they don't get enough sleep, which leads to them not being able to perform on the court or in the classroom. They think they need more, more, more: more workouts, more conditioning. But the big focus needs to be on nutrition, managing stress levels, and getting an adequate amount of sleep. It's so important for them to figure out how to relax, and how to manage their schedule using time management."

Karen's husband, Kevin Keyes, also attended the University of Notre Dame and played tennis his freshman and sophomore year. *"My husband Kevin played tennis at Notre Dame but he hurt his shoulder his sophomore year and that ended his tennis career. He was a tremendous basketball player* *in high school, along with tennis. When he was at ND, he would play a lot of pickup basketball with the guys from the ND basketball team on the courts behind the old bookstore. One of Kevin's friends, John Buscher (nickname – Booger), introduced Kevin and I at Bridget McGuire's Filling Station one night (a local watering hole in South Bend), and the next day we ran into each other playing basketball at the bookstore courts. He was tying up his Converses when he said hi to me. (Kevin and Booger won bookstore basketball together and Booger was named 'Mr. Bookstore.' They still talk about it today!) Kevin and I dated through undergraduate school, got engaged (on campus) while I was in graduate school, and were married at the Basilica in September of 1995. We also celebrated his parent's 50th wedding anniversary at the log cabin chapel on campus. A lot of our family history is wrapped around the University. In fact, our two oldest daughters just found out they were accepted to Notre Dame. We are ecstatic that they will be the third generation of Keyes to attend Notre Dame."*

Karen and her husband Kevin currently live in New Jersey with their three children, Katie (18), Cassie (18), and Johnny (13).

Karen (Robinson) Keyes, her husband Kevin, and their three children: Katie, Cassie, and Johnny. (Photo courtesy of Simon Luethi.)

Karen Keyes' Lessons from the Notre Dame Value Stream:

- As a high school student athlete, enjoy not only the game, but the recruiting process as well. It is unique and special to be a recruited athlete.
- When you get to college, enjoy every minute of wearing your college uniform because it truly goes so fast.
- Find a balance between your academics and your athletics. Focus on your nutrition, managing stress levels, and getting an adequate amount of sleep. It's so important to figure out how to relax, and how to manage your schedule using time management. This will be an often used skill for the rest of your life.

Portrait of football player Charles Stafford, May 1992.
(Photo courtesy of Notre Dame Archives.)

CHAPTER NINETEEN

The Mental Motivator

Charles Stafford

(Notre Dame Football – Class of 1995)

Charles Stafford grew up in a household with an older brother and an older sister who were both very active in sports, and a family that encouraged him to get involved himself. Growing up in a family that moved around several times, sports provided the perfect outlet for the Stafford children to easily establish bonds with their new peers each time they relocated. Coming from a family who moved so much, how did Charles become interested in playing football at the University of Notre Dame? This is Charles Stafford's story.

"I was born in Detroit, MI, and lived there until I was in fourth or fifth grade, at which point we moved to Norwalk, CA, near the Long Beach area. I always say my parents made us feel like we were in the military, without actually being in the military, with as much as we moved around. We lived in Norwalk until the middle of my junior year of high school, when my parents once again relocated to Barlett, IL, where I went to Elgin High School. There are two Elgin High Schools in that area, and I attended the Maroons. And finally, when I was at Notre Dame, my dad moved to Federal Way, in Washington, which is kind of funny because that was where Lake Dawson was from."

"Growing up my older brother and sister were always involved in sports, and as the youngest, you observe what your older siblings are doing. I noticed the attention they were getting when they were doing well at sports and I thought, 'Hey, I like attention, so maybe I should get into sports too.' My older brother loved football, and he played it a lot. He enjoyed the physicality of football, and eventually I decided that would be my path as well, and so I began to play football. I didn't actually start playing tackle football until my freshman year of high school, which is not the normal path that most kids take, especially for kids who end up playing football in college for a school like Notre Dame."

"Living and going to high school in the Chicago area, there are Notre Dame supporters, both fans and alumni, all over. It has one of the largest subway alumni followings in the world, and as a result of that I got a lot of exposure to Notre Dame. Many of my friends told me how special it was, and when they and others realized that I was being recruited by Notre Dame they would ask me, 'Why on earth would you look at any other school?' Being from California I also considered UCLA and Stanford, and within the Chicago area I was interested in Northwestern as well. During that time, my parents drilled into me that my education was going to be important, and thus I tried to make sure that every school I considered was known for their academics. Ironically, I may have been one of the few kids in America who didn't have a great appreciation for Notre Dame, but as I said, living in Chicago, that gap was bridged pretty quickly. I learned that ND had academics to go along with that rich history of football and thus it fit well."

"Adrian Jarrell was my host when I visited Notre Dame. At the time I felt pretty confident with his depiction of what it was like to be a student-athlete at Notre Dame. If you know Adrian, he's such a wonderful guy, and we still communicate to this day. What I remember most about my official visit to ND was this, I was very fortunate to have had Adrian as my host because he's a very *genuine guy. If you do enough recruiting visits, sometimes you find people who are concerned with how you're going to impact their playing time, and other times you're going to find people who are concerned with making sure you get an accurate feel for the University so that you make a good decision. I was fortunate, Adrian was definitely interested in making sure I had a good experience and that I understood Notre Dame and why he choose it. After my visit, Notre Dame just felt like a good place and a really good fit for me. Adrian did a superb job at getting me exposed to different aspects of the campus. You don't have a lot of time, if you will, when you're making those visits, and he definitely took the lead on my visit, so that helped me make my decision."*

As an alum of the University Notre Dame, I know from personal experience, from successes as well as failures, the rigors of being a student at Notre Dame. And as I do each and every one of these interviews, I am continually blown away. The internal fortitude, determination, and fearlessness that these men and women need to have to be a successful student-athlete at Notre Dame always makes me pause.

The Notre Dame Years

> ***It reinforced for me the importance that I better get my priorities in order quickly and start to understand what it takes to handle the student part of being a 'student-athlete.'***

"You know what, it was life altering for me. I thought I had a pretty good amount of structure growing up, but I quickly realized I may have had what I thought was structure, but I didn't have the kind of structure I needed to go along with the new amount of freedom I had: freedom to make not only good but bad decisions as well. Time management was something I had to come to terms with because there is no one making you do anything at this point. You get up, you go to class, and you have to make sure you're on time to practice. I remember in one of my earlier classes, being in an auditorium and the professor was speaking about the types of people that were in this class (it was a class of freshmen). He was asking us, 'How many of you were valedictorian? How many of you were salutatorian?' And all these other classifications that I had never heard of before. It quickly became very clear that I was the only one in the class that would never stand up. It reinforced for me the importance that I better get my priorities in order quickly and start to understand what it takes to handle the student part of being a 'student-athlete.'"

What so many of us took for granted during our time at Notre Dame was that we were not alone. Not only were our peers going through the exact same pitfalls that we were, but we also had this amazing safety net as we traveled along the *Notre Dame Value Stream*. A safety net of counselors, teachers, graduate assistants, upperclassmen and rectors among countless others to encourage us and keep us from sinking in the rough waters through which we were sailing.

> *"I was very fortunate. I had great upperclassmen who mentored me. I liked the fact that the football program made the freshmen go to the library to study, which reinforced the habits and behaviors which were necessary to be a successful student-athlete at Notre Dame. It was tough initially, but it definitely became something that was much easier for me to deal with as I got a couple of years under my belt, and started to understand how to manage my time. Time management was the key to my success. The funny thing about the exercise that my professor conducted in class, the composition of my classmates, that dynamic also existed on the football field. Every person who came to Notre Dame to play football (or any sport for that matter) was the Rocket Ismail of their school most likely. And then you get to Notre Dame and not only are you getting humbled in the classroom, you are also getting humbled on the field. I had roommates who could wake up, stroll to practice in flip flops, and run a 4.3 out of a dead sleep; that wasn't happening for me. Both sides of the student-athlete equation were very humbling, and tested your internal fortitude. As our hosts told us on our visit, you can fold up your tent and go home, or you can fight and try to make yourself better. It definitely took some soul searching to get through it, but like most things it was worth it once you got to the other side. And yes, there were a lot of calls home that first year. Fortunately, most of us decided to stay and try to figure it out."*

Want to know one of my favorite parts of doing these interviews and telling these stories? The fact that years, or even decades later, there is no shortage of love and respect for Coach Holtz, and for everything he did for them to guide them towards the various paths they are successfully traveling down today. Coach Holtz was as big of a part of the *Notre Dame Value Stream*, maybe bigger even than anything else they encountered during their time at Notre Dame.

> ***The experiences we went through with Coach Holtz are what every parent hopes for, I just wish I would have better understood how special it was when I had it, if that makes sense.***

> *"I think about my time playing for Coach Holtz, to this very day, and the first thing that comes to my mind is that I wish I would have appreciated it more in the moment. The majority of what I do in my life, especially in my*

professional career, is a direct reflection of my time spent under Coach Holtz and the guidance he gave me during my five years at Notre Dame. The best way to describe it is life altering. From the simple things he preached to us: 'Have a plan, focus on the plan, let it be the guide to your success so that if things aren't going well you can go back to the plan and get yourself back on track.' To his fundamentals of love, trust, and accountability. Things that I find myself saying daily in the business world, and to my kids. Little quips that he used to say to us. For example, Coach Holtz used to tell us to set our watches to LLH (Louis Leo Holtz) time. And he told us over and over, if you're on time you're late. If you want to be on time, get there early. My kids can recite those speeches because they hear them from me all the time. The experiences we went through with Coach Holtz are what every parent hopes for, I just wish I would have better understood how special it was when I had it, if that makes sense. I think about the types of people whom Coach Holtz exposed us to as players. We met former Secretary of State Colin Powell, and businessman and published author Harvey Mackay. He put you in contact and exposed you to people who had done pretty big things. They had to work for it, but yes, they had achieved great things. He always had a way of making you feel like you should expect the best, and you should get more, you just have to work for it. His philosophies fall right in line with being a parent, and everything you do in life."

Every successful coach, at any level of sports has their own unique set of fundamentals, work ethic, philosophies, and habits, that when you add them all together creates a recipe for achieving that coveted and triumphant victory: and the ability to achieve it week after week. Coach Holtz was no different.

"Ironically I think it's something fundamental: it's consistency. Every week he talked about 'How are we going to win this week?' And talked about going back to 'The Plan.' Even through the prayer he did every single Friday night at the Holiday Inn we went to down in Plymouth, Ind. 'The future is a whole string of nows.' He had consistency in using it week in and week out, and at some point you could recite it all by yourself. In that regard he got us all on the same page, going in the same direction, and with a common theme. I really think, especially as I've gotten older and think about how I conduct myself in the business world, at the end of the day that consistency is the key to a successful coach or leader. That coach or leader needs to make sure their people (whether it is players or employees) are clear in regards to what the objectives are, clear about how we are going to achieve those objectives, and then take accountability for their role in getting there. Coach Holtz did that

> *consistently during the five years I played for him. By the time I graduated from Notre Dame I felt like I could recite his whole spiel from memory. Which is great, because it shows the consistency in his message. That's where his strength comes from."*

Every athletic career at Notre Dame is filled with countless memories, both on and off the field. Picking one favorite memory is not easy to do, but most athletes discover that one memory does eventually rise to the top. Charles was no exception.

> *"Believe it or not, the particular memory which is my favorite Notre Dame Football memory, didn't involve me playing a significant role in the results we achieved. However, what I felt in that moment is something I won't soon forget. In 1993, I lived in Grace Hall, and we had a momentous win over Florida State. The Number 1 sign went up on top of Grace Hall and was lit up for everyone to see. The energy on campus that next week leading up to the ND vs. BC game, which we won't ever talk about <laughs>; it was just electric. We had the Pep Rally in front of Grace Hall, and I remember being on stage and getting to speak in front of the whole student body. The whole campus was just on fire, if you will; it was so alive. That Florida State game in 1993, even though I didn't play a major role in the game, is something I'll never forget. Mike Miller (who was a receiver like me) and I had a photo taken together after the game which ran on the AP Wire, and I got so many calls from friends and family. People who I didn't really even know were calling to say they saw my photo in the paper. That game and the whole week that followed: if that doesn't give you chills as a college athlete, I don't know what will. That was quite a memorable week for me. Obviously that season didn't end the way we wanted it to, so that was memorable for a different reason; no one can take that moment away from me or my teammates. I've never seen the campus with that much energy. I'm sure the current Women's Basketball Team (2018 National Champs) have that now, but when I was there it was the biggest moment that I had a role in, no matter how big or small. When you think about life and life's ups and downs, in a two week span I don't know if you could've had a more extreme up, followed by a more extreme down. But it was a life lesson for us for sure, because we learned that the sun will come up the next day, even if you don't want it to."*

College for most students and student-athletes is a time of discovery. A time to discover who you are at your core, who you want to become moving forward, and to decide what life path you will set out on, knowing that it will probably change multiple times during this adventure we call life. The challenges faced while at college may be different for each one of us, but at the end of the day we all can relate to the struggles that defined us as we headed onward towards adulthood.

> "My biggest challenge, when I think of on the field challenges anyway, was coming to terms with the fact that I was no longer the best player on the field. Every player on that Notre Dame squad had previously been the best player, and we all struggled to figure out, in this highly competitive dynamic, what is my role? How do I fit? What can I be the best in? One of the things I worked really hard to accomplish was this. I wanted to be the guy who practiced the hardest, who got to practice on time or even early, who stayed as late as he could, and who knew his plays. I tried to find ways that maybe weren't as physical as they would've been for me in high school, where things were much easier."

> "I tried to find ways in which I could still shine, that weren't in those traditional ways that I had done historically. That was a challenge for me. Psychologically coming to terms with that, and mentally trying to figure out, how do I find my way? That was tough. Similarly, as far as in the classroom goes, my challenge was realizing that I didn't have to be the valedictorian to do well. I just had to do my best. I felt good getting my degree, and then I felt even better in graduate school during my fifth year of eligibility. I got all A's in graduate school, and to this day I'll tell anyone who'll listen, I got all A's in graduate school at Notre Dame! I had one more year to finish, but while I was there, I got all A's. Being a student-athlete at Notre Dame, it was humbling. Being humbled at ND, both on and off the field, was probably the biggest challenge I faced. One of the most valuable lessons I got at Notre Dame was to be able to overcome failure, or as Coach Holtz called it, adversity. He'd always say at the beginning of every year, 'We're going to have three things this season that we can't control. We don't know when they're going to come, but they're going to happen. Our job is to get over that, find another way, and get it done.' And that's what life's really about."

I try, whenever I can, to toss in a bonus question from a fellow teammate, and before I interviewed Charles I caught up with Bobby Brown, who said to ask Charles about Culver Academy.

> "Oh my goodness, yes. The first word that comes to mind is, hot. It's funny that he brought that up because my favorite Coach Holtz story also involves Culver, believe it or not. I remember Culver first and foremost because it was hot. It was so hot that players slept in the stands of the ice rink just to try and get some relief from the heat, as none of the rooms had air conditioning. I still to this day wonder what lesson was I supposed to take from that experience,

> of being in that brutal heat day in and day out. <laughs> Other than the fact that to this very day I hate heat. It did, however, make me have a greater appreciation for water and the role that water plays in your life, because you absolutely need it. I think of that experience and all I can do is shake my head, because it was just so hot."
>
> "All of this talk about the Culver Academy brings me to my favorite Coach Holtz story. There were a number of players at camp that had this great idea that we should throw Coach Holtz into the lake that was on the property at the Culver Academy. It was so hot, and we figured, we're getting towards the end of camp, we should throw Coach Holtz into the lake. Keep in mind, that sounded great and all, but then you have another problem. Who is actually going to throw Coach Holtz into the lake? I knew I wasn't going to be the one to throw Coach into the lake. That kind of activity you reserve for the Derrick Mayes and Ron Powlus type of guys in the group. I'm not throwing Coach anywhere. We needed someone who had a little more of Coach's love than I did. So, we kind of hemmed and hawed, and then for whatever reason we decided not to do it. Now, let me flash forward to later in the year. Us not throwing Coach Holtz into the lake ended up being a very good idea because that ended up being the same year that Coach had neck surgery. I always think back on that decision to not throw Coach into the lake and think, man, if we would have done that, it could have ended very badly. We really could have accelerated that neck surgery. I don't know why that particular story sticks with me so much. Probably because of the fear that I felt just thinking about throwing Holtz into the water and knowing, yeah, I'm not going be a part of that. The funny thing about both of the memories I've shared about Culver Academy. . . they both involved the heat, and water. That's so funny that Bobby thought about that."

As Charles and I were walking down memory lane, we shifted back to that 1993 football season. The season that we all remember as not quite ending the way we had hoped it would. We have all, at one point or another, faced the stark reality that "life is not fair," but not everyone learns it in such a way that it leaves a lasting sting.

> "I'm not going to make myself sad, but I really thought that we had achieved that elusive national championship in 1993. Every year before that 1993 season, they would have split the polls and had co-champions. But not for us. Not for us. It's funny, we played Florida State again during my fifth year at Notre Dame, and we had a luncheon the Friday before the game. They had fake football helmets sitting on all of the tables as centerpieces. Each helmet was painted with ND colors on one side, and Florida State colors on the other

> side. And so I took the helmet from my table and had Coach Holtz sign the ND side, and Coach Bowden sign the Florida State side. Yep, I was that guy, 'Hey coach, I realize we're going to play you tomorrow, but can you sign this for me.' Yeah, I didn't care. So I have a helmet in my house to this day that has both coaches' signatures on it. And I still think that was such a great idea. And then I think, one day my kid is going to be smiling when he sells this. <laughs> And I'm going to be shaking my head somewhere."

At the end of four or five years at a school like Notre Dame, our journey along the *Notre Dame Value Stream* filled our tool box with the valuable skills and accessories needed for us to step forward toward our next adventure.

Today

> "Of course, every player convinces themselves that they have aspirations of playing in the pros. I did my Notre Dame pro day, and talked to some agents, but I knew deep down that it probably wasn't going to be in the cards for me. And it turned out that it wasn't. Unlike some players who have a difficult time wrapping their head around such a reality, the realization that I wasn't going to play pro wasn't problematic for me because in my mind, I already knew it. I knew in my heart, I probably wasn't as tall as I needed to be, or as fast as I needed to be; I also knew I had a good run and I was okay with that. At that point it became a matter of identifying what I wanted to do next. After graduation I worked with Tracy Graham, Cliff Stroud, and a few others and started a company in South Bend called CBD, with Jerome Bettis as the main principle. I didn't even have to leave South Bend right away after I graduated. It was an IT focused company, with internet access and websites, and we did that for three years or so. That was my first introduction to the business world. We were our own 'owners,' and we all had a lot of good intent, but not a lot of good experience. I learned so much from that experience which still pays me dividends to this day. That was my first entry to the work force as my own boss, which was a scary proposition."

> "That first job with CBD got me started in IT, and I have stayed in the IT realm ever since. I worked in telecom for quite a while for Lucent Technologies, which then became Avaya; I worked for them in Indiana, Kentucky, Texas and Denver. My experience in telecom helped me to expand and grow, and to understand what it meant to manage people. That's when I started to come into my own as far as starting to realize how to apply all of those things Coach Holtz told us over the years. It also made me realize that I had listened to Coach more than I thought I had back in college. I would be coaching people, and I'd hear myself say something and think, yep, I know where I've heard that

before. I knew that I had listened to what Coach Holtz had said to us back at Notre Dame, but I didn't realize how much his words had truly molded and shaped me. That was the path that got me into the IT world, and I'm still working in the IT business today."

"My degree from Notre Dame was in Psychology, and I chose that on purpose. I knew that no matter what I did, I would have to work with people. It's funny how insightful I was as a late teen, early twenty-something, to make that kind of decision. I like to think and analyze things, and my wife says I like to watch nerd TV; so it was the perfect fit for me. I always knew the more I could understand why people think the way they do, what motivates them, and what gets them up in the morning: the better I would be able to impact, influence and guide them (assuming I got into those type of roles). There's not a day that goes by I'm not thankful I chose the path I did because it helps me tremendously. IT people are smart, but at the same time very unique. My psychology degree has really helped me to better understand, relate and communicate with others. I'm thankful for my degree every single day. As I've gotten older, and developed a greater appreciation for the spiritual part of my life, I've realized that each one of us has been put on our specific path for a reason. It may not have seemed purposeful at the time, but I truly believe that a higher power has a plan for each and every one of us."

Embarking on the journey of a student-athlete at a Division I school such as Notre Dame is not something to take lightly. But when armed with the knowledge and wisdom of someone who has already gone through, it's not only possible to survive, but to survive and succeed at the highest of levels. The *Notre Dame Value Stream* arms each and every one of its travelers with the wisdom to not only sail it to their next destination, but to also pass that wisdom on to the next group of travelers who follow them.

"The biggest piece of advice that I would give to current student-athletes is to get involved in their community at large, beyond their sport and beyond their teammates. That is one of the things that I regret, not getting involved with my fellow students and peers as I truly should have done. When you think about the types of students who go to Notre Dame, these are people who are going to change the world, to put it bluntly. And their parents are people who are currently impacting the world. I wish I would have understood that when I was in college. I was so focused on going to practice, going to class, trying to fit in and have a good time; often I forgot that I was also there to catapult myself forward and help build the foundation for what I was going to do later on in life. I hope that student-athletes today understand the importance

> *of building those relationships. So that when they get out of school, and have certain interests, they can use those contacts to get in touch with their fellow alumni. It can not only help them professionally but personally and spiritually as well. Yes, student-athletes can use their networking skills to get into a certain job or industry, but even bigger than that, those skills can connect them with people who share their passion for faith or community and in turn impact those who need their help. Do your best as a student-athlete to set those connections in place while you are still in school. I wish I would have done a much better job at that."*

In learning about what sets Charles on fire as far as his spiritual passion goes, I asked him to talk about his involvement in his parish, St. Albert the Great, as a Vice Chair on their Pastoral Parish Council.

> *"Our Parish Pastoral Council is a body of parishioners who consult and assist our pastor with how the parish is supported. We work on the types of strategies that we need to help further the mission of our parish. It's something that I've always wanted to get more involved in, as far as my spirituality goes. It's a good avenue for me to make sure I'm developing myself spiritually, and since my children go to my parish school, it gives me an opportunity to make sure they are getting the proper education and spiritual direction. It is great for me both personally and from a community perspective. I like to say I'm a late bloomer. I've always had spirituality, but now I have come to understand what it means. I hope everyone gets that awakening at some point in their life because before this I didn't know what I was missing. My philosophy on having faith is this, it's not about what faith you are, it's about having faith. Just believe in something, please. Believe in something bigger than yourself. At the end of the day, as long as we're all looking up in the air when we're praying, at least we're all looking in the same direction."*

Charles also has two philanthropic organizations that are near and dear to his heart.

> *"There are two organizations that are special to me. One is the Muscular Dystrophy Association. I had an older brother who died when I was young from Muscular Dystrophy and so that has always been something that's been important to me. It hits me on a personal level. Obviously, anything that people can do to help the research and mission of the association, to continue to move that forward, that means a lot to me. And then, second, a woman that I work with, her daughter was at St. Jude Children's Hospital for many years, and through the power of their work, just attended her senior prom. St. Jude is an*

> *organization that impacts many lives and I have been fortunate to have seen firsthand the incredible work they are doing with children. I had never been exposed to St. Jude before this situation occurred, and I fell in love with not just their mission, but how they execute it. It's one thing to say you believe in something, but to execute in the way they do is pretty phenomenal. And what makes it more impressive is that it wasn't even my situation, and so to be an outside observer and to feel the way I do about St. Jude, is quite moving."*

Charles currently lives in Louisville, Kentucky, with his wife Shannon, and their two boys: Brandon (13) and Isiah (8).

> *"I love being a dad. Raising children definitely helps you to stay focused. Being a parent is a responsibility right now, and it is a responsibility for the future. My wife and I, we try and stay in the moment, which is not always easy when they are doing boy stuff. I was fortunate enough to meet my wife, Shannon, who was a student at St. Mary's while I was at Notre Dame. Everything else that I experienced at Notre Dame (football and academics) pales in comparison to meeting my wife. Her dad went to Notre Dame, and to be back in Louisville, and to have my sons attending the same elementary school that her father attended, is pretty great. You talk about how people are connected and how destiny plays a role in our lives. For me to see my kids taking the same path through the Louisville school system that her dad did, that is very special. Being fortunate enough to meet my soulmate while I was at Notre Dame, that is something which is very memorable for me. My wife and I have been married for 18 years, and together for much longer than that, and it is something that I am equally as proud of from my time at Notre Dame. And I'm not in the dog house. . . I'm not saying that because I'm in the dog house. <laughs>*

Since my initial interview with Charles, he lost his dad to cancer. *"This loss has been very difficult for me, but also has been an opportunity for me to reinforce my faith and focus. Life is difficult, and sometime feels unfair, but as I said earlier, you follow the plan and keep moving forward. We are all here to achieve something special, I believe my father simply completed his. I love you dad."*

Charles Stafford's Lessons from the Notre Dame Value Stream:

- Learn how to manage your time, and make it a priority to get good grades. Time management was something I had to come to terms with because there is no one making you do anything at this point. But once I figured it out, time management was the key to my success: both in college, and life after college.

Charles Stafford, his wife Shannon, and their two boys: Brandon and Isiah.

- Get involved in your community at large, beyond your sport and beyond your teammates. That is one of the things that I regret, not getting involved with my fellow students and peers as I truly should have done. When you think about the types of students who go to schools such as Notre Dame, these are people who are going to change the world, to put it bluntly. And their parents are people who are currently impacting the world. I wish I would have understood that when I was in college.

- Understand the importance of building relationships, so that when you get out of school, and have certain interests, you can use those contacts to get in touch with their fellow students. It can not only help you professionally but personally and spiritually as well. Yes, you can use your networking skills to get into a certain job or industry, but even bigger than that, those skills can connect you with people who share your passion for faith or community and in turn impact those who need your help. Do your best as a student-athlete to set those connections in place while you are still in school.

Marty Olosky (No. 74) and the 1963 Notre Dame football team.
(Photo courtesy of Notre Dame Archives.)

CHAPTER TWENTY

The Guidance Counselor

Martin 'Marty' Olosky

(Notre Dame Football – Class of 1964)

As a high school football player in the 1950s, you and your team were the main event in pretty much any town in America on a Friday night. Unlike today, where you can find a college or professional football game on television almost every night of the week, in the 1950s Friday nights were dedicated to watching your local high school football team play. And if you were looking for Marty Olosky on a Friday night as he attended Flint Holy Redeemer High school, that's exactly where you would have found him. As a standout football player in the Flint parochial football league, you would have expected Marty to go on to play football at any one of the excellent universities in the great state of Michigan, but Marty had other plans. How did Marty travel from Flint, MI to South Bend, IN to play football at the University of Notre Dame? This is Martin "Marty" Olosky's story.

> "Back when I played football, in the late 1950s, there was much less pressure placed on student-athletes to select which college or university they were going to play for as the recruiting process started much later than it does today. Today recruiters begin to urge the student-athletes whom they are pursuing to commit to a particular college or university as early as the ninth or tenth grade, but when I was in high school, the recruiters didn't really start contacting you until you were in your senior year. By the time you were a senior, though, if you were a decent football player, the scholarship offers would start rolling in. There were several Michigan schools that were interested in me coming to play football for them including Michigan State, the University of Michigan, Central Michigan University, Eastern Michigan University, Western Michigan University, and the University of Detroit. In addition to the Michigan schools that were interested in me, I was also being recruited by the University of Notre Dame. ND was the only out of state school that was looking at me, and so my dad and I flew down to South Bend for a visit. I really liked the campus and what I saw of the football team. Head coach Joe Kuharich, and line coach Dick Stanfield, also must have liked what they saw in me because I ended up getting a scholarship offer to play football for them at Notre Dame. I played high school football in Flint, Michigan, for Holy Redeemer High School, and we played in a parochial football league against other Catholic high schools, as well as some public high schools. In the 1950s and 1960s, Notre Dame recruited a lot of kids from parochial schools, and so I'm sure that helped me get on their radar."

As I was reading up on Notre Dame's 1960 football team, which was Marty's freshman year, they talked about the size of Marty and one of his teammates, "Of the ten guards on the freshmen squad Tom Finneran and Marty Olosky are the heaviest at 225 pounds, while Finneran is two inches taller than Olosky at 6-3."[7] Marty may have been big at the time, but in today's football standards, he would be considered somewhat small.

> "The thing about football is, back when I played, the players weren't as big as they are today. I was 6'1" tall and weighed 220 pounds, which was pretty big for a linemen, but today you wouldn't even be offered a scholarship for that size. You have to be at least 6'5" and weigh upwards of 280 pounds. They certainly weren't as big then as they are today."

1960 Football Team Stats from: www.archives.nd.edu/alumnus/vol_0038/vol_0038_issue_0005.pdf

Being a student-athlete at a school like University of Notre Dame has always been a challenging endeavor. Notre Dame requires her student-athletes to not only perform, but to excel, both on and off the field. But the *Notre Dame Value Stream* has perfected this journey over the years, and has this innate gift of knowing exactly what Her students need, in both good times and bad times. Marty spoke to me about what it was like to be a student-athlete at ND in the 1960s and the unique opportunities that Notre Dame offered that many other schools did not.

The Notre Dame Years

> *"Being a student-athlete at Notre Dame was a great experience for me. One of the things I particularly liked about being a student-athlete at Notre Dame was that as a freshman, they did not put you in a dorm with a bunch of other football players. You had to room with non-student-athletes, and I think that was a really good opportunity for us as football players to meet students on campus who were outside of the football team. Living in the dorm the way we did, with athletes and non-athletes mixed together, it was the perfect gateway to meet students who were first and foremost not on the football team with you, but to also meet students who weren't in your major as well. A lot of schools had football only, or athletic dorms. With Notre Dame not having dorms dedicated to student-athletes, they forced you to interact with students who were outside of your little bubble. By doing it this way, you had a chance to meet students from all walks of life, who were on all different kinds of academic paths. My freshman year roommate was a music major, and I was a history major with a minor in math. He was also from Michigan, which is probably why we got placed together, but I got along with him very well, and it was nice to come home from practice and hang out with someone who was not on the football team with me."*

Marty's first year at Notre Dame was the second year for head coach Joe Kuharich. The 1960 football season began with great optimism. Many believed that with a year under his belt, and a solid understanding of the football program at Notre Dame, Coach Kuharich would return Notre Dame to its tradition of excellence, after the average 5-5 record from his first year. Many of the pre-season polls even had Notre Dame ranked in the top ten. But, alas, the high hopes that so many had for Notre Dame that season did not come to fruition. Marty explained to me what it was like to play under the two head coaches he played for at Notre Dame, and the challenges that you face when things don't go as you want them to go out on the field.

> *"For my first three years at Notre Dame, Joe Kuharich was the head coach, and for my last year, Hughie (Hugh) Devore was our interim head coach.*

> *Joe Kuharich was a good coach, he just had a tremendous amount of pressure on him. The teams I played on at Notre Dame were average at best, (1960: 2-8, 1961: 5-5, 1962: 5-5, 1963: 2-7). And if you're the head coach at ND and you're not winning more than half of your games, you are going to be viewed under a very strong microscope. They actually forced him to resign at the end of the 1962 season. It's not as though he didn't have good athletes playing for him, because Notre Dame always manages to recruit good athletes. Some of the guys who played for Kuharich ended up doing quite well later on in the NFL (Jack Snow), and winning the Heisman Trophy while still at Notre Dame (John Huarte); it's not as though Coach Kuharich didn't have the guns in his arsenal. John Huarte hardly played during his first three years at Notre Dame, and then Coach Parseghian came in and turned him into a Heisman Trophy winner. Notre Dame always has talent out there on the field, they just didn't have the right leader at the helm when I was there."*

> *"And then following the departure of Coach Kuharich, Hughie Devore was selected as the interim head coach, and unfortunately, he was not well respected by his players. It was complete mayhem on the team that year. During my senior season at ND I got injured. I tore a ligament during the Pittsburgh game and had to sit out the rest of the season, but the guys who were still out there playing for him, they were really upset that he had been chosen to be our head coach that year. He had done really well with the freshmen team, but he just wasn't that good of a head coach, and many of the guys on the team felt he shouldn't have been given the head coaching reigns."*

The game of college football today is played quite differently from how it was played when Marty was at Notre Dame in the 1960s. It's even much different from when I was watching college football at Notre Dame in the 1990s. Marty spoke with me about challenges of playing such a violent sport, and the toll that injuries and the daily grind took on his body.

> *"During my senior season, I injured my knee (torn ligament) during the Pittsburgh game (at home), which was near the end of the season on November 9th. Sadly this prevented me from traveling with the team to New York City for the Yankee Stadium game versus Syracuse. I also had a ligament injury during my junior season in the Iowa game (at home), which was also near the end of the season on November 24th. And of course back in the 1960s they didn't have all of the knee braces and injury prevention techniques that they have today. Also, cut blocking, which is illegal today, was very prevalent when I played football. People would hit you from behind, which would*

> *oftentimes cause those ligament tearing injuries. Football certainly wasn't an easy sport to play, and it was definitely not for the faint of heart."*

As Marty was from Michigan, I asked him what it was like to return to his home state and play against the University of Michigan State, where many of his friends were attending college.

> *"It was actually really fun. When I was a sophomore, we traveled to East Lansing to play Michigan State University, and I remember that was definitely one of the highlights of my time playing football at Notre Dame. It was great to go back to Michigan, and play the Spartans in their stadium. That game, when I was a sophomore, was the first time I played Michigan State, as freshmen back then typically weren't allowed to play. Only sophomores, juniors, and seniors were allowed to play. And they had a different system back then as well. They didn't run an offensive squad and a defensive squad, but rather they had a first team, second team, and third team. Most of the playing was done by the first, second and third teams, not by offense and defense."*

As I looked at the football schedules during the years that Marty played football at Notre Dame, his first three years they played ten game seasons, and then his senior year they only played nine games. I had remembered my dad telling me that his junior year (Marty's senior year), they only played nine games because one game was cancelled due to the assassination of President Kennedy. I asked Marty to speak about how that day impacted him.

They assassinated our President.

> *"My senior year, I tore ligaments in my knee during the Pittsburgh game at home, and we had three games left in the season. Michigan State, Iowa and Syracuse. I remember being in the hospital (it was a Friday) and one of the nurses came in crying, and I had no idea why she was crying. I asked her what was wrong, and she said, 'They assassinated our President,' and at that moment she turned the television on in my room. That was definitely one of those events where everyone remembers where they were at that moment. It was a big thing. It was hard for any of us to believe that something like that could have happened to our President."*

I'm not sure if it's in the job description, but so many head coaches, no matter what the sport, seem to have personalities that are larger than life. Maybe that's what helps them reach their players, and hold their attention, but I love asking the student-athletes that I interview to tell a funny story about their head coach. Marty had one to share with me about head coach Joe Kuharich.

> "One of the funny things about Coach Kuharich was his voice. He had this squeaky voice by nature, and when he would yell and scream at us, it would come out even more high-pitched and squeaky. Try as we might, we couldn't help from chuckling and laughing to ourselves as he would yell at us in his shrill tone. But that was him, Mr. Squeaky voice." <laughs>

No matter how long it has been since a former Notre Dame Football player donned the golden helmet and played for Our Lady's University, the memories of their time under the dome are still as strong as if they were yesterday. When I asked Marty to share his favorite football memory from his time at Notre Dame, he didn't even pause before giving me his answer.

> "My favorite Notre Dame Football memory? There are two distinct memories that stand out from my time at ND. The first one that comes to mind was when we played the Naval Academy my sophomore year. It was my first year of actually playing football at ND, and it was just the sixth game I had ever played in at Notre Dame, and I had the opportunity to tackle Roger Staubach. Roger Staubach! What an incredible moment that was for sure, and most definitely a huge highlight of my career. It's a memory I will never forget. Not many guys got the chance to tackle Staubach. He was a legend indeed. My second favorite memory came in the spring of 1961. At the end of spring practice that year I won the Herring Award for most improved tackle. That was quite an honor."

Any journey along the *Notre Dame Value Stream* is filled with twists and turns. So often Her student-athletes set out to sail Her streams with one particular goal in mind, only to end up at a destination they could have never expected. But for each and every student, and student-athlete, who travels along Her streams, She makes certain that they step out into the world filled with everything they could possibly need to be successful in whatever career path they decide to follow post Notre Dame.

Today

> "With two knee ligament injuries at Notre Dame, I knew when I graduated it was time to hang up the cleats and follow my next path. I started a career in education, and then decided to head back to school and earn a Master's Degree from Eastern Michigan University in Guidance Counseling, after which I spent 30 years of my career in counseling as a high school counselor."

When looking for advice, I always head to someone who has already walked down the path that I wish to head down. This is why I always ask the former student-athletes I interview to share a few words of wisdom for those young men and women who wish to play college athletics at the Division I level. Who better to ask that someone who has already been there, and then spent 30 years counseling high school students? Marty shared with me his thoughts on what it takes to be successful in college sports at the Division I level.

> *"First and foremost, have humility, because when you reach the college level you are going to find out there are a lot of really great athletes there. When you go from playing sports at the high school level to the collegiate level, it's quite a transition. You may have been an All-State or All-American in high school, but when you get to college, pretty much everyone was an All-State or All-American in high school. Especially at a school like Notre Dame. Today they start recruiting kids when they're in ninth or tenth grade. When I played high school football, they didn't start recruiting us until we were seniors. There is so much more pressure on kids today to commit to schools, and to commit to them early; having humility is so important. But so is having a lot of self-confidence. If you have a good balance of both humility and self-confidence you will do well once you reach the Division I level."*

Marty and his wife Mary are now retired, and split their time between Florida and Michigan. His wife Mary also had a career in education, teaching at the high school, middle school, and elementary levels during her career. They have three children: Michael, who lives in California, Marianne, who lives in Florida, and Matthew, who lives in Michigan. Marty and his wife tremendously enjoyed their careers in education, and really thought one of their kids would follow in their path and go into education, but none of them did. In hindsight, though, they are happy their kids pursued other careers as they may have had more opportunities than they might have had if they'd pursued a career in education. Marty and Mary also have ten grandchildren, three of whom are in college: one at the University of Chicago, one at Georgetown, one at the Rochester Institute of Technology (RIT), and one who is a paramedic. In retirement Marty and his wife are still connected to education, as they still volunteer at the local elementary school in their community.

Marty Olosky and his wife Mary.

Marty Olosky's Lessons from the Notre Dame Value Stream:

- Have humility, because when you reach the college level you are going to find out there are a lot of really great athletes there. When you go from playing sports at the high school level to the collegiate level, it's quite a transition. You may have been an All-State or All-American in high school, but when you get to college, pretty much everyone was an All-State or All-American in high school.

- Balance your humility with a healthy amount of self-confidence. If you have a good balance of both humility and self-confidence you will do well once you reach the Division I level.

Notre Dame vs. Indiana, 1988. Notre Dame men's basketball player Joe Fredrick (#3) with the ball facing two defenders. Photo by Hans Scott. (Photo courtesy of Notre Dame Archives.)

CHAPTER TWENTY ONE

The Radio Guy

Joe Fredrick

(Notre Dame Basketball – Class of 1990)

If you've ever been to the mid-western river town of Cincinnati, Ohio, you can see why it was nicknamed "The Queen City." Originally given the nickname in the 1820s, the name was due to the culture, arts and civilization the city offered in the midst of the wildness of the westward expansion. Today, Cincinnati is a booming metropolis, filled with the arts, distinctive architecture, multiple impressive higher education institutions, and a storied sports tradition in addition to many other offerings. Joe Fredrick, who grew up in the Cincinnati suburb of Greenhills, OH, not only loved watching his local sports teams, but also loved playing sports from a very young age. As the youngest of four children, Joe followed in his siblings footsteps, and began playing the "family sport;" which was basketball. Even though his dad's sport of choice was football, the Fredrick kids all played basketball, and it was what they ate, slept and breathed as a family. How did the youngest of four from a strong Midwestern family come to dream of one day playing basketball for the University of Notre Dame? This is Joe Fredrick's story.

"I was born and raised in a suburb of Cincinnati, OH, called Greenhills. A lot of people don't know this but my father played football at Notre Dame in the 1950s, and then following his football career at Notre Dame he became the high school athletic director at a public high school in Cincinnati. Growing up I had two older brothers and an older sister, and they all played basketball. Even though my dad was a football guy, basketball became the sport of our household. And with me being the youngest, I really just wanted to emulate my brothers. I learned very quickly that if I wanted to spend time with my brothers I had to play basketball. It was truly the focal point of our life. It was everyone's focus at breakfast, lunch, and dinner. It was all we talked about. My mom and dad put a 20 x 20 foot slab of concrete and a goal in our backyard and that became our little mecca, my very own Joyce Athletic and Convocation Center right in my backyard. With my dad being an athletic director, he kind of stayed out of the way when it came to us playing sports. He hired good coaches and let them coach us. I was kind of blessed in that regard because I've seen plenty of crazy dads throughout the years, and I was lucky he wasn't one of them. He still managed to find ways to give us plenty of tough love. He taught us to play hard, and to do the right thing. He taught us to be respectful of our coaches. He always had these lines that he would say, being an athletic director. He used to say, 'I've never met a coach who didn't play their best players.' And that kind of became our family line, 'You better be good enough to play, and not leave it up to a coach to make the decision. You better be so good they have to play you.'"

"When I was a sophomore in high school, I was fortunate enough to make the varsity team. I went to a really good basketball school, Greenhills High School, and at that time we had an excellent basketball team. We had a legendary head coach by the name of Earl Edmonds, and he was never one to pump your tires or tell you how good you were. Basketball for him was all about the fundamentals and working hard. One day during my sophomore year of high school, after getting upset in a tournament, he said to me, 'Some schools have contacted us. I'd like you to come in to the coaches office, I have some letters for you.' When I went to his office he had 200 letters from schools

> *who were looking at me to play basketball for them. Up until that point, I didn't really understand where I was as a player."*

> *"I had been groomed from a very young age that if Notre Dame was looking at you, and made an offer for you to go play basketball there, you would go to Notre Dame. And so, I think I was the easiest recruit in the history of the school. Coach 'Digger' Phelps asked me to come play basketball at Notre Dame, and I said yes. I did take my official visit and go see Notre Dame. I was there for my official visit along with Keith Robinson and Scott Paddock (who both also ended up coming to Notre Dame), and we had a great time. But it wasn't my first time being at Notre Dame by any stretch of the imagination. Growing up in a Notre Dame house, we would go to Notre Dame Football games every year. I got Joe Montana's autograph in his dorm room before the USC game. I had grown up absolutely loving Notre Dame, and I knew all of the football players from the 70s and early 80s as a result of my dad's immeasurable love for Notre Dame. When I took my official visit we stayed at the Morris Inn, and our hosts that weekend were Sean Connor and David Rivers; it was incredible to get to spend time with the team. I also made an unofficial visit to Notre Dame my junior year when they played Syracuse, which was a huge game for them that year. I just remember thinking that Notre Dame was the mecca of college basketball, and it was exactly where I wanted to be. I committed early in my junior year, before the basketball season even started. To this day I think I'm the youngest recruit to commit to Notre Dame."*

As a high school athlete heads off to college, especially those athletes who experienced a great deal of success in high school, there is often a significant disparity between the expectation of what playing a college sport is going to be like, and the reality of what it ends up being. Of course, you understand that the competition will be more intense, and the work will be harder, and the hours will be longer; until you actually get in the thick of it, it is oftentimes hard to comprehend exactly what it takes to compete and succeed at the collegiate level. Fortunately, student-athletes at the University of Notre Dame have the *Notre Dame Value Stream* to show them how to put in the work both on and off the court, and maintain balance in all areas of their lives.

The Notre Dame Years

> *"Transitioning from playing high school basketball to playing at Notre Dame was the toughest thing athletically I've ever had to do. In high school you're a mega star, and you can pretty much do whatever you want to do. And then you go to a school like Notre Dame, and you're playing up against guys like*

> *Scott Hicks and David Rivers, where just taking the ball up the floor was a major task. It took me at least a full year to adjust to the speed of the game, and to be able to hang in with the incredible athleticism of my peers. I was blessed that Coach Phelps hung in there with me and gave me the opportunity to play basketball at Notre Dame. Today I'd probably be labeled as a bust as a freshman because I didn't play very much. In fact, I only scored 30 points the whole season. Nowadays people are so impatient and don't let kids develop. If they don't show great potential their freshman year they are benched or they end up transferring."*

For a student-athlete at a school like Notre Dame, there are not only athletic adjustments in moving from playing at the high school level to playing at the Division I level, but there are also academic adjustments as well. There are many skills that help make this transition doable, but above all else it helps to step back periodically and make sure that you are enjoying the process as well as the journey.

> *"For me personally, growing up dreaming of attending Notre Dame, I did my best to take it all in, and I greatly enjoyed student life. My freshman year I roomed with a basketball teammate, but after that I roomed with non-athletes. I knew I was going to see my teammates all the time (at practice, games, team meetings and travel), so my thought process was that it would be best if we didn't also live together. I definitely enjoyed having a non-athlete as a roommate, and I thrived off of the experiences I was having as a student. At 51 years old, I still miss those days. I know so many student-athletes today complain about not having time for school, and how feel they should be compensated monetarily. To those young men and women I say, you should go to Notre Dame because it was awesome. They were the greatest four years of my life, bar none. Yes, school was definitely difficult, but the University offered us tutors and every possible resource available to make us successful. . . which I needed. <laughs> I enjoyed dorm life so much. Hanging out with the guys in Alumni hall, those are some of my best college memories. I majored in American Studies when I was at Notre Dame, with a minor in business. My roommate (Mike Caponigro) teased me so much about being an American Studies major. And that could have contributed to why I enjoyed dorm life so much. I did not have the toughest major in the world. But I was quite confident that I was going to go into sales one day, and that's why I selected business as my minor. I truly enjoyed all aspects of my Notre Dame education."*

In doing my research about Joe, I saw several people talking about the "hop step" technique that he used in college. Joe spoke with me a little bit about how that developed and why it was successful for him.

> *Hey, I watched you at Notre Dame,*
> *and I remember you had that hop step.*

"Oh, that's funny! You know what, it's weird because I never really used it much in high school, but in college it gave me a way to get into the seams of a zone, doing that little hop step that I did. It allowed me to get into the heart of the zone. I had a lot of success using it, and it became my niche that I would always do. To this day people will come up to me and tell me, 'Hey, I watched you at Notre Dame, and I remember you had that hop step.' And honestly, I probably just wasn't athletic enough to do anything else. I was fortunate to find a little something that worked for me."

Coaches at the University of Notre Dame tend to have big coaching philosophies, and oftentimes even bigger personalities (and egos). Head basketball coach Richard Frederick "Digger" Phelps was no exception. Joe talks about what it was like to play for a demanding head coach, and how Digger's coaching style taught the guys not only about the game of basketball, but the game of life as well.

> **"Don't assume, always have a backup, and always have a follow up."**
> **– Coach Digger Phelps**

"What was it like to play for Coach Phelps? Challenging. You always knew that he was going to push you every single day to become the best possible player that you could be. What I admired most about Coach Phelps was that even with as difficult as the athletic part of the equation was, when it came to the academic and personal side of the equation, he truly cared about all portions of your life. He didn't only care about what happened on the court. Looking back on those days as an adult, father, and coach, I have a great deal of appreciation for what he did for us. He always talked to us about our life after school and after basketball, and emphasized the value of graduating and getting our degree. He had a phrase that he used quite often, that I still use this day, 'Don't assume, always have a backup, and always have a follow up.' And he would say it to us all the time. He literally drilled it into our heads. In addition, he would apply it to every life situation. If you were late to practice he would ask you, 'Why weren't you there early? Did you have a backup plan? Why did you assume we were going to start practice at 3 pm? You should have been here at 2:30 pm.' He basically eliminated every excuse you had and honestly to this day in business, I think that particular phrase of his is probably my number one core principle."

"We had practice at 3 pm, but practice really started at 2:15 pm with what was called 'pre-practice.' In hindsight, that 45 minute pre-practice was actually

harder than the regular practice. The first month of my freshman year I kept thinking to myself, are you kidding me? This is just pre-practice, and pre-practice is harder than the 'actual' practice. Coach would walk out for practice at 3 pm and I was dead, gassed, completely tired. I had to go through a significant adjustment period to gain the stamina to do both pre-practice and regular practice. He was a driver, make no bones about it, he pushed you every single day. He pushed you mentally, and physically. Every which way you could be pushed, he tried. He's a character. He's a one of a kind, that's for sure."

**He was a driver, make no bones about it,
he pushed you every single day.**

Every coach who coaches at a Division I school, especially a school so steeped in a winning tradition such as Notre Dame, wants his team to perform at their absolute best year in and year out. Joe explains some of the factors that contributed to head coach Digger Phelps being as successful as he was.

"First, candidly, back then the lack of network exposure (for teams other than Notre Dame), worked in Digger's favor. Today there are five or six ESPN channels, and the Fox Sports network of channels; every team has national exposure of some sort. Back then, Notre Dame was really the only school who was on TV weekly because we were not in a conference, and we played as an independent. This allowed him to recruit players from all over the country. The ability for him to get top, number one recruits was such a great asset for him. When you look through the years, he always had high level players. Second was his ability to push you, and get every ounce he could get out of you. He was a really good X's and O's coach. He understood the game, and knew how to motivate players. He always was able to keep you on edge. He never let you have a comfortable feeling, which meant you always felt like you were playing for your job. And from having friends who played football under Coach Holtz, the two coaches had very similar coaching styles."

And then, there it is, that dreaded point in every interview when I ask, "What is your favorite basketball memory from your time at Notre Dame." I always thought that question would be a slam dunk, but for so many of the athletes that I interview, that question is hands down the one they labor over the most. But without fail, as the conversation moves along, and the walk down memory lane gets a bit clearer, every single person has that a-ha moment and elatedly recites the story of their favorite Notre Dame memory.

"Honestly, my favorite memory from playing basketball at Notre Dame? Being in the locker room with my teammates. The bonds that I built with

guys like Jamere Jackson, Keith Robinson, Scott Paddock, Kevin Ellery, Tim Singleton, LaPhonso Ellis; those bonds never leave you. I coach at a local high school, and we were at a state tournament down in Lexington, and I got a text from Kevin Ellery who came to the game to watch my team play. When LaPhonso Ellis announces the Notre Dame Basketball games on TV, he and I text after the games. Jamere Jackson is super successful, he's the CFO of Hertz Rental Cars, and every time he gets a promotion we all text him and tease him about lending us money. Twenty plus years later and those bonds are just unbreakable. Every time we talk to each other we feel like we're right back there in the locker room. Like no time at all has passed. And I know the football guys feel the same way."

Catholics vs. Convicts

"Probably the most unforgettable, distinct basketball memory that I have, the one that is indelibly marked in my brain, is not really an on the court memory. It was the time when we were at Midnight Madness, and Coach Phelps called me over and asked me, 'Hey Fred, do you have anything to do with the Catholics vs. Convicts t-shirts?' And without missing a beat I responded, 'Coach, I have no idea what you're talking about. Nope, that's my roommate, Mike.' That was probably the most terrifying moment I ever had with Coach Phelps. But it's also my most lasting memory <laughs>... meanwhile I had thousands of dollars in my dorm room, and t-shirts flying out the door. Everywhere."

Speaking of Catholics vs. Convicts. So many of us have watched the ESPN 30 for 30 documentary on the Catholics vs. Convicts shirts that were all the rage during the 1988 football season. You may even have one in your closet, and if you do hold on to it. . . that thing is priceless! But what I wanted to know from Joe was this: what was the most important thing that you learned from the whole experience?

"The film did a really good job on a lot of the aspects of the shirt. The one thing that people may not understand is that it really was an Alumni Hall deal. I had sellers from Alumni Hall selling the shirts in every dorm. We had a lot of fun with it. The reality of it was, we honestly were just a bunch of broke college kids getting some money to go to Marci's Deli and get a break from the dining hall. That was our number one goal when I got the idea from my brother and ran with it. The idea was that if we could sell a couple hundred shirts, we could go with our buddies to Marci's Deli once a week. . . that was the end game. And the idea just caught on like nothing we had ever expected. We had shirts stacked up in our room. We were selling them in blocks of fifty.

I learned more about business selling those t-shirts than I did in any business class at Notre Dame. That's a true statement."

The reality of it was, we honestly were just a bunch of broke college kids getting some money to go to Marci's Deli and get a break from the dining hall.

"I learned about supply and demand, and everything else that comes along with it. The biggest lesson I learned from the whole experience was about being honest. When my roommate (Mike Caponigro) and I got called into Student Affairs, we went in there and were very transparent with them. Yes, we did do this. Yes, this is how much we sold. Yes, this is how much money we have left over, and we gave the money that we had back to the University. Part of it was clearly the fear that Digger had put into me the night before when he had asked me if I had any involvement with the Catholics vs. Convicts shirts. From that moment, I just wanted to get out of the deal. I wanted no trouble. I was on scholarship, I knew my mom and dad would kill me if I got in trouble, and I did not want to let my parents down. And so for me the biggest lesson was to just be honest. We knew, at some level, that we weren't allowed to sell unlicensed t-shirts around campus, but it was something that everyone did. Up to that point, the University had just looked away and not done anything about it. Up until we made the Catholics vs. Convict shirt, we weren't killing the bookstore by any means. We sold a couple hundred shirts from dorm to dorm. But the Catholics vs. Convict shirt became a whole other sensation. This became a University, branded, iconic t-shirt. And it was harming the University because we were taking business away from the bookstore that weekend. There was no question about it. The line was out the door of Alumni Hall and down past South Dining Hall. The line went on forever, just to get a shirt. So we learned a lot about business, trademarks, licensing, and if you're selling something on Notre Dame's campus, you better have a seller's permit or permission from the University. We learned a little too much too soon if I'm being honest. Those were some big life lessons."

"In addition to the fact that we were taking money away from the bookstore was the fact that the shirt had so much controversy around it. People really didn't grasp the intensity of the ND vs. Miami rivalry. The rivalry was as intense as anything I have ever seen to this day. In fact, I've never seen anything like it. As a Cincinnati guy, we have an extremely heated basketball rivalry here between the University of Cincinnati and Xavier, and I've attended Notre Dame vs. Michigan games. But I can tell you, that single event was the most heated thing that I've ever seen or been a part of as a fan, in my entire

> life. So that definitely added to the whole situation, and threw a little fuel on the fire if you will. It was covered in Sports Illustrated and USA Today. This wasn't just some campus t-shirt, it became an overnight sensation, and every single Notre Dame fan across the country wanted one. That's when I realized, this isn't some little campus t-shirt, this is a pretty mega deal."

And then it happens, just like that. In a flash you go from arriving on campus as a wide-eyed, eager freshman, ready to take on the world, to suddenly you're graduating and taking that next step towards your future. Fortunately, when you travel along the *Notre Dame Value Stream*, you are not only never alone, but you are also equipped with a support network, or some would say family, which is there to cheer you on in good times and bad.

The Professional Years

> "After I graduated from Notre Dame I got a free agent tryout from the Sacramento Kings and went to their pre-season camp. I made it through camp only to be cut on the last day, the day when rosters were due. That was absolutely devastating to me because I had made the team and then a player who had flunked his physical and was traded came back and took my spot. From there I went to a CBA team in Rockford, IL, which candidly turned into me fighting depression. I went from playing in the NBA to playing in the CBA. I went from Sacramento, California, with a big contract, to Rockford, Illinois, making $500 a week, trying to live my dream of playing basketball in the pros."

> "Honestly, I was so burned out at that point. I had given it so much, and had played as well as I possibly could have. I played out the year and then I went to the Milwaukee Bucks training camp. When I didn't get guaranteed money, I knew it was a sign that they liked you but they didn't love you. At that point I knew it was time to get on with my life's work, and quite frankly I've never looked back. The ironic thing was, when I was in the CBA, guys would sit on the bus or the plane and talk about, 'I should've made this team, or I should've made that team.' I was playing with guys who had been out of college for 8 or 9 years, still trying to reach that dream of playing in the NBA. After hearing that I told myself, I'm going to give it one year. I went to Notre Dame and I earned my Notre Dame degree. I'm not going to be like this and hang around forever chasing some elusive dream."

> "Overall, it was a good experience. The most significant thing I learned from playing in the CBA was that playing at that level was not something I wanted to do. I wanted to play in the show, and if that wasn't going to happen, it was

time to move on. There were guys I played against in college who I thought I was every bit as good as, if not better, who were already in the NBA. That is why I did give it that whole year. But I wasn't going to be one of those guys who kept going after it. I just didn't want to be that guy. I had friends from Notre Dame who had these amazing jobs, and there I was living out of a motel in Rockford, Illinois, chasing my NBA dream; and that wasn't sustainable long term. I knew, however, that I had to give it one good shot."

"My senior year at Notre Dame, pre-season we were ranked pretty high, and we thought we were going to have a solid team. Unfortunately, LaPhonso Ellis was ineligible that fall semester, and after that our season spiraled into a tailspin which we never quite recovered from. We had a lot of talent on that team, and after that season I wasn't ready to give up on my basketball dreams, but I also wasn't ready to invest five years of my life chasing NBA dreams. I saw that my brothers were successful in the radio business, and I saw my friends from Notre Dame being successful and getting good jobs, which made me all the more ready get into my work game."

Today

"After basketball I got into the radio business. I started as an account executive at a little radio station in Cincinnati called WKRC. The thing that made that station unique was that they carried the Cincinnati Bengals games, and I had a great passion for our hometown teams. I was able to be there for a year and then our company was sold to a larger radio conglomerate who owned a station called WLW which carried the Cincinnati Reds, the University of Cincinnati and Xavier basketball, and it was the number one rated station in the area. I was able to get on there at a pretty young age and worked my way up. Working in radio is a lot like basketball. You start at the bottom, work for playing time, taking your lumps, getting your teeth kicked in and then you find a little success, and a little more success, and work your way up. It was the best training I ever got. When I got interviewed, my boss at the time was a huge Kentucky basketball fan, and when I interviewed for the job I had no idea he knew who I was as far as my playing career at Notre Dame."

"At the end of the interview he looked me straight in the eye and said, 'Joe, can I ask you a serious question?' And I said, 'Well of course.' And he asked, 'Do you promise to play as hard for me as you did against Kentucky?' And I replied, 'Yes sir, I promise I will.' He hired me on the spot and told me I could start on Monday. That's how I got the job at WLW. Working my way up, the way I did in radio, was the best training ground for me. Where I really got hooked on the radio business was when I was interning for my brother

> *Mike, who is also in the radio business. I used to go into work with him in the summer to help him out. I went downstairs into the radio station kitchen, and there was Anthony Munoz, who was an iconic Cincinnati Bengal figure, (even though he went to USC). I was so excited. I went back upstairs to tell my brother who I just saw, and he said, 'Yeah, our sister station carries the Cincinnati Bengals,' and I said, 'I could do that all day. Everybody listens to the Bengals on the radio.' And that's how I got hooked on the radio business. I still am, I just love radio."*

Experience is one of the best teachers, both on and off the court. And sharing what we've learned in life with others is a big part of setting up future generations for success. Joe shared with me his words of advice for young athletes who wish to play at the Division I level someday.

> *"I have two nephews who play Division I sports. One plays football at Ohio State University, and one (who is the Kentucky state basketball player of the year) has signed to play basketball at Iowa. The advice that I've always given those guys is this, 'You only get one shot. You don't get a chance to redo this.' I think young people should try and mentally project themselves forward to 30, or 40, or 50 years-old, and look back at their current athletic experience. If they have zero regrets about what they're currently doing, then they're doing everything right. That's always been my advice to the kids I coach. And I see the kids who have become the most successful, they have the ability to look back like that. They understand they have to give it everything they've got to be sure they won't ever look back and say 'what if?' They understand they need to maximize every ounce of their ability and talent. That's the advice I give to young people all the time. Don't have any regrets and give the game everything you've got."*

> *"The other thing I tell young people looking to play a sport at the Division I level is this, enjoy your college experience. It's never going to get any better than this time of your life. You're on scholarship, you get to play in front of thousands of cheering fans, and you get academic help from the University with tutors. Enjoy every minute of your college experience, both on and off the court, and take advantage of all the resources at your disposal to be successful."*

For the students and fans of big time programs like Notre Dame Basketball, you see a particular image projected of the team's head coach, from how he coaches his team to how he carries himself on the court. But the relationship the players have with their coach is often much different. We all saw Coach Digger's larger than life personality on the court, and Joe shares with us what it was like to play for such an eclectic individual.

> *On his recruiting trip to visit me, I'm from Greenhills,*
> *OH, which is an extremely middle class area.*
> *He showed up wearing a full length fur coat.*

> *"On his recruiting trip to visit me, I'm from Greenhills, OH, which is an extremely middle class area. He showed up wearing a full length fur coat. And I can tell you, there were not men wearing full length fur coats in Greenhills, OH. I was 15 or 16 years old at the time, and he was larger than life to me. This guy had a fur coat. Coach was quite a character, he had a personality that could fill an arena. He would always come out and take heat from the other team's fans, and he would do it so that they wouldn't get to us. That was kind of his deal, he wanted to take the heat from the visiting team's fans, and they would yell at him and he would play up to it, to keep the fans off of us."*

Joe, born and raised in Greenhills, OH, still lives in his beloved hometown of Cincinnati with his family. When asked to share any philanthropic endeavors he was involved with, he shared his involvement with a local home town charity.

> *"I have been involved with the local Diocesan Catholic Children's Home, which houses sexually abused children. They do really great work in the Northern Kentucky/Cincinnati area. It's a sad situation. When my kids were little, their teams would play them in baseball. On our side of the field you'd have parents cheering and videotaping their kids. On the other side of the field you have these kids with no parents on the sideline, and these 22 or 23 year old volunteers helping them out. I was a young parent at the time, and seeing that really hit me. It made me think about how blessed our children were to have parents that cared about them. It's kind of turned into a pet peeve of mine, because I believe that every kid deserves a chance to have a good life. And so anything I can do to help a kid, that's my number one priority. I'm all in."*

Joe Fredrick's Lessons from the Notre Dame Value Stream:

- You only get one shot. You don't get a chance to redo this. I think young people should try and mentally project themselves forward to 30, or 40, or 50 years-old, and look back at their current athletic experience. If they have zero regrets about what they're currently doing, then they're doing everything right. Don't have any regrets and give the game everything you've got.

- Enjoy your college experience. It's never going to get any better than this time of your life. You're on scholarship, you get to play in front of thousands of cheering fans, and you get academic help from the

University with tutors. Enjoy every minute of your college experience, both on and off the court, and take advantage of all the resources at your disposal to be successful.

Joe Fredrick and his father, Charlie Fredrick (ND '59).

Notre Dame Women's Track Meet: Notre Dame vs. Michigan State (MSU), 2003. Left to right: Molly Huddle and Lauren King. (Photo courtesy of Notre Dame Archives.)

CHAPTER TWENTY TWO

The Ace Runner

Molly Huddle

(Notre Dame Track & Field – Class of 2006)

For some people, running is merely an activity you do to stay in shape, to lose weight, or that brings a competitive outlet. For others, running is more than just exercise; it is a spiritual, or cathartic experience. It's where you are able to get out of your head, solve the world's problems, and find some peace in your day. And finally, there are the people who would only be found running if someone was chasing them. For Molly Huddle, running is her everything. It started out as a bond between her and her dad, and ended up becoming a lifelong love, as well as her livelihood. How did a girl from Elmira, NY, become interested in running, and turn it into a lifelong passion? This is Molly Huddle's story.

"My dad loved to run, and he ran a lot. He was on the track team at the University of Notre Dame (class of 1969), and his events were the 400 and the 800. He continued to run well into his adult life, and when we were little he was running marathons. My mom would take us to watch him doing road races and we'd cheer him on. He had a passion for running, and he encouraged myself and my three sisters to all at least try track and cross country. I, however, was the only one who really loved and enjoyed running; and I was the only one who stuck with it. I also played basketball (that was my favorite sport for a long time), and soccer for a little while, but not for long. I remember my dad subtly trying to tell me that I was a better runner than basketball player, and that I might want to think about shifting my focus, but I didn't pick up on that right away. My dream was to play in the WNBA someday, and he kept nudging me towards running, and away from basketball. 'You know, you're really good at one of these sports, and basketball may not be it.'" <laughs>

"When I reached my senior year at Notre Dame High School, I decided to focus solely on running. I had always wanted to go to the University of Notre Dame, even before I began running, but eventually I realized that running could be my gateway to getting in to Notre Dame. When I became serious about running, I started to look at the schools which had the most successful running programs, and this pulled me away from Notre Dame a little bit. My top three schools were Stanford, Villanova, and Georgetown, but I did also keep Notre Dame on my list. At the end of the day, I had always wanted to go to Notre Dame, and I knew if I went there and running didn't work out for me, I'd still be happy there. The cross country team at Notre Dame wasn't very highly ranked before I got there, but our freshmen class ended up being very successful, finishing third in the country. Thankfully, I ended up getting the best of both worlds; I got to go to Notre Dame and I found a great deal of success with the track team."

"My dad took our family to two football games at Notre Dame when I was in junior high school, and on one of the trips my dad walked me up to the track office to say hello to the coaches. Which, looking back, is kind of funny because I was not good at running at that point. I was only 12 years old at the time, but the coach was very nice to us (Coach Connelly). I'm sure he was thinking, 'Oh look, another kid whose dad dragged them over to say hi. Who knows if I'll ever see this one again.' My dad and I always laugh about that story."

And then the journey along the *Notre Dame Value Stream* begins. The journey is different for each student and student-athlete who sails along Her waters, but

She always knows what they need. She makes sure they have the tools they need to be successful, the wind to fill their sails, and the support needed to lift them up in times of need; as no journey is without at least a little adversity. What She also knows is that adversity will help to make Her students stronger, and more successful, as they will most certainly face future adversity beyond the walls of Our Lady's University.

The Notre Dame Years

> *"When I first got to Notre Dame, my coach (Tim Connelly) brought me on pretty conservatively. I was running more than I was in high school, but he definitely didn't jump me up to the level that the upperclassmen were running at because he knew I could contribute to the cross country team right away, even if I was a little bit under trained. And so that was his plan for me. My freshman year went really well, and my transition from high school to college was very smooth. I would maybe struggle for a week or two with a class, and then I'd study really hard and make up for it on the next test. I remember getting through my freshman year with very few setbacks as far as injuries and academics went. When I was a sophomore he turned up the volume and intensity, and tried to push the team to win a national championship; that's when it got hard. That's when I started to get injured here and there, and was oftentimes too tired to put in the necessary work in regard to my academics. I'd say my freshman year was a false introduction to college; and then I got the real taste of what it took to be successful both on and off the track my sophomore and junior year. By the time my senior year came around I had adapted to the mileage, and had figured out what my biomechanical problems were. At that point I knew how to have a good run, and how to manage everything well."*

> **Sometimes when I look back on my college years,**
> **I have no idea how I did it.**
> **It is so very important to be able to manage your time.**

> *"Tutoring was very important to me, to be able to be successful in my most difficult classes: such as calculus my freshman year. I also tried to take some of my more intense classes in the summer, so that I could fully dedicate myself to them, and have less going on outside of classwork. Myself and a fellow teammate (Lauren King. . . 1500 runner) stayed at ND during the summer and took physics and organic chemistry together. It was really good. She was someone I trained with a lot, and so we spent a lot of time together in and out of class. Tutoring, and working one-on-one with fellow teammates, definitely helped me to be successful both on the track and in class. Study groups with my fellow classmates were difficult for me because they often met during the*

> *same time that I had practice, so being able to form study groups with my teammates was very helpful for me. I was a biology major, and I was very lucky that there were a lot of science majors on the team; it was great as there were upperclassmen around to ask for help, who had already been through the classes that we were taking. My long-term goal was to go to medical school, as I loved biology in high school, and studied it at Notre Dame. I took the MCATS during my fifth year at Notre Dame, but ended up deciding to keep running after college, and didn't end up going to medical school."*

In addition to having academic support through tutoring and study groups, it is also important to have support and guidance from your coaches, to provide you with the necessary tools to be athletically successful at the collegiate level. A good coach should not only elevate your skills in order to grow you and make you more successful at every step of your journey; they should also mentor you and advance your personal development as well. They should push you to your limits, let you fail some of the time, and be the safety net that shows you how to pick yourself up and propel you even further on your next try.

> *"Coach (Tim) Connelly was a father figure to a lot of us. He would give us good advice, and he had very high standards; he wanted us to get A's in our classes. I remember the head coach (Joe Piane) was a little more lenient with the team as far as grades went, but Coach Connelly wanted both for us. He wanted the best for us in our running careers, and in our academics as well. He brought us along pretty conservatively. One of the things I did in college that was new to me was strength training in the weight room, along with injury prevention training and drills before practice. He was pretty adamant as far as our participation in that for injury prevention. He was very detail oriented, and introduced that new facet of training to us, as he wanted to make sure we were well rounded athletes, which he believed would make us better runners. I have taken that with me into my professional running career. It was great to have that background as I transitioned into running at the professional level, to know your way around the weight room. Coach Connelly was passionate about running, but he also made it a fun experience for us. You could tell he really enjoyed his job, and enjoyed our successes along with us."*

Whether you are able to achieve great success at the collegiate level or not, there are always a few memories from your career that stand out from the rest. Molly was one of the lucky ones who was able to achieve a fair amount of success at the collegiate level, and shared with me some of her fondest memories from her time at Notre Dame.

> "Competing in the NCAA Cross Country Championships my freshman year was hands down one of my favorite memories from my time at Notre Dame. As a freshman who had never competed at that level before, it was surprisingly fun, and just an all-around good day. I remember the race, and I had rarely felt that good in a race up to that point. I finished 5th, which was very good for a freshman, and our team finished in third, which was such a surprise to all of us. Everyone was just in a really good mood, which absolutely set the tone for that fall. The championships were a great way to cap off my freshman year, and I had made some outstanding friends that year. Stephanie Madia, Lauren King, the other Lauren King and I were all in the top seven; and it was so fun hanging out with them all year and traveling to races. The championships were such a memorable moment because they were such a bright, happy way to wrap up our freshmen season; I definitely like to think back on that season. I still keep in touch with Stephanie and Lauren, as well as some of the guys who ran with my husband (Kurt Benninger), who was a year behind me."

Five years may seem like a long time to be in one place, but when those five years are spent at a place like Notre Dame, they seem to fly by much too quickly. Yes, when you arrive at college, you are told by upperclassmen, teachers and parents to enjoy every moment; in the blink of an eye you are walking across that graduation stage and headed out into the world to conquer the next mountain on the horizon of life. The *Notre Dame Value Stream* hasn't let you down yet, and She's still there to carry you through your future adventures; even though you are far away from Our Lady's campus.

The Professional Years

> "When I graduated from Notre Dame, I thought my collegiate running career had been a good one, but I wasn't sure if it had truly been good enough to get a contract from one of the shoe companies, and be able to run professionally moving forward. (That's how you support yourself at the professional level.) I hadn't won a NCAA title. My running times were good, but I wasn't sure they were good enough. Luckily I did get an offer to run for Saucony. They looked at my collegiate career at Notre Dame, and believed in me, which meant a great deal to me, as that told me they thought I was good enough. I probably would have tried to run on my own for at least one year, regardless of whether or not I got a contract."

> "My coach at Notre Dame knew the Providence College women's coach, Ray Treacy, who had a professional women's running group out in Providence, Rhode Island. I was quite familiar with their team because Notre Dame would race against them in the Big East Conference upwards of ten times

a year. My coach set up the meeting with Coach Ray Treacy, and within a month of graduating I had a professional coach, a professional running group, and a professional contract. Fortunately for me it just all flowed together, and I took it as a sign. I told myself if I kept improving every year, I'd keep running, and luckily I have done just that."

Everyone who participates in athletics at the professional level dreams of competing at the highest level, and, of course, winning at the highest level. But so many athletes, try as they might, never quite reach that pinnacle. Molly, however, has done just that. She has not only competed in the Olympics, she has also run in some of the elite running events, including the New York City marathon, and has been successful on multiple stages.

"There are definitely some events that I felt were larger than life. When I was on my first Olympic team, I was kind of awestruck by everyone there, and the event itself. I had tried two times previously to make the Olympic team, in 2004 and 2008, and didn't make it, and so I wasn't sure I would ever make an Olympic team. In 2012, when I made the Olympic team, I was trying to run well, but I was really just taking it all in and enjoying every moment of the experience. Running in New York City is always kind of dazzling, but even more so on the New York City marathon weekend. Running the New York City marathon was something I had wanted to do for years and years, and so it almost felt like a mini Olympics when I finally had the opportunity to do it. There are certain races where you have to make a conscious effort to concentrate on your running as if it were any old race, even though you truly are competing on a huge stage, whether it is the Olympics or the NYC marathon. When the event is so grand, and has so much meaning behind it, that can be really distracting. I learned how to deal with that pretty quickly."

"I am grateful to those experiences, of being able to perform and succeed on such grand stages. They are experiences that don't come around too often in a sports career, and I definitely wanted to make the most of them. The competition at the professional level is deeper for sure, and every race is important, which was difficult to wrap my head around at first. There are no small meets, and there are world class competitors at most races. But once I was able to wrap my head around that, I learned what I needed to do, personally, to be successful. I love focusing my whole day on running, recovery, and becoming a better athlete, one day at a time. Once I was able to narrow my focus on only running, and didn't have to worry about school work, or much else other than trying to be a better athlete; I took to that really well. I've discovered that one of my strengths is being able to focus on one thing at a time, really intensely,

and that lead to my being able to improve really quickly. I wasn't sure how I'd adapt to being a full time runner, as opposed to being a part time runner in college, but it was a perfect fit for me. You talk to some people that go from an intense academic institution, like a Stanford or a Notre Dame, who try to run at the professional level, and almost feel under stimulated, or maybe a little bored. Like maybe they should be doing a little more with their day. I definitely had that feeling the first year or two, but my body's response was really good. I was fresher, and more rested, and more recovered; and I was running personal records, which is all you can ask for as a runner. One of the best parts of running is when you can get to the point where your body is on autopilot, and you can just think about whatever."

Today

"I just turned 34 this year, and the 2020 Olympics are just around the corner, so I hope to be able to run through 2020 or 2021 if my body can handle it. The World Championships are in the United States in 2021 (in Eugene, Oregon), and it's been a long time since they've been held in the United States. I would love to end my career at that race in 2021. And as far as marathons go, as long as my body is still able to run them, I will continue to compete, but I'll take that one year at a time. Saucony has been my primary sponsor since I graduated from college 11 years ago. I'm extremely grateful that they've supported me for so long. I've had some other sponsors along the way, including Gatorade Endurance, KT Tape, Polar (the heart rate watch company); and all of their support has allowed me to train and be my best. Saucony has a bio-mechanical research lab at their offices, and sometimes they hook me up with all these little sensors and have me run on the treadmill to see the mechanics of how I run, and look at the metrics of how I'm performing; which I love being a science nerd and all. As I navigate towards the end of my running career, my husband and I look forward to starting a family in the next few years."

The lessons learned along a professional athletic career are many. As one looks back on the years, the collective lessons turn into a wealth of information that can then be passed along to the next generation of athletes. Molly gladly shared with me some of the lessons she learned along the way, from her collegiate running career through to her professional running career.

"Have a long term vision, when it comes to your collegiate athletic career, and don't feel like you need to make a huge jump right away, as you transition from high school to college. In running, in particular, just because your running times aren't competitive at a national level does not mean that you

won't get there. I've seen so many kids who weren't highly recruited become national class runners, and it just takes time. It's an experiment, to see what works and what doesn't work for you. Recognize that, and keep working at it, and you never know where it will take you. Never let where you currently are prevent you from trying to get to the next level. Running at the collegiate level is a great place to learn about competing, and to develop into a great athlete. Some of the best and deepest races in the world are in the NCAA. It's a great place to sharpen your speed and improve your skill set. Give yourself time and always keep trying."

"When I'm not training, or spending time with my husband, I currently sit on the board of a program called New England Distance. It's a professional distance running group here in Rhode Island, and they have a community outreach aspect to their organization. We fundraise to provide public schools with track and cross country teams in Rhode Island, and the professional athletes coach the kids. They've been providing that outreach since 2012. It's been a really fun program to be a part of, and for the last two years I've been involved in their cross country race, which is one of the fundraisers they hold. It's been awesome to expose junior high kids to cross country and track, most of which have never run before. And most likely neither their friends nor parents run either, and so they probably wouldn't even try it had it not been for programs like this. If you can get them running at a young age, they most likely will keep running. It also helps to keep them active after school and out of trouble as well. You can tell that they don't fully love running yet, and so we try not to coach them too hard. We just want to get them moving, and get them involved, and so what we provide them is a mix of mentoring and running and coaching. They love the coaches and so that's very rewarding for our volunteer coaches. My husband coaches professional athletes through the New England Distance group, so we're both active in the running community."

Molly Huddle running with her husband Kurt Benninger (ND '08).

Molly Huddle's Lessons from the Notre Dame Value Stream:

- Have a long term vision, when it comes to your collegiate athletic career, and don't feel like you need to make a huge jump right away, as you transition from high school to college. In running, in particular, just because you're running times aren't competitive at a national level does not mean that you won't get there. I've seen so many kids who weren't highly recruited become national class runners, and it just takes time. It's an experiment, to see what works and what doesn't work for you. Recognize that, and keep working at it, and you never know where it will take you. Never let where you currently are prevent you from trying to get to the next level. Give yourself time and always keep trying.

- Take advantage of the tutoring available to you. Tutoring was very important to me, to be able to be successful in my most difficult classes: such as calculus my freshman year. I also tried to take some of my more intense classes in the summer, so that I could fully dedicate myself to them, and have less going on outside of classwork. Tutoring, and working one-on-one with fellow teammates, definitely helped me to be successful both on the track and in class.

Notre Dame vs. Purdue, 1994. Mary O'Connor (center) and other student managers on the sidelines. (Photo courtesy of Notre Dame Archives.)

CHAPTER TWENTY THREE

The Sports Marketer
Mary O'Connor

(Notre Dame Football Manager – Class of 1996)

When Father Sorin set out to build the University of Notre Dame on a piece of land nestled between two lakes in South Bend, IN, he had grand dreams regarding the future of Our Lady's University, and all that She would give to the students who traveled to and through Her hallowed grounds. But I'm not sure that he truly understood what a magical and awe-inspiring place Our Lady's University would become, and all of the students, both men and women, that She would mold and shape throughout the years. Her students are drawn to Her from coast to coast, and each one has their unique story as to how they arrived at the often frozen campus that so many of us call home. Mary's introduction, like so many of ours, started from a very young age, and her love of Notre Dame grew as she grew up herself. How does a young woman from Ionia, MI, nestled in the heart of the Grand River Valley, end up leaving the state of Michigan and attend the University of Notre Dame? This is Mary O'Connor's story.

> *"My father, Rex O'Connor, was a 1951 graduate of the Law School at Notre Dame. Ironically, my dad did not have an undergraduate degree. After WWII (he was in the Army Air Corps), he attended Aquinas College in Grand Rapids, MI for two years on the GI Bill, during which time he was on their basketball team. He also attended Michigan State University for one summer. His admittance to Notre Dame's Law School was based on credit hours, which apparently was very common for veterans following the war. He was blessed to be able to attend Notre Dame on the GI Bill as well. He started taking me to football games at the age of five, and I became enamored with the campus and the Notre Dame family. Each football weekend, we would meet his fellow classmates at the '51 table in the JACC. I grew up knowing his classmates and witnessed their connection and the level of support they gave one another."*

> *"As I began looking at colleges, I looked at mostly east coast schools – Dartmouth, Seton Hall, Providence College, Duke, University of North Carolina, etc. I also looked at Georgia Tech."* But Notre Dame had already won her heart, and that is where she headed off to attend college.

The young men and women who are drawn to Our Lady's university are often the best of the best from their respective high schools. Quite often, they are the type of students who aren't challenged by schoolwork alone, but need to be involved in multiple areas of campus life in order to fully develop their mind, body and spirit. While many Notre Dame students do play sports at some level while they are traveling along the *Notre Dame Value Stream*, some of Her students find a different and unique way to be a part of the sports at ND. Mary heard about this program on campus, the "student manager program," and went to an informational meeting to learn about what the program had to offer. Little did she know how much that program would transform her years at Notre Dame.

> *"I loved sports; both watching sports and playing sports. I played basketball from fifth grade all the way through high school, both for my school team and the local AAU (Amateur Athletic Union) girls basketball team. It was a given growing up in our household that I would play basketball. My dad played college hoops at Aquinas College, and my mom is a die-hard Hoosier from Bloomington, Indiana. It also helped that I was 5'11" in 6th grade. I also participated in track & field in high school. Outside of sports, I was actively*

involved in activities including 4H (cooking, crafts and sewing), Fellowship of Christian Athletes, Debate Club, and National Honor Society."

The Notre Dame Years

> ***Being a part of the Student Manager Program was an incredible experience. It was a family within the Notre Dame family, packed with hard work, long nights, and a tremendous amount of fun.***

> "Truth be told, I would have loved to have played sports in college, however I wasn't good enough or big enough to play Division I basketball. I began Notre Dame studying engineering, but ended up altering my path and finished with a degree in Management Information Systems. As I was finding my way at Notre Dame, I was looking for something to get involved in, as I wasn't playing a sport. I had always been a Notre Dame Football fan, and the student manager program sounded exciting to me when I went to the informational session to learn more about it. Being a part of the student manager program was an incredible experience. It was a family within the Notre Dame family, packed with hard work, long nights, and a tremendous amount of fun. Most people don't realize that the student managers are working before practice starts and then long after it's over. The most wonderful part of the experience was that the athletes were truly appreciative of what we were doing. They were our friends. Some of my longest relationships from Notre Dame today are with other managers and the athletes we served."

In case you aren't familiar with the student manager program, I asked Mary to explain a little more about the program. She told me what the process was like to get into the program, what it was like to work so closely with the football team, and how you eventually get assigned to a sport of your own.

> "The way the student manager's organization worked at that time was everyone could sign up at the end of freshman year. Sophomore year, that group dwindled down to about 150 sophomore managers. The first and only elimination was from those 150 sophomore managers down to 19 junior managers. That was stressful! From there you were guaranteed to manage football junior year. After football season, we were ranked by our fellow managers and chose a sport based on our rank, and then we managed that particular team leading into and through our senior year. That was a lot less stressful."

> "I managed softball the second half of my junior year and through senior year. While it wouldn't have been my first choice at the time, in hindsight I wouldn't have changed it for the world. The work I did for the team was extensive, the

> head coach Liz Miller became a great mentor to me, and it set me up to get into graduate school one year after I graduated from Notre Dame."

The ability to manage athletics and academics in college takes a highly motivated and detail oriented person, who can manage their time and prioritize. But being a student manager for the various Notre Dame sports team was no easy task either. Mary talked to me about what it was like to balance the rigors of Notre Dame academics while simultaneously working in the student manager program.

> "What was it like balancing my school work and the student manager program? Hard! It was a lot of work. When I made the cut to junior manager, my friend Jenn Loynd gave me a card that said 'So proud of you. Congratulations on getting chosen to clean up sweaty uniforms and jock straps for the next 2 years!' While it made me laugh, it was true. The work as a student manager taught us about hard work, how to balance work and play, and how to work in a team."

When I interview athletes, I always ask them what their favorite memories were from playing sports at Notre Dame. In talking to Mary, I felt the question still applied. I asked her to share with me her favorite memory of her time spent working with the Notre Dame Football team. And while this is the question that everyone dislikes, it is also the question that makes them light up the most. Mary was no different.

> "My most memorable experience from my time working with the Notre Dame Football program was the first bowl game I worked – the Cotton Bowl in Dallas with the crew of sophomore managers. We all had to pay our own way, so we all stayed in 2 rooms at the team hotel. We were three to a bed, and I'm pretty sure someone was sleeping in both bathtubs. We worked our butts off at practice by day, and took over Dallas at night. It was my first trip to Texas, my first exposure to Lone Star beer, and the first time I had been on a field as big as the Cotton Bowl field. It was awesome! And it brought those of us who travelled to Dallas even closer. We felt like part of something bigger than Notre Dame. I still have that Cotton Bowl poster hanging in my house to this day, and it reminds me of that incredible week."

> "The other Notre Dame Football memory that I can remember like it was yesterday was being on the field for the No. 1 Notre Dame vs. No. 2 Florida State, 'Game of the Century,' during my sophomore year. We were 9-0 going into that game, and I was a ball spotter on the visitor side. During pre-game I found myself standing between OJ and Spike Lee (I still have that picture somewhere). It was the most electric atmosphere, and the experience on the

field at Notre Dame that day was amazing. Being down there for the win was the loudest, craziest, most incredible feeling I'd ever had."

There aren't too many people whom I've met in my life who have touched every single person they've met; Coach Holtz would definitely be on that very short list. Of course he touched all of the young men he coached, but he also touched each person he interacted with on that campus, including those incredibly valuable student managers who helped keep the Notre Dame Football program running smoothly. I asked Mary if she had a favorite Coach Holtz memory or encounter, and she responded yes without skipping a beat.

"What made Coach Holtz a great coach? His pure dedication to the sport, the school and most importantly the players and people who supported it, including the managers and trainers. He didn't accept mediocrity, he inspired people to be exceptional, to give 110% in everything they did, and to care. And he cared! And not just about winning, but genuinely about the people involved in his program."

"My favorite Coach Holtz memory? Well that's easy. In 1994, which was my junior year at Notre Dame, the majority of the junior student managers made the trip to Southern California for the USC game, which fell over Thanksgiving weekend. Because it was a long weekend, we actually buffed and painted the helmets there, in the tunnel of the Colosseum. At some point, we all decided that it was a good idea to also paint one wall of the tunnel ND gold. I wasn't in the hotel when Coach Holtz got the call from USC, or when he promptly instructed Matlock, the ND equipment manager, to get it put back to normal, but I was there when he instructed all of us to never do that again. You could see he was angry, but he couldn't help but crack a little smile. His sense of humor always prevailed."

Notre Dame does more for Her students than just give them book learning. She educates them: mind, body and spirit; makes sure that the education they receive along their travels on the *Notre Dame Value Stream* prepares them to seize all future opportunities placed in front of them. And not just give those future opportunities the good ole "college try," but to give them your 110% every single time. Mary did just that as she took what Notre Dame gave her and headed out into the world.

Today

"After I graduated from Notre Dame I did a volunteer teaching program in New York City for a year before attending Indiana University for my MBA. Since then I've worked primarily in sports and entertainment. I spent almost six years at General Motors managing sponsorships, one year at Carat in

New York City, 11 years at The Marketing Arm, building and leading the Olympic and Global Platforms division of the agency, a year as the President and CEO of the Dallas Wings, our Dallas WNBA team, and most recently I formed my own company, O'Connor & Advisors and started doing consulting work. I'm also working on a sports education start-up with two fellow class of 1996 graduates, Paul Berrettini and Derrick Mayes. I've been incredibly blessed that I have been able to follow my passions in my work, most of which have been centered around sports."

Every student at Notre Dame who travels along the *Notre Dame Value Stream* for four years of their lives learns a great deal about themselves. They learn what it's like to succeed, what it's like to fail, and how to pick themselves up and overcome just about any adversity placed in front of them. I asked Mary to share with me how her experiences and learning at Notre Dame prepared her for success in her post collegiate life.

"Notre Dame gave me four things that prepared me to be successful in my life, and for those I will forever be grateful. First and foremost, Notre Dame taught me the value of friendships and of a network. At Notre Dame, we were introduced almost immediately to the power of the Notre Dame family, and how valuable lifelong connections can be. I still treasure my Notre Dame family to this day. And being exposed to that at ND taught me how important networking and friendships are. I credit much of my success to the friendships and business network I have created since learning that invaluable lesson at Notre Dame."

"Second, Notre Dame, and especially the student manager program, taught me the value of hard work and time management. I have always prided myself on being able to juggle several things in life, and I credit that to my time at ND. Third, Notre Dame further ingrained in me the power and importance of giving back. Combined with the echoed sentiment from my parents, I left ND knowing that giving back should be a priority for the remainder of my life. Today, I still believe that volunteering time and/or sharing treasure gives us a feeling of joy, which in turn makes us more successful in all of the other things we do. It also gives us a purpose in those weeks or months we need it most."

"And most importantly, Notre Dame ingrained in me that with faith, anything is possible. It sounds crazy to the non-ND person, but there is something special about Notre Dame. You can't necessarily describe it; you have to experience it, to become immersed in it. As a student, there's this feeling that you get when you're on campus that anything is possible. Yes, we are encouraged

to pray, to visit the Grotto often, and to attend church weekly, but there's something about Our Lady in gold looking down on us that gives us that deep, internal belief that we can accomplish anything with faith. That's a feeling that I carried with me after Notre Dame, and still have today."

Mary currently lives in Dallas, TX.

Mary O'Connor

Mary O'Connor's Lessons from the Notre Dame Value Stream:

- First and foremost, Notre Dame taught me the value of friendships and of a network. At Notre Dame, we were introduced almost immediately to the power of the Notre Dame family, and how valuable lifelong connections can be. I still treasure my Notre Dame family to this day. I also credit much of my success to the friendships and business network I have created since learning that invaluable lesson at Notre Dame.

- Second, Notre Dame taught me the value of hard work and time management. I have always prided myself on being able to juggle several things in life, and I credit that to my time at ND.

- Third, Notre Dame further ingrained in me the power and importance of giving back. Combined with the echoed sentiment from my parents, I left ND knowing that giving back should be a priority for the remainder of my life.

Notre Dame baseball player Chris Michalak, September 1989.
(Photo courtesy of Notre Dame Archives.)

CHAPTER TWENTY FOUR

The Baseball Mentor

Chris Michalak

(Notre Dame Baseball – Class of 1995)

Have you ever been to Joliet, Illinois? If you live in or near the Chicagoland area, you probably have at least driven through Joliet. And if you haven't, you might have seen it on the big screen. The Joliet Prison is where the opening scenes of the 1980 movie, The Blues Brothers, which starred John Belushi as "Joliet" Jake Blues, was filmed. Chris Michalak is quite familiar with Joliet, IL. Born and raised just 15 minutes from the Southwest Chicago suburb, in a town called Lemont, IL, Chris went to school in Joliet along with his three siblings. What drew Chris to head east to Notre Dame, IN, and play baseball for the University of Notre Dame? This is Chris Michalak's story.

"I have two older brothers and an older sister. My sister is the oldest, and the three of them are 10, 11, and 12 years older than I am. They all participated in organized sports, which made it pretty easy for me; I just followed suit. If I wanted to spend time with them, I went to their games, and then played sports myself. My father was a pretty good athlete growing up in Lemont, and the four of us were natural athletes. I played baseball, football and basketball, and it was in our backyard where I learned how to play everything. We had a small home, sitting on two acres of land, and there was always some sort of game going on back there. Depending on what season it was, that's what we were playing."

"I was always trying to keep up with my brothers and they never cut me any slack. If I wanted to play, I had to play with the big boys, which meant I learned pretty fast. You know how brothers can be! Of all the sports I played, baseball was my first love. I loved playing the other sports, especially when they were in season, but no matter what time of year it was I couldn't wait for baseball season to come around. My cousin, who is eight years older than me, was a pitcher and a first round draft pick for the San Francisco Giants. I had the opportunity to watch him play from a young age, and he played in the big leagues for about seven years. As a result of that experience, I knew that playing professional baseball was exactly where I wanted to be; what I wanted to do. Notre Dame had always been a dream of mine. When you grow up in a Chicago suburb such as Joliet, and go to an all-boys Catholic school, in particular a Catholic school that is big in both football and baseball, you dream of going to Notre Dame and playing football for the Fighting Irish. Everyone in the Chicagoland area is well aware of Notre Dame. It's all we knew."

"To be honest with you, I got a letter in the mail from Notre Dame, a questionnaire, and I didn't even fill it out. I framed it. I thought it was awesome. But I also thought, 'I'm not getting in there.' I had offers from schools down south like Texas A&M, Arizona State, Florida State, and Duke; I never thought I could actually get in to Notre Dame. During the summer after my junior year of high school I got a call from Notre Dame's head baseball coach, Patrick Murphy. He asked me, 'Chris, did you get our questionnaire?' and I said, 'Yes, I got it coach. Thank you very much. I appreciate it, it's an honor!' Then Coach Murphy followed up with, 'You didn't send it back.' To which I replied, 'I'd love to go to Notre Dame, but I don't think I can get in there, Coach.' He asked me what my grades were, and I told him. He asked me what my test scores were, and I told him. And he said, 'Fill . . . Out . . . Your . . .

> *Questionnaire! Everything is fine!' I had this perception of Notre Dame that I'd had since I was a little kid, and it was larger than life to me. Thankfully Coach Murphy made that call, or I never would have sent that questionnaire in, or pursued getting an education and playing baseball at Notre Dame."*

So many of us who embarked upon our journey to Notre Dame, and down the *Notre Dame Value Stream*, were influenced by a parent who either went to Notre Dame, or just simply loved the place. Chris's story, however, is a little different.

> *"My dad, for whatever reason, was not a Notre Dame fan. He wasn't even a fan of Joliet Catholic High School. He didn't even really want me to go to Joliet Catholic, but my brother was teaching there, and I wanted to go there because of the excellent academics and athletics they offered. He finally agreed to let me go to Joliet Catholic, and he ended up absolutely loving the place. And then Notre Dame came knocking. My dad's brother was a big Notre Dame fan, and I think my dad ended up being a non-Notre Dame fan as a result of his brother being such a huge fan. He would always give his brother a hard time about Notre Dame. When I got my letter from Notre Dame, we took a trip to visit the school and attend a football game. It wasn't even my recruiting trip. We just went up, saw a game, did an informal tour of campus, and met with Coach Murphy. The game we happened to go to was the first home game of the 1988 season, the Notre Dame vs. Michigan game. Unbelievable. On the hour and a half drive home to Joliet with my parents, we're driving along and all of the sudden my dad asked me, 'You want to go there?' And I said, 'Yeah, it's pretty special.' He looked at me and said, 'Yeah, I think it's pretty special, too.' It was an awesome moment. And my mom was in the backseat going, 'Really?!' He's been the biggest Notre Dame fan ever since."*

The Notre Dame Years

> *"I never even made an official visit to Notre Dame because with my playing three sports, it was tough to get back during any of the official visit weekends. I was supposed to go back for a basketball game to do my official visit but, sure enough, there was a blizzard that weekend, and we couldn't get there. Typical Notre Dame weather. That should have been a sign right there. . . the weather in South Bend is definitely not the greatest. \<laughs\> I told Coach Murphy, 'I don't need to make my official visit, I know this is where I want to go.' Notre Dame was the place for me. I never even made any official visits to any other schools. After that football weekend at Notre Dame, that was it. My decision was made. I'll never forget, at that Notre Dame vs. Michigan game, we got to go out on the field before the game. We actually followed the team out onto the field. I was with Pat Pesavento, who was a shortstop on*

the ND Baseball team. He was also a Joliet Catholic grad, and a quarterback at Joliet Catholic like I was, and he was the one who showed us around campus and escorted us onto the field. That moment, when I walked out of the tunnel and the place was going crazy; I still get goosebumps talking about it. That was also when I met my future roommate, Eric Danapolis. 'Dino' as we affectionately called him. He and I were standing there on the sidelines looking around thinking, 'Holy cow.' That was also the game when they had the brawl in the tunnel, and it happened right in front of us. We were right there. We saw the fight coming and all we could say was, 'Oh my gosh.' If Coach Murphy would have had a letter of intent for me to sign right then and there on the sideline, I probably would have signed it."

"Everything about the Notre Dame experience was incredible, but looking back on it all, this is the craziest thing that I remember about being a student at Notre Dame and going to football games. We'd go to the games, stand for four quarters, be riveted to each and every play, and completely live and die with the team. Then we'd go home and watch the replay on NBC at 10:30 pm after the local news. We knew exactly what was going to happen, but we'd sit there and watch the whole thing again! It was crazy. After that weekend at Notre Dame for the Michigan game I cancelled the rest of my official visits. I had visits lined up with Texas A&M and Duke, and I called them both and said no thanks. I didn't need to look any further."

What are the type of students that Notre Dame attracts to come walk through Her hallowed halls? They are many things. They are smart, but they're not just smart, they also enjoy an academic challenge. They are also oftentimes athletic, even if they never earn a varsity letter or don a golden helmet. And, they are also driven, motivated, have a strong sense of self, and a passion to improve the world around them. But even the brightest student who steps foot on campus at Our Lady's University will learn some tough lessons during their journey along the *Notre Dame Value Stream*.

> **When you get to college and you're 18 and playing against young men who are 21 or 22 years old, that was a significant difference and quite an adjustment.**

"What was the transition like from being a high school student-athlete, to being a Division I student-athlete? It was a little eye opening, that's for sure. I realized very quickly that it was a full time commitment. In high school I played three sports. Whatever season it was, I played that sport in high school. But once I set foot on campus at Notre Dame, we immediately started playing baseball in the fall. We actually played games in the fall. The rules were a little

> *different, but we had a fall season. It was a full-time job. You had school, and you had baseball. And that was pretty much it. I learned that quickly. The other thing was, in high school, when you played against guys who were older than you, there wasn't much of a difference. But when you get to college and you're 18 and playing against young men who are 21 or 22 years old, that was a significant difference and quite an adjustment. It made you grow up fast. The college game was much more intense than the high school game. Just dealing with that transition was quite a challenge. I was lucky I had good people around me, and good teammates to help me along. You suddenly realize, this is for real. This is what you want to do for the rest of your life, so you might as well get started right now."*

With one week of school under his belt freshman year, Chris became sick and went to the infirmary. Not exactly the way you want to start out your college career, but Chris was determined to hold his own once he was well and made it back to baseball.

> *"I was in the infirmary for 10 days, my second week at Notre Dame; that made the transition to college even harder. They had no idea what I had, or what was wrong with me. My parents came up to visit me, and they would come in with masks on because they didn't know if what I had was contagious or not. Finally, they concluded that I had mono, and that I probably had it all summer long, because I was completely worn out. When I got to Notre Dame and jumped in full speed ahead, everything caught up with me. I lost 20 pounds. And you talk about a transition. I finally got out of the infirmary and I was behind in everything. Not just school but baseball, too. On my first day back at practice I was weak, the guys were making fun of me, and my clothes barely fit. Then, something happened at practice, and Murph was not happy. Undoubtedly we were screwing around, and then during a drill we messed something up. The next thing you know we were on the line, running from the foul line to center field doing sprints, just running. And I was dying. I was completely gassed, but I wouldn't let Coach Murphy know that I was gassed. Finally, Murph said, 'Michalak, go get off the field. I'm not going to watch you die out here.' Yes, I was a little bit behind once I got out of the infirmary."*

Finding the balance between academics and athletics can be a challenge once you reach the collegiate level. It's a challenge for every student, let's be honest, but when you add athletics to the mix, the challenge can almost become insurmountable.

> *"I majored in American Studies at Notre Dame, which (if you're not familiar) is a combination of History and English."* If you watched the tv show *The*

West Wing, President Bartlet had an American Studies degree from Notre Dame. But I digress. *"My first two years at Notre Dame I was pursuing a degree in Business. I really liked numbers and I thought that would be something I could do once my someday professional baseball career was over. And then sophomore year I had to take Finance, and I was hanging on by a thread. I could not wrap my head around what was going on in that class, but I did get through it by the skin of my teeth. Then statistics came along, which I ended up dropping, and at the end of my sophomore year my GPA was a 1.99 and I was put on academic probation. I had pretty much figured out halfway through that spring semester that getting a Business degree wasn't for me, and I let all of my teachers know that I was transferring out of the business school. I just couldn't handle it. I told them I would do whatever I could to make sure that I passed all of my classes. I would do extra work, whatever they needed to do, I just needed to pass; they were all very supportive of me. One teacher totally forgot, and I was right on the borderline between a C- and a D, and he gave me a D, which made me ineligible to play baseball in the fall."*

"My realization after my sophomore year was, who are you kidding? You are going to play baseball for as long as you can, and then probably after that you're going to get into some type of public relations or coaching, and they are most likely going to train you for it. But in order to be successful, you better have people skills and communication skills, and so getting a degree in American Studies was the way to go for me."

"In the fall, I switched majors from Business to American Studies, and my GPA went from a 1.99, to a 3.25 the following semester (culminating with a final GPA of 2.8). It was the best decision I made in college. As far as juggling baseball with my academics, they were both full time jobs. It was tough. Baseball might have been one of the tougher sports to play and manage your academics because you had both a fall and a spring season. I remember times when we would leave on a Thursday after class, fly to Arizona, play games at Arizona State on Friday and Saturday, and then play Arizona on Sunday. We'd fly back to South Bend on the redeye, get to campus at 6:30 am on Monday and were then expected to go to class on Monday. We were not excused from Monday classes. And then we'd do it all over again the next week. With the weather being not ideal in South Bend in the spring, we played a great deal of games on the road."

"As much as you tried to do homework on the plane, you were also exhausted from playing three or four games on the road, and you really just wanted to

sleep. On top of that you had practice. Back then there weren't restrictions on how many hours you could practice a week, and Murph practiced us every moment he could. I can remember being dead tired from traveling and changing time zones, and then staying up all night studying. Don't get me wrong, all students did that, but they weren't exhausted from traveling all over the country every week. But, if you wanted to continue to play the sport that you loved, you made it work. And then of course, returning to two feet of snow in South Bend after being in beautiful, sunny Arizona was no walk in the park either. As a result of there being two feet of snow on the ground, we were unable to practice outside, and so we had to practice indoors at Loftus practice facility. The problem with that was the football team was also practicing there to get ready for their spring game, and so many days the only time we could get in there was late at night or early in the morning. That didn't help our exhaustion either. No doubt about it, everything I went through at Notre Dame 100% prepared me for life after college. It gave me the confidence to be able to tackle anything head on. There are so many things that I can handle in my life today because of what I went through at Notre Dame. I learned how to figure out a way. If there was a challenge in front of me, I dug in and found a way to do it. You just learned how to adapt."

In the words of John Wooden, "A good coach can change a game. A great coach can change a life." As Chris and his teammate Eddie Hartwell have reminisced with me about their Notre Dame head coach, Patrick Murphy, they both commented on how Murph not only taught them about the game of baseball, but the game of life as well.

"A good coach can change a game. A great coach can change a life."
– Coach John Wooden

"I will say this, I still talk to him and am in contact with him to this day. Obviously part of that has to do with him being with the Milwaukee Brewers, and my still being in the game as well. Now that I am in coaching, I hope that there are players that say the same thing about me that we said about him. There were days that I would have run through a wall for him, and then there were days that I wanted to throw him through a wall. <laughs> But I think you can apply that to pretty much every coach. There are days that you absolutely love your coach, and then there are days when he drives you absolutely crazy. What I do know is that he was able to get the absolute best out of me. He probably wasn't the best coach for every player, but every coach isn't going to be a perfect fit for every player. He pushed me to the limits, and I was able to accept the challenge and handle the adversity placed in front of

> me. He taught us how to adapt to various situations and he challenged me on a daily basis. He got the best out of me and mentally he made me stronger both on and off the field. What I learned from Coach Murphy helped me achieve things I may or may not have been able to achieve had I not been challenged in the way that he challenged us."

Can answering a question be equivalent to both walking leisurely in the park and climbing Mt. Everest? You bet. Every time I ask the "What's your favorite memory" question I get all the moans and groans, but once they get going, it's almost always their favorite part of the interview. Chris shared with me some of his favorite memories from his time spent at the University of Notre Dame.

> "My favorite on the field memory, personally, happened during my senior year. We were down at Florida State playing at regionals. We beat Mississippi State in the first game of the tournament, and we didn't just beat them, we smoked them (15-1 if memory serves me correctly). It was amazing. On the second day of the tournament we played Florida State, and of course with Florida State hosting regionals, they had the 'home field advantage.' The game against FSU went to extra innings. I started the game playing first base, and then I came in from first base and pitched the final two innings of the game. I ended up giving up a grand slam to lose the game in extra innings. It was a double elimination tournament, so the next day we played South Florida and won, which meant we got a rematch with Florida State. In the rematch, I got the chance to pitch against Florida State once more. I went nine innings and we ended up winning the game 3-2. That loss eliminated them from the tournament, and that was the last game I pitched for the Irish, which was the feather in my cap. We made it to the championship game the next day against Long Beach State and lost, but that rematch win over Florida State was definitely an incredible accolade for me. That tournament was the epitome of going from the ultimate low to the ultimate high. I will always remember that win. Any time I get together or talk to any of the guys, that game and that tournament is the first thing we reminisce about; that 24-hour period was such an insane roller coaster ride."

> "One of the other things that I think about when I look back on my time playing baseball at Notre Dame, which also happens to be one of my favorite things, and this is going to sound weird but we rarely stayed in hotels when we went on the road. Instead, we stayed at the houses of alumni and booster club members. They were each responsible for two or three of us. They fed us and made sure we got to where we needed to be. It was such an amazing thing, and it just goes to show the strength of the Notre Dame family. There

may have been one or two cities where we actually stayed in hotels, but on pretty much every other trip we stayed with these families, families for all the players. A couple of the families whom I stayed with during my playing years at Notre Dame, I am still friends with and talk to them to this day. It was one of those things that made Notre Dame so special. These alumni and boosters were willing to open their homes to us, feed us meals, and take us to games, without even knowing who we were. That was amazing. A lot of the times you stayed with the same families every year, so you had the chance to develop relationships with them."

"I'll never forget, in either 1990 or 1991 I stayed with David and Sandy Sabey in Seattle, Washington. They were incredible people. We had an off day during the trip, and we went out for a ride on their boat, and they took us around and showed us the area. We were on Lake Washington, and they pointed out a house to us that was being built and they said, 'I don't know if you've ever heard of Bill Gates? He owns Microsoft. That's his house over there.' And I remember thinking, 'Yeah, I think I've heard of that guy.'"

The Professional Years

For a kid who decided early on that playing in the major leagues was his end game, he was going to do everything in his power to make his dream come true; what that dream looks like when it comes to fruition is often different from what was imagined for all of those years. That difference is not necessarily good or bad, it's just *different*.

"When I played baseball at Notre Dame, it was all about the team. You all had one common goal of getting to Omaha and playing in the College World Series. When you make it to professional baseball the team atmosphere is still there, and you still want to win as a team, but you also realize that there are some people who are in it for themselves more than they are in it for the team. And you also realize, this is your career. The drive that pushes you forward every day becomes a little bit more of a personal drive and not so much of a team drive. You go from the camaraderie that you had in college, to a very competitive atmosphere at the pro level, where you are competing for a starting job every single day."

"Suddenly you are playing with the best of the best, from all over the world, and you're all trying to get that professional baseball gig. It was the first time I had played with players from Latin America, and suddenly there were multiple languages being spoken. It was quite a culture shock. We all loved the game of baseball, and we all wanted to win, but at the same time we all wanted to keep moving and make it to the next level. In order to get to the

next level, you had to have personal success as well as team success. You had to take care of your own business because no one else is going to do it for you. It was a little cut throat, and very competitive. The sooner you realized that if you did your job and your teammates did their job, the team was successful; the sooner you were going to get an opportunity to move on and get one step closer to your goal of making it to the big leagues."

"That was the biggest transition. I had spent four years immersed in the Notre Dame 'family' atmosphere where we stayed at people's houses when we were on the road, and where you had such a tight bond and incredible camaraderie with your teammates. And then all of the sudden I'm in Medford, Oregon, a place I had never even heard of before playing for the Southern Oregon A's, a farm team for the Oakland A's. I was on my own for the first time. Fortunately, the A's provided each one of us with a host family, and I had a really great host family. I went from flying to games to being on these incredibly long bus rides to wherever we were playing. 13-hour bus rides were nothing, and then after being on a bus for hours on end you had to go out there and play. I think our closest trip was 5 or 6 hours, and our longest trip was probably 15 hours to Boise, Idaho. There weren't any 'short' trips, I can tell you that. And it wasn't as if you had your own seat, everyone was doubled up. We'd always say to each other, 'So you want to play pro ball, do ya?'" <laughs>

"My professional baseball career started in Medford, Oregon. I started there in June of 1993, after I graduated from Notre Dame, and finished the season there in August. From there, I went on to play 17 years in the minor and major leagues. I pitched until I was 38 years old. I ended up playing a portion of four seasons for MLB teams, and then I played 13 seasons in the minor leagues. Would I do it again? No doubt about it. I'd totally do it all over again. How does one play for 17 years, with 13 different organizations? That's the life of a left handed pitcher. . . you got bounced around a lot. 2009 was the last year that I pitched for a team, at which point I decided to try my hand at coaching. Every time I made it to a major league team, all of the trips, all of the sacrifices my wife and children made for me were all validated. Every time I got released or traded, they never missed a beat. Their response would always be, 'Where are we going?' If I didn't have their support, there was no way I could have done it. You talk about adapting, they did it without ever hesitating. And to be honest with you, having a degree from Notre Dame allowed me to chase my dreams for as long as I did. I always knew in the back of in mind that if tomorrow came and I could no longer pitch, I had that Notre Dame degree in my back pocket. I knew that degree was worth something, and no matter what, my family and I would be okay. It was a blessing to have that Notre Dame degree. If I had gone somewhere else, I would not have had that assurance. When you tell people you have a Notre Dame education, it opens doors. It gave me the opportunity to play a boys game for so long."

"It was a natural progression to move from playing the game to coaching it, especially towards the end of my career. When I got released by the A's in 1997 they told me, 'hey, we don't think you can pitch any more but we'd love to keep you in the organization as a coach. We think you're bright and could be a huge help to our upcoming pitchers.' While I thought that was flattering, I still thought I had a chance to play major league ball. And as fate would have it, the following year I was playing in the bigs with the Arizona Diamondbacks. As I got older, and was back playing Triple-A ball for a long, long time; I would get close with my pitching coaches. They would ask me if I planned on coaching when I was done, and all I could say was, 'I don't know. I love the game, but I just don't know.' Coach after coach would continue to encourage me, 'You're really good at coaching your teammates. You're good with people and you've been around the game for a long time, and you've seen a lot of stuff. I think you should do it.' My dad was a coach, and my brothers and sister were all coaches, so for me it was very much in the family."

Today

"When I started playing professional baseball my plan was to play for 10 years, make millions and millions of dollars and then be done; of course that didn't happen. Coaching was just a natural next step for me. In 2009, I couldn't get any invites to spring training. My first manger, Dick Scott, who managed me when I played in Medford, Oregon, was the minor league director for the Toronto Blue Jays. He called me and said, 'I hear you're looking for a pitching job, and I know you still want to pitch, but we need a rookie ball pitching coach here. Our guy who was supposed to do it has some family matters that he has to attend to, could you come out here? We'll allow you to keep pitching so long as you help out with the pitching coach duties.' And I agreed. He was looking out for me, he had always looked out for me, and I couldn't tell him no. He also told me that if I was pitching well, and another team wanted me, they'd let me go; if they needed me as a pitcher, they'd use me. How could I refuse? I went out there and I pitched for a little bit and I helped out with the coaching responsibilities. When it came time for the season to start, they told me that if I still wanted to pitch, I would have to find somewhere else to do it, but if I wanted to stay and coach, they needed a full time coach. I had no

> *other offers to play anywhere else and so I took the coaching job. The following year I got a job with the Washington Nationals as their pitching coach, and coached for them for eight years. And now I'm the pitching coordinator for the Miami Marlins."*

We've all heard the phrase, hindsight is 20/20, and it is never truer than when applied to the wisdom of age. We can all look back at our younger self and realize that if we had done x, y, z better or differently, the outcome would have been more positive. Chris takes a moment to apply what he learned as a student-athlete at Notre Dame and offers some advice for prospective Division I athletes.

> *"Here's the thing, if you love the sport, especially if you're talking about baseball, you need to look at schools for more than just their athletic department. I help kids out around here, in our area, and they ask me how they can get into a Division I program. Everyone here wants to go to Texas. The first thing I tell them is there are a lot of Division I schools. You need to go to a school where you are going to play, that is key. That is the only way you're going to get seen, and the more you get seen, the more opportunities you're going to have. The other thing I tell them is when you pick a school, make sure that if you get hurt the first day you're on campus and can never play your sport again, that it's a school you're going to be happy at for the next four years. And that was one of the things that my parents and I talked about when I was looking at colleges. I knew that if I went to Notre Dame, even if I never played a single game, I would be tremendously proud of my degree and would be happy to be at Notre Dame. I tell them over and over again, look at the whole school, not just the athletic program. 'If your arm blows out, and you can never throw another pitch, remember that you're going to be there for four years, and you better be happy.' I also remind them that their college decision will last them the rest of their life, so that's how they should make their decision about where they want to go."*

> **I had to go back to Notre Dame to finish up my degree because I was 12 credit hours short of graduating.**

> *"The other thing that I tell them is to start developing their time management skills now, because once you get to college, you're going to need them. I was so terrible at time management. I had to go back to Notre Dame to finish up my degree because I was 12 credit hours short of graduating. I went back and finished in the fall of 1994 thinking, 'Aw man, this is going to be so easy. I don't have practice to worry about, I don't have games to worry about; all I have is school. I am going to be so ahead in my classes. And... it was actually worse. I had so much time on my hands and didn't know how to focus myself.*

> *This was what was running through my brain, 'Oh look, there's Monday Night Football on at Coaches. I've got to watch that game.' And then, 'Oh hey, there are $2 Long Island Iced Teas at the 'Backer.' And then, Pat Leahy was also there, doing the same thing I was doing, and he would call and say, 'Hey, it's pretty nice out. Do you want to go play some golf today? How many classes do you have today?' And I'm thinking to myself, 'Oh my gosh, why are you doing this to me?!' <laughs> My time management was actually worse when I didn't have baseball, and so that's my biggest piece of advice to student-athletes, make sure you can manage your time. It's so valuable."*

> ***"For those who know Notre Dame, no explanation's necessary.***
> ***For those who don't, no explanation will suffice."***
> ***- Coach Lou Holtz***

> *"People, especially in the baseball community, love to give me a hard time about Notre Dame. They tell me, 'you think you're so special.' And I tell them, 'go to campus and you'll see how special it really is.' When you talk about Notre Dame, you talk about family, and it truly is a family. No matter where you go, if you see someone that has a Notre Dame class ring on, and you start a conversation with them, 'Flanner Hall, '93,' you have an instant connection with them. They talk to you just as though you were classmates, even though they might be 30 years older than you. It is special. And unless you've been there, you really don't understand it. My family is just in awe of it, and they love being on the campus, and experiencing all that is Notre Dame."*

Everyone loves hearing former Notre Dame Football players share their countless Coach Holtz stories. It never failed, as coach was trying to impart some incredibly important, worldly wisdom upon his players, some great hilarity would ensue. In talking with Chris, his memories of Coach Murphy were very similar. It would seem as if Coach Holtz and Coach Murphy were cut from the same cloth.

> *"On the field, Murph was a fiery coach, to say the least. I can remember, we were playing a game at Jake Kline field, which by-the-way was the worst field in college baseball. It was definitely the reason why we played most of our games at Coveleski Stadium in downtown South Bend, but we did play a few of our games at Jake Kline on campus. I'll never forget this one time. The backstop at the field at Jake Kline was just that; it was just a backstop. There were open areas between where the backstop ended and where the dugout began. There was a chalk line, on the field, that determined where 'out of bounds' began. If a ball went past that chalk line it was out of play, and the catcher couldn't go past that white line to catch the ball. At this particular moment, we were hitting, and whoever was up at bat hit a foul ball and it*

went towards the chalk line. The catcher for the other team went to catch the ball and he crossed the line, and the umpire called it out, which it should not have been out as the catcher was out-of-bounds."

"Murph just absolutely lost his mind. He came flying in from the third base coaching box to argue with the umpire. He took off running towards the umpire in a dead sprint. It was around 11 am and it was a typical spring day. The grass was wet, and unfortunately for Murph, he was wearing his turf shoes. As he approached the umpire he tried to stop but he lost his footing and fell right on his butt. As he fell he accidentally leg whipped the umpire. The umpire made noticeable noise when he went down, as he hurt his knee and was clearly in pain. Meanwhile Murph is laying on the ground and still chewing him out about the play. We're in the dugout trying as hard as we can to not laugh, or at least to not have Murph see us laugh, because that only would have made it worse. And, of course, Murph got tossed for running into the umpire. That was Murph."

So many of the men and women I have the opportunity to interview are active in their communities and volunteer with local charities, which to me is a shining example of the *Notre Dame Value Stream* still hard at work in their lives. Chris took the time to share with me the work he does with a charity in the Dallas, Texas area.

"There is a local charity that I help out with here in Texas, and it's called Coaches and Friends for the Military: **www.cfftm.org/about**. *It was founded by Tim Knight, one of Bob Knight's sons, and Tim is a good friend of mine. What he and the foundation does is raise money for military members and their families, and veterans as well. We have an annual golf tournament which raises some of the money, and then around Christmastime we go and visit the local VA hospitals and bring a little joy to them. The coaches who are involved with the foundation are from both the college level and the professional level, often bring t-shirts with them to give to the veterans. The foundation raises a ton of money to help out the veterans and active military personnel. He gets a ton of signed memorabilia from the various coaches which also helps raise money for the foundation. The NFL teams often send warm winter coats which we then take to the homeless shelter for veterans. It's a really terrific cause which enables us to share our abundant blessings with those who fight for our freedom."*

Chris and his wife Shannon currently live in Keller, Texas. Chris and his wife have two children, Madison and Ty.

Chris Michalak with his wife Shannon, and their two children: Madison and Ty.

Chris Michalak's Lessons from the Notre Dame Value Stream:

- If you love the sport you play, make sure to look at schools for more than just their athletic department. Of course you need to go to a school where you are going to play, that is key. That is the only way you're going to get seen, and the more you get seen, the more opportunities you're going to have. But, when you pick a school, make sure that if you get hurt the first day you're on campus and can never play your sport again, that it's a school you're going to be happy at for the next four years.

- Also, your college decision will last you the rest of your life, so keep that in mind as you make your decision about where you want to go to college.
- The other big thing is to start developing your time management skills now, because once you get to college, you're going to need them. This is my biggest piece of advice to student-athletes, make sure you can manage your time. It's so valuable. And you will use it for the rest of your life.

EPILOGUE

They've Only Just Begun

*I*f history is any indication, the journeys of these former Notre Dame student-athletes truly have only just begun. The question is, in future generations, what greatness will this University mold, shape and breed - a president? A supreme court justice? Corporate CEO? Nobel Prize winner? A scientific researcher? The potential is limitless and the children of these student-athletes will also be shaped by the *Notre Dame Value Stream*. The unique nature of this path is that it has the ability to change course and adapt to unknown future challenges; the stream maintains its foundation.

The foundation is Notre Dame and the values She instills in all who enter Her historic gates and emerge with not only the best academic education, but also having experienced the thrill and education of life as a student-athlete at the greatest of Universities. The toolbox She provides Her student-athletes also provides them with mentors and resources needed to help navigate those moments in life when failures happen, as they inevitably will, and redirect them toward a path of success.

Whether they achieve Olympic athlete status or toil as a walk-on, never realizing the excitement of playing in a game, each athlete who graduates today and tomorrow from Notre Dame will leave behind their legacy as a student-athlete. What is most significant are the accomplishments and pride we observe as these student-athletes become men and women, and what their mark on the world around them will be - how they will build families, how they will mold and shape their children and how they will be impacted by the *Notre Dame Value Stream*.

It has been my honor to be able to tell the stories of so many and I look forward to sharing the journeys and stories of many more of Her Loyal Sons and Daughters. Stay tuned!

Notre Dame alumna and author, Lisa Kelly. (Photo courtesy of Lynne Gilbert.)

ABOUT THE AUTHOR

*L*isa had no choice but to love Notre Dame Football. Ever since she can remember, Notre Dame Football has been a part of her life. She learned her first colorful word at the tender age of three during the Notre Dame – USC game on a Thanksgiving weekend spent at her grandparents' house. She and her family made annual pilgrimages to Notre Dame to spend football weekends with her dad's college roommate and his family. Notre Dame Football has always been an integral part of her life.

As a business major at Notre Dame, Lisa made sure she took advantage of three things in her four years. First, becoming a student of theology at the most renowned theologian institution in the world. Second, studying English to support her passion for effective communications no matter her career direction. Finally, and most importantly, leaving this great University with a degree in business and a specialty in marketing. Armed with these tools she engages the world, continuing to use what she so aptly calls, the *Notre Dame Value Stream.*

Lisa began her professional career in the not-for-profit sector, working for the Better Business Bureau (BBB). She taught people how to be better-informed consumers and served as a dispute resolution arbitrator. She expanded her career horizons by branching further into her career field, working 13 years as a marketing professional in yellow page advertising. The fast-paced environment in an agency setting and the creative outlet energized her career.

In 2007, she took a leap from the advertising world and accepted a job with a marketing and communications company, Katey Charles Communications. Their specialty was web design and maintenance, and e-mail newsletter design and production. She knew little about HTML programming or copy writing, but was confident that she could learn how to do anything. She spent two amazing years working for Katey Charles and learned much about copy writing, web design and HTML programming. What she learned there was the stepping off point to where she is today.

When the economy took a downturn in 2009, Lisa, like so many others, was faced with a job loss. But such a loss with the right mental attitude turns into an opportunity. For Lisa, her loss turned into a marketing research position running in-house advertising, marketing and social media for a small company. She also took the lessons and skills she was learning and began her own blog which was a mishmash of digital marketing best practices, motherhood, music flashback, and sports. Blogging is hard work, taking patience and perseverance. Lisa's perseverance was the catalyst for a major life change.

In 2011, Lisa was contacted by an advertising agency on Twitter who was working on a contest sponsored by Volvo and the Big East Conference to determine the "Biggest Fan of the Big East Conference." She was selected along with 15 other alumni writers representing the 16 schools in the Big East Conference, to compete for the title of "Biggest Fan." As basketball is not really her forte, Lisa had to dig inward for this contest. After eight writing assignments, a trip to New York City for media day, a trip to her Alma Mater for the Notre Dame – Syracuse match-up and endless self-promotion on social media, Lisa rose to the top and was crowned the "Biggest Fan of the Big East Conference." In all honesty, Lisa never expected to win this contest, but the more she thought about it, losing really is not in her vocabulary. If you're going to do something, give it your all and shoot for the top.

Shortly after the contest, Lisa realized she was constantly defending Our Lady's University. People were quick to find the shortcomings of Notre Dame and those associated with it, and she really wanted to do something that would showcase all of the positive things that emerge from Our Lady's University. And that is how her first book, *"Echoes From the End Zone: The Men We Became"* took shape. Her first interview was with former tight end Oscar McBride. It was more like two friends catching up, but it was a wonderful walk down memory lane with Oscar and a discovery of how Notre Dame helped shape him into the man he is today. She realized that this was the beginning of something special. One interview lead to another. As she completed each interview, it was clear that a theme was emerging. Even though Lisa and these former players all came to Notre Dame from vastly different backgrounds, they all had similar experiences and each credited their time at Notre Dame and the *Notre Dame Value Stream* with playing a huge role in molding them into the people they are today.

Currently Lisa is an eContent Specialist in the eCommerce Department at Nestle Purina PetCare. Eighty interviews and three books later, Lisa is still enjoying how wonderful it is to be able to share these positive stories about Our Lady's student-athletes. In Lisa's words, there are so many of these stories yet to be told and she hopes that you have enjoyed her journey through the lives of these Loyal Sons and Daughters of Our Lady's University and the stories they tell. These three books only touch the surface. She looks forward to continuing the journey and sharing more remarkable stories of Her Loyal Sons and Daughters.

www.ingramcontent.com/pod-product-compliance
Lightning Source LLC
Chambersburg PA
CBHW071332080526
44587CB00017B/2811